COLLECTIONS AT RISK

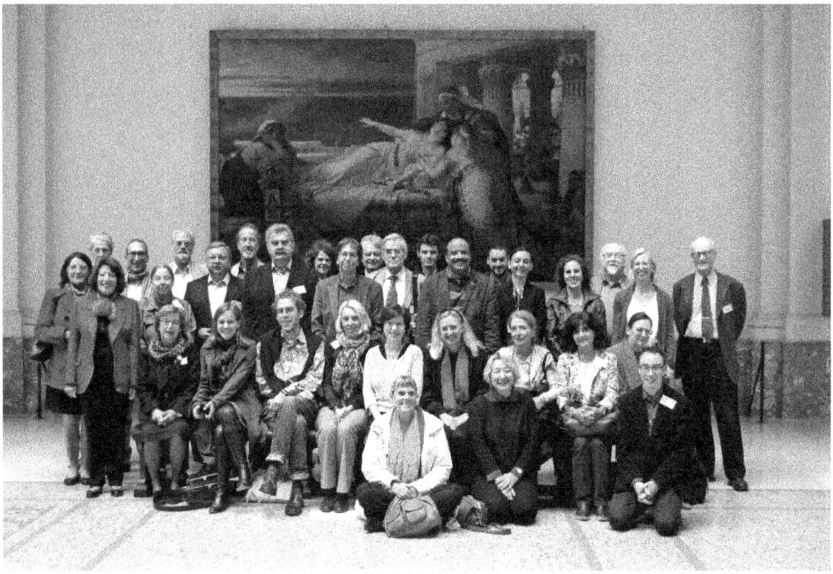

CIPEG members taking part in the Brussels meeting 2012

COLLECTIONS AT RISK

New Challenges in a New Environment

Proceedings of the 29th CIPEG Annual Meeting in Brussels, September 25–28, 2012, Royal Museums of Art and History, Brussels, Belgium

Edited by

Claire Derriks

LOCKWOOD PRESS

2017

Collections at Risk
New Challenges in a New Environment

Library of Congress Control Number: 2017934787

ISBN: 978-1-937040-60-4

Cover design by Susanne Wilhelm.

Cover image credits: Background photo: Museo Arqueológico Nacional, Madrid, © Carmen Pérez-Die. First overlay: Statue of Amenemhat III in the Neues Museum, Berlin, by Miguel Hermoso Cuesta, courtesy Wikimedia Commons. Second overlay: Ancient Egyptian models of boats in the Louvre – Room 3, by Vania Teofilo, courtesy Wikimedia Commons. Third overlay: View of the collections, © Musée royal de Mariemont, courtesy Arnaud Quertinmont.

Printed in the United States of America on acid-free paper.

Contents

Acknowledgments

Je souhaite exprimer ma profonde reconnaissance à M. Draguet, Directeur a.i. des Musées royaux d'Art et d'Histoire de Bruxelles pour avoir accueilli dans ses locaux, dans une situation d'urgence, le 29e Congrès Annuel du Comité International pour l'Égyptologie au sein de l'ICOM.

Une reconnaissance toute particulière va à nos sponsors, sans lesquels l'organisation de cet événement n'aurait pas été possible. Je soulignerais le généreux engagement de la Région de Bruxelles Capitale, l'accueil de l'Ambassade de la République Arabe d'Égypte et de La Fondation Boghossian, ainsi que le service d'Egyptair.

Mes remerciements vont aux hommes et aux femmes du personnel logistique des Musées qui nous ont assisté de manière fantastique. Que soient remerciées aussi les membres du service des bénévoles qui ont assuré avec beaucoup de générosité un accueil chaleureux aux participants au congrès du CIPEG.

Luc Delvaux, Conservateur des antiquités d'Égypte dynastique et Greco-romaine, et Martine Gruselle, secrétaire de l'Association Egyptologique Reine Elisabeth (AERE), ont été les chevilles ouvrières de cette organisation. Nous leur devons beaucoup.

Merci à tous les participants d'avoir apporté une riche contribution au thème d'une actualité brulante choisi par le CIPEG : « Collections at Risk. New Challenges in a New Environment".

Ce volume contribuera, nous l'espérons, à mobiliser les énergies au profit de la préservation de notre patrimoine culturel.

Au moment de publier ce volume, je voudrais exprimer toute ma gratitude à Diane Bergman, Simone Burger, Aidan Dodson et Emily Teeter pour leur soutien et leur aide précieuse.

Claire Derriks, Présidente du CIPEG

Foreword

Egypt, the homeland to one of the oldest civilizations, having various sites under the UNESCO's world heritage list, has always supported and will continue to contribute to all endeavors aiming at preserving Egypt's cultural heritage.

In that regard, I would personally like to seize this opportunity to express Egypt's appreciation and support to all the efforts that have been taken during and after the 29th Annual Meeting of ICOM's International Committee for Egyptology (CIPEG) that took place in Brussels in September 2012 and was devoted to the "New Challenges in a New Environment".

I would also like to reaffirm Egypt's commitment to working with and supporting various international institutions aiming at helping with the preservation of Egypt's own cultural heritage.

One must admit that new challenges have emerged in the last couple of years; the violence that Egypt has been facing in the wake of the 25th Revolution effectively threatened Egypt's culture heritage in various unfortunate incidents such as the burning of the Institut d'Egypte with its unique collection of manuscripts, the pillaging of the Mallawi Museum, and the bomb attack damaging the Islamic Museum.

Yet, it needs to be noted that Egyptians themselves are aware of such challenges and are keen on preserving their own cultural heritage. Photos captured during the 2011 revolution of Egyptians protecting the Egyptian National Museum from robbery were truly a vivid example of such unique commitment and ownership.

At the same time, the Egyptian government itself, specifically the ministry of Antiquities and the ministry of Culture have dedicated most of their resources to protecting and preserving Egyptian cultural heritage. Moreover, our embassies all over the world are indeed doing their utmost efforts, both bilaterally and multilaterally, in order to safely return illegally traded heritage material to its rightful owner, the Egyptian people.

Let me express my sincere appreciation and support to all endeavors and initiatives taken with the view of helping Egypt preserve its cultural heritage for the entire world civilization.

Ehab Fawzy, Ambassador of the Arab Republic of Egypt

Preface

Les contributions qu'on lira dans ce volume, brillamment présentées et mises en contexte dans l'essai introductif de Maarten Raven, reflètent, à juste titre, les préoccupations des conservateurs de collections égyptiennes face à des situations de conflit ou à divers types de catastrophes, naturelles ou accidentelles. Mais de tels événements cependant, s'ils sont très graves et peuvent engendrer d'immenses pertes patrimoniales, n'en sont pas moins relativement ponctuels et éphémères. En revanche, les Musées en général, et les collections égyptologiques en particulier, sont aujourd'hui confrontés à d'autres périls, bien plus profonds, fondamentaux et durables, nés, quant à eux, de la marchandisation du monde et des énormes mutations qu'elle engendre. Dans cette économie globalisée, les Musées n'échappent pas à la logique des dogmes de la mondialisation financière, qui veulent que l'utilité sociale d'une initiative culturelle soit mesurée essentiellement à l'aune de sa rentabilité commerciale ou de sa conformité à la culture dominante. Dans cette optique, le taux de fréquentation des Musées par le public s'impose trop souvent comme le critère principal, voire exclusif, de leur évaluation par les autorités politiques qui en ont la tutelle, indépendamment des enjeux sociaux dont ils devraient être les acteurs.

Ce débat sur le rôle des musées, sur leur ancrage social et, surtout, sur leur appropriation par le public traverse toute leur histoire récente, mais il est loin d'être neuf. Ainsi, en 1930 déjà, l'égyptologue belge Jean Capart (1877-1947), alors Conservateur en Chef des Musées royaux d'Art et d'Histoire de Bruxelles, publiait un article visionnaire, au titre inattendu et provocateur : « Un essai de communisme »[1]. Capart, fervent catholique et conservateur dans tous les sens du terme, n'avait à l'évidence aucune sympathie pour les structures économiques et politiques mises en place en Russie après la Révolution d'octobre 1917, ce qu'il exprime d'ailleurs d'une manière particulièrement virulente dans les premières lignes de son article. Mais, jouant habilement des paradoxes, il s'attache ensuite à démontrer que les Musées dont il a la responsabilité constitueraient « un exemple très curieux d'une application du communisme ». En effet, pour lui, le communisme se résume simplement à l'abolition de toute propriété privée. Or, selon sa démonstration, les collections des Musées appartiennent précisément à l'ensemble la collectivité, chaque citoyen en étant dès lors, en quelque sorte, le propriétaire, susceptible d'en jouir à volonté. Cette argumentation permet ensuite à Capart de déplorer que « ce propriétaire aux millions de têtes » ne fréquente guère les

1. J. Capart, « Un essai de communisme », in : *La Belgique en 1930* ; repr. in : *Le Temple des Muses* (Bruxelles 1936), 137–40.

Musées et ne manifeste que de l'indifférence à l'égard des trésors qu'ils contiennent. Ce triste constat imprègne de manière récurrente de nombreux écrits de Capart, consacrés à la gestion des Musées. Il y regrette sans cesse que les citoyens ne s'approprient pas les lieux en les fréquentant massivement, malgré tous les efforts consentis par la direction des Musées pour les y attirer. En 1930, la légitimité des Musées se mesure donc essentiellement à leur nombre de visiteurs, l'évidence de leur utilité sociale, en tant que lieux de culture et de savoir, allant manifestement de soi.

Plus de quatre-vingt ans plus tard, au Brésil, dans un monde en mutation, l'échec exemplaire d'une appropriation collective et populaire d'un lieu muséal aurait sans doute interpellé Jean Capart, même s'il n'est pas question, en l'occurrence, d'un musée d'égyptologie. Entre 1953 et 1977, à Maracana, un quartier au nord de Rio de Janeiro, un bel édifice du XIXe siècle abrita le « Musée indien » (*O Museu do Indio*), créé par le célèbre anthropologue brésilien Darcy Ribeiro (1922–1997) et dédié aux cultures autochtones. Riche de plusieurs milliers d'objets et de très importantes archives, le Musée fut transféré en 1978 dans le quartier plus aisé de Botafogo, au sud de la ville, où il est toujours actif. Depuis, cependant, le bâtiment de l'ancien musée était resté dans la mémoire collective des Indiens du Brésil comme un lieu emblématique de leur identité, où s'était progressivement développée, après une période d'abandon du bâtiment, une intense vie sociale et culturelle. En août 2012, le gouvernement brésilien et le Gouverneur de Rio de Janeiro annoncent leur intention de démolir le bâtiment, et d'en expulser ses occupants, suite à une demande de la FIFA (*Fédération Internationale de Football Association*), désireuse de dégager les abords d'un nouveau stade à ériger dans la perspective de la Coupe du Monde de Football 2014. Le 22 mars 2013, la police, appuyée par des blindés militaires, expulse les Indiens par la force, non sans de sérieuses échauffourées avec la population venue soutenir les occupants des lieux. Aujourd'hui, le sort de ce bâtiment qui, selon le gouverneur de Rio, n'aurait « aucune valeur patrimoniale », est toujours incertain. Le cas de l'ancien *Museu do Indio* montre de manière éloquente combien une institution muséale ou le lieu qui l'incarne peuvent s'inscrire dans la conscience collective d'une population qui les fait vivre et y affirme son identité et sa dignité. Mais surtout, et de manière plus inquiétante, il démontre que l'appropriation d'un musée, ou dans ce cas-ci d'un ancien musée, par une population, ce que Jean Capart appelait de ses vœux, n'est aucunement une garantie de pérennité de celui-ci dans un monde globalisé où dominent outrancièrement les jeux des intérêts financiers et commerciaux.

La viabilité des musées et, de manière plus large, la conservation des patrimoines culturels, sont donc avant tout des questions de choix politiques et économiques. Le cas de l'Égypte d'après janvier 2011 est à cet égard très représentatif. Les nombreux exemples de déprédations infligées au patrimoine archéologique et muséal égyptien au cours des soubresauts de la Révolution seront largement évoqués dans les contributions qui suivent. Mais, au-delà de la tragédie que représentent ces destructions, il importe avant tout de s'interroger sur les racines du problème et de rappeler, même si c'est là une banalité et une évidence, que la protection du patrimoine est avant tout une question de développement et d'éducation. Or, il faut bien constater que l'État égyptien a été confronté à de multiples obstacles lorsqu'il a voulu, dès les premiers mois qui ont suivi la chute de l'ancien régime, décréter quelques mesures élémentaires de progrès social. Suite à ces tentatives, l'Égypte a été immédiatement la cible d'attaques de la part de plusieurs puissances financières internationales, au point que, en avril 2014, elle était le quatrième pays au monde à subir le plus de plaintes, devant les tribunaux internationaux du commerce, pour avoir pris des mesures sociales risquant de réduire quelque peu les bénéfices des entreprises multinationales qui travaillent sur son territoire. Ainsi, par exemple, le seul projet d'une hausse, pourtant bien modeste, du salaire minimum légal, a immédiatement suscité une plainte (toujours en cours) du groupe français Veolia contre l'État égyptien[2]. Depuis, de tels recours en justice se sont multipliés, alimentant indirectement pauvreté et précarité, un terreau sur lequel prospèrent naturellement l'insécurité et les atteintes au patrimoine archéologique et muséal.

Cependant, dans ce contexte troublé, c'est à une autre sorte d'appropriation d'un Musée et de son patrimoine par la population, bien plus positive et rassurante, que l'on a assisté, au Caire, en janvier 2011. Dans le cadre des grands rassemblements de la Place Tahrir, des individus s'introduisent dans le Musée, durant la nuit du 28 janvier, et y dérobent ou y endommagent plusieurs dizaines de pièces. Le déroulement précis de ces événements, ainsi que l'identité des pillards, demeure, aujourd'hui encore, relativement flous. Cependant, la conséquence la plus remarquable de ces déprédations fut la mobilisation des manifestants et des habitants du Caire qui, spontanément, dès le lendemain, formèrent autour du Musée une impressionnante chaîne humaine destinée à le protéger concrètement et surtout, de manière très éloquente, à affirmer l'attachement de la population égyptienne envers son patrimoine.

Les Musées sont par essence des lieux où sont donnés à voir les contrastes des identités, la beauté des différences et la richesse des influences entre civilisations, un rôle social aux multiples facettes qui devrait s'avérer particulièrement pertinent dans un monde globalisé où règnent en permanence les coexistences, les échanges et les relations entre cultures, qu'elles soient harmonieuses ou conflictuelles. Sous cet aspect, les collections égyptiennes peuvent incontestablement jouer un rôle central, en montrant comment une civilisation fondée sur un système de pensée très différent du nôtre, et dont la vie était rythmée par une série de cycles naturels fondamentaux, s'est perpétuée, sans mutations notables, pendant trois millénaires. Cependant, il ne suffit plus aujourd'hui de démontrer l'utilité sociale des Musées pour garantir leur pérennité. Face à des pouvoirs publics qui ont trop souvent renoncé à se donner les moyens d'assumer leurs missions, dans un monde où la culture pèse peu par rapport aux stratégies du profit, les Musées, s'ils veulent survivre, doivent devenir de véritables enjeux de société, ancrés dans le quotidien des villes et des milieux sociaux où ils sont

2. Voir à ce sujet : F. Rey, « Veolia assigne l'Egypte en justice », Jeune Afrique, 11 juillet 2012.

implantés et qui doivent d'urgence se les approprier. Espérons que la chaîne humaine de la Place Tahrir soit un symbole d'avenir...

Abbreviations

CIPEG	International Committee for Egyptology (ICOM)
DRTF	Disaster Relief Task Force
ICA	International Council on Archives
ICCROM	International Center for the Study of the Preservation and restauration of Cultural Property
ICOM	International Council of Museums
ICOM-CC	International Committee for Conservation (ICOM)
ICOMOS	International Committee on Monuments and Sites
ICMS	International Committee of Museum Security (ICOM)
ICTOP	International Committee for the Training of Personnel (ICOM)
IFLA	International Federation of Library Associations and Institutions
INTERCOM	International Committee for Museum Management (ICOM)
KMKG-MRAH	Koninklijk Musea voor Kunst en Geschiedenis -Musées royaux d'Art et d'Histoire, Bruxelles
MEP	Museum Emergency Programme
SCA	Supreme Council of Antiquities, Egypt
SPNHC	Society for the Preservation of Natural History Collections
UCL	University College London
UMAC	International Committee for University Museums and Collections (ICOM)
UNESCO	United Nations, Educational, Scientific and Cultural Organization

Bibliographic Abbreviations

ASAE	Annales du Service des Antiquités d'Égypte
BdE	Bibliothèque d'Étude. Institut français d'archéologie orientale
BIE	*Bulletin de l'Institut d'Égypte*
BIFAO	*Bulletin de l'Institut français d'archéologie orientale*
CdE	*Chronique d'Égypte*
JARCE	*Journal of the American Research Center in Egypt*
JEA	*Journal of Egyptian Archaeology*
JNES	*Journal of Near Eastern Studies*

LÄ	*Lexikon der Ägyptologie*
MDAIK	*Mitteilungen des deutschen archäologischen Instituts, Abteilung Kairo*
OLA	Orientalia Lovaniensia Analecta
PSBA	Proceedings of the Society of Biblical Archaeology
SAK	Studies zur altägyptischen Kultur

Contributors

Mohamed Ismael Badawi
Conservation Department, Faculty of Archaeology, South Valley University, Egypt. Consultant to the National Museum of Egyptian Civilization, Egypt.

Tine Bagh
Ny Carlsberg Glyptotek, curator, Egyptian Art. Copenhagen, Denmark.

Simone Burger Robin
Independent scholar, Brussels, Belgium.

Marek Chłodnicki
Senior curator, Archaeological Museum in Poznań, Poznań, Poland.

Luc Delvaux
Curator, Dynastic and Greco-Roman Egypt, Royal Museums of Art and History, Brussels, Belgium.

Claire Derriks
Chair of CIPEG 2007–2013. Curator emeritus, Royal Museum of Mariemont (Belgium). Professor, Royal Institute of History of Art and Archaeology, Brussels, Belgium.

Hedvig Győry
Museum of Fine Arts, Budapest, Hungary.

Christian E. Loeben
Egyptian Collection, Museum August Kestner, Hannover, Germany.

Sabina Malgora
Director, Milan Mummy Project: mummyproject@libero.it. Curator of the Egyptian Collection at Buonconsiglio Castle, Trent, Italy.

M. Carmen Pérez-Die
Keeper of Egyptian and Near East Department, Museo Arqueológico Nacional, Madrid, Spain.

Esther Pons Mellado
Curator of Egyptian and Near East Department, Museo Arqueológico Nacional, Madrid, Spain.

Madlen Tomorad
Assistant professor, Croatian Studies (Studia Croatiaca), University of Zagreb., Croatia.

Arnaud Quertinmont
Attaché au service Inventaire et Numérisation, Musée royal de Mariemont. Morlanwelz, Belgium.

Annamaria Ravagnan
Regione Lombardia. General Direction: Culture, Identita' e Autonomie della Lombardia; Service: Musei, Ecomusei, Biblioteche e Archivi. Milano, Italy.

Maarten J. Raven
Curator, Oudheidkundige Museum van Oudheden, Leiden, Netherlands.

Regine Schulz
Member of the executive council of ICOM. Director/CEO, Roemer and Pelizaeus Museum, Hildesheim, Germany.

Badrya Serry
Director, Antiquities Museum, Bibliotheca Alexandrina. Alexandria, Egypt.

Ben van den Bercken
Master of Archaeology, Leiden, Netherlands.

Willem van Haarlem
Curator, Egyptian Department, Allard Pierson Museum, Amsterdam, The Netherlands.

Paula Veiga
Researcher in Egyptology, Lisbon, Portugal.

Eugène Warmenbol
Centre de Recherches en Archéologie et Patrimoine, Université libre de Bruxelles, Belgium.

Collections at Risk: New Challenges in a New Environment

Maarten J. Raven

"Everything of value is defenseless"
(Alles van waarde is weerloos)

This line from the poem "The Very Old One Sings," written in 1974 by the Dutch poet and painter Lucebert (pseudonym for Lubertus Jacobus Swaanswijk, 1924–1994), may serve as an appropriate motto for the present volume. It has become one of those set phrases that everyone in the Dutch language community knows by heart and appropriates for his own purposes. In political discussions in the Netherlands, Lucebert's line is often quoted in the ongoing dispute about the necessity of government support for anything cultural. Written in neon lights on the roof top of an insurance office, the phrase acquired a rather cynical commercial character. No doubt closer to the poet's intentions is a copy of the same phrase on the façade of an art school in Rotterdam, whereas yet another version (rather mysteriously) graces the entrance of a pub in Ghent.

But do we really know what the poet meant by this phrase? In order to understand it,[1] we should not read it in isolation but have to include the context of the poem as a whole. The *old one* of the title refers to the philosopher Parmenides (ca. 515 BC) who stressed that reality only exists in the here and now. We have to treasure the things that surround us, because they are all we have got: we do not always know where they come from; we do not know where they will go. The poem ends with the lines:

Everything of value is defenseless
At a touch it becomes
Rich
And equal to everything

1. For the following analysis, I borrow from Peter Hofman in the newspaper *Trouw* of 31 January 2006; see http://www.trouw.nl/tr/nl/4324/Nieuws/archief/article/detail/1681924/2006/01/31/De-filosofie-van-een-weerloos-citaat.dhtml.

As the heart of time
As the heart of time

So indeed, Lucebert's phrase can be used as an appropriate motto by all those who take culture to heart. When applied to cultural remains from antiquity, such as the monuments and artifacts of ancient Egypt that form the background of the contributions in the present volume, we might paraphrase as follows: these vulnerable remains are all we have of a world that has vanished long ago. We have inherited them from a distant past, and though we do not know what will come after us, on us rests the responsibility to preserve and protect them for the future. Being able to enjoy these mysterious objects in the here and now, or even to touch them—though most museum curators would object we do not have to take the poet's word literally there—is an experience that both enriches our lives and adds new significance to the objects themselves. Our confrontation with the original object thus becomes a timeless event that cannot be matched by any replica, copy, or illustration. Therefore we have to combine all our efforts to ensure that future generations, too, can benefit from the same sensation, and to prevent that they will only know these ancient treasures from books or other media.

International Efforts

Such considerations are far from new, of course. In fact, they lay at the basis of the well-known The Hague Convention for the Protection of Cultural Property of 1954. The direct motivation for the drafting of this protocol was formed by the dreadful experiences of the Second World War with its great losses of cultural, artistic, religious, and historical heritage. Indeed, the convention explicitly stated that it was meant to apply *in the Event of Armed Conflict*, which at the time was understood as international conflict. Gradually, however, the awareness spread that intranational conflicts such as civil wars and revolutions could have equally disastrous effects. This gave rise to a rephrasing of the protocol in 1999, in which this aspect is explicitly stressed, as pointed out in an article on the The Hague Convention by Karl von Habsburg.[2] The rapid changes that have taken place in the world since the end of World War II have resulted in the current situation, in which interethnic, intercultural, and interreligious conflicts play a larger role in the destruction of cultural heritage than the large-scale international wars we have somehow learned to suppress. As Von Habsburg argues, such intranational conflicts are sometimes far more detrimental to the survival of monuments and art treasures than the traditional international wars, because quite often the opposing parties intentionally seek to wipe out each other's cultural identity.

2. *ICOM News*, 67 (April 2014), 26–27; see http://archives.icom.museum/icomnews2014–1_eng/index.html.

Another change brought about by the shaping of postwar society is that far-away places that used to be utterly inaccessible (except by a few hardy explorers and adventurers) have suddenly become the holiday resorts and playgrounds of the masses. Large-scale tourism not only destroys the natural habitat of many exotic paradises, but also wreaks havoc on their cultural heritage, either directly by the construction of airports, roads, or hotels, or indirectly because the advent of mass tourism creates a demand for cheap and easily transportable souvenirs and antiquities, and thereby stimulates illicit excavations and vandalism. At the same time, the boom of economy has created an affluent clientele in the western (and recently also in the eastern) hemisphere, where auction houses and art galleries sell high-priced archaeological or ethnographical objects to collectors or museums. Often, these are objects freshly excavated from hitherto unexplored sites or, even worse, intentionally broken off from standing monuments. In order to curb these unwanted developments, yet another international convention was drafted, the 1970 Convention on the Means of Prohibiting and Preventing the Illicit Import, Export and Transfer of Ownership of Cultural Property. Though pessimists will say that this admirable initiative has not been very successful, it has at least raised a public awareness for the aspect of legitimacy in handling antiquities and other art objects. Today, no dealer or auction house can ignore specifying the provenance or pedigree of their merchandise, and no bona fide collector or museum can acquire illegitimate objects and display them without exposing themselves to public criticism.

Protecting cultural heritage in times of armed conflict is a matter best left to trained law enforcement officers and the military. The coordination of such actions is often undertaken by the Blue Shield organization, a cooperation of the International Council on Archives (ICA), the International Council of Museums (ICOM), the International Council on Monuments and Sites (ICOMOS) and the International Federation of Library Associations and Institutions (IFLA). Again, I refer to the article by Blue Shield chairman Karl von Habsburg for further details and examples of its invaluable work. On the other hand, the prevention of illicit export during more peaceful conditions cannot very well be enforced by armed troops. Here a major part has to be played by education of the local population, the organization of efficient institutions such as regional museums, information centers, and archaeological commissions, the training of police officers and customs personnel, and the codification of national and international law (such as the 1995 Unidroit Convention on Stolen and Illegally Exported Cultural Objects).

Local Conditions

There is of course another category of events that may result in the massive destruction of cultural heritage. Natural disasters such as earthquakes, volcanic eruptions, tsunamis, or hurricanes usually cause extensive damage, both to freestanding monuments and to museum constructions and other cultural institutions. Apart from their direct detrimental effects, they may also create lasting social problems such as impoverishment and economic decline or even downright anarchy, which in their turn increase the risk of illicit digging and dealing in antiquities.

Another type of disaster, smaller in scale but potentially of equal effect to public (or private) collections, is of course the flooding or conflagration of the building where they are kept. Such risks of water and fire, and those of theft and robbery, can be minimized by good maintenance, the installation of proper technical devices, and the care for museum security. Inevitably, the efficacy of museum management in these areas depends on local conditions, on the financial means available for modernization, and on the political negotiations with governing bodies. Yet here, too, international cooperation can be helpful. The International Council of Museums has various subcommittees that can advise on these matters,[3] such as the International Committee for Museum Security (ICMS) and the International Committee for the Training of Personnel (ICTOP), or even the International Committee on Management (INTERCOM). In case of disasters, international rescue of art treasures is also available through institutions such as the Museums Emergency Programme (MEP), the Disaster Relief Task Force (DRTF), the International Centre for the Study of the Preservation and Restoration of Cultural Property (ICCROM), or more independent organizations such the Getty Foundation or the Prince Claus Fund.

A final aspect of the care for art treasures, whether from the past or the present, is the proper conservation and restoration of the objects in question. Here, too, the ultimate responsibility lies with the management of the monument or museum in question and their local, regional, or national financing institutions and politicians. Yet international help and advice is again available, for instance via the International Committee for Conservation (ICOM-CC).

Egypt: New Conditions, New Risks

Unfortunately, all of these aspects of risk management come together in the care for the heritage of Egypt. To a certain extent, the antiquities and monuments of the pharaonic, Coptic, and Islamic periods (the latter including the memorabilia of the recent past) have of course always been under threat. However, the rate of deterioration of their condition has increased over the years, to find a quite horrifying climax in the last few years. Down to about 1800, Egypt was a relatively stagnant backwater where the antiquities rested safely under their cover of wind-blown sand of many centuries, while the freestanding monuments were left to the elements and were slowly decaying but not generally vandalized. All this changed with the advent of the Napoleonic armies, when all of a sudden the antiquities and the portable monuments acquired

3. See the ICOM website, http://icom.museum/.

the fateful status of mere merchandise and were exported by the shipload to Europe, and later America.

With the foundation of the Egyptian Museum and the national Antiquities Service in 1858, several decades of commercial digging and pillaging gradually gave way to a more organized and scholarly type of exploration. However, the growing involvement of the European powers with the Nilotic region certainly did not have beneficial effects only. The other side of the medal was a rapid modernization and industrialization, the construction of railroads, canals, and factories, and finally the construction of the first Aswan Dam in 1898, all of which led to an ever quicker loss of antiquities which had been perfectly safe for millennia. The effects of the rapid growth of the local population and their increasing need of housing, transport, agricultural fields, irrigation water, and electricity has quite transformed the country in the course of the twentieth century. Such modern demands also brought about the construction of the new High Dam at Aswan (1960–1970) and the ensuing drowning of Nubia's monuments. The development of mass tourism in the same period changed many formerly unviolated landscapes into airstrips, parking areas, hotel resorts, and facilities for cruise ships, whereas the walls of tombs and temples now get covered in graffiti and their floors erode under the shuffle of countless feet. Even more worrying is the fact that the very structure of several monuments is giving way due to the spill of sewage water and the vibrations of tourist buses. At the same time, air pollution starts to cause major damage to the vulnerable stone surfaces and their sculpted or painted decorations.

Egyptologists thought they were used to such modern conditions, and had found certain ways to curb their evil effects. We have been naïve, because we have been blind to the social, economic and religious tensions which built up in the Egyptian population and which were suddenly released during the Egyptian revolution of January 2011. Nobody could have foretold that within three days most of the Egyptian sites and monuments would be exposed to looting and illicit excavations, and that the national collection of antiquities in the Egyptian Museum on Tahrir Square would be robbed of a number of irreplaceable objects. Since then we have witnessed the burning of the Institut d'Égypte with its unique collection of manuscripts (December 2011), the pillaging of the Mallawi Museum (August 2013), and the bomb attack damaging the Islamic Museum (January 2014). At the same time, numerous archaeological sites are still being plundered by gangs of robbers, with widespread destruction being reported from the Aswan west bank, Abydos, Antinoopolis, and Abusir el-Meleq, to mention only a few (and this is only the first letter of the alphabet!). In some cases, archaeologists have been chased away from their concessions by armed gangs, regional storage facilities have come under attack, and local museums have been robbed. Quite often, the destruction is totally meaningless because the finds will have a very limited financial value, while the resulting losses of scientific knowledge are considerable and irreparable. This state of anarchy is still continuing, and together with their past the people of Egypt are now destroying their own future. However, we can hardly blame individual members of this community, because it is not their fault that they are uneducated and destitute.

Egyptian Museums: Preserving the Past for the Future

Under these challenging circumstances, the role of the international museums of ancient Egyptian art and antiquities becomes ever more important. We all know that in most cases these collections owe their existence to practices that would be considered illegitimate according to modern standards. However, the current events in the country of origin of these treasures of human experience has clearly shown that there may be a benefit in the dispersal of the objects over the globe. At least, this means that the risks of wholesale damage and loss of the Egyptian heritage has been reduced, and that, even though tourism to Egypt may be slow in taking off to the same level as before the revolution, there are many other places where we can educate our visitors to appreciate the eternal values of these heirlooms, and to instruct them that these should never be lost for humanity as a whole.

Also, the recent events increase the responsibility of each representative of our museum community to do his or her utmost for the preservation of the Egyptian heritage, both inside Egypt and in the many collections and scientific institutions abroad. Therefore, it was very appropriate that the 29th Annual Meeting of ICOM's International Committee for Egyptology (CIPEG) was devoted to the theme of *Collections at Risk: New Challenges in a New Environment.* The present volume contains several of the papers read during those sessions in Brussels in 2012, and thereby gives a clear example of the multifarious means that lie open to us in order to gain our objectives.

Thus Regine Schulz stresses how museums have to fight the cultural dementia of politicians and the whims of the public, while Anna-Maria Ravagnan and Hedvig Györy show the importance of proper training and museum pedagogy for the purpose of increasing cultural awareness and preventing attacks to heritage. Arnaud Quertinmont discusses the various risks facing a museum collection and how to prevent them, whereas Ben van den Bercken discusses the role of university collections in the preservation of Egyptian heritage. Badrya Serry highlights the intimate bond existing between the Alexandria museum and local archaeology, while Marek Chlodnicki shows how newly excavated finds can reshape the presentation of Egypt's national collection. Mohamed Ismael Badawi gives a vivid picture of methods of handling art developed for the displays in Egypt's new museums, whereas Willem van Haarlem introduces new methods of storing a fragile and neglected papyrus collection in Amsterdam.

New displays offer a fresh chance to focus on the themes that are considered important today and to educate our visitors. Thus Carmen Pérez-Die and Esther Pons Mellado share with us their plans for the future display of the Madrid Museum. On the other hand, the full inventory of existing collections still has to be refined, as

Mladen Tomorad shows in his overview of the Egyptian collections in Croatia. Old and new can also meet, as Sabina Malgora stresses in her presentation of the virtually unknown Camille Leone collection of Vercelli.

The loss of monuments or museum objects is always a very painful experience, yet various papers show that such losses can sometimes be reconstructed: if not in actuality, then at least on paper. Thus Luc Delvaux demonstrates what the Brussels Museum can do to repair the damages of a fire, even seventy years after the event, and Paula Veiga shows how the collection at Porto (which was likewise damaged by fire recently) has started rising from its ashes. Christian Loeben tries to reconstruct the losses sustained by the Museum August Kestner in Hannover, Germany during World War II, whereas Eugène Warmenbol revivifies a mummy from Brussels lost during an autopsy in 1942. Tine Bagh illustrates how a now-lost monument from ancient Memphis can be reconstructed inside the Ny Carlsberg Glyptotek in Copenhagen, and Simone Burger tries to recreate a statue from Karnak on the basis of petrographic research of the now-dispersed fragments.

Taken together, all these initiatives show that museum specialists can indeed contribute to reduce the risks to the Egyptian heritage, both in Egypt itself and in their own community, and that in some cases they may succeed in redressing some of the damage done in less-enlightened periods or resulting from unfortunate events in the past. We can only hope that this spirit of optimism and enterprise will also convince the managers and politicians of our time that something can be done. In that case, *everything of value* may yet find the much needed protection, to quote Lucebert once again, until *it becomes rich and equal to everything*. For it is our heritage that shows us who we are, where we came from, and where we are going. Our cultural treasures can form the basis for the education and economic prosperity that this world needs.

I. Collections at Risk: Cultural Heritage Preservation

Museums in Danger and How They Can Survive

Regine Schulz

"Collections at risk," the theme of the 2012 annual meeting of CIPEG in Brussels, is a topic relevant not only in Egypt, but in many other countries as well. The dangers for the collections in museums are diverse. They range from destruction and theft by looters and criminals in unstable political situations to neglect and disregard by the responsible authorities, as well as misuse, damage, or sale for financial reasons.

We all know about the difficult situation in Egypt after the Arab Spring in 2011 and in other Middle Eastern countries because of unstable political situations and a lack of security. We can only hope that the situation will improve. However, many thefts in museums and looting in cultural sites of Egypt were not the direct result of turmoil but of the financial crisis that followed, together with an increase of criminality.

Many collections and museums in Europe and the United States are increasingly in danger because of financial problems, changing expectations, and the lower esteem in which they are held. Politicans are asking the questions, Do we have too many museums? Do we still need museums in the era of internet? Must museums change to become more attractive?

Let us look for a moment at numbers. In the first decade of the twenty-first century, the number of museums in Egypt has increased to forty-nine and more were planned (listed by the Supreme Council of Antiquities in 2012). The major goal for these additional museums was to increase the amount of places of interest for visitors, to spread tourist activities all over the country, and particularly to support structurally weak areas. To raise awareness of the Egyptian population for their own culture was only a secondary goal. After the Arab Spring, many projects (e.g., the new Minya Museum) have been halted because of changing priorities and financial problems.

The number of museums has increased also in Europe and the United States during recent decades. In Germany, for example, the number of museums has nearly doubled during the last thirty years from 3,200 official museums in 1980 to 6,200 in 2008; this is one museum for every 13,200 inhabitants. Let us compare with some other countries: in 2011, the United States had one museum for every 17,600 inhabitants, Switzerland one for every 8,200, and France one for every 6,500 inhabitants.[1] Since 2009 the increase has slowed down and some assume that 20 percent of the museums are in danger of closing for financial reasons.

The role of museums in society has been discussed intensively since the time of the first collections in "Cabinets of Wonders and Curiosities" at royal and princely courts in the late Renaissance and Baroque. Intensive discussions on the role and function of museums reflect not only their diversity, but also their importance for the development of society.[2] They act as loci for a collective memory,[3] of interdisciplinary activities,[4] and places that make their own and foreign views and ideas visible.[5] Therefore they assist in building identity, raising awareness and understanding, and inspiring creativity.

However, politicians, administrators, and even stakeholders more and more question this important role for different reasons. Therefore we have to ask what are the major challenges and threats for many museums; what are the possible chances and opportunities; and which strategies can museums develop to keep alive and fulfill their mission.

In the United States and Europe many museums face:

- a lack of funding, intensified by the financial crisis
- a lack of expertise
- fast-changing expectations
- heteronomy by politics, external administrators, trustees or other nonexecutive directors, foundations and donors/sponsors.

These problems create a variety of challenges, including:

- to care in an adequate and professional way for the needs of the collections in storage, on display, and during travel as loans
- to preserve the objects of the collection
- to keep the collection and avoid de-accessioning for financial reasons
- to care for the needs of the visitors
- to compete with other cultural and educational institutions
- to fulfill the guidelines of ICOM's Code of Ethics.

The main problem for many museums is a lack of funding. This is the reason why they cannot care for their collections in a professional manner, nor hire specialists to provide the expertise needed to act or react in a timely manner to the changing ex-

1. Senseng 2011.
2. For ICOM's definition of museums see http://icom.museum/the-vision/museum-definition/.
3. Rivera-Orraca 2009.
4. Beuys 1980, 47–74.
5. M. Kröger, "nicht-wirklich. wo sind wir, wenn wir im museum sind?" http://www.kunstgeschichte-ejournal.net/discussion/2008/Kroeger.

pectations of the visitors. Some of these challenges have been discussed openly in the media, others not. Only if dramatic situations threaten a museum do the media and the public become aware of the problems. An intensive debate started in the United States when Brandeis University in Waltham, MA planned to close its Rose Art Museum and sell the collection in 2009, and when in Germany the existence of famous museums, such as the Museum of Natural Science in Leipzig, the Art Museum in Bochum, and the City Museum in Hildesheim were in danger.

Other problems are less in the forefront, particularly the problem of heteronomy. The Northampton Museum in the United Kingdom, run by the town, was considering selling its Egyptian statue for two million GBP to use the money for other projects. The defence for the sale is quite interesting; the city administration had argued that since they do not have the capacity to safely secure a statue of such a high value and that the object is not part of the regional culture it therefore can be sold. The city had also planned a citizen survey to discuss how the money should be used. Also in this case an open debate started not only on the regional and national levels, but also internationally.[6]

Another barely discussed challenge is the heteronomy of museums. Professional administrators working for the state or city, boards of trustees, or other supervisory boards, donors, and sponsors all have their own ideas, which are sometimes not in accordance with professional and ethical rules and regulations. The dependence of the museums on outside decision makers and on the interest of private supporters and foundations is often a real challenge. One of the main problems is conflicts of interest or decisions that are to the detriment of the museum. This kind of heteronomy concerns all parts of the institution: funding, accessioning, and deaccessioning, decisions on exhibitions and loans, and so on.

What are the opportunities for museum professionals to avoid the possibility that their museum will be one of the 10 to 20 percent of museums that may close in the next one or two decades? How can museums survive and continue to play an important role in the social and the cultural life of the people? In other words, how can museums enhance their profiles as important partners not only for other institutions, but for each individual visitor. A possibility would be to strengthen or modify the museum's profile to become:

- an advisor, mentor, educator
- an open-minded discussion partner

6. After this lecture was given in 2012, the statue was sold on July 10, 2014 at Christie's London for 15.76 million GBP to a private buyer. The Northampton borough council, the owner of the statue, received 45% of the proceeds and Spencer Compton, the 7th Marquess of Northampton and descendant of the donor of the statue, 55%. The Museums Association UK had not endorsed the sale, and the British Arts Council withdrew the accreditation of the museum. Shortly before the Egyptian Minister of State of Antiquities Dr. Mamdouh Eldamaty appealed to stop the sale and CIPEG-ICOM had sent out a statement criticizing the sale for ethical reasons (ICOM Code of Ethics § 2.16).

- an inspirator and animator
- an innovative project partner
- an experimental platform for projects and presentations
- and last but not least, a place of participation

Such a profile could result in an increase in the museums's attractiveness to different audiences, partners, donors, and sponsors. Hopefully this would also result in greater financial support, and volunteer participation.

Although such thoughts may be helpful in the discussion with outside administrators, sponsors, and political decision makers, each museum is different and so is the community it serves. Only a close analysis of its own dependences can help it to make the right decisions or to convince the decision makers to do so. There is no doubt that not all museums will survive. But if the collections can survive and the professional goals are met, changes can help to fulfill the museum's mission even if the place of the museum in the community and administrative structure may change.

References

BEUYS, J. 1980. "Das Museum: Ein Ort der permanenten Konferenz." Pp. 47–74 in H. Kurnitzky (ed.), *Notizbuch 3: Kunst, Gesellschaft, Museum*. Berlin: Medusa.

Rivera-Orraca, L. 2009. "Are Museums Sites of Memory?" *The New School Psychology Bulletin* 6, 32–37.

SENSENG, S. 2011. "Museen in der Krise? Eine Problembeschreibung." In *Verband Rheinischer Museen, 8. Rheinischer Museumstag, 6. Juni 2011,* http://www.museumsverband-rheinland.de/wp-content/uploads/Sensen_Museen-in-der-Krise-06062011.pdf.

Training against Attacks on Cultural Heritage

Annamaria Ravagnan

The risk of attacks to cultural heritage is still high in many countries of the world and therefore the importance of training in their prevention is essential. As understood from press releases, in 2011, following protests and clashes in Egypt,[1] known as the Revolution of the Nile, many objects were damaged and removed not only within the Museum of Egyptian Antiquities in Cairo but also in deposits belonging to a large number of archaeological sites in Egypt.

A. Biasiotti, an electrical engineer in charge of security systems both in institutions in Italy and abroad and a UNESCO expert, had travelled throughout Egypt in 2010 to examine the security measures in place at several sites and museums. Biasiotti in general pointed out gaps in security and suggested creating an emergency action plan for natural and man-made disasters.[2] Despite Biasiotti's recommendations, security measures remained substandard as the following year would highlight.

There was wide media coverage on the attacks perpetrated by unknown assailants against the Egyptian Museum in Cairo in January 2011. The intruders took advantage of the lack of control and the lack of emergency procedures. After the attack on the museum, there were also other intrusions elsewhere, as at Saqqara for example, where many graves are not yet excavated and where storage facilities for archaeological finds do not measure up to security standards.

In December 2011, another disastrous event occurred when the Institut d'Égypte in Cairo was destroyed by fire. This institute is a short walk from the U.S. Embassy and is well known to scholars, although quite unknown by tourists. The fire developed on the lower floors of the building and reached the upper floors. The Institute is considered the oldest scientific institute in Egypt and its library contained more than 200,000 volumes, including the original volumes of the *Description de l'Égypte* written by savants as a result of the Napoleon's expedition to Egypt.

Many volunteers came to help after the disaster. They were invited to recover the books and provided with white coveralls, gloves, and masks. Unfortunately, most of

1. Bertini 2005.
2. Biasiotti 1998, 2005.

the volunteers had no experience in the intervention of recovery of wet and partially burned volumes. Fortunately, a library in Cairo made available a machine for vacuum packing of books and this helped in saving many volumes. The lack of an updated catalog of books and manuscripts kept in the Institut d'Égypte still makes an accurate assessment of losses difficult.

These dramatic episodes remind us that most of our museums worldwide and archaeological sites lack specific programs for the preservation of cultural heritage, and above all lack appropriate training for employees of museums and archaeological sites in order to make them prepared to deal with acts of violence, vandalism, and dramatic events such as fires or earthquakes.

The defense of cultural heritage, including monuments, archives, libraries, and museums, is certainly very difficult because of its inherent weakness and its exposition to all kinds of attacks, even vandalism.

We can thus separate the problem of cultural heritage protection into two main categories: Protection and preservation, including restoration, (1) in times of peace and (2) during armed conflicts.

Despite the fact that several countries signed The Hague Convention for the Protection of Cultural Property in the Event of Armed Conflict[3]—the first international instrument exclusively dedicated to the protection of cultural heritage in the event of armed conflict—it remains very difficult to preserve cultural heritage during armed conflicts.[4] Egypt subscribed to the Convention on 30th December 1954 but to sign an agreement is not enough to protect cultural heritage, as recent events have evidenced.

In 2011, for the very first time, libraries, archives, and museums in the Lombardy Region of Italy decided to collaborate in order to preserve their properties from all kinds of damage and to create an emergency plan. The working group, which was organized by Ornella Foglieni, Superintendence Heritage Books Lombardy Region, and Adalberto Biasiotti, UNESCO expert, prepared a working document as a first standard procedure for staff and the public inside museums, libraries, and archives to make stakeholders aware of emergency procedures for the safeguard of cultural heritage. The most important problem is security and prevention of disasters in the library/archive/museum; while the safety of people, of course, is the first priority, particular care must also be taken also to safeguard collections.

The Italian working group believes that it is important to practice and to prepare triage treatment of cultural heritage and to invest in training and education acting on two different levels:[5]

---

3. Convention for the Protection of Cultural Property in the Event of Armed Conflict with Regulations for the Execution of the Convention 1954, The Hague, 14 May 1954: First Protocol, The Hague, 14 May 1954; Second Protocol, The Hague, 26 March 1999.
4. Gwinn and Wellheiser 2005.
5. Biasiotti and Beccaro Migliorati 2006.

1. Training for people on different levels for the protection of cultural heritage (guards, policemen, conservators, and museum directors, volunteers, cultural associations, firefighters, and so on)
2. Creating in all citizens a civic conscience in defense of cultural heritage

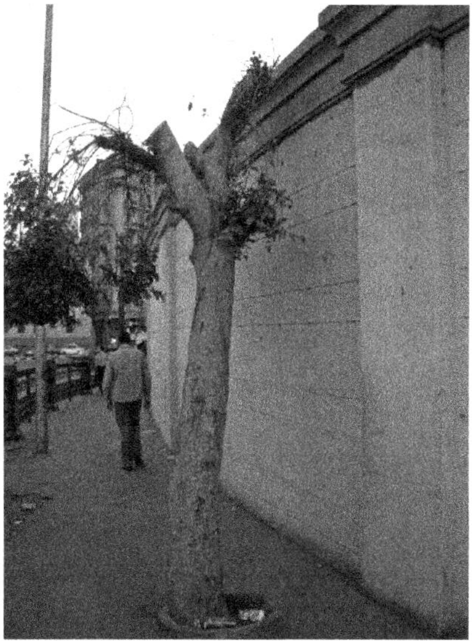

Fig. 1. Egyptian Museum Cairo, outside wall. © Adalberto Biasiotti.

For these reasons, in the Lombardy region, we have stressed the importance of volunteers at all levels and the invaluable involvement of the Civil Protection Staff, such as firemen and policemen, as additional protagonists before, during, and after the disaster.

In the last months Lombardy Region hold intensive courses in Emergency training for Cultural Heritage. The courses was addressed to museum staff, which has responsibility for movable cultural properties, such as museum directors, conservators, museum curators but also to volunteers and to the public in order to create a sense of belonging and to defense the cultural heritage.

Lombardy Region together with the offices of the Civil Protection has prepared a checklist for the"disaster plan" which is attached to this article.

During the Convention of the Cultural Heritage Professionals held in Milan on 22 November 2012 the topic of cultural heritage emergency has been particularly enhanced. The Galleries, Libraries, Archives and Museums Association ("Musei Biblioteche e Archivi"), has issued a final document on "Partnering for emergencies: how to intervene during disasters." GLAM has identified several lines of actions including:

- Activation in emergencies handled by the Department of National Civil Protection through voluntary professional resources that can operate in an interdisciplinary logistic to immediately make available expertise;
- Provision of update training dedicated to interdisciplinary cultural heritage professionals;
- Organization of training including the involvement of the Department of National Civil Protection on safety by preventing the emergences on cultural heritage.

As stated by A. Biasiotti, consultant in Lombardy region for disasters, a common sense is essential and it is really important to face the *status quo* to prevent damages. For example, as discussed above, even the simple elimination of a tree near the wall of the Museum of Egyptian Antiquities in Cairo could prevent or delay the access of the invaders (fig. 1).

An important strategic action is to improve knowledge and consciousness in implementing emergency plans to avoid dramatic consequences. Only through continuous training especially for young people we can protect our cultural heritage.

References

Bertini, M. B. 2005. *La conservazione dei beni archivistici e librari: prevenzione e piani di emergenza*. Rome: Carocci.

Biasiotti, A. 1998. *Arte sicura: tecniche e procedure per la difesa dei musei e delle mostre temporanee*. Bologna: Edis.

———. 2005. *Il piano di emergenza per i beni culturali: guida pratica all'applicazione della circolare n. 132 dell'8 ottobre 2004 del Ministero per i beni e le attività culturali sulla protezione del patrimonio artistico mobile*. Rome: EPC LIBRI.

Biasiotti A. and B. Beccaro Migliorati. 2006. *Security at Museums: 1. Di Cultural Heritage Protection Handbook*. Paris: UNESCO.

Gwinn, N., and J. Wellheiser (eds.). 2005. *Preparing for the Worst, Planning for the Best: Protecting four Cultural Heritage from Disaster*. Munich: Saur.

Checklist for setting up a disaster plan. Document drawn up by the federal office of civil defense protection of cultural heritage against the effects of disasters.

SCOPE	MEASURES	PENDING	DONE	COMMENTS
List of cultural properties to be evacuated	Keep copies of the inventories in another place than that in which the collections are kept. Prepare a list of the goods to be evacuated in case of a dramatic event. Mark cultural properties to be evacuated (note that the mark should not be an invitation to thieves!). Give instructions on how to access and deal with objects (unplug from the wall, remove etc.). The list of goods to be evacuated should be distributed in a targeted manner.			
Security documen-tation	Record the buildings according to the terms of the safety documentation. Make an inventory of the movable cultural properties. Microfilm archives and books.			
Technical installations	Ensure control of electrical systems (including emergency lighting). Ensure control of pipelines and ductwork. Check the water drain fire protection. Install fire and water infiltration detectors, hygrometers and burglar alarms. Test fire safety of buildings (walls and doors). For the most valuable buildings consult the protection of monuments.			

	Install fire hydrants, install fire extinguishers and ensure their maintenance. Check the locks on the doors, on the windows, as well as on general access. Ensure objects in simple and uniform way. Adopt uniform application to lock the windows and the cabinets. Check the quality of the deposits. Mark emergency exit. Install lightning rods and check these regularly and mark the locations of fire hydrants. Provide for necessary material for the evacuation (packaging, transportation, gloves, etc.).			
Refuges for cultural heritage	Promote the construction of shelters for cultural heritage. Grant temporary or permanent shelters for people.			
Staff information and education	Include specialists in the detachment of a disaster. Train in advance for the detachment of disasters, Arrange exercises with staff intervention (e.g. handling of fire extinguishers) and train for a fast evacuation			

Other areas	Prepare and update a detailed plan of the buildings (access, safety exits, fire hydrants, fire extinguishers, alarm panel, locations of collections and packing material etc.) Report the locations of cultural heritage on the action plans of the municipalities (fire brigades, civil protection organization, police). Reduce the possible sources of fire. Record the locations where to freeze paper documents damaged by water. Prepare a list of companies that have extendable ladders to evacuate through windows. Set up a list of experts to be convened in the event of a claim. Post a list with the addresses of agency to contact in case of emergency. Make sure access to deposits Train bodies of local intervention about appropriate performing. Distribute targeted lists of addresses and cultural heritage to evacuate enclosed in a sealed envelope.			

Tell el-Farkha: The Life of Discovered Objects after the Excavations

Marek Chłodnicki

The site of Tell el-Farkha has been excavated by the Polish Archaeological Mission to the eastern Nile Delta for fifteen years.[1] The site constitutes a settlement and a cemetery dated to Predynastic and Early Dynastic times and is already well known to scholars working on the beginnings of the ancient Egyptian state.[2] The excavations have delivered not only material of a high scientific value, but also hundreds of thousands of archaeological artifacts. Most of them are pottery and stone fragments, but almost twelve hundred selected objects have been registered in the Register Book of the Supreme Council of Antiquities in Dakahliya Inspectorate in Mansura. Among them are masterpieces of Egyptian art, including gold and ivory figurines. All of the objects, after the excavations, were packed into wooden boxes and transported to Mendes where the main stores of the Dakahliya Inspectorate are located.

Although the Polish excavations at Tell el-Farkha began in 1998,[3] the discoveries became famous after 2006 when the deposit of ivory and golden figures was found. The deposit of sixty-two small objects—ivory figurines and other items—were packed in a small jar and deposited in the shrine on the western Kom. The golden figures, found on the opposite side of the site (eastern Kom) were completely demolished, hidden in ancient times under the wall of a simple house.[4]

All of these pieces were probably hidden in the storerooms for a long time, but in 2007, the Polish Centre of Mediterranean Archaeology, organized an exhibition in the Cairo Egyptian Museum showcasing seventy years of Polish excavations in Egypt.[5]

1. Mission was organized by Poznań Archaeological Museum and Institute of Archaeology Jagiellonian University in Kraków with cooperation with the Centre of the Mediterranean Archaeology Warsaw University.
2. Results of the excavations were published many times, the complete summary of the results of the research are in Chłodnicki, Ciałowicz, and Mączyńska 2012.
3. These excavations were proceded by the Italian Archaeological Mission of the Centro Studi Ricerche Ligabue in 1988–1990 and partly published in Chłodnicki, Fattovich, and Salvatori, 1992.
4. Chłodnicki and Ciałowicz 2007; Chłodnicki and Ciałowicz 2010; Ciałowicz 2010.
5. Laskowska-Kusztal 2007.

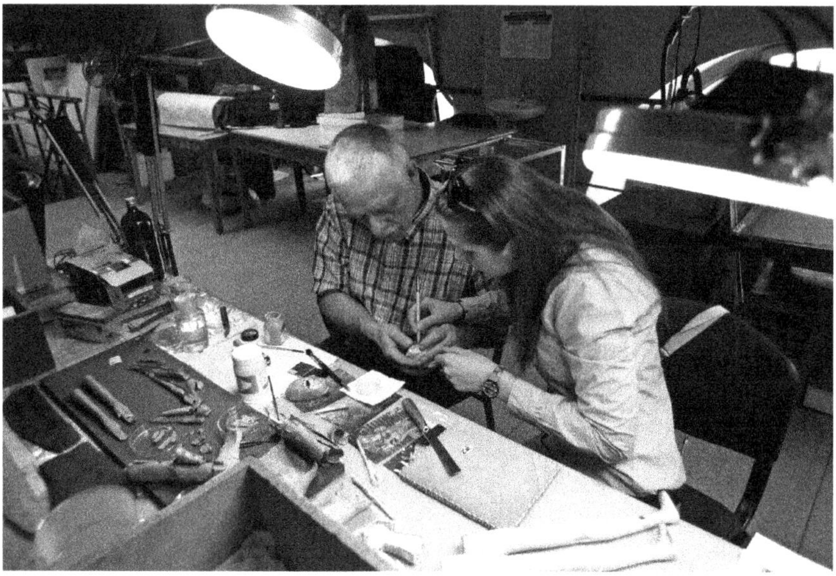

Fig. 1. Conservation work in Egyptian Museum. © Robert Slabonski.

Because of this, selected pieces from Tell el-Farkha have been taken to the Egyptian Museum in Cairo.[6]

After short, preliminary conservation, the objects have been placed on the gallery. They were a central attraction of that display, and masterpieces from Tell el-Farkha were kept in the Egyptian Museum for permanent exhibition and presented in the main hall in the vicinity of the Narmer palette.

Conservation work began before the exhibition in Egyptian Museum and was continued until 2013 (fig. 1).[7] Every year for one month a small team has conducted the work. In the mission, which was financed by the Polish Centre of Mediterranean Archaeology Warsaw University, conservators from the State Archaeological Museum in Warsaw and the Poznań Archaeological Museum participated[8] The conservation season in 2011 was postponed because of Egyptian Revolution. The objects fortunately survived that time in good condition and without any damage.

The objects from the ivory deposit were in quite good condition. They needed only to be strengthened and cleaned. The process of restoration was completed in 2010 and after that only the state of preservation was checked. They were checked in 2012 and it seems that the process of the erosion was stopped.

6. Ciałowicz 2007.
7. Longa and Weker 2011.
8. The works were conducted by Władysław Weker with the assistance of Anna Longa and later Małgorzata Żukowska and the photographer Robert Słaboński.

The situation with the figurines made of sheet gold was initially very bad. The foil of the golden figures was broken into many pieces, smashed, folded, cracked, and very deformed. The provisional reconstruction made already in the field in 2006 revealed two figurines of standing, naked males, one approximately 60 cm high and the second 30 cm high. Gold rivets indicated that the gold was mounted probably on the wooden core.

The objects were transported to the Egyptian Museum in Cairo, where with the cooperation with Conservation Department of the Museum the works were continued. Because of the lack of time before the anniversary exhibition, the gold of the smaller figure was mounted on the paper-maché corpus and presented in standing position. The bigger figurine was only provisionally modeled and recomposed, presented in lying position.

In 2008 the work began again. The small pieces were carefully joined and carefully modeled into their original form. A model of the core was prepared in jeweler's wax and then replaced in gypsum. In the next steps small pieces were also connected, changing their shapes a little, and all the gold was transferred onto the wooden core (fig. 2).

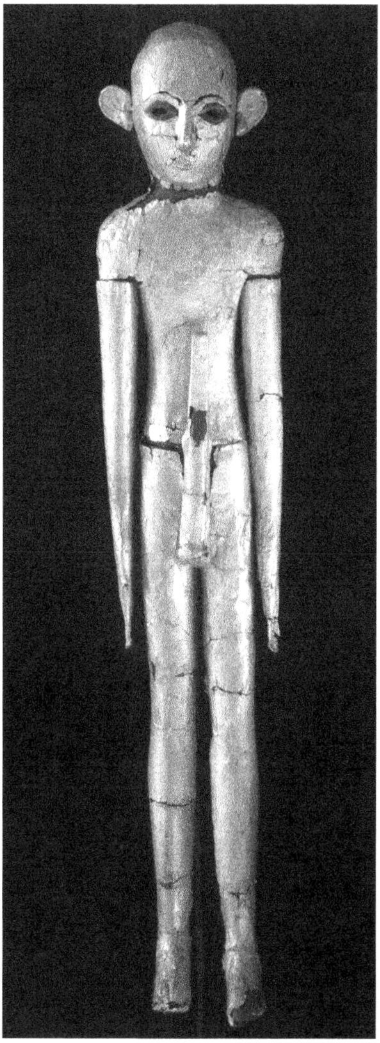

Fig. 2. Golden figure, Naqada IIIB. © Robert Slabonski.

The golden figurines with eyes of lapis lazuli were found in the Naqada IIIB context, but the flint knives found in the deposit suggest that they could be older. The style of the figures, their large protruding ears and large phalluses fit very well into Predynastic art.[9] The whole deposit was presented complete together with the coil of the carnelian and ostrich eggshell beads.

In the same display case in the exhibit, five objects dated to the beginning of the First Dynasty are also presented. These are three ivory figurines, a spoon with a handle in the shape of crocodile, and a falcon-shaped palette found in the administrative/cult building on the western Kom.

9. Ciałowicz 2012, 203.

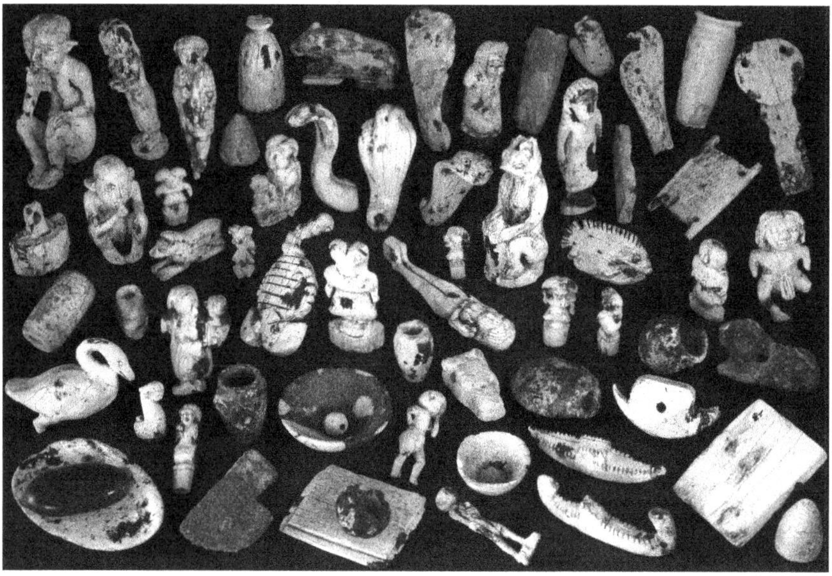

Fig. 3. Content of the deposit. © Robert Slabonski.

In the second display case we can see all sixty-two objects that were deposited in the small jar (fig. 3). Between them the most interesting was a group of human figurines made of hippopotamus ivory. Many of them are masterpieces of art. All of them are already published so I will not go into more detail about them.[10] The decorated jar that the deposit was found in is also presented there. At Tell el-Farkha, wine jars with the *serekh* have also been found. One of them with Narmer's *serekh* is on exhibit.

The objects found at Tell el-Farkha call attention to the organization of the exhibition in the newly created Grand Egyptian Museum. The curators selected an additional collection to be presented in the exhibit together with the Tell el-Farkha material. The selection was made in 2008, unfortunately without the consultation with the excavators, and the criteria for the selection are not always clear. We do not know the framework of this display. We don't know if the objects from Tell el-Farkha will be presented together as a collection from one site or will be placed in combination with objects from other sites according to the categories of the objects. For this reason, it is difficult to criticize the decision. Despite this objection we can say that almost all of the important artifacts discovered until 2008 are on the list for the exhibit. They represent the full range of objects: pottery, stone vessels, stone palettes, flint, copper, jewelry, seals, and pieces of art. If we could change anything, it would be to ensure that objects found are not separated and to replace some of the objects selected in 2008 with other, better samples found later.

10. Ciałowicz 2010, 86–98; 2012, 207–21.

However, I can offer my opinion about the selected objects from the point of view of the scientists who took part in the discoveries and have knowledge about the whole collection of the objects from Tell el-Farkha site.

The most abundant category of the selected objects is pottery. It is reasonable that only a sample of them was selected. It represents the most frequent type of the vessel dated to Protodynastic and Early Dynastic times. Among them are very popular cylindrical jars and wine jars. Worthy of special mention is a cylindrical jar with an incised gazelle. It is the only pot that survived after the Italian excavations in 1988–1990. This pot was not discovered on the site but was found in a house in Gazala village where it was used as a flowerpot.

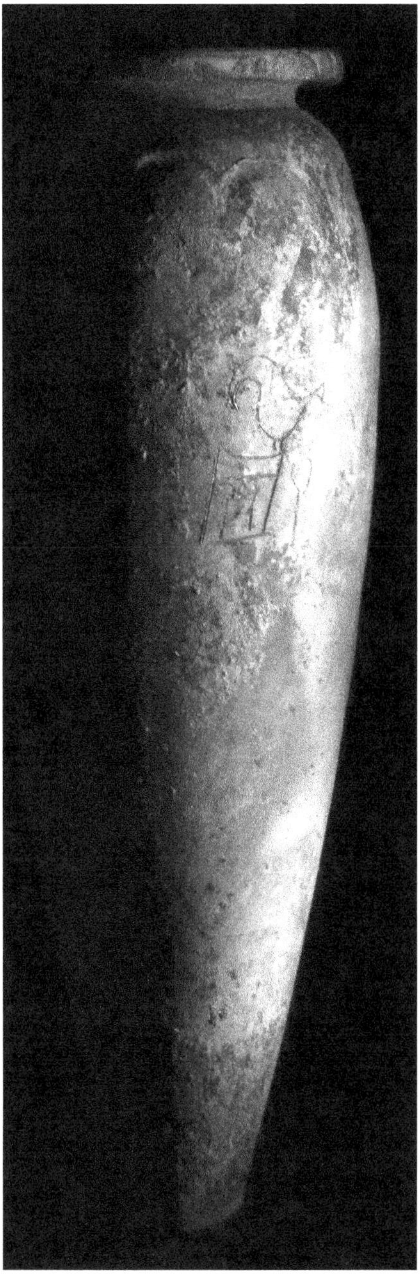

Fig. 4. Wine jar with a *serekh* of Iry-hor. © Robert Slabonski.

A second group of pottery are bowls and a selection of smaller pots. Among them are imitations of the Levantine forms and Predynastic vessels of Lower Egyptian culture.

Pottery is always a very common archaeological find and sometimes too many pots are exhibited so I wouldn't suggest augmenting the collection on display. But it may be good to replace some simple bowls or cylindrical jars with wine jars with the *serekhs* or potmarks with the names of the early rulers of Egypt, like *Iry-hor* (fig. 4).

Also vessels of Lower Egyptian culture decorated with a zigzag pattern should have their place in the exhibition; not many complete pots of this kind are in the museum's collections (fig. 5). A spinning bowl dated as early as Protodynastic times is also worthy of presentation.

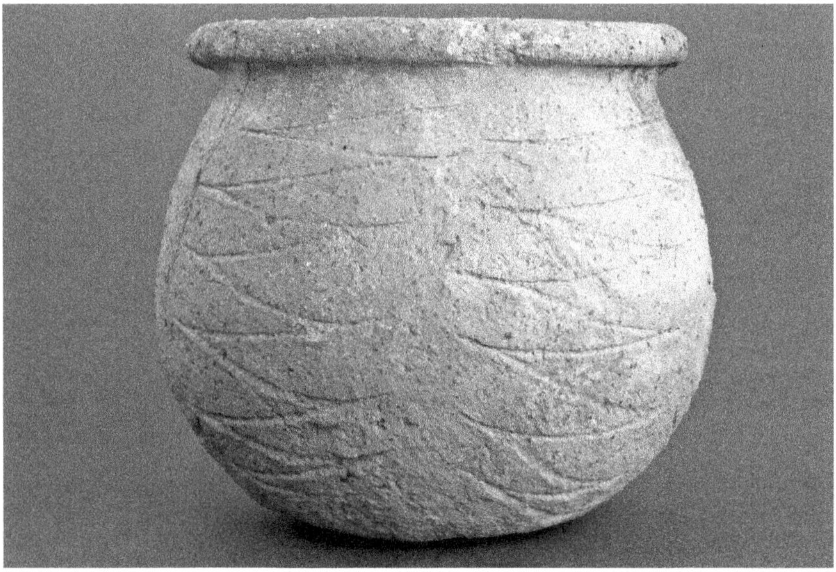

Fig. 5. Pot decorated with zigzag. © Robert Slabonski.

From Tell el-Farkha, mostly from the graves, comes quite a good collection of stone vessels.[11] From these a good selection was made for the exhibit. We can only add to it a few pots made of other raw materials with different shapes. Noteworthy is a mortar-like pot, designated as "Libyan" by Petrie,[12] found in the Lower Egyptian context.

We can certainly replace some of the previously selected samples of cosmetic palettes. There are much more interesting objects, found after 2008, in the collection. Most of them are simple oval or rectangular shapes but the palettes in the animal shape or decorated with animal representation are more unique.

The Supreme Council of Anquities selected only two copper harpoons for the exhibition at the Giza Museum. This list should be augmented with other implements, such as axes, chisels, hooks, knives, and netting needles. All these objects need conservation and permanent observation and it is better to move them to a museum with well-equipped laboratories than store them in boxes.

The selection of flint implements is big enough and it is not necessary to augment it. It consists of different types of knives as well as sickle blades, scrapers, and only one flint arrowhead found at Tell el-Farkha. Perhaps some of the broken knives should be removed from the selection or replaced by complete ones.

11. Pryc 2012.
12. Pryc 2012, 299, fig. 1.7.

The selection of the seals is also good. Among those selected we found geometric impressions as well as the impressions of the early hieroglyphs. All three cylindrical seals found on the site are in the collection. Especially noteworthy is a clay seal dated to the Naqada IIIA2/IIIB period. This crudely made seal contains royal names written in the forms of a *serekh* and *nebti*. It is the oldest one known from northern Egypt. On the other cylindrical seals we can find representations of the ostrich and gazelle.[13] These two animals were often found together in Tell el-Farkha. Both of them were also depicted on the vessel with the ivory figurine deposit. It seems that they are in some way connected with the ancient name of Tell el-Farkha.[14]

Objects of figural art have been found not only in the mentioned above deposit on the western Kom. Single finds are not very common but they occur in Predynastic as well as Early Dynastic layers. Most of them were made of clay but some bone objects also occur. Often found among them are representations of birds (awl, falcon) and quadruped animals (the last ones are mostly without legs and heads). The representation of a pig, dated to Naqada IIIB period, is rare in ancient art. Also unique is a rectangle ladle decorated with four lions on the corners, found in the one of the graves dated to Dynasty 0.[15]

The selection of beads and amulets includes four golden beads that are probably the oldest golden objects found in the Nile Delta. Unfortunately, in the selection process for the exhibition these beads were separated from the others found together with them,[16] probably because they are registered in separated numbers. All the beads should surely be reunited.

It is also necessary to reunite the first deposit found at Tell el-Farkha in 2001. From this deposit faience baboons, a figurine of a ram, clay rattles, and a few small objects were selected for the Giza Museum. Unfortunately, another faience figurine of a prostrate man, undoubtedly a captive; a fragment of a crocodile figurine; aclay figurine of naked man with a beard; and three miniature vessels were left in storage.

It is good for Tell el-Farkha that so many objects from the site soon will find their place in exhibitions. This is not so easy in the overcrowded museums in Egypt. Another thousand objects are still left in twenty-eight boxes stored in Mendes. Unfortunately, some of the objects have spent fifteen years there, moved many times from place to place. Preliminary conservation made during the excavations is not enough. A few years ago, it was not possible to do even inspect the condition of the objects in the overcrowded, small stores of Mendes. Fortunately in 2008 new, safe storerooms were built in Mendes and the finds from Tell el-Farkha have been placed in separate storage for Predynastic and Early Dynastic objects. The conditions for the conservation work and storage the objects there are quite good.

13. Chłodnicki 2007, 81, pl. VII.3.
14. Ciałowicz 2008.
15. Ciałowicz 2012, 240.
16. Chłodnicki 2011.

Generally about 20 percent of the objects from Tell el-Farkha have a chance to be presented to the public, which is a very good result. It is well-known that the best place for artifacts is in a museum. Of course it is not possible for all objects to be on display, but in museums they are more accessible to scientists and it is easier to control their condition. We hope that the rest of the artifacts from Tell el-Farkha will find their place in the new museum planned in Mansura.

References

CHŁODNICKI, M. 2007. "Excavations at the Central Kom." In M. CHŁODNICKI AND K. M. CIAŁOWICZ (eds.), "Polish Excavations at Tell el-Farkha (Ghazala) in the Nile Delta, Preliminary Report 2004–2005." *Archeologia* 57, 80–84.

———. 2011. "The Central Kom of Tell el-Farkha: 1000 Years of History (c. 3.600–2600 BC)." Pp. 41–57 in R. F. FRIEDMAN and P. N. FISKE (eds.), *Egypt at Its Origins 3: Proceedings of the International Conference "Origin of the State. Predynastic and Early Dynastic Egypt." London 27th September–1st August 2008*. OLA 205. Leuven: Peeters.

CHŁODNICKI, M. and K. M. CIAŁOWICZ. 2007. "Golden Figures from Tell el-Farkha." *Studies in Ancient Art and Civilization* 10, 7–22.

———. 2010. "Excavations at the Eastern Kom." In M. CHŁODNICKI AND K. M. CIAŁOWICZ (eds.). "Polish Excavations at Tell el-Farkha (Ghazala) in the Nile Delta, Preliminary Report 2006–2007." *Archeologia* 59, 118–23.

CHŁODNICKI, M., CIAŁOWICZ, K. M., and MĄCZYŃSKA, A. (eds.). 2012. *Tell el-Farkha I, Excavations 1998–2011*. Poznań, Kraków: Poznań Archaeological Museum and Institute of Archaeology Jagiellonian University.

CHŁODNICKI, M., R. FATTOVICH, and S. SALVATORI. 1992. "The Italian Archaeological Mission of the C.S.R.L., Venice to the Eastern Nile Delta: A Preliminary Report of the 1987–1988 Season." *Cahiers de Recherches de l'Institut de Papyrologie et d'Egyptologie de Lille* 14, 46–53.

CIAŁOWICZ, K. M. 2007. "Tell el-Farkha." Pp. 67–78 in E. LASKOWSKA-KUSZTAL (ed.), *Seventy Years of Polish Archaeology in Egypt*. Warsaw: University of Warsaw Press.

———. 2008. "Gazelles and Ostriches from Tell el-Farkha." *Studies in Ancient Art and Civilisation* 12, 21–34.

———. 2010. "Excavations at the Western Kom." In M. CHŁODNICKI M., K. M. CIAŁOWICZ, "Polish Excavations at Tell el-Farkha (Ghazala) in the Nile Delta, Preliminary Report 2006–2007." *Archeologia* 59, 86–98.

———. 2012. "Early Egyptian Objects of Art." Pp. 201–44 in M. CHŁODNICKI M., K. M. CIAŁOWICZ, and A. MĄCZYŃSKA (eds.), *Tell el-Farkha I, Excavations 1998–2011*, Poznań, Kraków: Poznań Archaeological Museum and Institute of Archaeology Jagiellonian University.

LASKOWSKA-KUSZTAL, E. (ed.). 2007. *Seventy Years of Polish Archaeology in Egypt*. Warsaw: University of Warsaw Press.

LONGA, A. and S. WEKER. 2011. "Gold from Tell el-Farkha: Conservation Project in the Egyptian Museum in Cairo." *Polish Archaeology in the Mediterranean* 20, 171–75.

PRYC, G. 2012. "Stone Vessels." Pp. 297–314 in M. CHŁODNICKI, K. M. CIAŁOWICZ, and A. MĄCZYŃSKA (eds.), *Tell el-Farkha I, Excavations 1998–2011*. Poznań, Kraków: Poznań Archaeological Museum and Institute of Archaeology Jagiellonian University.

The Role of the Antiquities Museum in Preserving the Archaeological Heritage of Alexandria, Egypt

Badrya Serry

The Bibliotheca Alexandrina Antiquities Museum (BA) as a cultural establishment has the principal role of preserving archaeological heritage, and supports all cultural and artistic activities and exhibits. Since its inauguration in October 2002, the BA has maintained an effective and active role in the different fields of cultural and civilization heritage.

The Museum plays an important role in spreading the news of cultural and archaeological discoveries in Alexandria. Its mission is to promote research and creativity to all through various programs and activities. The Museum is the first in Egypt to exhibit a rare collection of antiquities that had been submerged and found at Abukir and the eastern harbor (fig. 1). The most important of these are royal heads and tools (pots) of daily life that were found at the sites of the cities of Heracleion, Canopus, and Menouthis. The collection includes coins, jewels, amphorae, and a unique collection of statues.

A new project in our museum is the exhibition of the archaeological discoveries that were found on Nelson's Island. Nelson's Island is located in Abukir Bay off the coast of Alexandria. It is a local site for picnics and recreation and is the location of a group of British graves dating from Napoleonic Wars.

This collection will be exhibited permanently in a new hall of the Antiquities Museum in the library. The Italian excavations on Nelson's Island are being directed by Prof. Paolo Gallo from the University of Turin. These discoveries consist of more than two hundred finds of high archaeological importance, fundamental for understanding the life and material culture of the ancient inhabitants of the place. Ceramics with very unusual shapes are dateable from the period of the foundation of Alexandria to the present day, showing the cultural daily life of the first Greeks of Alexandria through archaeological artifacts (figs. 2 and 3).

It is essential that such important material for the history of Alexandria be shown to tourists and scholars visiting the town, especially after restoration (fig. 4).

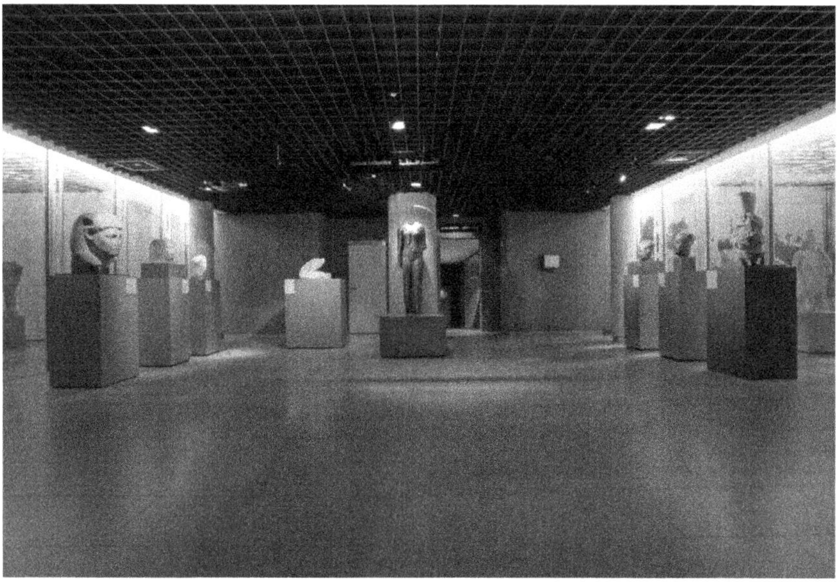

Fig. 1. Antiquities Museum, sculpture room, Bibliotheca Alexandrina, Alexandria. © Bibliotheca Alexandrina Antiquities Museum.

These discoveries include monuments that date back to the Twenty-Sixth Dynasty of the Egyptian pharaohs.

Prof. Gallo has even discovered some artifacts including graffiti and burials that are believed to relate to the British occupation of the island from shortly after the Battle of the Nile in August 1798.

However, based on archaeological activities, it has been proved that the Macedonians, the followers of Alexander the Great, and the new inhabitants of the island had established a massive fortress above the Egyptian cemetery. A residential area was found, consisting of large houses established according to the Greek style with

Fig. 2. Ceramics for daily life among the discoveries on Nelson's Island. © Museion, Shaboury & Associates JLT.

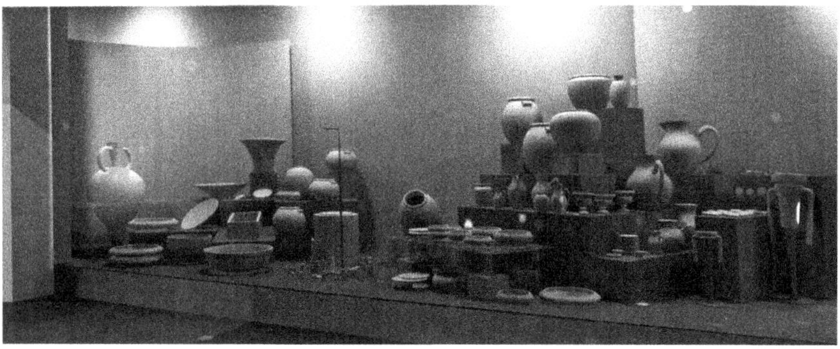

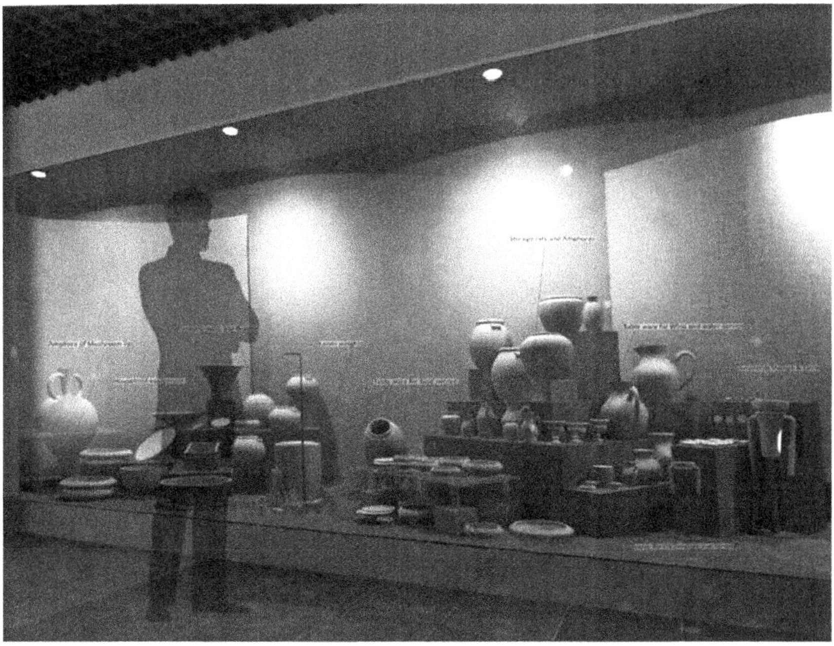

Fig. 3. Ceramics discovered on Nelson's Island. © Museion, Shaboury & Associates JLT.

Fig. 4. Labels on the Nelson's Island excavations. © Museion, Shaboury & Associates JLT.

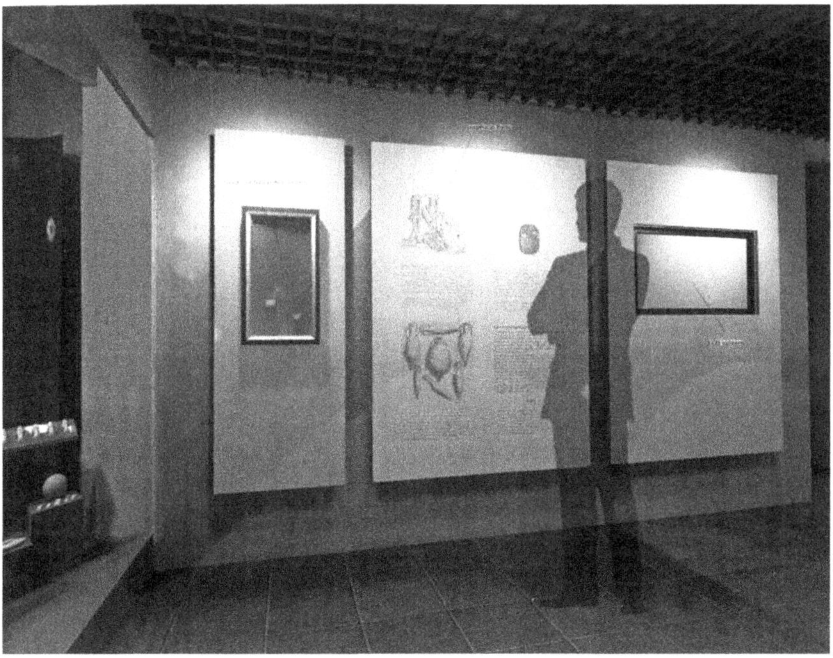

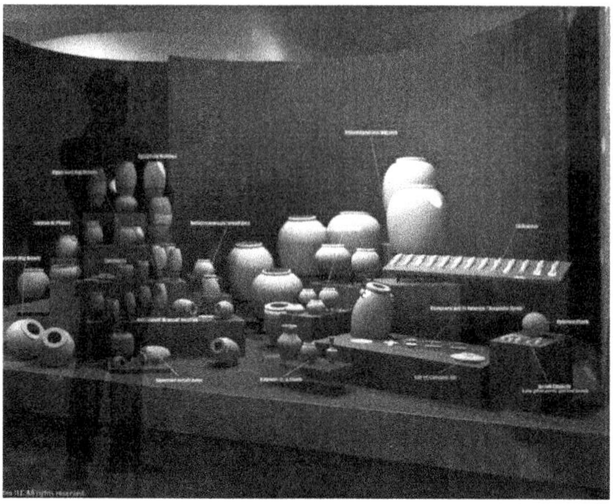

Fig. 5. Pharaonic ceramics. © Museion, Shaboury & Associates JLT.

decorated walls, complete kitchens, bathrooms, and bedrooms with sewing utensils. Notably, all artifacts from the island were found inside the houses.

The forms of construction on Nelson's Island gave us a model on which to base our museum display where we could use two neighboring areas, the first displaying Egyptian civilization, the second displaying Greek civilization.

The Pharaonic Section

Nelson's Island is the only site in Alexandria with large Egyptian tombs cut in the rock cliff dating back to the late Egyptian periods containing mummies and Egyptian funeral scenes and decorations. Preserving these artifacts and their historical context allows for creating a unique museum display where every detail in construction highlights an artifact (fig. 5). Nelson's Island has the only Pharaonic cemetery in Alexandria.

The presence of the cemetery guarantees the existence of yet undiscovered artifacts such as coffins made of pottery, amulets, and valuable offerings of faience representing the only collection in the Delta dating back to the Late period.

This section of the exhibit is arranged in three parts. In the first are displayed amulets, scarabs, ushabtis, and other small funerary objects. In the second is a mummified body inside a coffin made of pottery covered by a net of shells. It also contains amulets of faience and a heart-shaped scarab. Behind the head is an amphora containing food offerings for the afterlife. The third contains vessels and urns from the Egyptian period set as offering jars.

The Greek Section

The Greek section contains objects of daily life from one of the Macedonian houses (end of the fourth–beginning of the third century BC; fig. 6). We now have an ex-

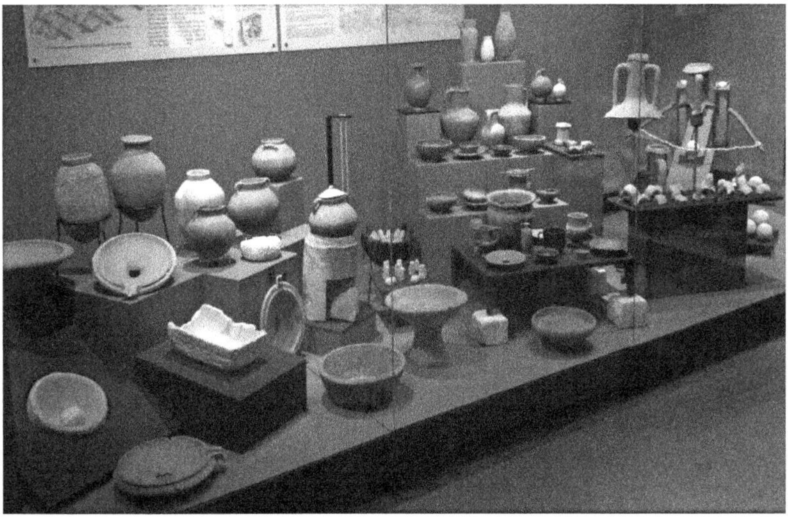

Fig. 6. Greek ceramics. © Museion, Shaboury & Associates JLT.

traordinary collection of artifacts, debris and objects, evidence of life at that time, such as jars and utensils used as tableware and for cooking and utensils used for sewing and for domestic activities.

This section is arranged in two parts. The first includes tableware consisting of Kantharos cups for wine, water jugs, serving plates and baskets, ointment and cream bottles and flasks, and oil lamps. The second features kitchen tools, a basin made of pottery, a jar to preserve liquids and food (wine, oil, salt), kitchenware to produce different sorts of food, and plates and mortars to crush and mix food.

The Objectives

The Antiquities Museum displays only a few artifacts from Alexandria and, as all artifacts are displayed out of their archaeological context, they have to be positioned in their correct places. In this manner the characteristics of both the Egyptian and the Greek civilizations which flourished on the coast of the Mediterranean are demonstrated.

One of the main objectives of this exhibition is for it to be able to tour the world's most famous Museums in order to make viewers aware of Egyptian culture and to engage them in a cultural heritage dialogue.

Egyptian Oinochoe

The pottery of the last seven hundred years before the conquest of Egypt by Alexander the Great is among the least defined of all (fig. 7), though studies of material from several sites are in progress to clarify the picture. Pottery was classified into two phases according to material, one extending from the Twenty-First Dynasty to the

Fig. 7. Egyptian oenochoe. © Museion, Shaboury & Associates JLT. Ramy Rifaat.

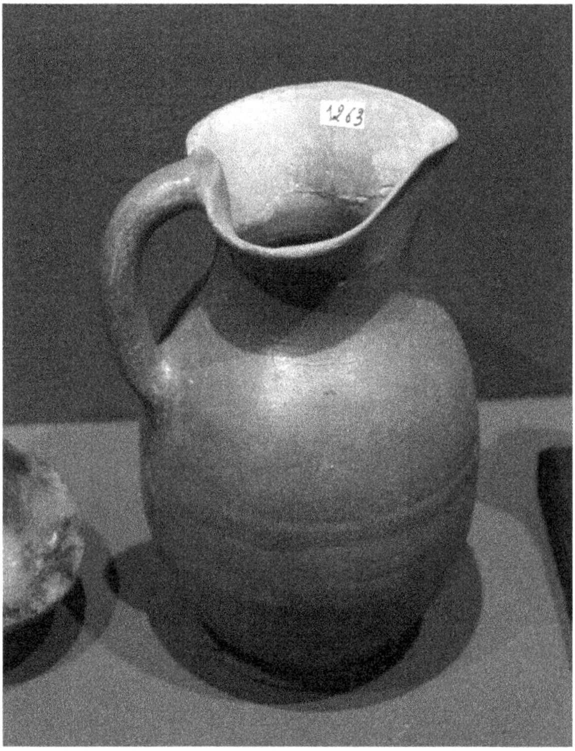

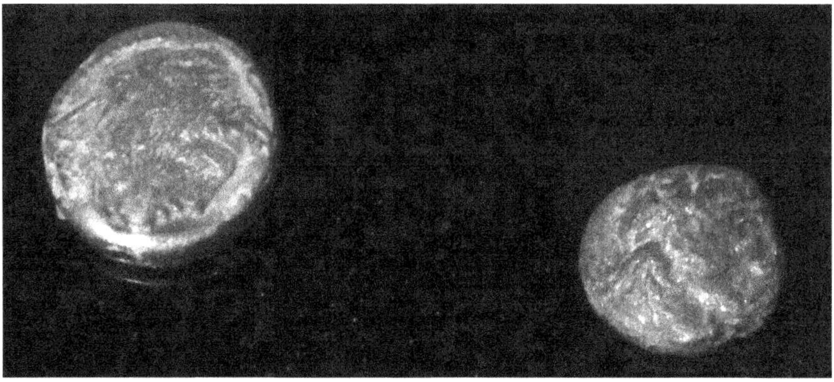

Fig. 8. Coins. © Bibliotheca Alexandrina Antiquities Museum. Ramy Rifaat.

Twenty-Fifth, and another from the Twenty-Sixth to the Thirty-First, which extends into the following Ptolemaic period.

During the first of these phases the pottery resembles that of the Late New Kingdom, though painted decoration disappeared almost completely and marl clays were less commonly used. During the second phase, vessels made from marl clay were

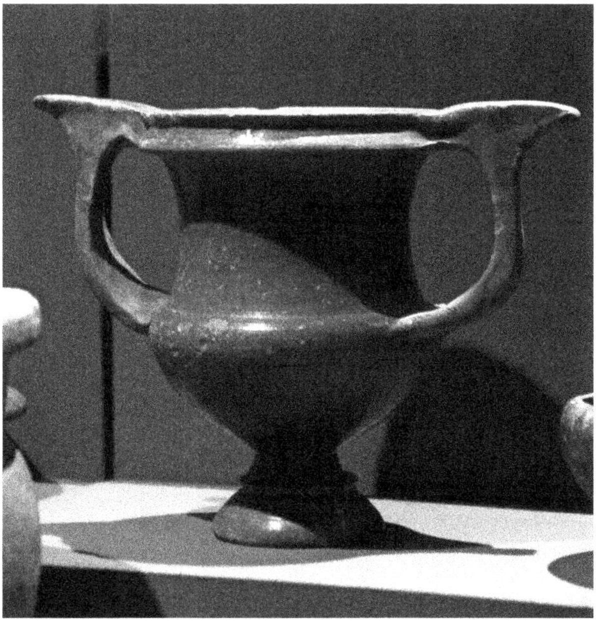

Fig. 9. Kantharos.
© Bibliotheca Alexandrina Antiquities Museum. Ramy Rifaat.

manufactured in greater abundance and new shapes developed, some of which were inspired by vessels imported from the Mediterranean countries, particularly Greece.

Coins

Almost all of the coins found in the Greek settlement on Nelson's Island date from the reign of Ptolemy I (fig. 8). These two coins feature the head of Alexander the Great. Such coins were not only minted during Alexander's lifetime but their issue was continued in the two decades following his death by the Macedonian generals who divided the empire between them and created the Hellenistic kingdoms. Even as the successor kings initiated coinage in their own names and with their own types the "Alexanders" lived on for two centuries during which time they were issued by independent cities as an international coinage.

Kantharos

The Kantharos (fig. 9), which in its early stages is closely related to the cup, has two handles set vertically. A normal size is 10 to 15 cm across, but there are very many smaller Kantharoi and some larger. The proto-geometric Kantharos has low handles and a conical foot. In the geometric Kantharos, this foot is rejected, the handles rising high above the rim and sometimes without a distinct lip. This type of Kantharos is still found at the end of the Hellenistic period.

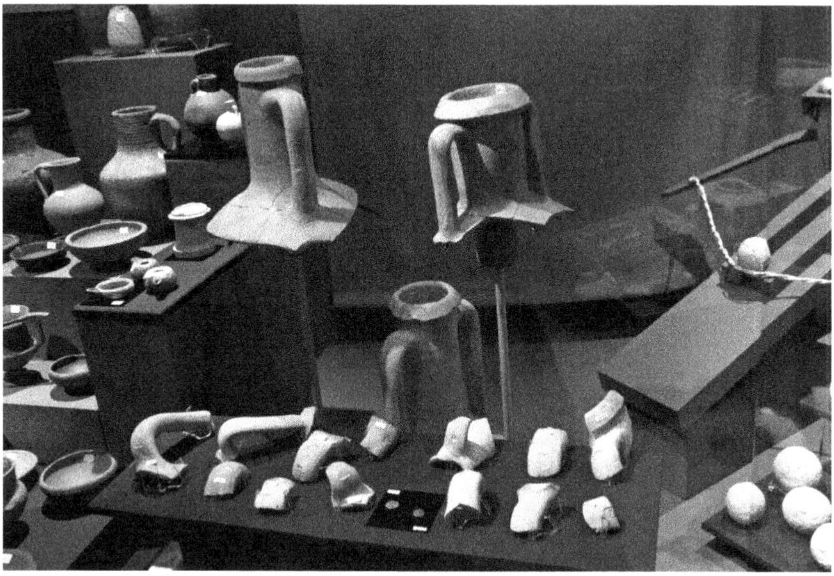

Fig. 10. Amphorae and amphorae stamps. © Bibliotheca Alexandrina Antiquities Museum. Photographer Hassan Mady.

Amphorae and Amphora Stamps

In the early Hellenistic period, the potters began to stamp their names, a mark or a little picture/symbol (a lion's head for instance) on the handles of the amphorae they produced before firing them (fig. 10). This distinctive stamp, regularly renewed, also served to help customers identify the different wines exported from the many countries of the Greek world. These handle marks allow scholars to date these productions and to reconstruct the routes of the wine and oil trade in antiquity. When found in an excavation, the amphora stamps provide a helpful tool for understanding stratigraphy and the chronology of the archeological site.

Conclusion

Since 2002, Egypt's archaeological heritage has expanded significantly due to submarine research at Abukir, the eastern Harbor, but also thanks to the discovery of lost cities like Heracleion, Canopus, and Menouthis, along with the excavations conducted on Nelson Island.

These tremendous discoveries highlight Egyptian daily life during the Ptolemaic and Roman periods, as well as religious and social habits, and political and commercial activities along the Mediterranean coast. Now exhibited in the Antiquities Museum in the Bibliotheca Alexandrina, these important objects enrich our knowledge of these times. They contribute significantly to educating a large public, including children, scholars, tourists, scientists, and archaeologists, about Egyptian civilization. These new discoveries also show how essential the preservation of Egyptian heritage is. In this way, the Antiquities Museum of Alexandria helps new generations create their future.

Sauvés des flammes: destruction et reconstruction de sculptures monumentales de la collection égyptienne des Musées royaux d'Art et d'Histoire, Bruxelles

Luc Delvaux

Les situations de conflit ne sont pas les seuls dangers que courent les collections d'art égyptien des musées, puisque des accidents ou catastrophes de natures très variées peuvent également survenir : inondations, tremblements de terre et sinistres divers. Ainsi, dans la nuit du 19 au 20 février 1946, un violent incendie a ravagé l'aile de l'Antiquité des Musées royaux d'Art et d'Histoire de Bruxelles, sur le site du Cinquantenaire, détruisant ou endommageant sévèrement cinq des monuments les plus importants de la collection égyptienne[1].

Avant cette catastrophe, la collection égyptienne avait connu de fréquents déménagements depuis son transfert, dès 1889, sur le site des expositions universelles du Cinquantenaire, dans la banlieue est de Bruxelles. D'abord installée dans l'aile nord des palais[2], puis dans la galerie courbe de l'aile sud à partir de 1901[3], la collection prend place dans trois des nouvelles salles consacrées à l'Antiquité, inaugurées le 3 août 1905[4]. En 1928, son accroissement important oblige à la répartir dans une succession de sept salles, toujours au sein de l'ancien bâtiment de l'Antiquité. Cependant, après plus d'un demi-siècle d'existence, celui-ci, conçu comme un édifice temporaire pour l'exposition de 1880, s'avère particulièrement vétuste. Aussi, la transformation du hall de l'Antiquité en un bâtiment définitif, plus apte à accueillir les collections, étant programmée pour 1936, les objets égyptiens sont temporairement déménagés dans une série de six salles situées à l'étage de la nouvelle Galerie Albert-Elisabeth, inaugurée le 30 décembre 1930[5]. Le mastaba de Neferirtenef, pièce maîtresse de l'Ancien

1. Pour l'historique général de la collection égyptienne des Musées royaux d'Art et d'Histoire, voir : van de Walle, Limme & De Meulenaere 1980.
2. Deltour-Levie 1985, 35, fig. 2 ; van de Walle, Limme & De Meulenaere 1980, 15–16, fig. 2.
3. Deltour-Levie 1985, 37, fig. 3.
4. Deltour-Levie 1985, 40–41 ; [Anonyme] 1905, 73–76.
5. [Anonyme] 1933, 226 ; [Anonyme] 1934, 23–24 ; [Anonyme] 1937, 74.

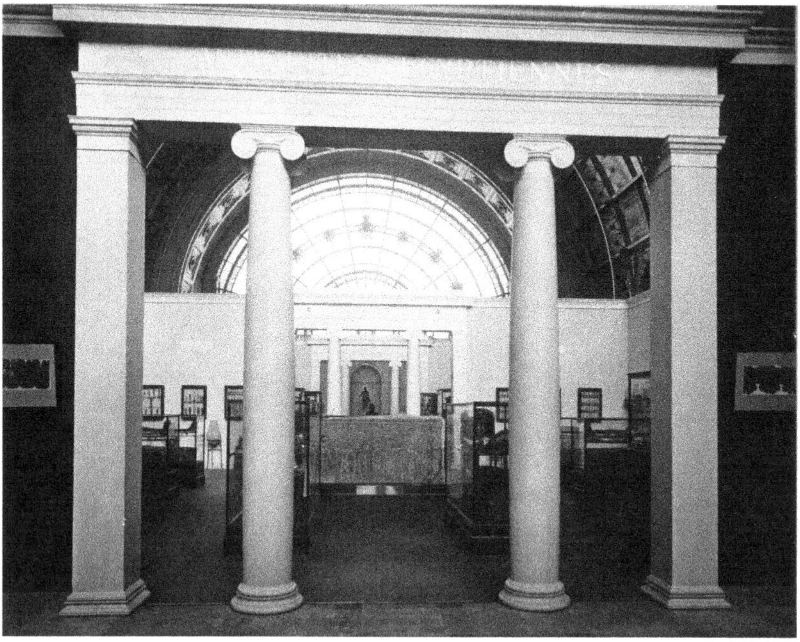

Fig. 1. Le linteau de Séthi Ier au centre de la collection égyptienne avant 1930. © Archives AERE.

Empire, est alors démonté et ses blocs sont provisoirement entreposés dans les réserves[6]. Seules restent dans l'ancien bâtiment, outre une maquette en plâtre de l'île de Philae (Inv. E.M.225)[7] et une reproduction en bois de la pyramide de Kheops (sans n°), cinq lourds monuments en pierre, trop pesants pour être aisément transportés:

1. Un grand linteau de porte en granit gris montrant Sethi Ier recevant une libation de Seth et Behedety (Inv. E.407) (fig. 1)[8]. Ce monument impressionnant avait été donné au Musée en 1900 par un riche Arménien d'Alexandrie, Tito Pacha Hekekyan[9], par l'intermédiaire du roi Léopold II. Au début du 20e siècle, il trônait au centre de la collection égyptienne dont il constituait une des pièces essentielles[10]. Exposé ensuite

6. Sur le mastaba de Neferirtenef et les circonstances de son acquisition, voir Bruffaerts 2005.

7. Van Rinsveld 2011, 27, fig. 1.

8. Inv. E.407 : granit gris ; L. : 2,48 m. ; H. : 1,08 m. : PM IV, 64 ; [Anonyme] 1901, 5 ; Capart 1902a, 82 ; Capart 1902b, pl. 39 ; Speleers 1923a, 64 ; Gardiner 1950, 5, pl. I ; van de Walle, Limme & De Meulenaere 1980, 23–25, fig. 6. Le linteau est réputé provenir d'Héliopolis ; il aurait longtemps servi de linteau de porte dans une maison d'Alexandrie ; il était visible avant 1855 en un emplacement inconnu de la ville, sans doute à demi enfoui dans le sol : voir Sharpe 1855, pl. 30.

9. Tito Hekekyan (né en 1840) est le fils de Joseph Hekekyan (1807–1875), ingénieur civil arménien qui a notamment réalisé des fouilles à Memphis ; sur celui-ci, voir : Bierbrier 2012, 251 ; sur la famille Hekekyan, voir notamment : Le Gall-Kazazian 2011.

10. F. B., « Le Musée des Antiquités », *Revue nationale* , [c. 1905], 9.

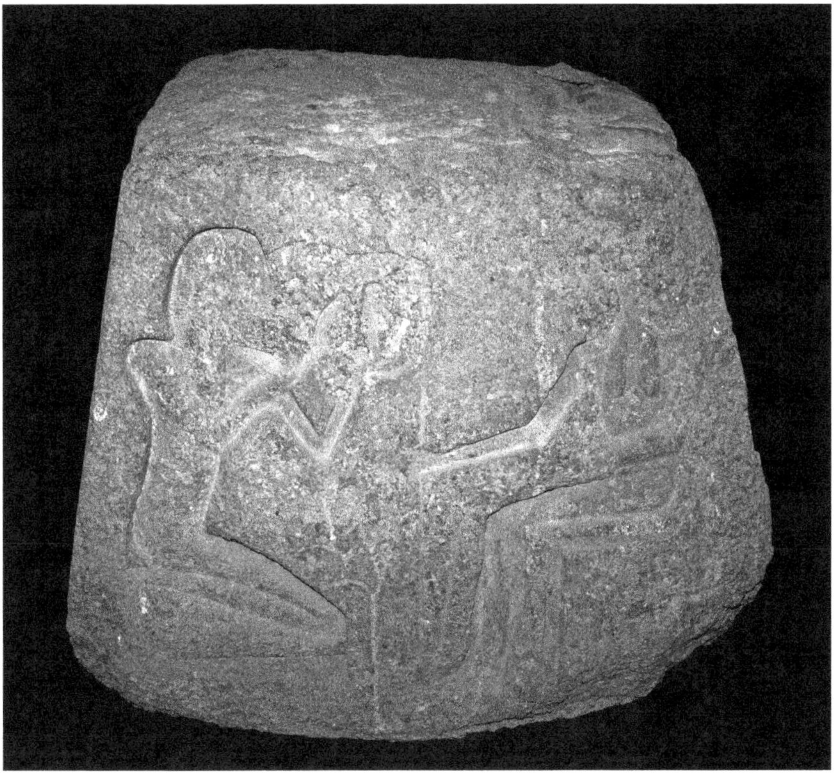

Fig. 2. Pyramidion. Provenance : probablement Tanis. Granit rose. 19e dynastie. Inv. E.1836. © KMKG-MRAH, photo Luc Delvaux.

dans la salle V de la section égyptienne[11], il resta en place dans le hall de l'Antiquité, en compagnie des deux pièces suivantes (2 et 3), lors du déménagement de la collection vers la Galerie Albert-Elisabeth.

2. Un grand pyramidion ramesside en granit rose (Inv. E.1836) (fig. 2)[12]. Ce monument est décoré sur ses quatre faces de scènes montrant un roi agenouillé, offrant Maât à diverses divinités assises : Rê-Horakhty, Atoum, probablement Amon-Rê et un dieu non identifié. Tant le style et le modelé très accusé du relief que le type des scènes rappelle les obélisques de Ramsès II mis au jour à Tanis, et qui proviennent certainement, pour la plupart, de Pi-Ramsès[13].

3. La statue colossale d'une divinité faucon en quartzite (Inv. E.5188) (fig. 3)[14], provenant du temple de Khonsou à Karnak et issue de l'ancienne collection de Léopold

11. Capart 1928, 55–56; Guide 1928, 20.

12. Inv. E.1836: achat au Caire en décembre 1900 ; granit rose; H.: 0,80 m. ; l. : 0,95 m. : Capart 1902a, 82.

13. Voir Montet 1935–1937; Uphill 1984, 72–84.

14. Inv. E.5188: provenant probablement du temple de Khonsou, à Karnak; ancienne collection Léopold II, acquis par les musées en 1914 ; quartzite ; H. : 2,10 m. ; l. : 0,92 m. ; pr. : 0,95 m. : PM II², 244 ; van

II, transmise aux Musées en 1914. Chef d'œuvre de la statuaire divine de l'époque d'Amenhotep III, cette statue, représentant probablement le dieu solaire faucon Rê-Horakhty, a été transformée à la Troisième Période Intermédiaire, sous le grand prêtre Masaharta, en une statue de Khonsou.

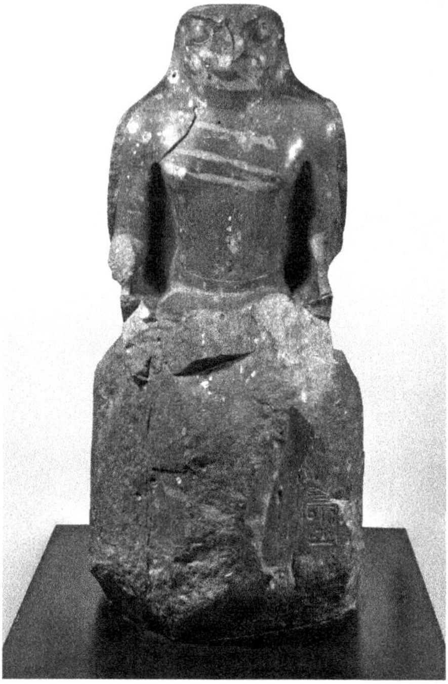

Fig. 3. Statue d'une divinité faucon, état actuel. Provenance : Karnak, temple de Khonsou. Quartzite. Fin de la XVIIIe dynastie. Inv. E.5188. © KMKG-MRAH

4. L'énorme sarcophage du grand intendant Youpa, contemporain de Ramsès II, au couvercle en quartzite et à la cuve en granit rose (Inv. E.5189) (fig. 4)[15]. Lui aussi issu de la collection du roi Léopold II, il avait été longtemps exposé dans un couloir et une salle des écuries royales, où la cuve servait d'ailleurs de bac à fleurs ! Quant au couvercle, il était dressé devant un mur des écuries, comme le montrent les deux seules photographies conservées de la pièce, probablement réalisées par Jean Capart avant le transfert de la collection royale aux Musées. Au début du 20e siècle, le sarcophage était exposé dans les salles égyptiennes, à proximité du grand linteau de Sethi Ier, le couvercle reposé sur la cuve[16]. Ensuite, il fut placé dans la salle IV de la section égyptienne, devant la porte de la salle V, où il resta lors du déménagement des collections[17].

5. Un monumental naos en granit au nom de Psammétique II (Inv. E.5283) (fig. 5), donné au Musée en 1900 par Tito Pacha Hekekyan, par l'intermédiaire du roi Léopold II[18]. Outre le relevé des inscriptions publié par Louis Speleers en 1923, ce

de Walle, Limme & De Meulenaere 1980, 26–27 et n. 59, fig. 7 ; Van Rinsveld 1991 ; De Putter 1991 ; Warmenbol 2012, 83.

15. Inv. E.5189 : quartzite (couvercle) et granit rose (cuve) ; L. : 2 ,30 m. ; l. : 1,18 m. ; H. : 1,38 m. : Eisenlohr 1889, 261 ; Schmidt 1919, 126, fig. 647 ; Speleers 1923a, 66–68, n° 278 ; Speleers 1923b, 30, pl. 15 ; Capart 1928, 57–58, § 54 ; Werbrouck 1930, 78 ; Werbrouck 1935, 63 ; van de Walle 1974, 176 ; Ruffle & Kitchen 1979, 58, pl. VII ; van de Walle, Limme & De Meulenaere 1980, 29–30, fig. 8 ; KRI III 197, 15 - 198, 4.

16. Son contour se distingue à l'arrière du linteau sur une vue générale de la collection, prise à une date indéterminée entre 1914 et 1928 : Photo Association égyptologique Reine Elisabeth 2066.

17. Capart 1928, 57–58 ; Guide 1928, 18.

18. Inv. E.5283 : granit ; H. : 2,50 m. ; l. : 1,20 m. ; pr. : 0,67 m. : Capart 1902a, 82 ; [Anonyme] 1901,

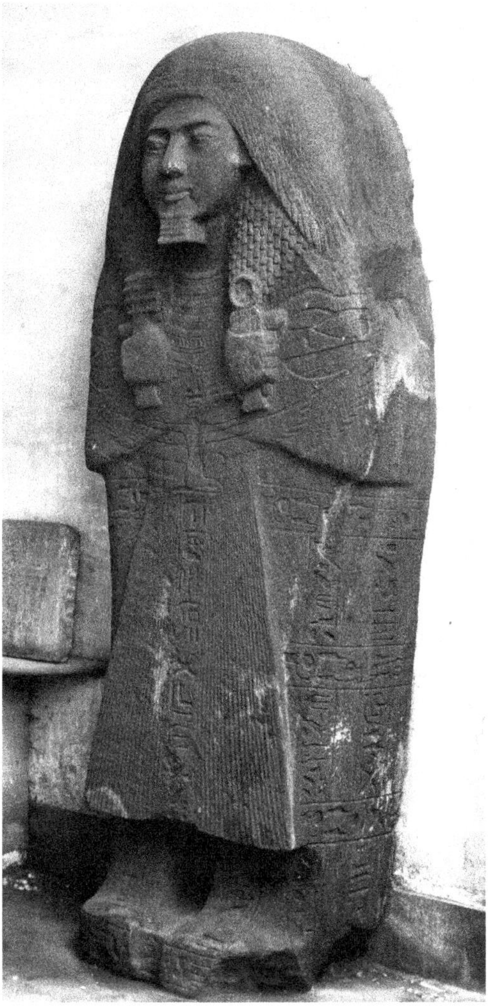

Fig. 4. Couvercle du sarcophage de Youpa. Provenance inconnue. Quartzite. 19e dynastie. Inv. E.5189. © Archives AERE

naos n'est connu que par une ancienne photographie[19], et par un cliché qui le montre en place, sur une vue d'ensemble des anciennes salles égyptiennes du Musée, probablement en 1905[20]. En 1928, et jusqu'au déménagement des collections vers la Galerie Albert-Elisabeth, il était exposé dans la salle VI de la section égyptienne, en compagnie d'autres pièces d'époque saïte[21].

Durant la nuit du 19 au 20 février 1946, pour des raisons mal connues, un incendie se déclenche au niveau du toit du bâtiment de l'Antiquité et, malgré l'intervention rapide des pompiers bruxellois et des militaires britanniques casernés à l'École Royale Militaire toute proche, il se propage très rapidement, entraînant l'effondrement des structures en métal et verre de l'édifice. Si les locaux de la Fondation égyptologique Reine Elisabeth, qui occupent le pavillon de l'angle nord-ouest du hall, sont miraculeusement épargnés, il n'en va pas de même des cinq monuments égyptiens, attaqués par la chaleur de l'incendie et sur lesquels s'écroule la structure du bâtiment.

Les articles de presse publiés dans les jours qui suivent l'incendie sont d'abord assez imprécis quant aux dégâts subis par les objets égyptiens monumentaux, les

5 ; Speleers 1923a, 87, n° 331. Dans l'article anonyme du Bulletin des Musées royaux des Arts décoratifs et industriels de 1901, le naos est décrit comme « un grand sarcophage en granit, [qui] porte un nom royal que l'usure de la pierre n'a pas permis de déchiffrer jusqu'à présent ».

19. Photo Association égyptologique Reine Elisabeth 1278.

20. F. B. 1905, 8.

21. Capart 1928, 70 ; Guide 1928, 22.

Fig. 5. Naos de Psammétique II. Provenance inconnue. Granit. XXVIe dynastie. Inv. E.5283. © Archives AERE

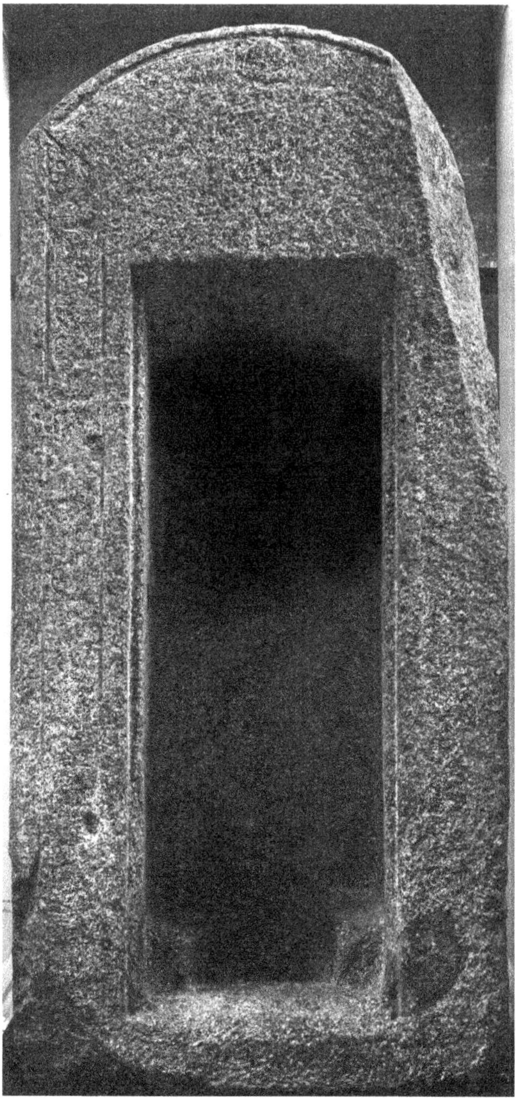

premières rumeurs faisant même état de la destruction complète de la collection et de la bibliothèque de la Fondation égyptologique Reine Elisabeth[22]. Les journalistes envoyés sur place décrivent d'abord l'ampleur de la catastrophe et l'aspect dantesque des ruines, d'où émergent les monuments égyptiens : « Nous sommes allés voir ce que la sauvagerie des flammes en avait laissé : quatre hauts murs auxquels s'appuie un ramassis de ferrailles tordues et noircies et, au milieu, quelques statues égyptiennes qui viennent d'avoir chaud. »[23]

Rapidement cependant, la description des dégâts se fait plus nuancée :

« L'énorme statue du dieu Khonsu à la tête de faucon est partiellement fendue mais à restaurer. Le superbe bas-relief de Séthi Ier, ainsi que le sarcophage en granit rose de la XVIIIe dynastie[24], ont littéralement éclaté sous l'intensité du feu. Il reste peu d'espoir pour leur reconstitution. »[25]

Ce n'est qu'au début de mars 1946 qu'un premier véritable bilan des pertes subies par la collection peut être rédigé par le Conservateur en Chef, Henry Lavachery : « Des

22. Brasseur-Capart 1974, 181–182 .

23. Bastien 1946.

24. Il s'agit du sarcophage ramesside de Youpa. Inv. E.5189.

25. Langhi 1946.

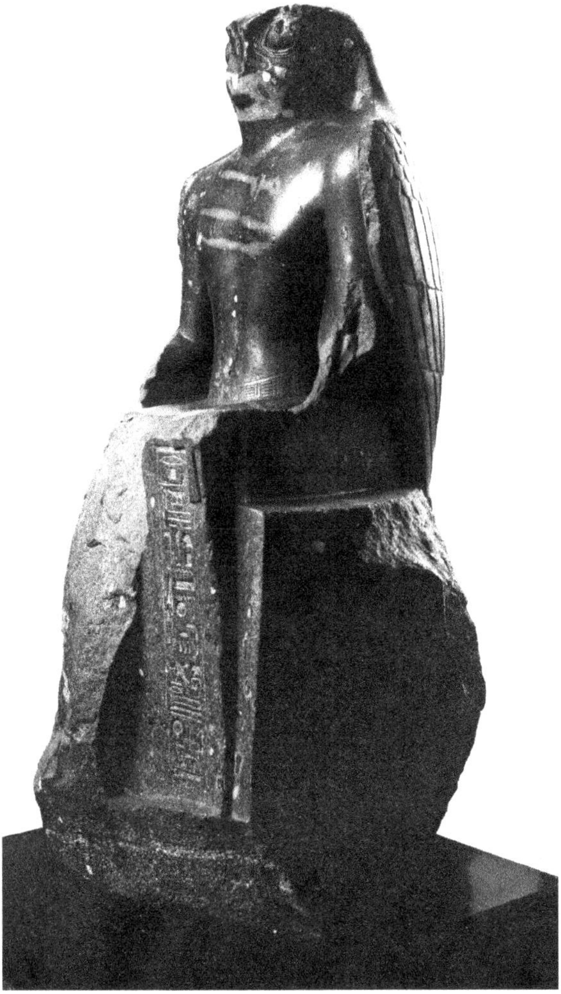

Fig. 6. Statue d'une divinité faucon ; état avant l'incendie. © Archives AERE

cinq pièces originales, de grandes dimensions qui se trouvaient dans le hall incendié, deux sont peu atteintes : une statue datant probablement de la IVe dynastie, du dieu Khonsou, homme assis, à la tête et aux ailes de faucon, a perdu quelques éclats et est fendillée dans tous les sens ; un tronçon d'obélisque, de Ramsès II, s'est un peu écaillé. Les trois autres monuments sont détruits : un naos saïte de granit rose a commencé par être rongé en surface par le feu, puis s'est émietté en tellement de morceaux qu'il sera vain de tenter sa reconstitution. Le sarcophage de granit rose, à couvercle de grès, de Youpa, intendant de Ramsès II, est aussi réduit en débris, mais des reconstitutions partielles pourront être tentées. Notre plus regrettable perte est celle d'un linteau en granit noir, de Séthi Ier, dont presque toute la face sculptée a éclaté en menus fragments. Nous les avons ramassés avec soin, mais ils sont loin de couvrir toute la surface du relief original, qui représentait le roi purifié par les dieux Horus et Seth et, de part et d'autre faisant des offrandes au dieu Atoum et au dieu Horus. C'était une très belle composition. Tout ce que l'on pourra faire sera d'en encastrer les fragments dans un moulage teinté ; car le moule existe au musée. »[26]

26. Lavachery, 1946. Ce texte est repris, avec quelques légères variantes, dans plusieurs journaux de mars et avril 1946 ; voir par exemple : [Anonyme] 1946 ; *La Dernière Heure* 1946 ; etc.

Une estimation financière des pertes subies est transmise par Marcelle Werbrouck[27], conservatrice de la collection, au Conservateur en Chef, Henry Lavachery, en date du 18 mai 1946. Pour le sarcophage de Youpa, le linteau de Séthi Ier et le naos de Psammétique II, les valeurs d'après sinistre sont estimées respectivement à 200.000, 150.000 et 100.000 francs de l'époque. L'état de la statue de Khonsou est considéré comme précaire, la valeur qui lui est attribuée (65.000 francs) n'étant validée que si la statue « se maintient dans son état actuel, ce qui n'est pas encore assuré ». Enfin, comme l'écrit Werbrouck, « le pyramidion a été assez préservé pour qu'on puisse estimer sans valeur réelle la perte subie ». Des annotations manuscrites portées par Marcelle Werbrouck sur une lettre de H. Lavachery, datée d'octobre 1947[28] confirment ce constat : trois pièces (le linteau de Séthi Ier, le sarcophage de Youpa et le naos de Psammétique II) sont alors considérées comme « perdues », et deux autres comme simplement « en danger » (le pyramidion ramesside et la statue de Khonsou).

Dès les premiers jours après l'incendie, de nombreux fragments des monuments endommagés sont récupérés, notamment par Pierre Gilbert[29], alors conservateur-adjoint, qui écrit à Henry Lavachery, le 26 février 1946 : « Je n'ai pas besoin de vous dire combien je suis absorbé par le souci des salles égyptiennes à parachever[30], des pièces égyptiennes brûlées dont il importe de recueillir au plus tôt les débris, de celles qui ont résisté et qu'il faut consolider, protéger… »[31].

Les monuments égyptiens atteints par l'incendie passent le reste de l'hiver 1946 en plein air, exposés au gel et aux intempéries, sans aucune protection[32]. Ce n'est qu'à la mi-juin 1946 que le démontage de la charpente métallique ruinée peut enfin s'achever et que, parmi les travaux à entreprendre d'urgence, le Conservateur en Chef préconise de « construire un abri pour les quelques pièces égyptiennes qui ont échappé à l'incendie et qu'il est impossible, vu leur poids, de transporter ailleurs. »[33]. Cette demande se heurte à l'opposition du Ministère des Travaux publics qui considère qu'il incombe au Musée de construire lui-même cet abri, avec ses propres ressources techniques[34]. Une structure en « carton bitumé » sera finalement érigée, qui protègera sommairement les pièces égyptiennes des intempéries, mais ne les mettra aucunement à l'abri du gel et de l'humidité, une situation alarmante que souligne plusieurs fois Marcelle Werbrouck

27. Sur Marcelle Werbrouck (1889–1959) : Bierbrier 2012, 572–573.
28. Lettre de Henri Lavachery, Conservateur en Chef, concernant l'inventaire des biens de l'État, en date du 1er octobre 1947 (Archives MRAH).
29. Sur Pierre Gilbert (1904–1986) : Bierbrier 2012, 212.
30. Il s'agit des salles de la Galerie Albert-Elisabeth où était hébergée la collection égyptienne, à l'exception des cinq objets monumentaux.
31. Lettre de P. Gilbert à H. Lavachery, 26 février 1946 (Archives MRAH).
32. Une photographie (Archives MRAH), réalisée probablement dans les jours suivant l'incendie, montre les vestiges du linteau de Sethi Ier sous la neige.
33. Lettre de H. Lavachery à Mr. Poelman, Directeur à la Direction des Bâtiments du Brabant, 16 juin 1946 (Archives MRAH).
34. Lettre du Ministère des Travaux publics, Direction générale du Bâtiment, à H. Lavachery, 13 juillet 1946 (Archives MRAH).

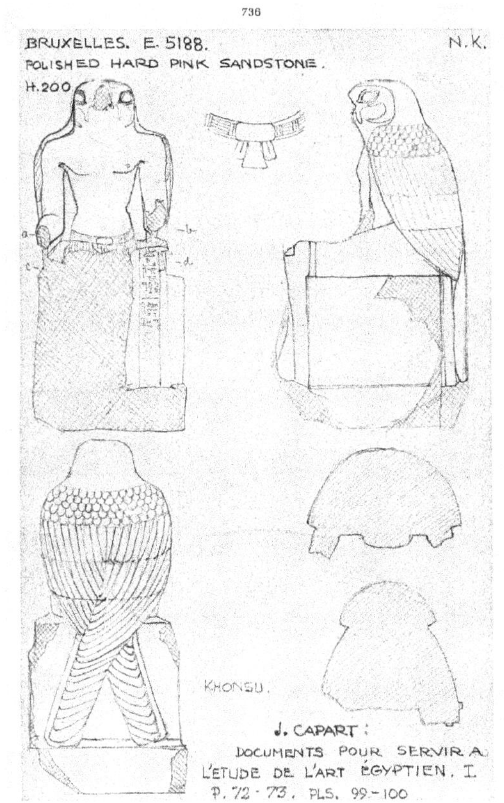

Fig. 7. Statue d'une divinité faucon ; croquis réalisés avant l'incendie. Inv. E.5188. Hornemann 1957, n° 736

dans ses rapports d'activité et sa correspondance avec le Conservateur en Chef[35] :

> « Les trois grandes œuvres pharaoniques qui n'ont pas été détruites par l'incendie de 1946 sont actuellement sous un hangar dans le hall ruiné. J'ai dit plusieurs fois combien cet abri était néfaste surtout à la statue de Khonsou et, dans mon rapport d'octobre, j'ai dû avertir que la base calcinée du Khonsou cédant peu à peu, il y avait une grave menace de chute. Cette chute réduirait probablement l'œuvre en morceaux et risquerait aussi d'écraser le pyramidion, seule pièce intacte sauvée de l'incendie. Il est urgent de déplacer le pyramidion tout d'abord, puis le Khonsou, enfin la cuve du sarcophage de Ioupa dont le couvercle est entièrement détruit. Ces objets, pourraient être transportés avec le minimum de difficultés, et de plain-pied, dans l'antichambre, sèche heureusement, du pavillon de la géologie auquel on vient de travailler. »[36]

35. Cet abri est mentionné pour la première fois dans une lettre de M. Werbrouck à H. Lavachery, 21 décembre 1950 (Archives MRAH).

36. Lettre de M. Werbrouck à H. Lavachery, 20 novembre 1951 (Archives MRAH).

Ou encore :

> « Les trois monuments sauvés de l'incendie de 1946 nécessitent, eux aussi, une intervention rapide et énergique. Le grand Khonsou, fendu dans toute sa masse et dans une humidité constante, sur un socle de bois calciné, risque de s'effondrer de façon irréparable. J'ai demandé qu'on le traîne jusqu'au pavillon de la géologie, pour le préserver lui ainsi que le pyramidion et la cuve du sarcophage de Ioupa qui seraient détruits si le Khonsou s'effondrait. Je sais que ce travail présente de grandes difficultés et même peut-être du danger pour les hommes. Mais le retarder c'est augmenter les risques. Il faudra s'entourer de toutes les précautions possible pour éviter les accidents ou bien renoncer à sauver le Khonsou la pièce le (sic) plus monumentale du musée, don de Léopold II. »[37]

Plusieurs fragments du grand Khonsou se sont probablement détachés durant cette période, comme le montrent les multiples zones de cassures dépourvues de patine ou de noircissement révélées lors des examens récents de la statue, notamment au niveau du bras droit et du siège.

L'édifice ruiné restera à ciel ouvert pendant dix ans, jusqu'à sa démolition complète[38]. Celle-ci, qui doit précéder la reconstruction du bâtiment, est programmée en 1956. On prévoit dès lors le « déplacement des statues et autres objets pondéreux : ces œuvres d'art devront être évacuées pendant les travaux »[39]. Cependant, alors que les travaux de démolition ont commencé, les statues égyptiennes sont toujours en place, à la consternation du conservateur Pierre Gilbert : « ... les chocs répétés que subit le sous-sol, à chaque chute de matériaux dans le bâtiment que l'on démolit, me font craindre que le colosse de Khonsou, qui est fissuré, ne finisse par se disloquer. J'ai demandé à M. Peiffer de l'entourer d'un cerclage provisoire avant de pouvoir le transporter, avec les pierres du mastaba[40], dans notre nouvelle réserve du « palais mondial [41] »[42].

Le déménagement des pièces égyptiennes a probablement lieu peu après et leur remise en place dans les nouveaux locaux peut être envisagée[43]. Dès octobre 1958, le gros-œuvre du nouveau bâtiment est achevé[44] ; il faudra cependant attendre le 25

---

37. Rapport de M. Werbrouck, octobre-décembre 1951 (Archives MRAH).

38. Voir la lettre de J. de Borchgrave d'Altena, Conservateur en Chef, à P. Caso (Journal Le Soir), 14 février 1956 (Archives MRAH) : « Depuis 10 ans, l'aile sud du Cinquantenaire est sans toit... ».

39. Procès-verbal de la réunion du 11 juillet 1956 : « Transformation et reconstruction du Musée de l'Antiquité » (Archives MRAH).

40. Le mastaba de Neferirtenef avait été démonté en 1937, dans la perspective d'une rénovation complète du vétuste bâtiment de l'Antiquité ; voir : Bruffaerts 2005, 25–26.

41. Il s'agit du grand hall sud des Palais du Cinquantenaire, dont les Musées royaux d'Art et d'Histoire ont été amputés en 1986, pour la création du Musée Autoworld.

42. Lettre de P. Gilbert à J. de Borchgrave d'Altena, Conservateur en Chef, 4 février 1957 (Archives MRAH).

43. Voir notamment lettre de P. Gilbert à M. De Trock, ingénieur-directeur, Service des Bâtiments, Ministère des Travaux publics, 4 septembre 1956, préconisant la réinstallation de la statue de Khonsou dans les futures salles égyptiennes (Archives MRAH).

44. Lettre de A. Boereboom, directeur d'administration du Ministère des Travaux publics, à J. de Borch-

novembre 1966 pour que les nouvelles salles soient inaugurées[45] et que la collection égyptienne y retrouve progressivement sa place, au troisième étage de l'édifice[46]. Quant aux pièces endommagées par l'incendie, leurs vestiges seront entreposés dans les nouvelles réserves de la section égyptienne, aménagées dans la moitié nord du quatrième étage du nouveau bâtiment de l'Antiquité. Seule la statue de Khonsou sera exposée au public. Les projets de remise en place de la statue au sein de la collection égyptienne n'ayant pas abouti, probablement à cause de problèmes de résistance des sols[47], elle sera d'abord placée dans une niche latérale du sas d'entrée, puis déplacée le 21 juin 1994 vers le centre du hall d'accueil des groupes scolaires, où elle se trouve toujours aujourd'hui.

En 2012, un projet d'étude des sculptures atteintes par l'incendie de 1946 a été mis en œuvre avec pour objectifs leur éventuelle restauration, leur potentielle réintégration dans les salles d'exposition permanentes et leur publication scientifique. La première phase de ce projet a consisté en une évaluation de l'état des monuments et un inventaire complet des fragments subsistants. Il est rapidement apparu que le monumental naos en granit au nom de Psammétique II (E.5283) semble avoir été totalement détruit lors de l'incendie, et, malgré l'exploration systématique des réserves de la section Égypte, aucun fragment n'en a été identifié à ce jour. Comme l'avaient noté les documents d'archives, le grand pyramidion ramesside en granit rose (E.1836) a vu sa surface gravement détériorée par la chaleur des flammes, des plaques entières de granit s'en étant désolidarisées.

La statue colossale de Rê-Horakhty/Khonsou (Inv. E.5188) a, quant à elle, très sévèrement souffert de l'incendie ; l'ensemble du bloc de quartzite s'est fendillé sous l'effet de la chaleur et de nombreux éclats se sont détachés sur la totalité de la surface. Deux photographies anciennes (fig. 6)[48], ainsi que des croquis antérieurs à 1946 (fig. 7)[49] , montrent que c'est essentiellement l'avant de la statue qui a été affecté. Après l'incendie, quatorze fragments de la statue, de dimensions variables, ont été récupérés dans les décombres[50]. Certains de ces morceaux sont minuscules mais les deux plus importants sont un grand fragment du haut de la colonne d'inscription au nom du grand prêtre d'Amon Masaharta, inscrite à l'avant du siège, du côté gauche[51] et un grand segment du pagne plissé provenant du haut de la cuisse gauche[52].

Enfin, le dernier important monument réduit en fragments par la chaleur de l'in-

grave d'Altena, Conservateur en Chef, 27 octobre 1958 (Archives MRAH).

45. Ruyssinck 1985, 63–64.

46. Gilbert 1968.

47. Selon une estimation réalisée par le géologue Thierry De Putter, le poids de la statue est évalué à environ 2800 kg.

48. Photos Association égyptologique Reine Elisabeth 4133–4134 (reproductions : van de Walle, Limme & De Meulenaere 1980, 26, fig. 7 ; Van Rinsveld 1991, 17, fig. 1 ; p. 19, fig. 2).

49. Hornemann 1957, n° 736.

50. Inv. E.5188/1–7.

51. Inv. E.5188/1 : Van Rinsveld 1991, 27, fig. 4.

52. Inv. E.5188/2.

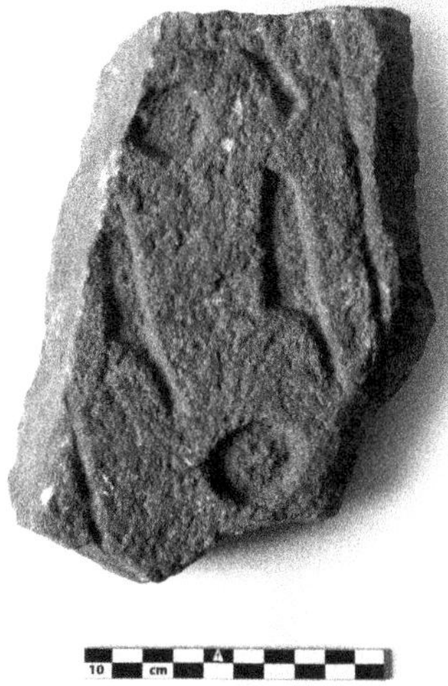

Fig. 8. Fragment du couvercle du sarcophage de Youpa, avec inscription. Inv. E.5189. © KMKG-MRAH

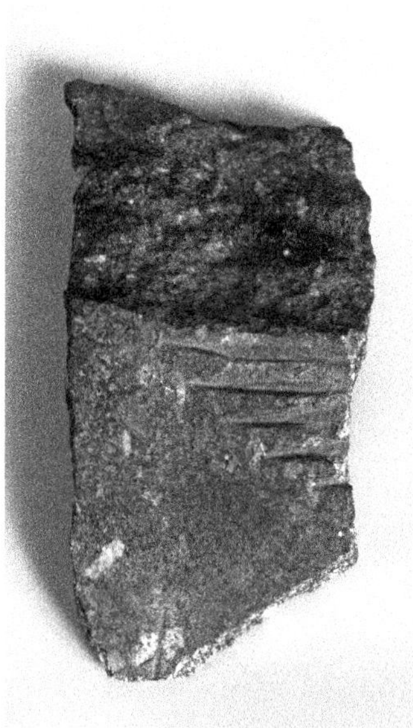

Fig. 9. Fragment du linteau de Sethi Ier. Inv. E.407. © KMKG-MRAH

cendie est l'énorme sarcophage du grand intendant Youpa, contemporain de Ramsès II, au couvercle en quartzite et à la cuve en granit rose (Inv. E.5189). Lors de l'installation des nouvelles réserves de la collection égyptienne, les débris de ce sarcophage (fig. 8), souvent noircis par la fumée de l'incendie et fragilisés par les flammes, ont été entreposés en un grand tas, qui n'a pas été examiné ou inventorié jusqu'au début de l'année 2012. Dès ses débuts, l'opération de tri de ces fragments a donné des résultats surprenants. Elle a en effet amené, de manière totalement inattendue, à la découverte, parmi les débris, de nombreux fragments des autres monuments endommagés ou détruits dans l'incendie de 1946. Ainsi, cinq fragments de granodiorite grise, appartenant au grand linteau de Sethi Ier (Inv. E.407) ont pu être identifiés. Selon les sources d'archives, des fragments de la surface décorée du monument avaient été récupérés après l'incendie, mais ils n'étaient cependant pas localisés dans les réserves de la section Égypte. Certains de ces fragments conservent quelques éléments du décor sculpté, dont le tracé de l'extrémité des plumes de l'aile droite du disque solaire qui surmonte la scène (fig. 9), ou une portion de la coiffure du dieu Rê-Horakhty ou du dieu Seth. D'autres ne portent aucun élément de décor et proviennent de la masse interne du monument. Ces fragments très ténus sont insuffisants pour pouvoir envisager une restitution de ce magnifique linteau mais certains pourront cependant être remis en place, par exemple au sein du moulage du monument, que conserve heureusement la collection. En revanche, d'autres portions du décor sculpté, qu'une photographie d'archives montre encore en place dans les jours suivants la catastrophe[53], restent à ce jour introuvables.

Ensuite, il est très vite apparu que plusieurs fragments de quartzite, parfois importants, n'appartenaient pas au couvercle du sarcophage de Youpa mais bien à la grande statue de Rê-Horakhty/Khonsou de l'époque d'Amenhotep III (Inv. E.5188). Comparé au quartzite du sarcophage, le matériau de la statue de Rê-Horakhty/Khonsou est aisément repérable, d'aspect très différent, plus compact et caractérisé par la présence de nodules de couleur jaune crème. Si l'on y ajoute les fragments récupérés après l'incendie, l'examen des débris du sarcophage de Youpa a ainsi permis d'identifier pas moins de vingt-huit nouveaux fragments de la grande statue de Rê-Horakhty/Khonsou, inconnus jusqu'à présent. Parmi ceux-ci figurent notamment un important fragment du siège, appartenant probablement au côté droit de celui-ci[54], ainsi qu'un beau fragment de l'aile gauche du faucon, permettant de combler une grande lacune et de restituer le profil complet de l'aile[55]. D'autres fragments de dimensions restreintes appartiennent probablement à la surface du siège. Certains enfin, de très petites dimensions, ne sont parfois que des écailles de la pierre, dont il sera très malaisé de déterminer l'emplacement d'origine. Aujourd'hui, ce sont donc pas moins de quarante-deux fragments du grand Khonsou qui pourront être remis en place, ce qui permet d'envisager une restauration globale et une remise en valeur de cette statue qui est certainement une des plus impressionnantes de la collection au plan esthétique, mais aussi une des plus riches au point de vue de sa signification historique, dans le contexte de la fin de la 18e dynastie et de la genèse de la période amarnienne.

Le tri des fragments du sarcophage de Youpa a été facilité par le fait que le couvercle et la cuve du sarcophage sont réalisés dans des matériaux distincts, respectivement en quartzite et en granit rose. Après la réalisation de relevés au trait des fragments portant des inscriptions ou des portions de décor, les phases finales de l'opération consisteront à proposer une reconstitution virtuelle du sarcophage, puis, si les éléments conservés s'avèrent suffisants, à entreprendre sa restauration et sa ré-érection dans les salles permanentes, ainsi que sa publication complète. Un premier bilan de ce travail permet à présent d'affirmer que les fragments du sarcophage sont suffisamment nombreux pour permettre, à moyen terme, une reconstitution partielle du monument. Cependant, plusieurs obstacles subsistent. Il semble en effet que, durant les journées chaotiques qui ont suivi l'incendie de 1946, un nombre considérable de fragments n'aient pas été récupérés. En effet, si les colonnes d'inscriptions longitudinales du couvercle pourront être à peu près complètement reconstituées, il n'en va pas de même des côtés, dont de nombreuses portions sont manquantes. Il semble aussi que beaucoup de fragments non décorés, voire même la majorité d'entre eux, n'aient

53. Photographie numérotée « 684 », montrant les restes du linteau sous la neige, tombée avec abondance dès le lendemain de l'incendie (Archives MRAH).

54. Inv. E.5188/8.

55. Inv. E.5188/9.

pas été récupérés en 1946. Il s'agit notamment de fragments de la masse interne du sarcophage, ne comprenant aucune surface travaillée, mais aussi de portions du vêtement plissé de Youpa. Plus préoccupant, à ce jour, et pour l'instant inexplicable, aucun fragment de la partie supérieure du couvercle n'a pu être identifié, à l'exception de la bouche. Enfin, certaines reconstitutions risquent d'être relativement hypothétiques. En effet, nous ne possédons que deux photographies anciennes du couvercle du sarcophage[56] et il semble qu'aucun cliché de la cuve en granit rose ne soit conservé. En dehors de ces deux photos, le seul document que nous possédons sur l'emplacement des divers textes est la copie, souvent assez peu claire, réalisée par Louis Speleers en 1923 et publiée dans son recueil d'inscriptions hiéroglyphiques[57]. Il est parfois difficile, sur la base des indications de Speleers, d'identifier avec précision l'emplacement des inscriptions. Les seules pistes de travail seront donc fournies par le matériel comparatif des grands sarcophages ramessides en pierre, présentant les défunts en habits des vivants.

Comme on le voit, si l'archéologie égyptienne s'exerce le plus souvent en Égypte, les fouilles effectuées dans les réserves des musées offrent parfois de belles surprises, un travail parfois décourageant et même pénible car, avant inventaire, il s'agit de nettoyer les fragments de l'épaisse gangue de poussière et de suie dans laquelle ils sont incrustés depuis des décennies… Dans ces cas-là ce sont plutôt les conservateurs et les restaurateurs qui sont « at risk », mais le jeu en vaut la peine s'il aboutit à réintégrer dans les salles d'exposition permanentes d'authentiques chefs d'œuvre de la statuaire égyptienne.

Bibliographie

[ANONYME]. 1901. « Dons ». *Bulletin des Musées royaux des Arts décoratifs et industriels*, 1e année, n° 1, 3–5.

[ANONYME]. 1905. « Le pavillon de l'Antiquité au Cinquantenaire ». *Bulletin des Musées royaux des Arts décoratifs et industriels*, 4e année, n° 10, 73–84.

[ANONYME]. 1933. « Musée ». *CdE* 8, 226.

[ANONYME]. 1934. « Musée ». *CdE* 9, 23–24.

[ANONYME]. 1937. « Nouvelles ». *CdE* 12, 73–79.

[ANONYME]. 1946. « La portée exacte des dégâts au Musée du Cinquantenaire ». *La Nouvelle Gazette de Bruxelles*.

BASTIEN, A. 1946. « Des trésors uniques dans un hangar ». *Le Drapeau Rouge* (Archives MRAH).

BIERBRIER, M. L. (ed.). 2012. *Who Was Who in Egyptology*, 4th rev. ed. London: Egypt Exploration Society.

BRASSEUR-CAPART, A.-M. et A. BRASSEUR-CAPART. 1974. *Jean Capart ou le rêve comblé de l'égyptologie*. Bruxelles: Lucien De Meyer, 1974.

56. Photos Association égyptologique Reine Elisabeth 419–420. Il est probable que ces clichés ont été pris par Jean Capart dans les écuries du palais royal de Bruxelles, avant le transfert de la collection Léopold II vers les Musées, en 1919 (voir Schmidt 1919, 126, fig. 647).

57. Speleers 1923a, 66–68, n° 278.

Bruffaerts, J.-M. 2005. « Un mastaba égyptien pour Bruxelles ». *Bulletin des Musées royaux d'Art et d'Histoire* 76, 5–36.

Capart, J. 1902a. « Antiquités égyptiennes (suite) ». *Bulletin des Musées royaux des Arts décoratifs et industriels*, 1e année, n° 11, 81–83.

———. 1902b. *Recueil de monuments égyptiens*, 1ère série, Bruxelles.

———. 1928. *Musées royaux du Cinquantenaire. Guide du visiteur. Égypte*, Bruxelles.

Deltour-Levie, Cl. 1985. « 1889–1946 ». In *Liber Memorialis 1835–1985*, Brussel-Bruxelles, Koninklijke Musea voor Kunst en Geschiedenis – Musées royaux d'Art et d'Histoire, 31–56.

De Putter, Th. 1991. « L'identification et l'origine du matériau de la statue du dieu-faucon des Musées royaux d'Art et d'Histoire ». *Bulletin des Musées royaux d'Art et d'Histoire* 62, 47–52.

Eisenlohr, A. 1889. "Egyptian Antiquities in Brussels." *PSBA* 11, 254–66.

Gardiner, A. H. 1950. "The Baptism of Pharaoh." *JEA* 36, 3–12.

Gilbert, P. 1968. « Aux Musées Royaux d'Art et d'Histoire : nouvel aménagement de la collection égyptienne ». *Brabant* 3, 20–28.

Guide. 1928. = *Musées Royaux du Cinquantenaire. Guide sommaire du visiteur*. Wetteren, Belgium: De Meester.

Hornemann, B. 1957. *Types of Ancient Egyptian Statuary*. Vol. 3. Copenhagen: Munksgaard.

KRI = K. A. Kitchen, *Ramesside Inscriptions. Historical and Biographical*, Oxford 1975–1990.

Langhi, E. 1946. « La portée exacte du sinistre au Musée du Cinquantenaire. Bilan et conclusions ». *Le Peuple*, 23 février 1946 (Archives MRAH).

Lavachery, H. 1946, « Note sur les pertes du département égyptien dans l'incendie du 20 février 1946 », document du 1er mars 1946 (Archives MRAH).

Le Gall-Kazazian, A. 2011. « Deux familles arméniennes dans l'Égypte du XIXe siècle, les Tcherakian et les Nubarian ». *Cahiers de la Méditerranée* 82, 341–58.

La Dernière Heure. 1946. « Après l'incendie du Cinquantenaire ». *La Dernière Heure*, 25 avril 1946 (Archives MRAH).

Montet, P. 1935–1937. « Les obélisques de Ramsès II ». *Kêmi* 5, 104–14.

PM = B. Porter et R. B. Moss. 1934–. *Topographical Bibliography of Ancient Egyptian Hieroglyphic Texts, Reliefs and Paintings*. Oxford: Clarendon.

Ruffle, J. et K. A. Kitchen. 1979. "The Family of Urhiya and Yupa, High Stewards of the Ramesseum", in : *Glimpses of Ancient Egypt. Studies in Honour of H.W. Fairman*. Warminster: Aris & Phillips, 55–74.

Ruyssinck, M. 1985. « 1946–1984 ». *Liber Memorialis 1835–1985*, Brussel-Bruxelles, Koninklijke Musea voor Kunst en Geschiedenis – Musées royaux d'Art et d'Histoire, 57–69.

Schmidt, V. 1919. *Sarkofager, mumiekister, og mumiehylstre i det gamle Aegypten: typologisk atlas med inledning*. Copenhagen: Frimodt.

Sharpe, S. 1855. *Egyptian Inscriptions from the British Museum and Other Sources (Second Series)*. London.

Speleers, L. 1923a. *Recueil des inscriptions égyptiennes des Musées royaux du Cinquantenaire à Bruxelles*. Bruxelles: Musées royaux du Cinquantenaire.

———. 1923b. *Les figurines funéraires égyptiennes*, Bruxelles: Fondation Universitaire.

Uphill, E. P. 1984. *The Temples of Per Ramesses*, Warminster: Aris & Phillips.

van de Walle, B. 1974. « La publication des textes des musées: Bruxelles (Musées Royaux d'Art et d'Histoire) ». In *Textes et langages de l'Égypte pharaonique. Cent cinquante années de recherches, 1822–1972. III. Hommage à Jean-François Champollion*. BdE 64/3. Le Caire : IFAO, 169–80.

VAN DE WALLE, B., L. LIMME et H. DE MEULENAERE. 1980. *La collection égyptienne. Les étapes marquantes de son développement.* Bruxelles : Musées royaux d'Art et d'Histoire.

VAN RINSVELD, B. 1991. « Le dieu-faucon égyptien des Musées royaux d'Art et d'Histoire ». *Bulletin des Musées royaux d'Art et d'Histoire* 62, 15–45.

VAN RINSVELD, B. 2011. « Les moulages, reproductions et maquettes de la collection égyptienne des Musées royaux d'Art et d'Histoire: vrai, faux-semblant et hyperréalité ». *Bulletin des Musées royaux d'Art et d'Histoire* 82, 17–54.

WARMENBOL, E. 2012. *L'Égypte vue par Florent Mols et Jacob Jacobs (1838–1839). L'orientalisme en Belgique.* Bruxelles: Racine.

WERBROUCK, M. 1930. « Léopold II et l'égyptologie ». *La Gaule*, 76–79.

———. 1935. « La collection Léopold II ». *Bulletin des Musées royaux d'Art et d'Histoire*, 7e année, 3e série, 63–67.

Collections at a Loss: The Looting of Egyptian Objects in 1945 after the End of WWII as Illustrated by an Exhibition at the Museum August Kestner, Hannover

Christian E. Loeben

From 21 June to 6 November 2011, the Museum August Kestner Hannover showed the special exhibition "Lost! Die Ägypten-Sammlung und ihre (Kriegs-) Verluste," which was organized in close cooperation with the Stadtarchiv Hannover (the main archive of the City of Hannover). The exhibition and its catalogue intended to introduce the public to 734 ancient Egyptian objects, about one third of the holdings at that time, that had been missing from the museum since World War II (fig. 1).

These objects were lost immediately *after* World War II, when the storage facilities for Hannover's art holdings were plundered. It is therefore not the case that they were "destroyed as a result of enemy action" (*Durch Feindeinwirkung vernichtet*) as the stamp on the inventory files in the Stadtarchiv Hannover of the lost objects indicates. This stamp was used mostly for the objects that were in fact destroyed during the severe air raids over Hannover in 1943, and then incorrectly used again for the objects lost in the postwar turmoil (fig. 2).

The visitors were informed about the theme largely by means of large printed banners. Photographs of the inventory cards of all 734 lost items were displayed on two whole walls of the exhibition section on the museum's second floor, immediately adjacent to the entrance to the permanent exhibition of the museum's Egyptian holdings (figs. 3, 4).

Two display cases provided comprehensive information about the private collection of the former professor for Egyptology in Munich, Friedrich Wilhelm Freiherr von Bissing (1873–1956), which was acquired by the city of Hannover in 1935. Purchased for 61,500 reichsmarks, the museum came into possession of over 1,500 Egyptian items all at once, increasing the older holdings of *aegyptiaca*—from August Kestner (ca. 800 objects) and Friedrich Culemann (ca. 150 objects)—by over 150 percent! The acquisition for Hannover is owed to the museum's then director, the

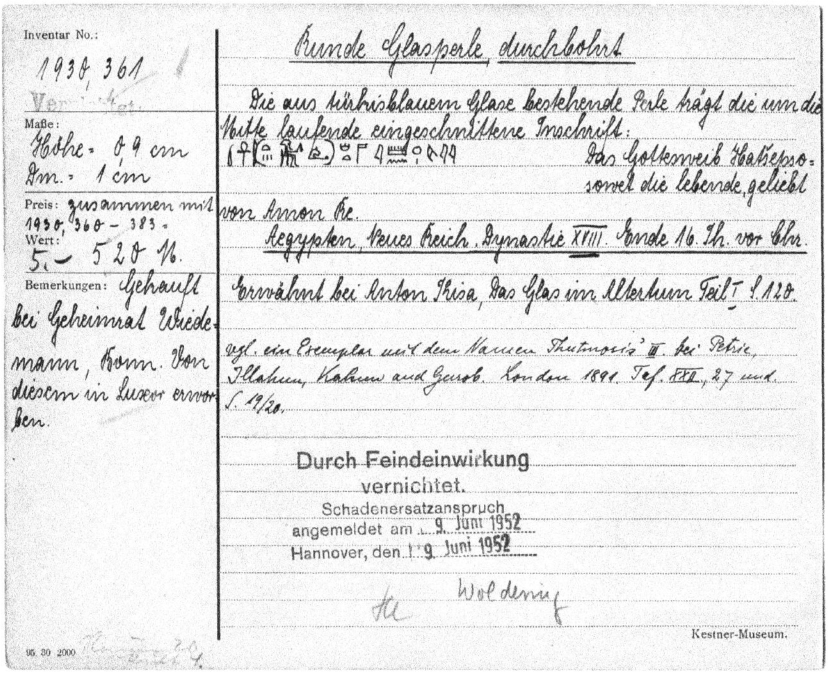

Inventar No.: 1930, 361

Maße: Höhe = 0,9 cm
Dm. = 1 cm

Preis: zusammen mit 1930, 360 – 383.
Wert: 5,– 520 M.

Bemerkungen: Gekauft bei Geheimrat Wiedemann, Bonn. Von diesem in Luxor erworben.

Runde Glasperle, durchbohrt

Die aus türkisblauem Glase bestehende Perle trägt die um die Mitte laufende eingeschnittene Inschrift: Das Gottesweib Hatschepsowet die lebende, geliebt von Amon Re.

Aegypten, Neues Reich. Dynastie XVIII. Ende 16. Jh. vor Chr.

Erwähnt bei Anton Kisa, Das Glas im Altertum Teil I S. 120.

vgl. ein Exemplar mit dem Namen Thutmosis' III. bei Petrie, Illahun, Kahun and Gurob. London 1891. Taf. XXII, 27 und S. 19/20.

Durch Feindeinwirkung
vernichtet.
Schadenersatzanspruch
angemeldet am 9. Juni 1952
Hannover, den 9. Juni 1952

Kestner-Museum.

95. 30. 2000

Fig. 1. Inventory card of a glass bead bearing the ring name of the female pharaoh Hatshepsut (1479–1458 BC); the card shows the rubber stamp "Durch Feindeinwirkung vernichtet" ("destroyed as a result of enemy action") (Stadtarchiv Hannover). © Museum August Kestner, Hannover, Christian Tepper.

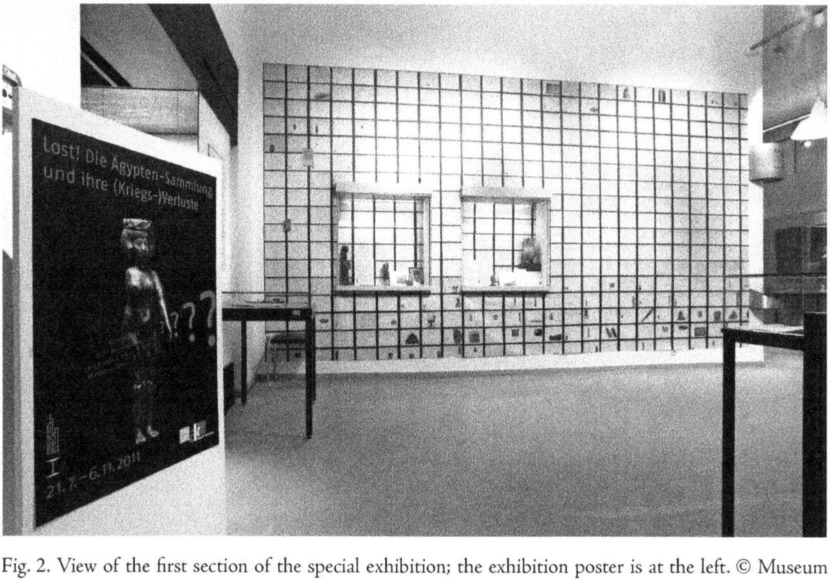

Fig. 2. View of the first section of the special exhibition; the exhibition poster is at the left. © Museum August Kestner, Hannover, Christian Tepper.

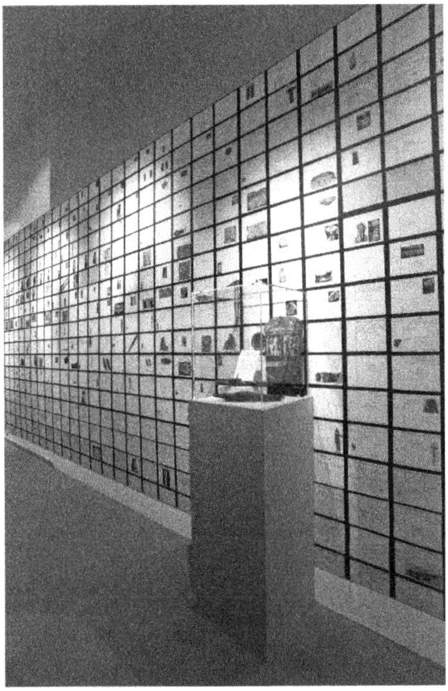

Fig. 3. View of the long exhibition wall with the facsimiles of the inventory cards of the lost Egyptian items. © Museum August Kestner, Hannover, Christian Tepper.

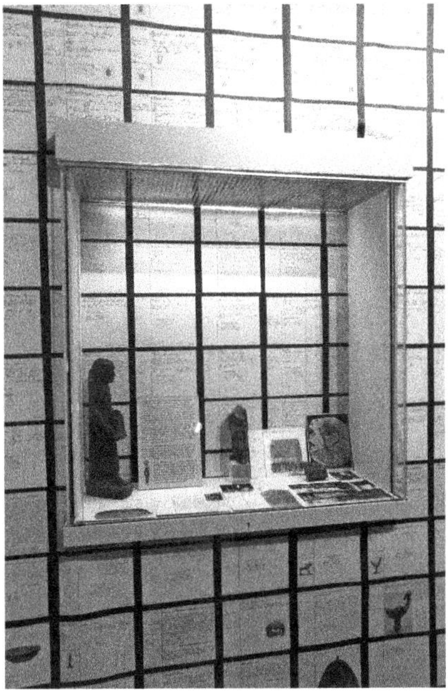

Fig. 4. A wall display case with items from the former collection of Friedrich Wilhelm Freiherr von Bissing. © Museum August Kestner, Hannover, Christian Tepper.

Egyptologist Carl Küthmann (1885–1968, museum director 1920–1937 and 1945–1951), who was a close friend of his colleague von Bissing. Küthmann is now largely forgotten as an Egyptologist and is not even mentioned in the latest edition of Who Was Who in Egyptology.[1] His services on behalf of the museum were furthermore extraordinarily forward-looking. Seen in retrospect it was fortunate that the inventorying of the von Bissing Collection proceeded much too slowly, causing him to have photographs made of all the items. We therefore also possess good pictorial documentation of the many lost pieces from this collection.

The next thematic complex concerned the evacuation of the museum's holdings during the war, the losses incurred afterwards, and the rediscovery of pieces that were believed lost in addition to items that were returned from the evacuation damaged. The gaps that the losses inflicted on the museum's Egyptian collection were illustrated based on works still present in the museum's holdings or acquired later (figs. 5, 6).

But the centerpiece of the exhibition was the over-30 m-long wall featuring photographs of the destroyed city of Hannover, behind which illustrations of the most

1. Bierbrier 2012.

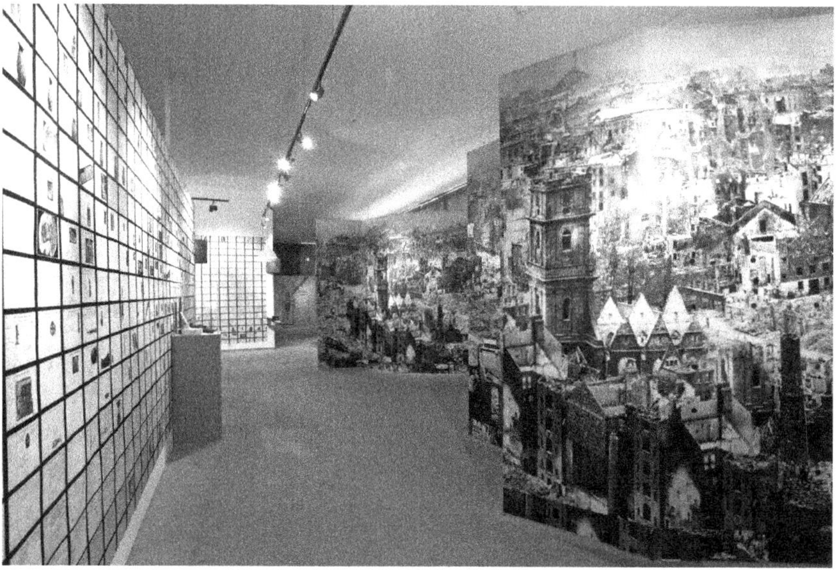

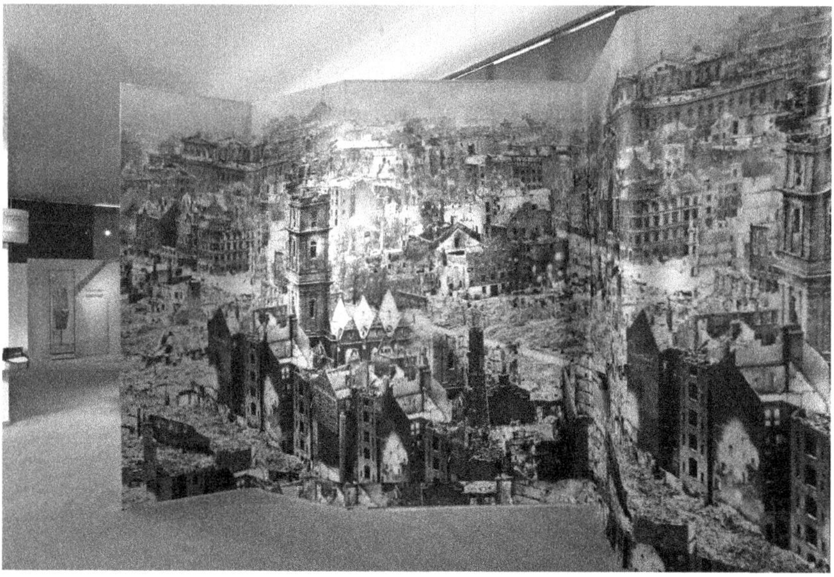

Figs. 5 and 6. Views of the zigzagged exhibition wall with the photographs of the destroyed city of Hanover. © Museum August Kestner, Hannover, Christian Tepper.

important of the lost items were "concealed" and could be "discovered" through one hundred peepholes (fig. 7–8).

Why were there so many losses particularly in the Egyptian collection of the Kestner Museum? Even before Hitler's Germany invaded Poland on 1 September 1939, a flood of directives were issued to the German museums that occasioned an

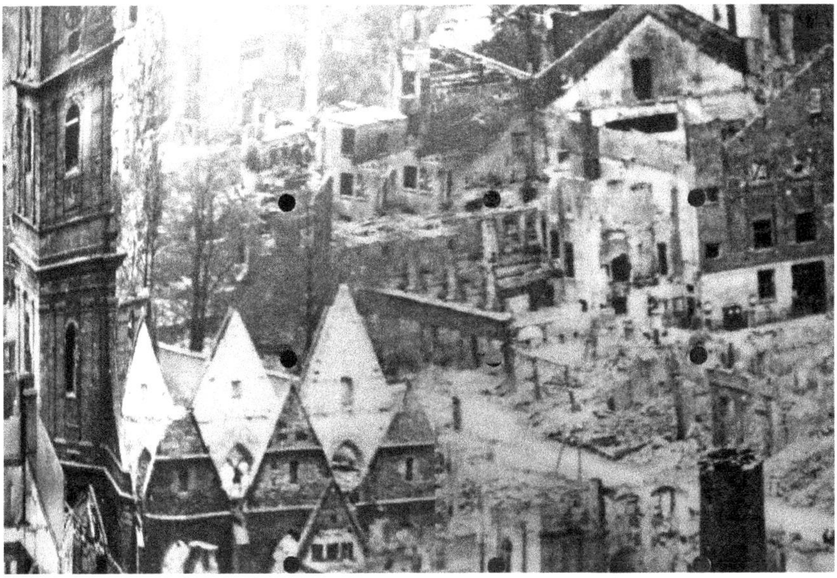

Fig. 7. Detail of the exhibition wall with the photograph of the destroyed city of Hannover. © Museum August Kestner, Hannover, Christian Tepper.

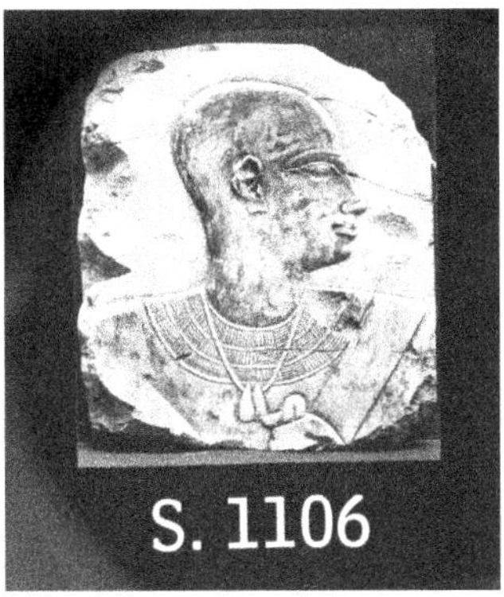

Fig. 8. View through one of the 100 peepholes at a photo of a lost object: limestone relief from the Theban necropolis with head of a high official of the Twenty-Fifth Dynasty (ca. 700 BC) from the von Bissing Collection. Inv. S.1106. © Museum August Kestner, Hannover, Christian Tepper.

awareness of the impending danger to the cultural items they administered. During the second year of the war, the Kestner Museum's then director Ferdinand Stuttmann (1897–1968)[2] wrote:

> "On the evening of 11 February 1941, shortly before 10 o'clock, the Kestner Museum was damaged (for the first time) by bombs dropped by enemy aircraft ... Fortunately, no very serious damage was done to the art objects ... Over the course of the work, a large percentage of the art objects were removed from

2. Stadtarchiv Hannover, folder: AAA 2346

> the building. [Author's note: the objects were taken to the ground floor of the Landesmuseum; the vault in the Landschaftliche Brandkasse; the vault in the new City Hall; the strong room in the municipal salaries department] ... An even larger percentage of the collections however had to remain in the Kestner Museum itself. These are assembled for the most on the ground floor."

The account clearly shows that—as opposed to the art department of the Landesmuseum, which Stuttmann was also responsible for—neither the collections of the Kestner Museum were far from completely evacuated at the outbreak of the war, nor were other safety measures taken.

The 1943 air raids on Hannover were also calamitous for the museums. Storing the artworks within the city limits was increasingly being viewed as unsafe, so that their "distribution to the countryside" was organized. The first shipment of the Kestner Museum's artworks from the storage facilities in the city to Loccum Abbey (ca. 50 km to the west of Hannover) took place on 3 May 1943. Other rural storage facilities included Bad Wildungen (ca. 200 km to the southwest of Hannover);[3] the Weser Renaissance Hämelschenburg Castle near Hameln (ca. 50 km to the southwest); Idensen near Wunstorf (ca. 30 km to the west); Wiebrechtshausen near Northeim (ca. 90 km to the southwest); Moringen near Northeim (ca. 100 km to the south); Medingen Abbey near Bevensen (ca. 110 km to the northeast); Sachsenhagen (ca. 40 km to the west); Liebenau near Warburg (ca. 125 km to the south) in addition to the Grasleben salt mine near Helmstedt (ca. 100 km to the east).

The Grasleben salt mine was the most important—and unfortunately also the most ill-fated—of the Kestner Museum's evacuation sites. The extensive system of passageways over 400 m below ground provided excellent protection for works of art because of their aridity. Six transports of 136 crates from the Kestner Museum to the Grasleben salt mine took place between 2 February and 30 March 1944. Significant holdings from the State Museums in Berlin were likewise brought to Grasleben, including twenty shipments between 6 June and 19 November 1944.

Grasleben was taken by the 35th Infantry Division of the Ninth United States Army on 12 April 1945. The salt mine and its contents were apparently handed over by the mine director in perfect condition. The indecision about whether the Americans would retain control of this region or whether it would become a part of the British zone—which ultimately occurred—occasioned a period of uncertainty, during which devastating plunderings took place at Grasleben, in part by the forced laborers who formerly had to work in this mine. All of the 136 crates from the Kestner Museum stored there were broken into. A terrible fire that broke out on 18 June 1945 at 12:30 in the afternoon further made the part of the mine used for art storage uncontrollable until 26 June 1945. On 14 September 1945, 118 crates were returned

3. On Bad Wildungen, see now: Jelusic 2011, 111–34.

directly to Hannover, followed by about ten more on 7 November 1945.[4] Even today, there is still no information about the whereabouts of eight crates from the Kestner Museum stored at the Grasleben salt mine! As late as 1948, objects that were feared lost were found on the floor of the salt mine, including a small decorated gold foil that was once sewed onto mummy bandages.

Although only a few such original Egyptian objects were on show at the exhibition of 2011, it did attract numerous visitors, particularly colleagues from Germany and abroad who were interested in seeing how the "unexhibitable" could be exhibited.

The contents of the temporary exhibition are documented in an accompanying publication (320 pages, 627 illustrations and a CD-ROM).[5] The book's scope extends beyond the exhibition, encompassing a history of how the internationally important Egyptian Collection in Hannover came about,[6] the story of the evacuation and losses in addition to a catalogue of the missing items in the third part of the catalogue with all the documentary illustrations. The included CD-ROM features these illustrations again, but in better digital quality, in addition to facsimiles of the inventory cards of all lost objects. As such, it is now possible to identify and thus perhaps rediscover the losses anywhere in the world and the information provided about these lost objects furthermore makes it possible for them to be taken in consideration by scholarship. The publication is thus not only the first catalogue of losses of a Hannover museum but also the first one of the many Egyptian museums—not only in Germany—that have suffered far-reaching losses.

The extensive archival research made in conjunction with these loses has definitively shown that none of the 734 lost objects from the Egyptian Collection in Hannover can be proven to have been destroyed. As such, there is hope that the one or other item can be identified thanks to the exhibition and its publication, and returned to the museum one day. The Museum August Kestner naturally hopes very much that this will happen—it would be the perfect long-term achievement of a modest exhibition project.

References

Bierbrier, M. L. (ed.). 2012. *Who Was Who in Egyptology*, 4th rev. ed. London: Egypt Exploration Society.

Jelusic, M. 2011. "Ein Zufluchtsort für weltbekannte Kunst. Bad Wildungen als Bergungsdepot für das Landesmuseum und das Kestner-Museum Hannover während des Zweiten Weltkrieges." *Hannoversche Geschichtsblätter*, NF 65, 111–34.

Loeben, C. E. 2005. "Ägyptische Sammlung des Kestner-Museums." In E. Hornung, C. E.

4. Account by Ferdinand Stuttman to city finance director Weber from 8 November 1945: Stadtarchiv Hannover, folder: HR 10, nr. 1280.

5. Loeben 2011.

6. For English versions of the history of the Egyptian collection in Hanover see now also: Loeben 2005, 192–95; 2012, 18–23; 2013, 54–65.

LOEBEN, and A. WIESE (eds.), *Immortal Pharaoh: The Tomb of Thutmose III* (exhibition catalogue Edinburgh, City Art Centre 2005–2006), 192–95.

———. 2005. "The Egyptian Collection at the 'Museum August Kestner,' Hanover (Germany): Assembled Privately with Connoisseurship – Given Generously to the Public." Pp. 18–23 in *Ancient Egypt: Masterpieces from Collectors and Collections*. Brussels: Brussels Ancient Art Fair.

———, (with contributions by T. HENKE, B. LÜSCHER, A. V. SIEBERT, and A. WIESE). 2011. *Die Ägypten-Sammlung des Museum August Kestner und ihre (Kriegs-)Verluste*. Museum Kestnerianum 15. Rahden/Westf.: Leidorf.

———. 2013. "Museum August Kestner, Hanover, Germany, Part 1: History of the Egyptian Collection." *KMT* 24.2, 54–65.

Pharaoh's Palace: From the Ruins of Memphis to Copenhagen

Tine Bagh

A large relief from the palace of King Apries at Memphis was the centrepiece of the Petrie exhibition "In the Shadow of the Pyramids" at the Ny Carlsberg Glyptotek from November 2011 till March 2012. Many years ago it had been reduced to a sorry heap of fragments of limestone and old plaster restorations, but it was restored to its former glory for the exhibition. When the exhibition closed, another temporary exhibition space was found in the museum's exhibition area "The Ancient Mediterranean." For two years it could be viewed there together with palace fragments from Assyria, Babylonia, and Persia. The story recounted here concerning the relief's long journey from Pharaoh's Palace in Memphis to this appropriate place among equals in the Glyptotek can thus be said to have had a happy ending (fig. 1).

Ny Carlsberg Glyptotek

The brewing magnate Carl Jacobsen (1842–1914) bought his first Egyptian antiquities in 1884 for the original Ny Carlsberg Glyptotek, founded in his home in Valby in 1882. Jacobsen's collection of Egyptian and classical antiquities grew steadily, together with that of his Danish and French art so the Valby Glyptotek was extended, but proved too small in the end. Jacobsen and his wife Ottilia then donated their collection to the Danish state on condition that the latter provided a site for a museum where it could be displayed. The first building of the present Ny Carlsberg Glyptotek, now on Dantes Plads in Copenhagen, was opened in 1897 and the part housing the Collection of Antiquities in 1906. In 1892 Jacobsen had engaged Denmark's founder of Egyptology at the university, Valdemar Schmidt (1836–1925) to buy Egyptian antiquities in Egypt and Europe. The Ny Carlsberg Foundation was established in 1902 and after the Glyptotek was completed in 1906 Schmidt suggested to Jacobsen that he support Flinders Petrie's excavations through the Foundation. In this way the museum would be able to receive finds from documented excavations. From 1908–1913 and again in 1920–1922 the Ny Carlsberg Foundation supported Petrie on behalf of Carl Jacobsen and the Glyptotek which thus every year received finds from Petrie.

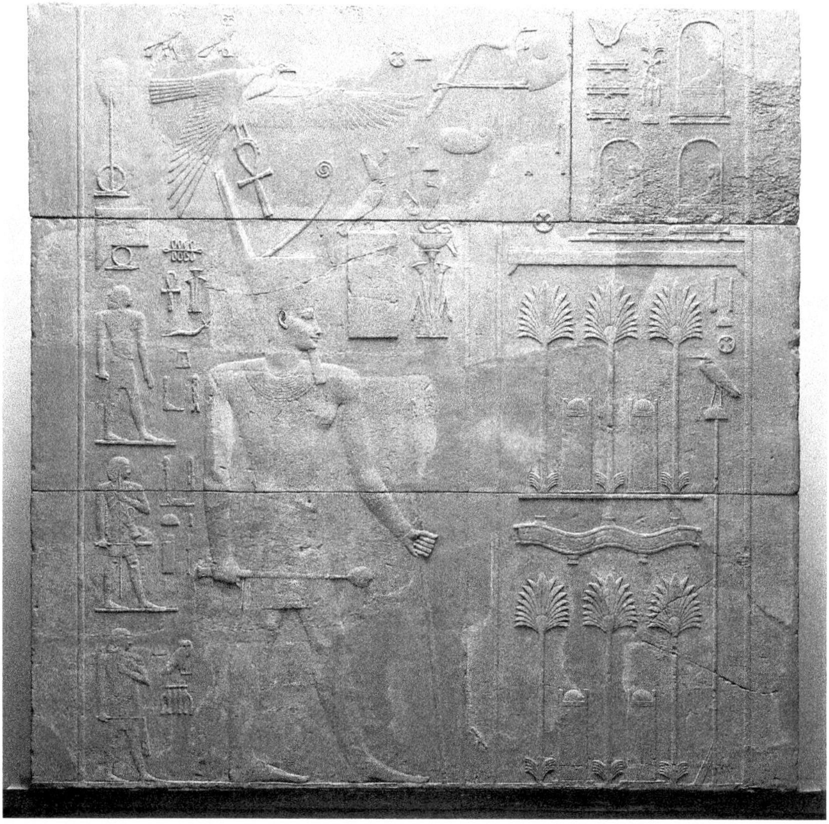

Fig. 1. The Apries relief in the Ny Carlsberg Glyptotek. Inv. AEIN 1046. © Ole Haupt.

Maria Mogensen (1882–1932) had been a student of Schmidt and from 1910 she was officially engaged at the Glyptotek as his assistant.

W. M.F . Petrie's Excavations in Memphis

Petrie considered the excavations of Memphis as of the utmost importance because of the historical significance of the former capital. Another reason to work there was to investigate and document what was still left of the site, which was at that time already rapidly deteriorating. The head of the Department of Antiquities, the Frenchman Gaston Maspero, had also urged him to start in Memphis and by 1908 Petrie thought that finally the finances of his British School of Archaeology were sound enough for him to embark on such a large project. During the six excavation seasons 1908–13 he uncovered various parts of the city and the work was only stopped by the Great War, although Petrie had anticipated that it would take at least twenty years

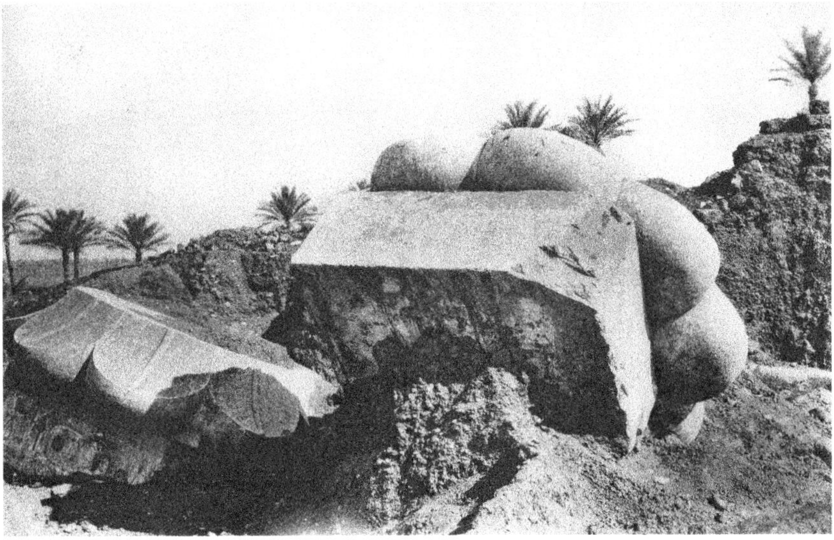

Fig. 2. Palm column capitals with the name of Apries in the Palace of Apries. Petrie 1909b, pl. XI.2.

to "clear the temple sites alone."[1] The Glyptotek received finds from every season in Memphis; these ranged from a colossal statue of Ramses II and Ptah-Tatenen to a rusty nail from a Roman house.[2]

The Palace of Apries

During his first season in Memphis, Petrie discovered the name of Apries of the Twenty-Sixth Dynasty on a column fragment at the so-called fort in the northern part of the city.[3] Further efforts to uncover the secrets of the large mound, Kom Tuman, had been stopped by the groundwater. The following year, however, when work was concentrated there, the mound was shown to contain the royal palace of Apries built on a high mud-brick platform.[4] The palace walls were also of mud brick and lined with limestone slabs on the floors and lower parts of the larger rooms. The columns, as well as doorways and stairways, were also of stone (fig. 2). The name of Apries on columns confirmed, as mentioned, the ownership of the palace, but no other wall decorations or inscriptions were brought to light.

On the south side of the palace what Petrie termed a fosse separated the building from the southern approach. In the west end of this fosse, on a lower level than the

1. Petrie 1909a, p. 1.
2. Cf. Bagh 2011, p. 25–78 for all the Memphis finds and ibid. passim for all Petrie's excavations supported by the Ny Carlsberg Foundation for the Glyptotek.
3. Petrie 1909a, p. 4.
4. Petrie 1909b, p. 1. Cf. also Kemp 1977.

palace itself, limestone relief fragments of a large gateway were discovered that Petrie thought had belonged to an earlier building. There was no royal name preserved on the relief fragments and the date earlier than Apries he based on its lower find position as well as on the fine style that made him date it to the Middle Kingdom, the reign of Senusret I.[5] However, the gateway more likely belonged to an earlier version of the Palace of Apries as concluded by the studies of H. Kees,[6] B. Kemp[7] and W. Kaiser.[8]

The Large Gateway of the Palace

Petrie must have spent many hours with the large jigsaw puzzle of the fragmentary gateway with many missing pieces. He drew everything full size and explained in detail how he had reached the conclusions causing him to publish the fragments as the two sides of the gateway.[9] In the text he recommended to the readers that if they only wanted to read about the results they should skip the chapter with his argumentation for the reconstructions of the scenes and the gateway.[10]

Petrie reconstructed the gate with three scenes on each side of the doorway, each about 2 × 2 m with the king in large format. The scenes were all representations of the king performing *heb-sed* rituals. He explained that he was able to do so based on the fact that the depictions of the king all had a smooth edge behind him and a rough edge before him which would match a gateway with images of the king oriented as "walking out" of the gate. The preserved fragments included elements of at least five kings, three on the left side of the gate and two on the right. Petrie concluded that this meant that the original number of scenes must have been six. Enough was preserved of the kings to show that he was wearing the white crown on the left side of the gate and the red on the right side. All of the scenes were framed in the same way by a sky with five-pointed stars in the familiar Egyptian style above the scenes. In the corner above the king was a bird with an *ankh* or *shen* in its claws and Petrie reconstructed all the birds as the vulture Nekhbet. W. Kaiser (fig. 3), however, has since proved that some were the falcon Horus Bedehty instead—a fact that is clear from the preserved parts of the inscriptions naming the birds[11] (cf. below). In front of the king is in all cases a Wepwawet standard and a *serekh* that in all the surviving fragments with this part preserved were empty. Behind the king were courtiers, about a third of the king in size and with their own registers.

5. Petrie 1909b, p. 5–6 ; Mogensen 1930, n° A 703 even suggested a date to the Third Dynasty after the discovery of similar reliefs in the Djoser Complex in Saqqara.
6. Kees 1912, p. 197–200.
7. Kemp 1977.
8. Kaiser 1987.
9. Petrie 1909b, pl. IX.
10. Petrie 1909b, p. 6.
11. Kaiser 1987, fig. 9. Cf. also Bagh 2011, p. 38.

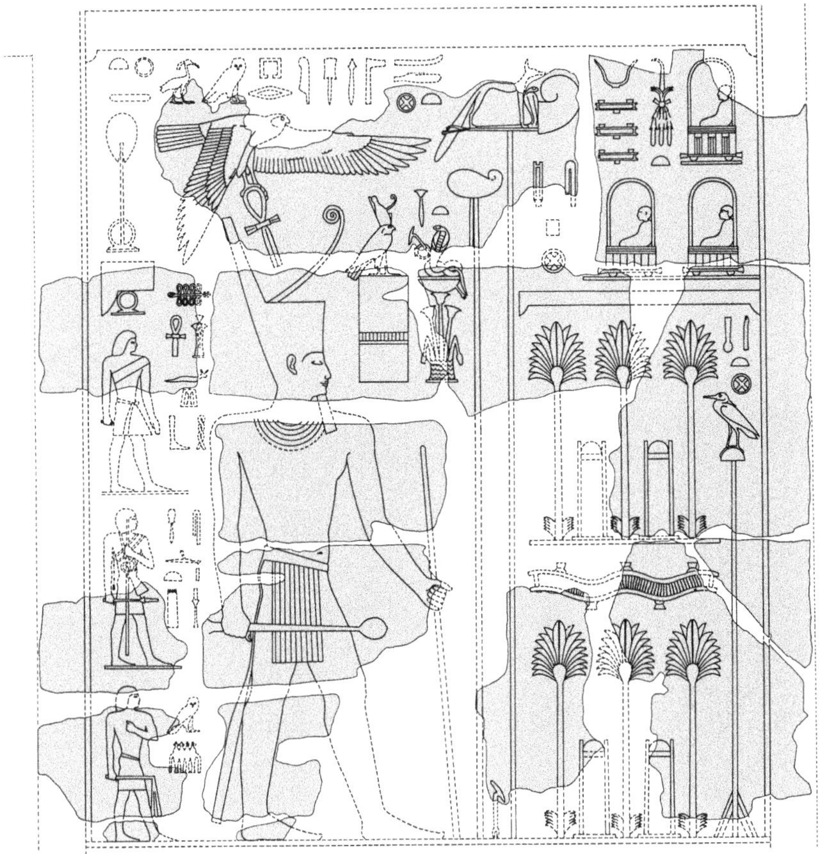

Fig. 3. Drawing of the Apries relief; the coloured areas show the original parts. Kaiser 1987, fig. 9.

The Relief Destined for Copenhagen

Carl Jacobsen and his daughter Paula visited Egypt in 1909 while Petrie was excavating the Palace of Apries in Memphis. Jacobsen mentioned his visit to the site on March 5th in his travel diary[12].

> To Flinders Petrie and his excavations in Memphis
> [...]

12. The diary is kept in the Ny Carlsberg Glyptotek together with the letters referred to below. Cf. also Bagh 2011, p. 17 for the page in the diary.

> We saw the location of the fortress[13] where they were still digging up the fragments. Very fragmentary but lovely work of relief rivalling (Petrie thought even surpassing) Abydos
>
> The stone is from Abusir and had been relocated to be used in the building in the fortress.

No doubt the mention of the "relocated" "lovely work of relief" refers to the fragments of the great gateway. It is not clear why it is described as "from Abusir" but that was probably what Petrie told Jacobsen at the site and, as mentioned above, Petrie was convinced that the gateway predated the reign of Apries.[14]

More explicitly the gateway scene from the Palace of Apries that was destined for Copenhagen was mentioned in a letter from Schmidt to Jacobsen dating from July 5th the same year. Schmidt visited Petrie's London exhibition and reported to Jacobsen what he saw, listing the objects that he considered appropriate for the Glyptotek. Every summer Petrie arranged an exhibition in London with finds from the previous excavation season that were to be distributed among his sponsors. In 1909 the objects on display were from Memphis.

> I took a quick look round the exhibition, it is mainly trifling antiquities – and fragmentary, but not of great value for the Glyptotek.
>
> 1) I stopped at no.10 and he [Petrie] said that he thought that it would suit the Glyptotek. It is 2m long and 2m wide in several fragments. Parts of it can be completed with a "cast from what we will obtain. It is the largest and best piece that we will receive. The best with the dancing crown prince has been claimed by Maspero.

Schmidt knew that Jacobsen did not want small or insignificant antiquities for the Glyptotek so the 2 × 2 m relief was obviously an appropriate candidate for the collection. Petrie was also well aware of Jacobsen's preferences, although it was only the second time that the Ny Carlsberg Foundation had supported Petrie, and hence the second time the Glyptotek was going to receive finds from the excavations. Since the relief scene was fragmentary it was also important for Schmidt to state that it could be reconstructed with casts. In addition he pointed out that it was the largest and best, even though the one with what he termed "the dancing crown prince" had stayed in Cairo. According to the laws of the time the Antiquities Service and the Egyptian Museum would keep the excavated finds that were considered unique.[15] And this was obviously the case with the scene with the *heb-sed* race of the king ("crown prince").

13. I.e., the Palace of Apries.

14. In Bagh 2011, 17 it was suggested that the reference to Abusir might have been connected to the fact that Petrie was thinking of the *heb-sed* scenes from the Sun Temple of Niuserre in Abusir.

15. Petrie 1930, 123. With an explanation about "unique" (*sans pareil*) finds.

Reconstructions

Since many of the individual details were similar in the various scenes, it was possible to reconstruct parts of some motifs with parts of others. This fact Petrie made use of in his drawings of the various scenes where he copied parts from some scenes to reconstruct them in others, always showing the reconstructions in dotted lines.[16] In Valdemar Schmidt's correspondence with Carl Jacobsen it also becomes clear that reconstructions of scenes were attempted through actual cast copies made from parts of scenes that were more complete in one scene than in another and these seem to have been exchanged between the various collections that received the various relief scenes of the gateway.

On August 17, 1909, Schmidt writes again to Jacobsen about his visits to Petrie's July exhibition in London with the finds from Memphis.

> During my first stay in London July 4–7 I had to make do with studying Petrie's Egyptian exhibition piece by piece, fragment by fragment. Not least in order to be able to see if there was anything for the Glyptotek other than the large monument [i.e. the Apries relief].
>
> During my last stay the large monuments were still in place and I helped making casts of details of parts that were destined for New York, Manchester, Liverpool etc. and which could be used to fill the empty spaces in the monument that the Glyptotek will receive - (as, in reverse, casts were made of details of the piece for the Glyptotek for use for New York etc.

His letter continues with an account of Maria Mogensen's first visit to Petrie's exhibition and it is clearly important to Schmidt that she should know how to help with the restoration of the relief.

> I met Miss. Mogensen in London [...] I took Miss. Mogensen to see the remains of Petrie's exhibition and she is now well informed about the restoration with the aid of the casts to fill in the gaps – so that I will not be the only one who can help arranging the monument and filling the empty spaces with casts that will fit exactly.

On 23 August, Jacobsen answers Schmidt and he is obviously very dissatisfied that parts of the Memphis monument are destined for other collections. When he had seen fragments of the monument while they were being excavated during his visit in Memphis in March (see above) he may have imagined that it would be possible to obtain all of them.

16. Petrie 1909b, 5.

> Thank you so much for your kind letter of the 17th this month. I cannot deny that I am very disappointed not only that - as I knew already – Maspero has taken the best part of the large wall but that also part of it will go to New York, Manchester and Liverpool etc.
>
> [...]
>
> I suppose there is unfortunately nothing to be done about that now, but I am really not very keen on donating more to Petrie Flinders [sic] excavations for the benefit of 'New York Manchester Liverpool etc.'!
>
> It would be good to know how much the others have paid and what they have received - in relation to what I have paid and we have received.

In a letter from 26 August, Schmidt then makes it even clearer to Jacobsen that the relief section for the Glyptotek was indeed the very best and that the many fragments including the ones for other collections did not fit directly together as one large monument with the scene selected for the Glyptotek.

> The pieces that are destined for New York and Liverpool are considerably smaller (the biggest about a third of the size of the one for the Glyptotek) - and they are very likely from the same building, but they are not directly organically connected to the Glyptotek piece. It is merely fragments, but they probably belonged to pieces that formed part of a kind of counterpart to the Glyptotek's piece, but not enough is preserved to be able to see exactly how they looked. It is only possible to see that several of the figures were of the same size as on the piece for the Glyptotek and that is why it is possible to make use of the fragments to fill the empty spaces (with plaster casts). But the original fragments themselves could not be used. The fragments that are preserved do not correspond to the empty spaces and they are extended in other directions.

Schmidt thus also elaborated on the cast issue and assured Jacobsen that the parts for New York and Liverpool were much smaller than the one for the Glyptotek. The threat to stop supporting Petrie was obviously also not carried out and in the end Jacobsen must have been satisfied with the 2 × 2 m relief. In addition, a palm column capital with well-preserved paint, likewise from the Palace of Apries, was part of the 1909 finds from Memphis that were presented to the Glyptotek together with fragments of scenes similar to the large gateway with well-preserved color and another column fragment.[17] In order to visualise the size of the palm capital Schmidt had explained in the letter of July 5th that it could not be carried by a single camel but had to hang between two of them.

17. Bagh 2011, 43.

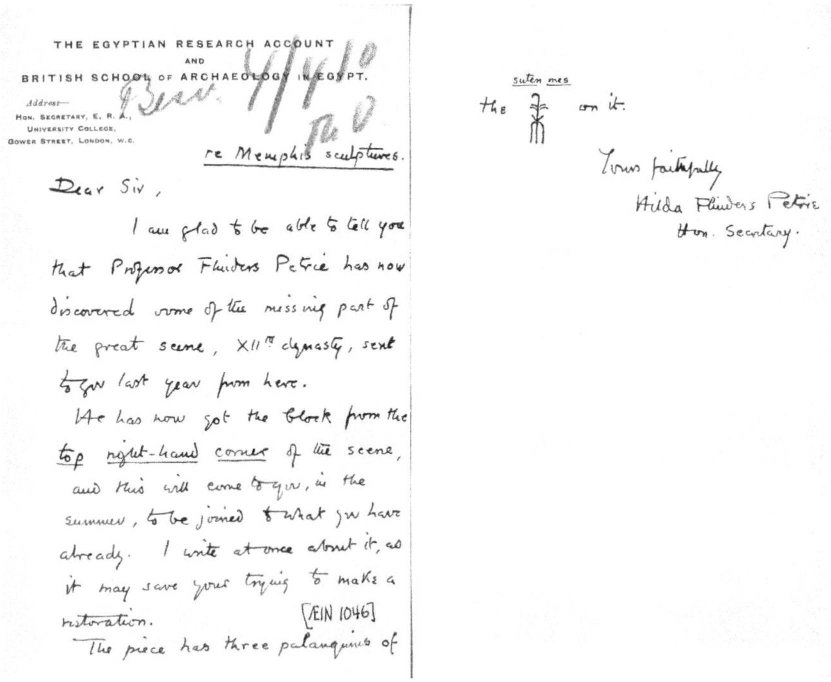

THE EGYPTIAN RESEARCH ACCOUNT AND BRITISH SCHOOL OF ARCHAEOLOGY IN EGYPT.

Address— Hon. Secretary, E. R. A., University College, Gower Street, London, W.C.

re Memphis sculptures.

Dear Sir,

I am glad to be able to tell you that Professor Flinders Petrie has now discovered some of the missing part of the great scene, XIIth dynasty, sent to you last year from here.

He has now got the block from the top right-hand corner of the scene, and this will come to you, in the summer, to be joined to what you have already. I write at once about it, as it may save your trying to make a restoration. [ÆIN 1046]

The piece has three palanquins of the suten mes on it.

Yours faithfully
Hilda Flinders Petrie
Hon. Secretary.

Fig. 4. Letter from Hilda Petrie in the archives of the Glyptotek.

An Addition to the Relief in Copenhagen

When the relief fragments arrived in Copenhagen from London, the motif with the king was apparently not immediately restored. This was lucky as Petrie located an additional fragment of the scene during the 1910 season. It was found in the fosse, like the fragments from the previous year, and Petrie immediately recognized it as "belonging to the Copenhagen scene."[18] Hilda Petrie wrote a note about this to the Glyptotek that was answered on April 4 (fig. 4):

> re Memphis sculpture.
> Dear Sir,
> I am glad to be able to tell you that Professor Flinders Petrie has now discovered some of the missing part of the great scene, XIIth dynasty, sent to you last year from here.
> He has now got the block from the top right-hand corner of the scene, and this will come to you, in the summer, to be joined to what you have already. I write at once about it, as it may save your trying to make a restoration.

18. This was mentioned in his notebook on February 28, 1910. See Bagh 2011, 18.

The piece has three palanquins of the suten mes [also the hieroglyphs] on it.
Yours faithfully
Hilda Flinders Petrie
Hon. Secretary

The relief scene was subsequently restored in Copenhagen with the additional fragment from 1910 and with details from the casts mentioned from other scenes and from the Copenhagen relief itself. This is clear since the reconstructed parts on the relief, being made from casts, are not as sharp as the original parts. The restorations of missing parts largely followed Petrie's published drawing with, for example, the bird in the corner as a vulture[19].

In the Copenhagen scene the king stands with the red crown of Lower Egypt and with his mace and staff in front of the Lower Egyptian chapels, *per-nu* placed between palm trees on both sides of the mythological winding channel[20]. The king's Horus name in the *serekh* in front of his face is, as mentioned, missing and may never have been completed or it was executed in paint and is no longer visible. A few traces of paint on the fragments show that the relief was originally painted in bright colours. Behind the king are three courtiers in a smaller scale and above the chapels in front of him are three so-called royal children in litters. This latter was the part found in 1910 mentioned above. The sky with stars that existed above all the scenes is not part of the Copenhagen relief.

The scene was originally divided into three horizontal parts and it is apparent from older photographs (fig. 5) that the surface of the 2 × 2 m relief scene was originally restored with smooth transitions between the three parts. It was initially put on display in the large Egyptian hall in the Glyptotek where it was mounted on a stone base in a wooden frame with glass front (fig. 6). At some subsequent point in time it was decided to move the large relief to the study collection of the Glyptotek. It was probably when this was to take place that it was again cut into three horizontal parts and the additional corner fragment from 1910 was also cut free again. That this had happened is apparent from a photograph from 2004 (fig. 1).[21] When the area of the study collection was to be utilised for another purpose around 2005 the relief was moved again and very unfortunately tipped over. The upper third part was the most damaged as it hit the floor first. Altogether it was principally parts of the restored plaster elements that suffered at the fall, which was also unfortunate. As mentioned they were not just restorations but details that had been copied from other parts of the gateway in order to make the restorations as authentic as possible. It was not immediately planned to have the relief on display and the three, once more fragmentary

19. See above in the text about the bird that ought to have been a falcon.
20. See Jørgensen 2009, 82–87.
21. Published in Jørgensen 2009, 83 and Bagh 2011, fig. 1.28.

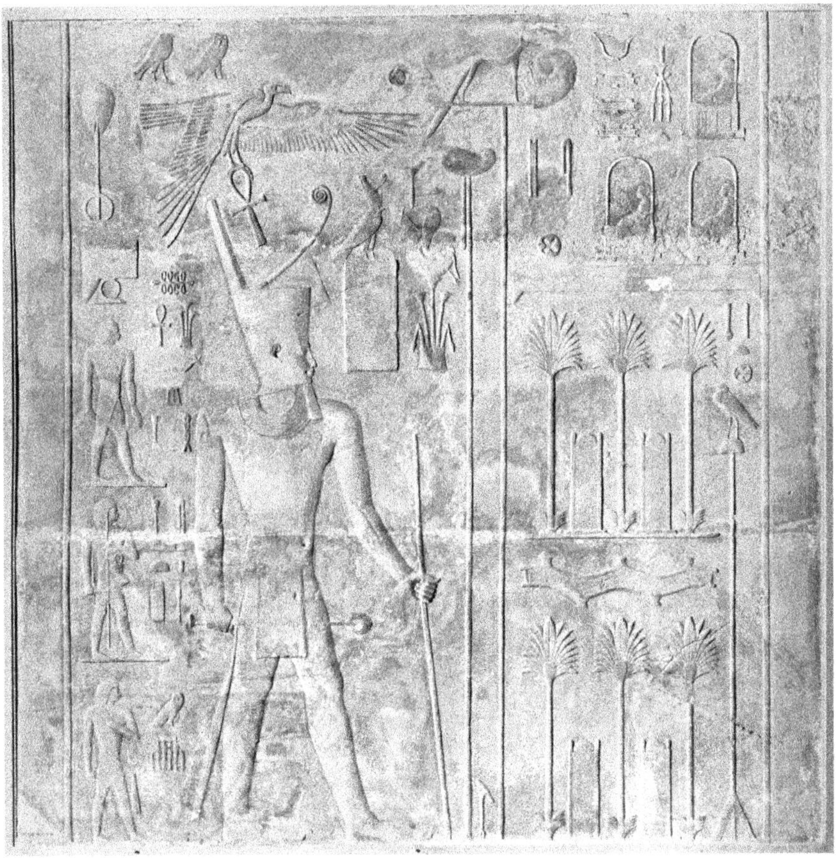

Fig. 5. Photo of the Apries relief published in Mogensen 1930, pl. CII.

parts were placed in three boxes in a store room and although important, a new restoration was initially postponed.

The Petrie Exhibition 2011

When the Petrie Project was initiated in 2009 it very soon became clear that the large Apries relief had top priority for the Petrie exhibition planned for November 2011. As mentioned, the Glyptotek houses a number of finds from Petrie's excavations in Memphis and it is essentially the most important Petrie site represented in the museum. So obviously Memphis would also play an important role in the Petrie exhibition.

What first catches the eye of a museum visitor to the Egyptian collection is the huge granite statue group of Ramses II and Ptah-Tatenen already mentioned. To the left of Ramses is a portal from the time of Siamun of the Twenty-First Dynasty that was the first large monument from Petrie's excavations in Memphis in 1908 that was

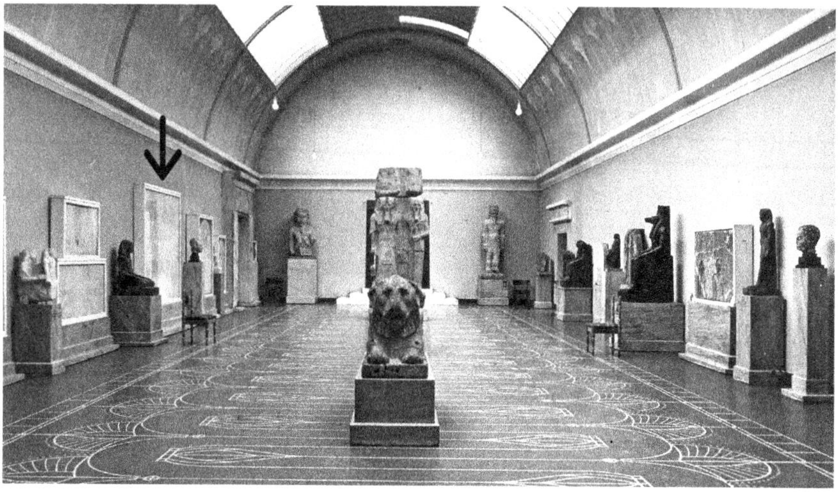

Fig. 6. The large Egyptian hall in the Glyptotek in 1939. The arrow shows the position of the Apries relief.

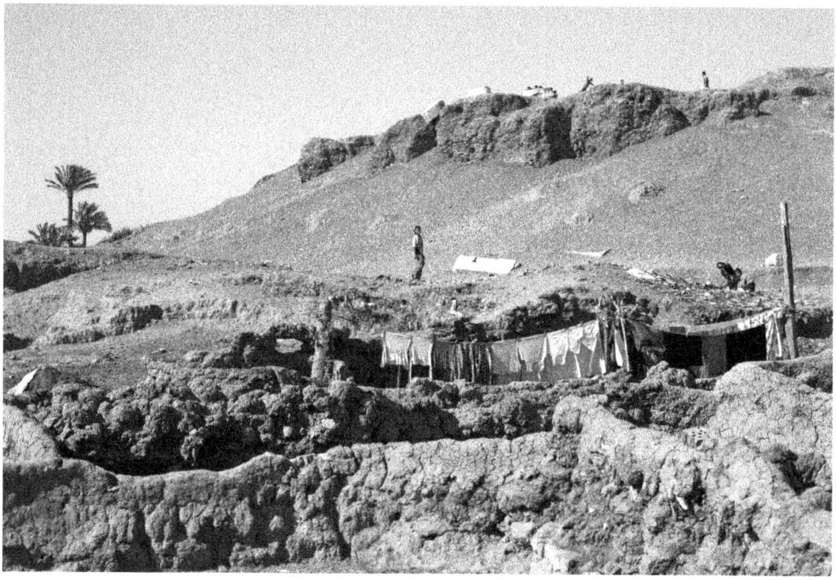

Fig. 7. The Palace of Apries 2011. © Janne Klerk.

presented to the Glyptotek. It is built-in around a doorway and, with a reconstructed right panel, forms a real portal to the smaller Egyptian hall here to the left of the large Egyptian hall. Like the colossal Ramesses dyad statue, the Siamun portal could obviously not be moved for a special exhibition. Other relatively "grand" monuments from Memphis are normally in the store room and were to be displayed in the Petrie exhibition: part of a granite column with Ramesses II offering to Ptah, a decorated quartzite corner block with reliefs of Amenhotep III offering to Sekhmet, a limestone wall relief with Ptah, a granite upper cornice corner part of a portal with the name of Ramesses VI and part of a door post with the name of Merenptah. A large African head that is normally on display in the aforementioned smaller Egyptian hall above the door could be moved and thus displayed with the other Memphis monuments. In order to have a focus point to visually unite the Memphis part of the Petrie exhibition with these fragmented monuments mentioned a genuinely grand monument was needed.

The location where the exhibition was held was a large long hall with a kind of portico with two columns at each end, by the entrance and at the end of the hall furthest away. For the Petrie exhibition the hall itself was divided into smaller niches by pylon shaped showcases and in this way the "niches" could frame the various Petrie sites represented in the Glyptotek. Walking down the hall would convey the impression of walking through an Egyptian temple, that is, being in Egypt. The displayed objects' relationship to the sites where they were found was further emphasised by large panorama photographs between the pylons of the sites as they look today (fig. 7). The entrance area with two columns was the obvious place to introduce Petrie and the story of his connection to the Glyptotek. The end of the hall furthest away, after the last set of pylons, was left larger than the niches between them, and this area was obviously best suited for "Memphis." And here against the back wall between the two columns was the natural position for an object of principal focus in the exhibition, viewable from the start of the exhibition down past the row of pylons. The 2 × 2 m Apries relief was without doubt the best suited candidate for this prominent position. It was thus of the utmost importance that it would be restored once again for this occasion which would celebrate the 'Father of Archaeology' and his importance for the Egyptian collection in the Glyptotek.

Back to Life

Lars Henningsen, the Glyptotek's conservator, embarked on the restoration project in December 2009 and lifted out the most damaged upper third part of the relief from its crate (fig. 8). The restoration work would be time consuming but not a hopeless task as the motif was still basically intact, except for, in particular, serious cracks and loose parts of the plaster.

One of the questions was how much of the originally restored plaster one should attempt to reconstruct and in what respect the plaster restorations should be remade. Some of the original plaster parts were obviously too tiny to be of use while others it would be sensible to reuse. The final restoration of all three parts of the relief took its time with many other conservation tasks also to be taken care of.

One of these was the preparation of objects and settings for the "Cleopatra's World" exhibition that opened in the spring of 2011. The first (upper) part of the

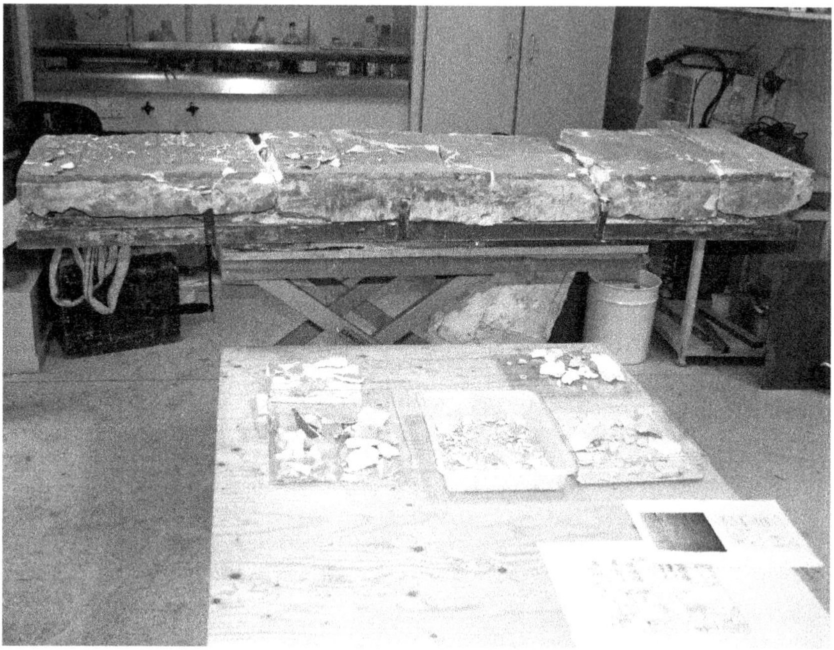

Fig. 8. The top part of the Apries relief in the conservator workshop 2010.

relief took the longest but when this was completed, and wooden boxes for each of the three parts were ready, hopes were high that the project would, in fact, be accomplished in time for the Petrie opening night on 10 November 2011.

About a week before this date, this was indeed the case and the next hurdle was then how to transport the three heavy relief parts up to the second floor where the exhibition hall was located. Well before they were ready it was clear that they were too big and heavy for the passenger lift to the exhibition hall. Consequently it was necessary to call upon strong men who normally carried pianos with straps and they arrived three days before the opening. While they carried the wooden frames with their valuable re-restored relief and plaster contents up the stairs we could only watch with trembling hearts till they were all three in the hall. This task accomplished, they of course also had to be hoisted and put on top of each other, which, although also a hard job, was nothing compared to the transportation up the stairs.

The in-house carpenter Henrik Hansen who had made the pylons as well as the relief frames could then finish the back of the relief so the frames of the three parts would be securely bound together. Lars Henningsen put the final touches to the surface restorations leaving the electrician finally to work his wonders so that the delicate relief was indeed once again viewed in all its glory on the opening night (fig. 9). The restored plaster parts were not gleaming white but colored in a shade similar to that of the original limestone relief. In the right light the original and restored parts blend

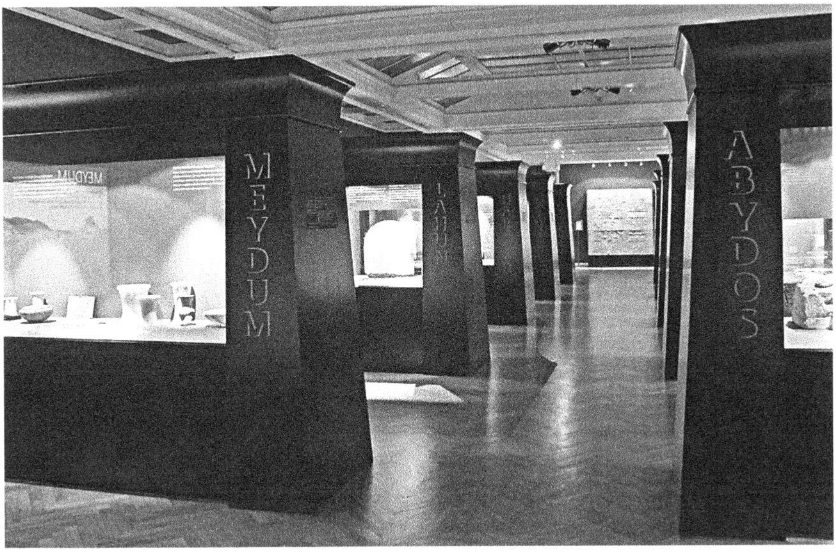

Fig. 9. The Petrie exhibition 2011 with the Apries relief at the back. © Ana Cecilia Gonzalez.

while they are still recognizably different. In this way one is given the best impression of the original fine workmanship while not being tricked into believing that all is still original. Other solutions of how to display the Apries relief scenes are to be found in the Metropolitan Museum in New York where their Apries relief is on the wall without restored parts as they have more readily combinable fragments as well as larger missing parts.[22] In the World Museum in Liverpool, their relief is also without restored plaster but with a colored drawing of missing parts on the wall.[23] In this way it is possible to indicate how the relief was originally colored. Both approaches also make sense in relation to the preserved parts. The Cairo relief with the running king is not currently on display, but a photo shows that is has partly been restored with plaster with some details reconstructing the original relief and others not.[24]

A Suitable Home

During the period of the Petrie exhibition, November 2011 through March 2012, the Apries relief drew visitors from the entrance to the end of the hall with the Memphis area (fig. 9). Very few people had a chance to realize the entire story of the relief's long journey from the ruins of Memphis to the present location. Its origin as part of a gateway in the Palace of Apries and Petrie's discovery of the fragments more than 2500

22. Bagh 2011, fig. 1.33.
23. Bagh 2011, fig. 1.31 without the coloured drawings.
24. Kaiser 1987, pl. 44; Bagh 2011, fig. 1.32.

years later was recorded on a board next to the relief, but of course it was not possible to recount all the chapters of the story here related.

When the exhibition closed it was not the end of the story. On one hand, it would have been a great disappointment if the relief was confined to the storeroom once again now that it had been re-restored. On the other, it was not easy to fit it into the Egyptian collection as it is now. Armed with a ruler we went in search of a suitable home in the museum and found one in the area termed The Ancient Mediterranean, where the Etruscan collection has been put into context with the surrounding Mediterranean world. In the first part of this exhibition area is a room called "Princely Palaces" where three Assyrian reliefs, three Babylonian glazed-brick reliefs, and one Persian relief were on view. Obviously an Egyptian palace was missing from this ancient world of great empires and, in addition, the era of King Apries (ca. 589–568 BC) was not so far removed from that of the Assyrian king, Assurnasirpal II (ca. 883–859 BC) and the relief from Persepolis dated to ca. 500 BC). The small Persian relief could be moved to another wall thus freeing up its original location: a wall next to a doorway with exactly enough space for the 2 × 2 m relief. The Apries relief was brought down the stairs the same way as it had come up and erected here among equals, with the palm column capital likewise from the Palace of Apries already back on permanent display in a niche in the adjacent room. In this way the Apries relief story had so far found a happy ending from the decision of probably Apries himself to have his great —perhaps not completely finished—gateway torn down and the fragments deposited in front of the palace where they were discovered by Petrie some 2500 years later. The rest is now history.

References

BAGH, T. 2011. *Finds from W.M.F Petrie's Excavations in Egypt in the Ny Carlsberg Glyptotek.* Copenhagen: Ny Carlsberg Glyptotek.

JØRGENSEN, M. 2009. *Egypt* IV. Copenhagen: Ny Carlsberg Glyptotek.

KAISER, W. 1987. "Die dekorierte Torfassade des spätzeitlichen Palastbezirkes von Memphis," *MDAIK* 43, 123–54.

KEES, H. 1912. *Der Opfertanz des ägyptischen Königs.* Diss., Munich.

KEMP, B. J. 1977. "The Palace of Apries at Memphis," *MDAIK* 33, 101–8.

MOGENSEN, M. 1930. *La collection égyptienne, La Glyptothèque Ny Carlsberg.* Copenhagen: Ny Carlsberg Glyptotek.

PETRIE, W. M. F. 1909a. *Memphis* I. Publications of the Egyptian Research Account 15. London: School of archaeology in Egypt, Bernard Quaritch.

———. 1909b. *The Palace of Apries* (*Memphis* II). Publications of the Egyptian Research Account 17. London: School of archaeology in Egypt, University college.

———, E. Mackay and G. Wainwright. 1910. *Meydum and Memphis* (III). Publications of the Egyptian research account 18. London: School of archaeology in Egypt.

———. 1931. *Seventy Years in Archaeology.* London: Sampson Low, Marston.

Les collections égyptiennes et proche-orientales du Musée royal de Mariemont: Risques encourus et préventions de ceux-ci

Arnaud Quertinmont

Les conditions de conservation, d'exposition, de manipulation d'objets archéologiques et artistiques ainsi que les nombreux réaménagements scénographiques sont les premiers responsables des risques encourus par les œuvres. Bien que ceux-ci soient inhérents à la gestion d'une collection, c'est au personnel du musée qu'incombe la responsabilité de les atténuer autant que possible et de réussir à concilier la préservation de l'objet dans son intégrité pour les générations futures avec sa présentation au plus grand nombre dans un but d'éducation et de délectation.

Le Musée royal de Mariemont ne fait pas exception à la règle. Au cours de son histoire, les collections égyptiennes et proche-orientales ont, à de nombreuses reprises, été soumises à des manipulations, des réaménagements, des restaurations, mais également à des évènements tragiques comme deux guerres mondiales et un incendie. C'est la raison pour laquelle il nous a semblé opportun de revenir brièvement sur l'évolution scénographique des collections égyptiennes et proche-orientales, de développer les risques encourus par ces objets à Mariemont mais également de présenter les solutions qui ont été développées depuis lors.

Du Château au Musée en passant par le Château-Musée[1]

La genèse du musée et celle de la collection ayant déjà été présentées à de nombreuses reprises, nous n'en aborderons que quelques éléments qui se rapportent à notre propos. Nous renvoyons également vers les travaux de C. Derriks[2] et de M.-C. Bruwier[3].

Le Musée royal de Mariemont doit son existence à Raoul Warocqué (1870–1917). Dernier descendant d'une riche famille d'industriels, il fait partie de ces grands

1. Pour l'histoire scénographique de la collection, on consultera Quertinmont (à paraître)

2. Evrard-Derriks 1981, 57–61 ; Derriks 1987–1988, 76–81 ; Derriks 1988, 3–5 ; Derriks 1997, 3 et sqq. ; pour une synthèse complète voir Derriks et Delvaux 2009, 16–38.

3. Bruwier 1987–1988, 46–75 ; Bruwier 1989, 25–43 ; Bruwier 1989–1990, 25–52 ; Bruwier 2001, 35–43.

collectionneurs de la fin du 19e et du début du 20e siècle qui prônent une culture accessible au plus grand nombre. Il ouvre d'ailleurs régulièrement les portes de son château au public. Son intérêt se manifeste principalement pour les antiquités extrême-orientales, méditerranéennes, régionales ainsi qu'envers la bibliophilie. C'est à l'âge de 18 ans à peine que Raoul Warocqué se procure une édition originale de la *Description de l'Égypte*, ou *Recueil des observations et des recherches qui ont été faites en Égypte pendant l'expédition de l'Armée française*. Cet ouvrage scientifique est, entre autres raisons, à l'origine de la curiosité que l'industriel porte aux antiquités égyptiennes. Cet intérêt est d'abord bibliophilique et sa collection comprend non seulement des imprimés (livres d'égyptologie, photographies et cartes postales) mais également des documents manuscrits. Raoul Warocqué consulte George Van der Meylen (1871–1935) qui acquiert pour lui de nombreux autographes d'égyptologues et orientalistes du 19e siècle. La correspondance suivie qu'il entretient avec quelques savants de son temps lui permet également d'accroître sa collection.

C'est à partir de 1903 que Raoul Warocqué se met à rassembler des antiquités égyptiennes parmi lesquelles plusieurs représentations de la déesse Isis. Ce choix est peut-être à mettre en relation avec son entrée en loge maçonnique quelques années plus tôt[4]. Il se fait alors conseiller par plusieurs grands noms de l'époque : Franz Cumont, Georges Bénédite et Jean Capart, fondateur de l'égyptologie en Belgique. En 1911, Raoul Warocqué entreprend un voyage au pays des pharaons. Il y rencontre Albert Daninos-Pacha, archéologue résidant en Égypte et jouant le rôle d'intermédiaire dans le lucratif commerce d'antiquités. On lui doit l'acquisition de quelques-unes des plus belles pièces de la collection de Mariemont, notamment du buste colossal de reine ptolémaïque dit « de Cléopâtre ». C'est également Daninos-Pacha qui obtient, en 1912, une concession de fouilles sur le site d'Héliopolis dans la banlieue du Caire. Raoul Warocqué finance la campagne mais, devant la maigreur des trouvailles, y renonce quelques mois plus tard.

Les prémices de la Première Guerre mondiale inquiètent l'industriel qui interrompt ses acquisitions. Il s'engage alors au sein du *Comité national de secours et d'alimentation* et accueille, au sein du château et du domaine, l'aide des volontaires américains de la *Commission for relief in Belgium*. Fort heureusement, le conflit ne semble pas avoir été préjudiciable aux collections. Le décès de Raoul Warocqué en 1917 met temporairement un terme au développement des acquisitions pour Mariemont. Sans héritier, il lègue son domaine, son château et ses collections à l'État belge pour qu'il devienne un Musée public. Celui-ci ouvre ses portes en 1920.

C'est à Paul Faider, conservateur du Musée-château de 1934 à 1940, que l'on doit de nouveaux assemblages scénographiques visant à transformer le château en une véritable institution muséale. En effet, comme il l'écrit lui-même en 1939, « le château de Mariemont [...] a subi [...] des rajeunissements et des aménagements [...] qui ont eut pour effet de transformer en un musée proprement dit ce qui se présentait jusque

4. Bruwier 2001, 37.

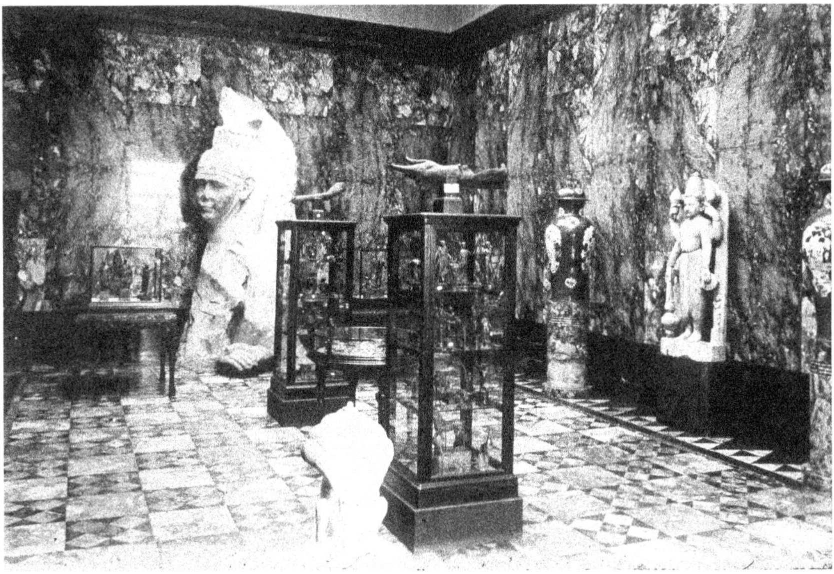

Fig.1. La salle des marbres avant 1936. © Musée royal de Mariemont.

là comme une collection particulière »[5]. Dès lors, « les vitrines s'allègent des œuvres fausses, douteuses ou simplement médiocres, qui sont reléguées dans les réserves »[6]. Les antiquités méditerranéennes, qui étaient logées depuis 1910 dans l'aile sud du château vont bénéficier d'une nouvelle présentation au sein de cet espace privilégié. Bien que le rez-de-chaussée accueille principalement le lapidaire grec et romain, on doit toutefois relever la présence de quelques objets égyptiens et proche-orientaux. Ils sont situés au départ de l'escalier menant à l'étage et donc à la « salle des marbres », salle au décor égyptisant d'inspiration maçonnique. C'est notamment le cas d'un sarcophage en plomb provenant de Tyr (Inv. B.214) et d'un cylindre de Nabuchodonosor II (Inv. B.509). Le guide illustré de 1935[7] nous apprend que cette salle doit être le salon d'honneur du musée et que les pièces de sculptures les plus curieuses et les plus impressionnantes de la collection Warocqué y ont été rassemblées, en ce compris des pièces d'Extrême-Orient. Sur un cliché contemporain, on remarque que la salle s'articule autour de six vitrines en bois contenant principalement des bronzes romains même si quelques objets égyptiens et proche-orientaux y sont visibles, notamment une tête d'ibex en bronze (Inv. B.395) localisée dans la partie inférieure droite de la première vitrine (fig. 1). Le buste colossal occupe, quant à lui, une place qu'il conservera jusqu'à son transfert dans le nouveau musée en 1968.

5. Faider 1939, 269.
6. Donnay G. (dir.) 1975, 27.
7. Faider 1935, 39.

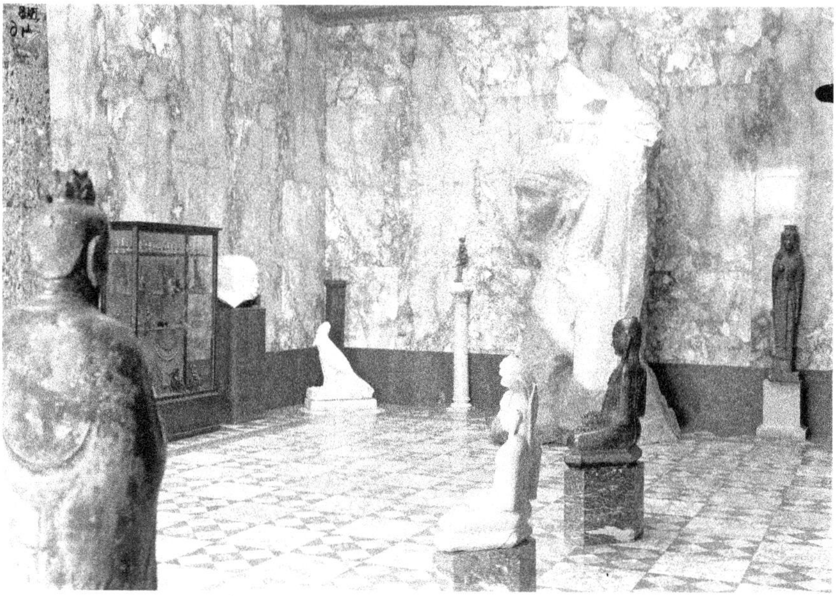

Fig. 2. La salle des marbres entre 1936 et 1960. © Musée royal de Mariemont.

L'année 1936 voit les travaux de redéploiement des collections se poursuivre avec, notamment, la création d'une salle dédiée aux bronzes antiques. Ceux-ci sont enlevés de la salle des marbres remplacés par « deux vitrines contenant, l'une, des albâtres provenant du Caire et de la nécropole d'Abydos, et l'autre des statuettes de bronze [égyptiennes] »[8]. Il s'agit vraisemblablement des objets qui étaient présentés jusqu'alors au bas de l'escalier. Il faudra attendre la publication du guide illustré de 1937[9] pour apprendre que le mortier du roi Den (Inv. B.101), la statue de faucon (Inv. B.126), une statue d'Isis (Inv. B.130) ainsi que d'autres pièces ont rejoint cet espace dédié aux antiquités égyptiennes. Notons toutefois que certaines sculptures extrême-orientales sont encore présentes dans la salle (fig. 2).

La mort de Paul Faider, en 1940, voit la nomination de son épouse Germaine à la tête du musée-château. Sa première mission sera de protéger le domaine et ses collections durant la Seconde Guerre mondiale. Bien que le château n'ait pas été occupé par les autorités allemandes, Germaine Faider craignait le pillage comme l'indique une demande visant à faire armer les gardiens du château. Celle-ci sera cependant rejetée par la Kommandantur[10]. « Le conflit s'étant éteint sans causer de dommages au château et à ses collections, la jeune conservatrice pourra sortir le musée de sa léthargie ».

8. Faider 1936, 41.
9. Faider 1937, 41–42.
10. Communication orale d'Y. Quairiaux, ancien responsable de la section Histoire régionale du Musée royal de Mariemont.

Elle n'a alors de cesse de poursuivre les réaménagements de son époux, de développer les recherches archéologiques et scientifiques du musée mais également d'acquérir des objets d'arts.

Un incendie ravage le corps de logis du château le jour de Noël 1960. Les deux nouvelles ailes ajoutées par Raoul Warocqué en 1910 sont en béton armé et résistent ainsi mieux au feu. La collection d'œuvres liées à l'histoire régionale et le « Musée de famille » sont irrémédiablement détruits. Certaines pièces bibliophiliques ainsi que des porcelaines de Tournai ont également énormément souffert. Fort heureusement, la part la plus importante des collections se situait dans les deux ailes qui sont demeurées pratiquement intactes. Le bilan aurait pu être beaucoup plus lourd. Bien qu'aucune pièce égyptienne ou proche-orientale n'ait souffert de l'incendie, un objet semble manquer à l'appel : un petit groupe érotique en faïence[11].

Sur les ruines du château sera construit le musée actuel. Il est l'œuvre de Roger Bastin et s'inspire des théories de l'architecte français Le Corbusier[12]. Seule l'annexe de l'aile qui abritait les collections d'antiquités méditerranéennes est préservée, le reste du château est abattu. L'ensemble des collections est alors repensé dans le but de présenter une scénographie cohérente et moderne, capable de répondre pleinement aux missions essentielles que sont celles d'un musée. C'est à Germaine Faider et Guy Donnay, futur directeur du musée, que l'on doit cette réflexion ainsi que sa mise en œuvre. L'un des moments les plus spectaculaires fut, à n'en pas douter, le transfert du buste colossal de reine ptolémaïque (Inv. B.505.1), de la salle des marbres à son emplacement actuel, suspendue à plus de cinq mètres de hauteur et fixée dans un voile de béton. Le but de ce déménagement était, notamment, de mettre en valeur la pièce en restituant sa hauteur initiale et de l'isoler des marbres très colorés de la pièce où elle était présentée à l'origine[13] (fig. 3).

Le nouveau musée ouvre en 1975. Dès ce moment, et ce jusqu'en 1991, les collections d'Occident, d'Orient et d'Asie sont présentées de façon synchronique et chronologique. Ainsi des objets égyptiens font face à des objets grecs et proche-orientaux et sont associés de façon à former un discours thématique et non plus simplement basé sur leurs origines (fig. 4). Si les civilisations occidentales sont présentées à gauche, les civilisations orientales le sont à droite, dans un souci de délimiter les grandes aires géographiques. En rassemblant les pièces par chronologie, on permettra au visiteur d'apprécier en un seul ensemble les différentes cultures du monde à une période donnée. « À Mariemont, ... les témoins des diverses civilisations sont présentés de façon synoptique, dans une cadre rigoureusement chronologique : la Grèce et l'Italie côtoient l'Égypte, la Mésopotamie, l'Iran, la Chine »[14]. Cette présentation se révèle vite problématique en raison du manque de pièces à confronter pour certaines périodes.

11. Van de Walle 1952, n° E.129, 51, pl. 16.
12. Donnay G. (dir.) 1975, 43–50.
13. Donnay G. (dir.) 1975, 61.
14. Donnay G. (dir.) 1975, 53.

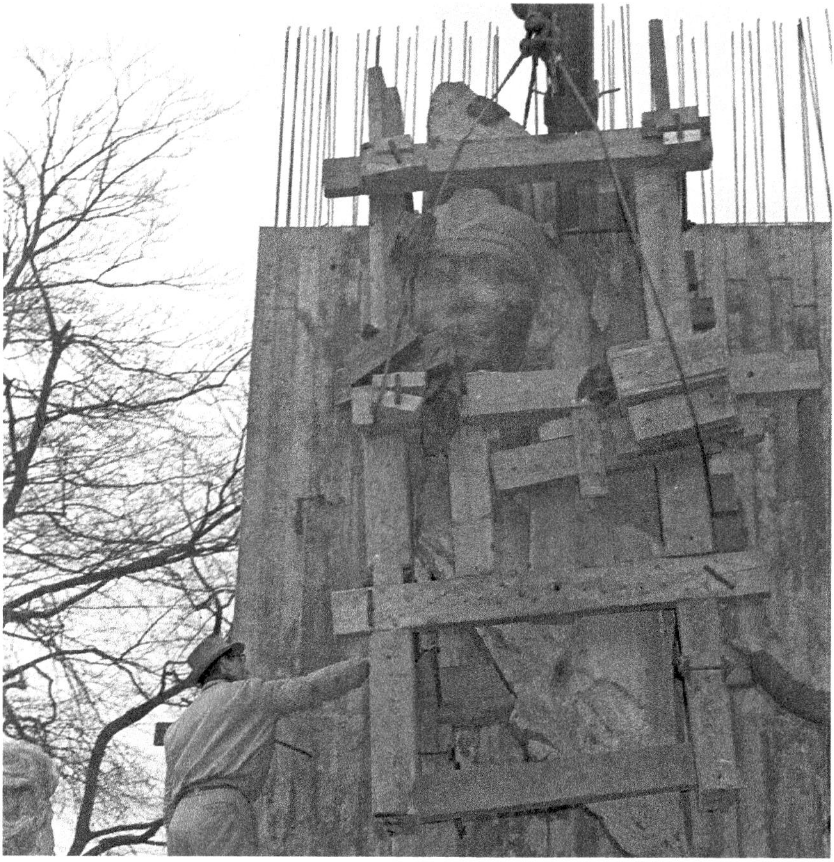

Fig. 3. Fixation du buste colossal de reine ptolémaïque dans l'un des murs du nouveau musée. Inv. B.505.1. © Musée royal de Mariemont.

En effet, cette volonté de comparaison des civilisations n'est pas celle qui a guidé les achats de Raoul Warocqué.

Les travaux de désamiantage du bâtiment qui eurent lieu de 1991 à 1993 furent l'occasion de redéfinir la présentation des collections et de pouvoir exposer de nouvelles acquisitions. Il fut décidé de scinder la présentation comparée des civilisations en deux niveaux[15] : le premier concernera le bassin méditerranéen antique (civilisations égyptienne, proche-orientale, grecque, italiques, étrusque et romaine) qui occupera deux salles et demi, tandis que l'Asie (Chine, Japon, Vietnam, Asie du Sud-Est…) sera présentée dans les salles restantes. Les pièces durent cependant toutes être précautionneusement emballées de façon à attendre la fin des travaux. La présentation

15. Note de service de A. Verbanck, C. Noppe et M.-C. Bruwier (pour C. Derriks) datée du 11 janvier 1991.

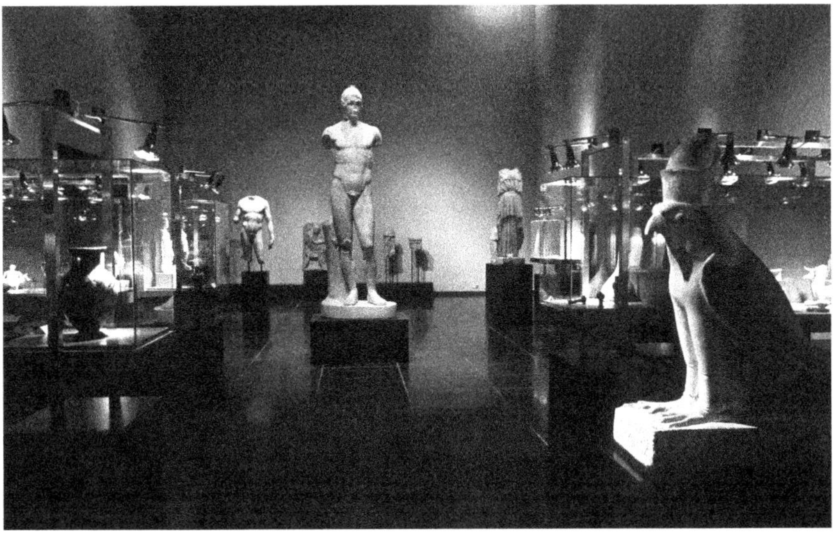

Fig. 4. Présentation des collections entre 1975 et 1991. © Musée royal de Mariemont.

des pièces égyptiennes et proche-orientales se fit alors dans la même salle, de façon essentiellement thématique : croyances funéraires, beauté, mythes et dieux… (fig. 5).

L'ajout de nouvelles acquisitions, dont le cercueil d'Irethorerou (Inv. Ac.95/1), rendait un nouveau réaménagement des collections égyptiennes et proches-orientales inévitable. C'est ainsi qu'au dernier trimestre 1998, une présentation différente de la section fut proposée[16]. Le début de la salle A est réservé à la seule présentation de l'Égypte antique. Certaines œuvres jugées de moindre qualité sont mises en réserve de façon à accentuer les pièces maîtresses de la collection.

Plus de dix ans après ce dernier réaménagement, il était temps d'offrir au département des antiquités égyptiennes et proche-orientales une nouvelle présentation. C'est en 2009 que le Musée royal de Mariemont entreprend une rénovation en profondeur des salles du premier étage qui abritent certaines de ses collections les plus illustres. La première phase fut l'occasion de proposer une nouvelle scénographie pour l'Extrême-Orient et l'Empire romain, en ce compris les provinces orientales, mais également pour les pièces issues de l'Égypte et du Proche-Orient copte et musulman conservés en salle C. Le projet architectural du Musée fut relu et la présentation des objets et des vitrines repensée. Celles-ci furent désolidarisées des murs de façon à occuper la totalité de l'espace disponible. Les quatre faces vitrées permettent au visiteur d'en faire le tour, sans privilégier aucune des faces et en offrant les objets sous différents angles. Les structures internes sont beaucoup plus légères, offrent plus de modulations sur la hauteur et permettent une meilleur présentation des objets. C'est

16. Dartevelle 1997, 3.

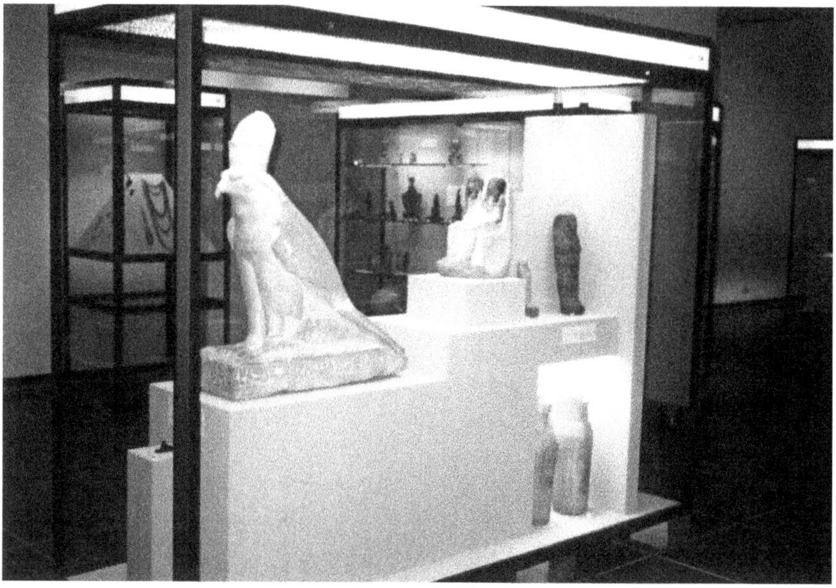

Fig. 5. Présentation de la collection égyptienne et proche-orientale de 1993 à 1998. © Musée royal de Mariemont.

donc au sein de cette salle C que l'on retrouve certaines des œuvres emblématiques du Musée, comme une statue d'Isis en diorite (Inv. B.130), un sarcophage en plomb (Inv. B.214), un flabellum égyptien du 13e siècle (Inv. III.G.76.B) ou encore quelques pièces islamiques (fig. 6).

L'année 2013 verra la finalisation de cette campagne de réaménagement avec le redéploiement des objets pharaoniques et ptolémaïques présentés dans les salles A et B. Grâce à de nouvelles acquisitions prestigieuses et à un soclage ambitieux, ce sont plus de deux cent cinquante objets qui seront ainsi magnifiés et présentés au public. Bien que la majeure partie des thèmes soient conservés, la présentation des objets est plus adéquate, les modulations sur la présentation en hauteur ou au niveau du regard des adultes, des personnes à mobilité réduite et des enfants sont plus nombreuses et un travail important a été réalisé en ce qui concerne l'éclairage direct et indirect des objets.

Des transferts et des accidents...

Les missions fondamentales d'un musée et d'un établissement scientifique impliquent malheureusement toujours un risque, fut-il minimal pour les objets. Les nombreux réaménagements scénographiques dont nous venons de parler en sont un témoin : disparitions de pièces, transferts dangereux, manipulations excessives... Le déplacement de certains objets, le plus souvent pondéreux, nécessite parfois d'intervenir

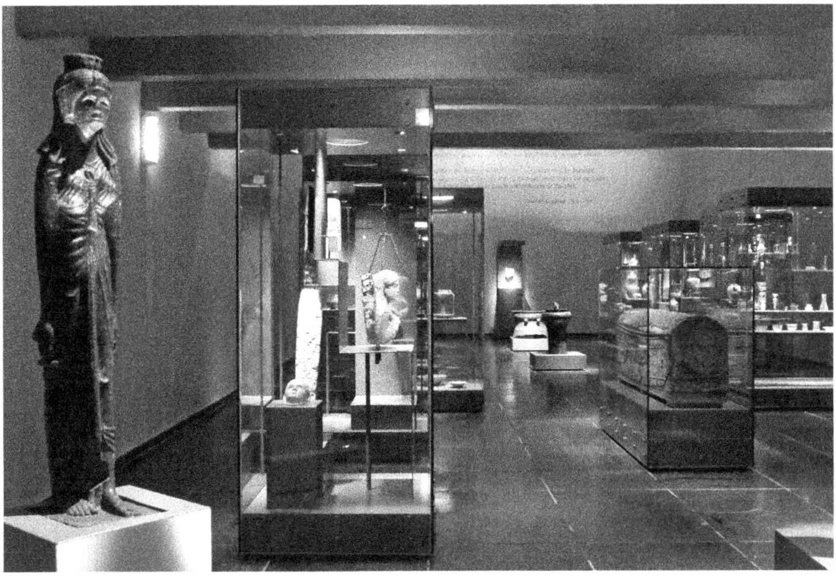

Fig. 6. Présentation des collections des pièces issues des provinces orientales romaines ainsi que de l'Égypte et du Proche-Orient copte et musulman, 2009. © C. Derriks.

directement sur la nature physique de la pièce. Lorsqu'en avril 1968 le buste colossal de reine ptolémaïque, de près de 5 tonnes, quitte la salle des marbres au moyen d'une grue, il se retrouve suspendu dans les airs et n'est pas à l'abri d'une défaillance technique ou humaine. Sa fixation dans le voile de béton au moyen d'une résine époxy est complétée par l'adjonction de trois broches à l'arrière de la pièce visant à en faciliter la mise en place[17]. Trois carottages sont ainsi prélevés, polis et envoyé en laboratoire de façon à confirmer la nature granitoïde de la pierre[18]. L'aventure de cette statue ne s'arrête pas là. En effet, une fois solidement arrimée au béton, elle est couverte d'une bâche de plastique visant à la protéger pendant la suite des travaux et, notamment, la pose du plafond de la salle B (fig. 7). Il est inutile de préciser les risques qu'encourent alors l'œuvre.

Un autre transfert délicat, celui d'un sarcophage en plomb (Inv. B.214), eut lieu récemment. La pièce fut déménagée de nombreuses fois à l'époque de Raoul Warocqué et nécessita même l'intervention d'un zingueur pour maintenir la cohésion des différentes plaques de plomb soutenant le décor. Elle fut à nouveau restaurée en 2009 en vue de son installation dans une nouvelle vitrine. Les opérations furent délicates en raison de la fragilité de l'objet.

17. Donnay G. (dir.) 1975, 61.

18. Le rapport, ainsi que les trois prélèvements, sont conservés au musée et inventoriés sous le numéro d'inventaire B.505.doc.

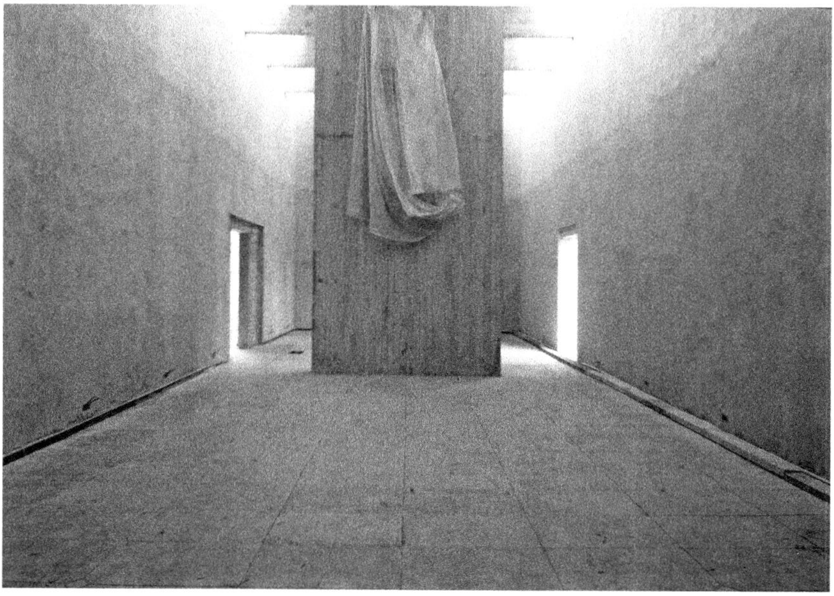

Fig. 7. Le buste colossal de reine ptolémaïque durant les travaux de construction du nouveau musée. © Musée royal de Mariemont.

La seconde phase du réaménagement prévu pour 2013 verra également des manipulations complexes comme le transfert de la vasque de Den (Inv. B.101), d'un fragment de sarcophage (Inv. B.1) ou encore du cercueil d'Irethorerou (Inv. Ac.95/1) dont la polychromie rend le déménagement techniquement assez difficile.

Ces manipulations sont parfois tellement complexes que l'objet en souffre et peut parfois s'abîmer, voire se casser. Ce fut le cas en 1988, à l'occasion du retour de prêt d'une statuette en bronze d'Isis (Inv. B.482). La pièce, représentant la déesse assise et couronnée d'un croissant et d'un disque lunaire, fut brisée en plusieurs morceaux[19] (fig. 8). Les opérations de restauration furent alors l'occasion d'analyser la pièce et de procéder à un examen minutieux des anciennes restaurations. Il apparut à cette occasion que la pièce était en réalité constituée de deux parties distinctes, la couronne lunaire ayant une composition chimique totalement différente de la pièce principale. La statue fut alors restaurée sans lui adjoindre cette couronne ajoutée postérieurement. Les bras semblent également avoir été ajoutés postérieurement, cependant, le geste qu'ils forment correspond tout à fait à ce que devaient être les bras originaux. Ils ont donc été conservés de façon à préserver l'unité de lecture de la pièce.

Un débat constant entre professionnels des musées est la question de l'accessibilité des œuvres. Faut-il, dans un but de conservation et de protection des œuvres, les enfermer dans une vitrine ou faut-il, dans le but d'en favoriser l'appropriation intel-

19. Derriks et Urban 1986, 6–24.

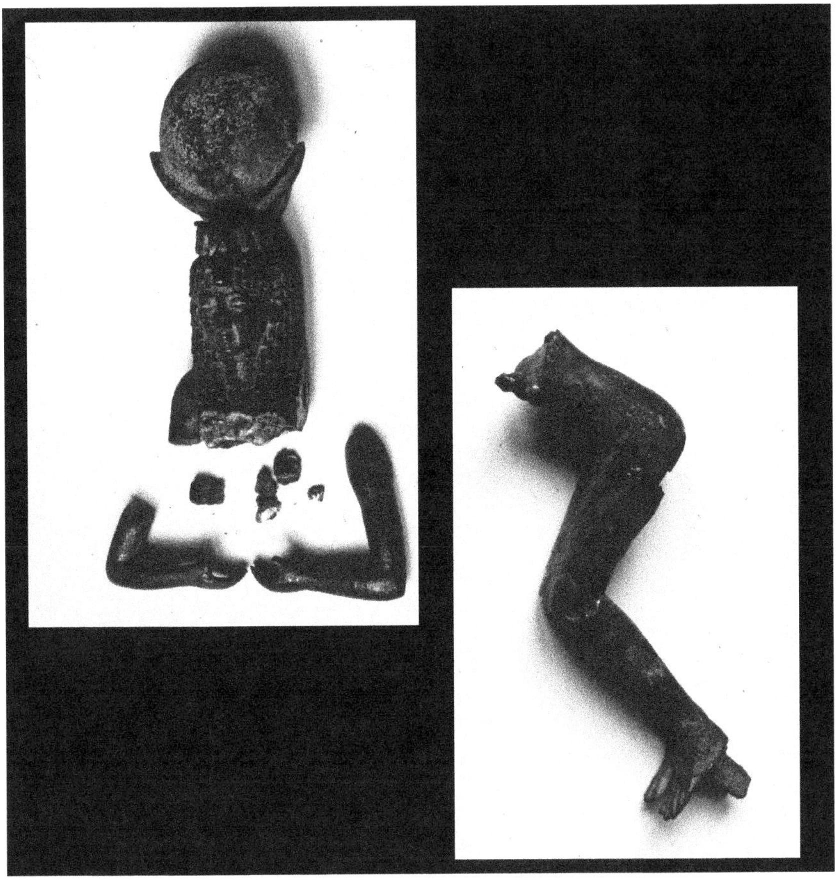

Fig. 8. Statue d'Isis brisée. Inv. B.482. Photos © Fr. Urban.

lectuelle et esthétique, les sortir de vitrines ? Cette question est sujette à l'interprétation du conservateur ayant en charge la collection. Plusieurs dégradations viennent malheureusement alimenter ce débat. Prenons l'exemple d'une vasque inscrite au nom du roi Den (Inv. B.101). Elle fut présentée dans le nouveau bâtiment Bastin sur un support d'une cinquantaine de centimètres de haut tout comme elle l'était dans le château Warocqué. Cette hauteur, tout à fait inadaptée, causa de nombreux torts à la pièce qui fut vandalisée à plusieurs reprises. À la suite des travaux de désamiantage il fut donc décidé de protéger l'objet en le plaçant à l'intérieur d'une vitrine. Il apparut cependant que la pièce ne pouvait réellement être appréhendé que sortie de sa vitrine et placée à niveau de regard de façon à pouvoir pleinement profiter du nom du pharaon inscrit sur la face avant de la vasque. C'est la raison pour laquelle elle fut placée sur un support de plus de 150 cm de haut. Cette volonté de contemplation hors vitrine est maintenue dans la nouvelle présentation. Le déplacement de cette pièce, d'un

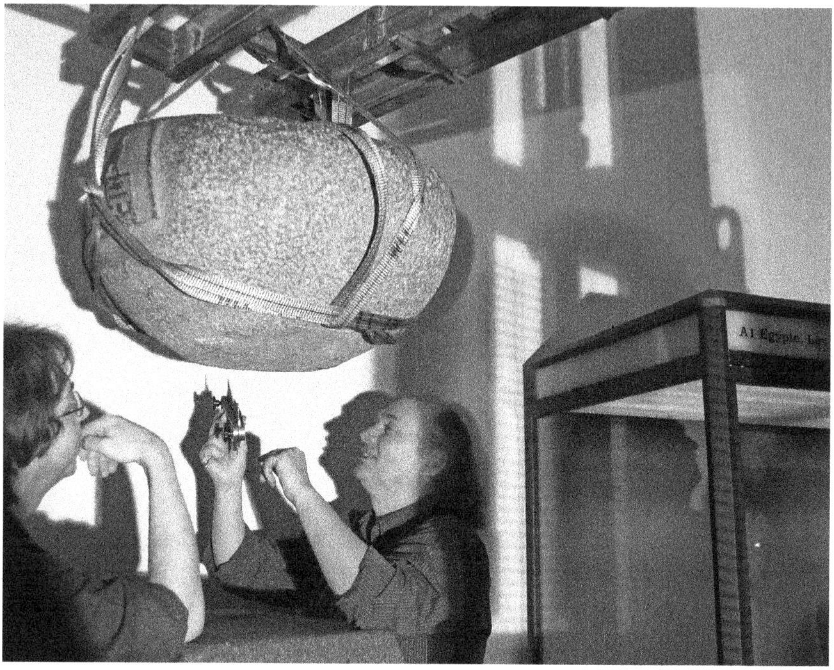

Fig. 9. Étude de la vasque du roi Den. Inv. B.101. © Musée royal de Mariemont.

poids certains, est également délicat comme l'atteste son étude par Stan Hendrickx en 2008 (fig. 9).

De manière préventive, la statue d'Horus-faucon (Inv. B.126) dont le bec a subi à plusieurs reprises des dégradations fut protégée, dès 1993, par une vitrine. À l'occasion du réaménagement, l'option retenue fut de restituer son amplitude en le sortant de vitrine, mais en le présentant sur un socle avec un séparateur visuel empêchant les visiteurs d'y accéder directement et de le toucher.

Il nous faut également mentionner les marbres exposés au musée, victimes de ces nombreux actes de dégradation. Ceux-ci consistent essentiellement en des traces de crayon ou de marqueur ainsi que le dépôt de substances (essentiellement du sable) sur les œuvres (fig. 10). Même si ces accès de vandalisme sont connus depuis de nombreuses d'années, une recrudescence a été observée ces derniers années. Il convient donc d'entreprendre un nettoyage des pièces et de lancer un processus de réflexion sur les moyens qui pourraient être mis en œuvre pour éviter que ces faits ne se reproduisent à l'avenir (sensibilisation des publics, ronde adaptée pour les agents de sécurité selon les fréquentations, dispositifs de sécurité sonores, surveillance caméra, etc.). Dans ce cadre, nous assistons actuellement à une professionnalisation du personnel de surveillance du musée avec une formation en tant que gardien de patrimoine. Les moyens techniques sont également accrus (caméra, détecteurs, alarmes ...) de façon à réagir face à l'augmentation des dégradations et des vols dans les musées.

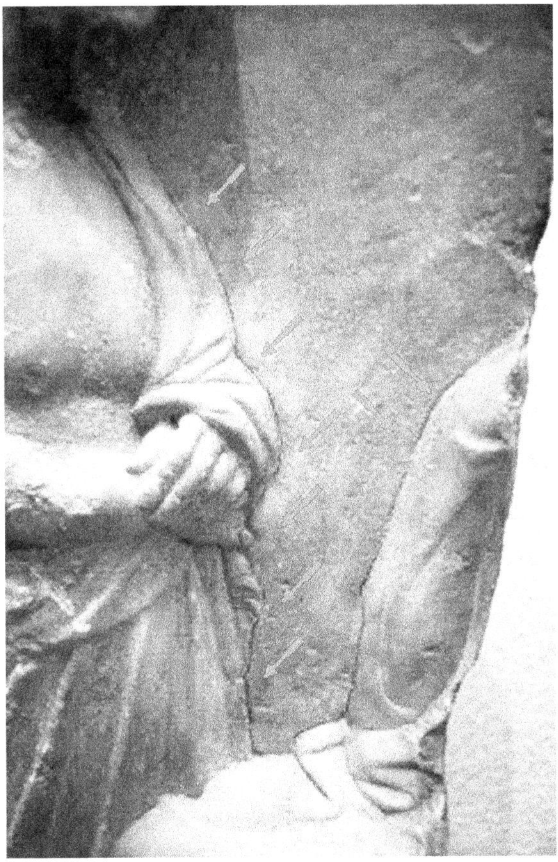

Fig. 10. Traces de crayon sur le contour des figures d'une stèle en marbre. © Musée royal de Mariemont.

C'est parfois la nature même de l'objet qui est responsable de son état. Albert France-Lanord, dans un rapport de 1980 adressé l'UNESCO et relatif à la conservation des bronzes du Musée du Bardo écrit *Tout objet conservé dans un musée possède une double personnalité. En premier lieu, il est «objet matière» en fonction de la matière ou des matériaux dont il est constitué, en second lieu «objet message» en fonction de la signification historique, artistique, technique, etc... dont il est chargé et qui justifie son séjour dans les collections d'un musée*[20]. C'est exactement dans le cadre de cette première personnalité que se situe un fragment de calcaire portant un fragment d'inscription hiéroglyphique (Inv. B.425). La mauvaise qualité de la pierre fait que le relief est aujourd'hui pulvérulent et perdu pour les générations futures. Il est cependant parfois possible d'intervenir sur ces objets comme en témoigne le relief de Qen provenant de Deir el-Médineh (Inv. Ac.78/11). Celui-ci est aménagé dans un calcaire de mauvaise qualité qui présente de nombreux éclats lamellaires[21]. Déjà stabilisé en 2002, il devra à

20. http://unesdoc.unesco.org/images/0004/000413/041367fo.pdf
21. Derriks et Garcia Gomez 2003, 149–57.

Fig. 11. Dague proche-orientale atteinte de la maladie du bronze. Inv. Ac.2007/172. © Musée royal de Mariemont.

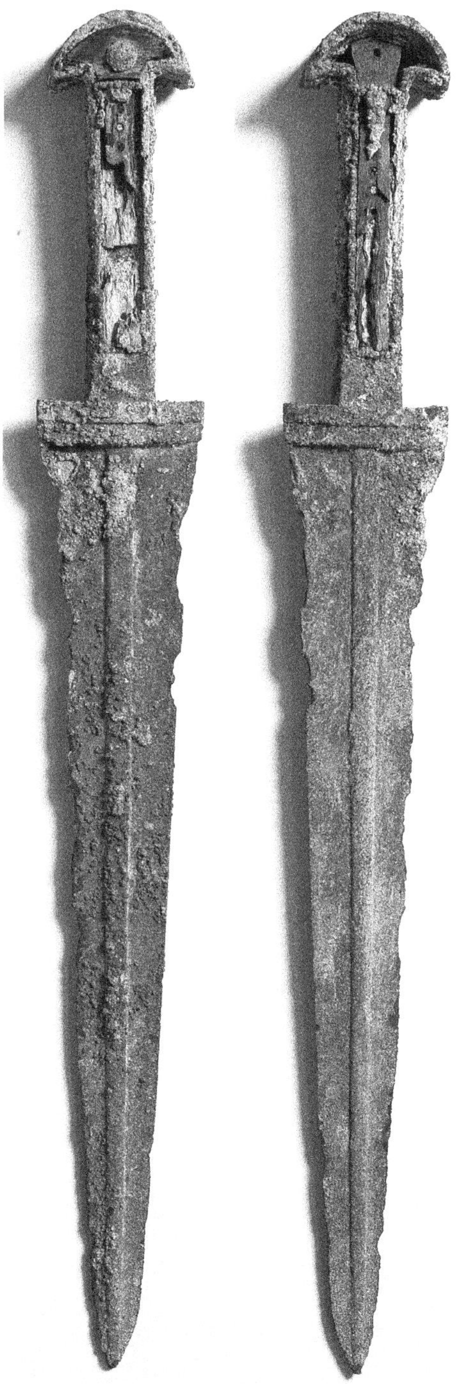

nouveau l'être en 2013 de façon à le protéger au mieux et à le conserver autant que possible.

Il arrive également que certains objets arrivent au musée en mauvais état, celui-ci résultant de mauvaises conditions de conservation. En 2007, le Musée reçu une dague proche-orientale en don (Inv. Ac.2007/172). Elle est réalisée en bronze et son état est très préoccupant (fig. 11). Elle est atteinte de ce qu'on appelle la maladie du bronze qui est un développement de produits de corrosion à base de chlore qui rendent le métal poudreux jusqu'à tomber en poussière. Actuellement, elle présente une patine hétérogène à corrosion active avec des surfaces pulvérulentes, granuleuses et pustuleuses. Celle-ci détériore l'objet et laisse d'ailleurs apparaître l'âme de bois de la garde qui a subit de sévères dommages. La seule option qui semble s'offrir à nous est de stabiliser rapidement cet objet au risque de le voir définitivement détruit. Parce que les produits de corrosion sont très volatiles, ils se répandent facilement sur les autres objets de collection au moindre courant d'air. C'est la raison pour

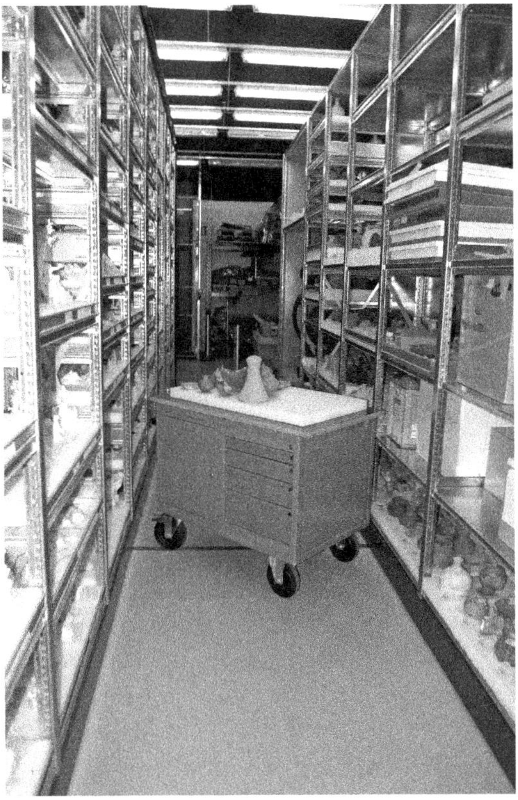

Fig. 12. Vue du Compactus installé en réserve principale. © Musée royal de Mariemont.

Fig. 13. Présentation générale du conditionnement de la collection égyptienne. © Musée royal de Mariemont.

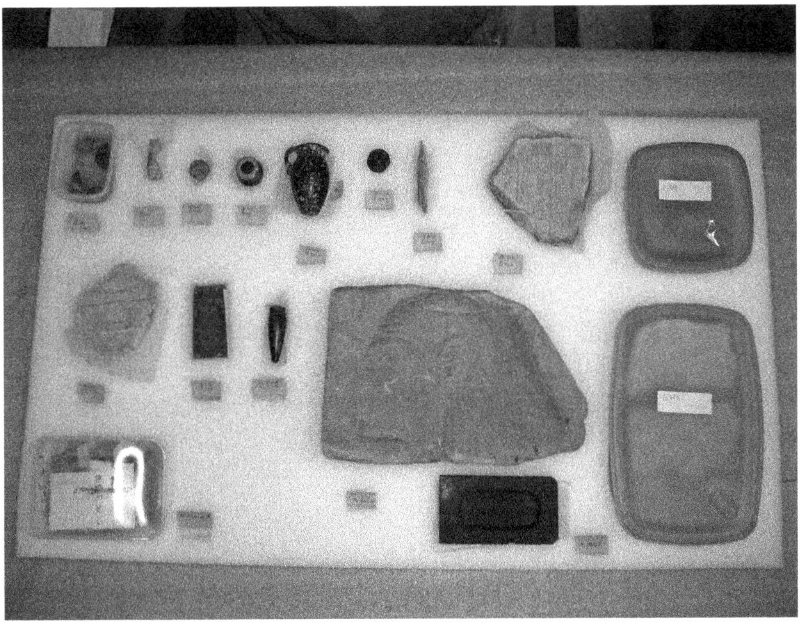

laquelle cette dague a été isolée des autres objets archéologiques de façon à éviter toute contamination.

Le chantier des collections, des opérations visant à diminuer les risques

Bien qu'une réflexion sur les dangers encourus par les objets lors de leur manipulation et de leur présentation ai été amorcée, il restait encore énormément de travail en ce qui concerne la conservation préventive et le stockage des objets au sein des réserves. C'est ainsi qu'en 2006 fut mis en place un important chantier des collections dont la durée était prévue pour plusieurs années en fonction des opérations à mener sur les collections et leur conditionnement : dépoussiérages, constats d'état, récolement, photographies et intégration à l'inventaire. L'installation d'un meuble Compactus et de zones d'entreposage adéquates fut la première étape (fig. 12). La seconde consista au récolement des collections et à leur transfert dans ce nouvel espace de stockage, avec un emplacement spécifique reporté dans l'inventaire informatique (fig. 13). Les réserves furent sécurisées par le biais d'un badge d'accès et de caméras. Au sein de cet espace se trouve divers appareils de mesures visant à enregistrer et maintenir des conditions constantes de conservation (température et hygrométrie). La collection égyptienne et proche-orientale fut l'une des premières à bénéficier de ces intentions.

De nombreux objets égyptiens, comme ce très beau cartonnage funéraire (Inv. Ac.65/40), profitèrent également du chantier des collections et de la rédaction du catalogue scientifique[22] pour être analysés et restaurés. Certains vases en pierre prédynastique nécessitaient une restauration visant à boucher les lacunes et nettoyer les anciennes traces de colle qui avaient vieilli (Inv. B.400). D'autres, comme les bronzes ou les momies animales, furent analysés en laboratoire ou radiographiés. La radiographie permet de visualiser l'intérieur d'un « paquet funéraire » sans en altérer la nature ou l'apparence. Les examens nous ont ainsi permis d'en apprendre plus sur les momies animales et les fragments de momies humaines conservés au musée.

Plus un objet est manipulé, plus grand sont les risques de le voir se détériorer. C'est la raison pour laquelle, dans une volonté d'ouverture du musée et de diffusion des connaissances, nous avons entrepris depuis plusieurs années une campagne de numérisation de nos collections. Les différentes opérations comprennent le tri des objets, le récolement et l'encodage au sein de l'inventaire informatisé, le travail photographique (prises de vue, traitement de l'image et retouches photographiques) ainsi que le conditionnement des objets. La dernière phase est celle de la mise en ligne des collections. Dans le cadre de la collection égyptienne, c'est au sein du *Global Egyptian Museum*[23] que nous avons choisi de valoriser plusieurs de nos pièces. Un soin tout particulier a également été apporté aux ressources disponibles en ligne à l'usage des chercheurs mais également du grand public et du public enseignant. Les publications

22. Derriks et Delvaux 2009, 441–48.
23. http://www.globalegyptianmuseum.org/

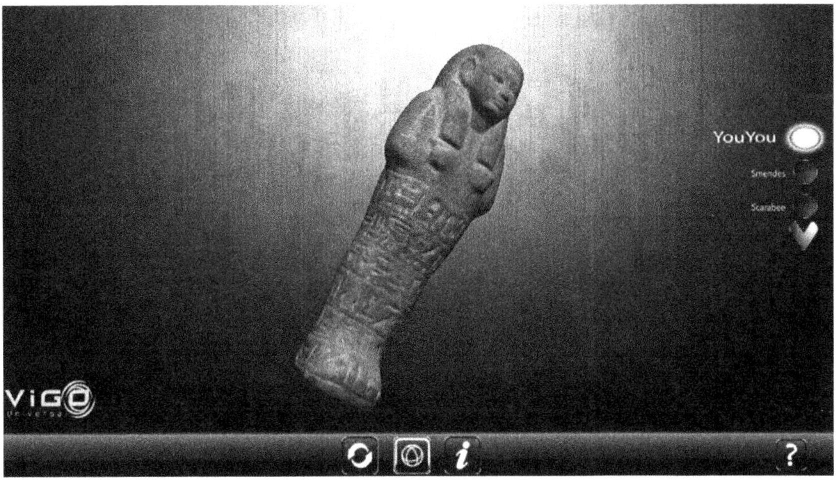

Fig. 14. Vue 3D d'un oushebti. Inv. B.127. © Vigo Universal.

épuisées, les audio-guides d'expositions ainsi que les guides du visiteur et des vidéos pédagogiques ont ainsi été mis en ligne. Outre le fait de faire connaitre les objets, ces nouvelles technologies réduisent de façon considérable les manipulations des objets et permettent ainsi de les conserver dans des conditions plus adéquates de conservation. C'est à présent au tour de la numérisation en 3D d'être expérimentée à Mariemont avec la collection égyptienne choisie comme test (fig. 14).

Un autre chantier fut également mis en œuvre de façon à pouvoir diffuser les résultats des études en laboratoire et des recherches stylistiques et contextuelles des objets. C'est dans ce cadre que s'inscrit la publication du catalogue scientifique de la collection permettant ainsi à celle-ci d'être connue et accessible par le plus grand nombre.

Depuis la disparition de son fondateur, en 1917, les responsables successifs du Musée n'ont eu de cesse d'accroître ses collections. Le département des antiquités égyptiennes et proche-orientales vient d'ailleurs de bénéficier d'une donation exceptionnelle ainsi que d'un dépôt de la Wallonie. Ces deux ensembles accroissent la qualité des collections ainsi que la quantité d'œuvres conservées. Mariemont peut actuellement être considéré comme conservant la première collection égyptienne de Wallonie, deuxième de Belgique. On y découvre, notamment, plus de deux cents *chaouabtis* égyptiens ayant appartenu à des hommes ou des femmes répartis entre le Moyen Empire et l'époque ptolémaïque, des vases en calcite, un gobelet au nom de Ramsès II, de petits récipients d'un dépôt de fondation, des bracelets et boucles d'oreille en or. Parmi les centaines d'objets provenant de Mésopotamie figurent des tablettes cunéiformes en terre cuite, dont des tablettes scolaires. Un grand nombre portent des inscriptions concernant des comptes de terrain ou de denrées agricoles. D'autres objets inscrits,

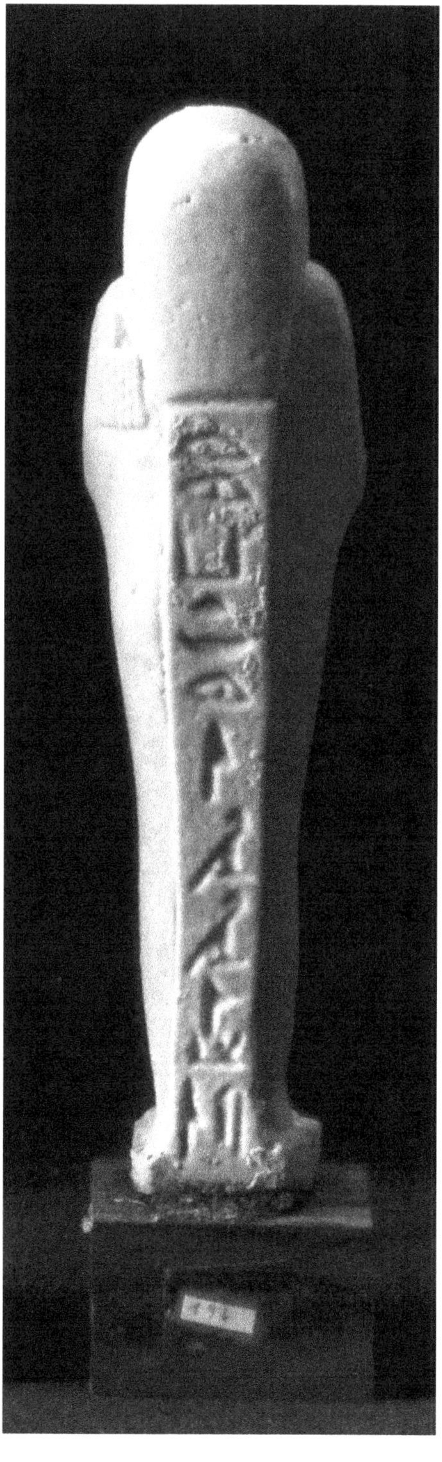

Fig. 15. Utilisation de colle inadéquate ainsi que d'un socle inadapté. © Musée royal de Mariemont.

tels des sceaux-cylindres, un clou et une brique de fondation, un barillet au nom de Nabuchodonosor II, se trouvent aussi dans la collection. Cet accroissement des collections illustre la nécessité de suivre certains protocoles. En effet, à leur arrivée au Musée, ces objets ont été placés en quarantaine, de façon à s'assurer qu'ils étaient stables et que nous ne risquions pas de contaminer les autres œuvres du musée en matière de corrosion ou de sels. Ils ont alors été inventoriés et encodés. Un gros travail devra également être fait en ce qui concerne leur désoclage, certains d'entre eux subissant des tensions dues à l'utilisation de colles inadéquates ainsi que par des socles inappropriés (fig. 15). La collection comporte également des amulettes zoomorphes, des bracelets et boucles d'oreille achéménides en or. Il convient de sécuriser ceux-ci au sein d'un espace approprié. De plus, la taille parfois réduite de certaines amulettes, notamment un chat en cornaline d'un centimètre de longueur, implique un conditionnement particulier visant à assurer à l'objet une visibilité suffisante. Si certains d'entres eux trouveront leur place dans les nouvelles vitrines accessibles dès l'automne 2013, leur mise en ligne, visant à faire connaitre l'intégralité de la collection, est prévue pour début 2014.

Le travail à accomplir dans le but de protéger au maximum les œuvres reste cependant énorme comme en témoigne les dégradations récentes de certaines statues du parc ainsi que certaines tentatives de vol au sein du domaine.

Bibliographie

Bruwier, M.-C. 1987–1988. « La collection égyptienne de Raoul Warocqué, I, De 1888 à 1911 », *Cahiers de Mariemont* 18–19, 46–75.

Bruwier, M.-C. 1989. « Deux fragments d'une statue colossale de reine ptolémaïque à Mariemont », *Chronique d'Égypte* 64, 25–43

Bruwier, M.-C. 1989–1990. « La collection égyptienne de Raoul Warocqué, II, De 1912 à 1917 », *Cahiers de Mariemont* 20–21, 25–52.

Bruwier, M.-C. 2001. « Motifs égyptiens dans le décor intérieur des châteaux de Mariemont et d'Enghien », *Les Cahiers de l'Urbanisme* 35–36, 35–43.

Dartevelle, P. 1997. « Editorial », *Bulletin du Musée royal de Mariemont* 80, 3 et sqq.

Derriks, C. 1987–1988. « Activités de la sous-section Egypte et Proche-Orient de 1975 à 1985 », *Cahiers de Mariemont* 18/19, 76–81

Derriks, C. 1988. « Exposition permanente », *Bulletin du Musée royal de Mariemont* 42, 3–5.

Derriks, C. et L. Delvaux (éd.). 2009. *Antiquités égyptiennes au Musée royal de Mariemont*, Morlanwelz: Musée royal de Mariemont.

Derriks, C. et I. Garcia Gomez. 2003. « Le sculpteur Qen et le culte d'Amenhotep 1er », *Cahiers de Mariemont* 30–31, 149–57.

Derriks, C. et F. Urban. 1986. « Étude et restauration d'une statuette d'Isis en bronze au musée royal de Mariemont », *Cahiers de Mariemont* 17, 6–24.

Evrard-Derriks, C. 1981. « Aspects muséologiques et présentation des collections égyptiennes au musée royal de Mariemont suivis d'un choix d'œuvres post-ramessides ». *Göttinger Miszellen* 51, 57–61.

Donnay, G. (dir.). 1975. *Les Cahiers de Mariemont* 8. Morlanwelz: Musée royal de Mariemont.

Faider, P. 1935. *Mariemont : le château, les collections, le parc : guide sommaire illustré ; précédé d'une notice biographique sur Raoul Warocqué et d'un aperçu historique sur l'ancien domaine de Mariemont*. Gembloux: Duculot.

Faider, P. 1936. *Le Château et le domaine de Mariemont : guide illustré et aperçu sommaire des collections précédés d'une notice biographique sur Raoul Warocqué et d'un historique de l'ancien domaine de Mariemont*. Gembloux: Duculot.

Faider, P. 1937. *Musée royal de Le Château et le domaine de Mariemont : guide illustré ; précédé d'une notice biographique sur Raoul Warocqué et d'un historique de l'ancien domaine de Mariemont*. Gembloux: Duculot.

Faider, P. 1939. « Le Musée de Mariemont ». *Revue belge d'Archéologie et d'histoire de l'art* IX, 269–73.

Quertinmont, A. 2014 (à paraître). « Du Château au Musée en passant par le Château-Musée. Histoire de la scénographie des collections égyptiennes et proche-orientales de Mariemont ». *Cahiers de Mariemont* 41.

Van de Walle, B. 1952. *Les Antiquités égyptiennes, grecques, étrusques, romaines et gallo-romaines du Musée de Mariemont*. Bruxelles: Librairie encyclopédique.

New Methods of Handling and Care of Collections in the Grand Egyptian Museum and the National Museum of Egyptian Civilization

Mohamed Ismael Badawi

Part 1: Design of Anoxia and Nitrogen Systems

Cultural heritage objects such as mummies, wood, and archives are often subject to deterioration as a result of attacks by insects, and by microorganisms such as fungi and bacteria. In the past, various toxic gases such as ethylene oxide and methyl bromide have been used extensively to eliminate pest infestation, but the employment of such gases can give rise to serious health problems,[1] as well as risks to the collections themselves.[2]

Owing to the hazards arising from the utilization of chemical substances, non-traditional methods, such as anoxia (the exclusion of oxygen), have been applied to sterilize affected cultural heritage objects. The dynamic system of nitrogen anoxia is performed by exposing these objects to an oxygen atmosphere containing less than ten parts per million of oxygen. A continuous flow of nitrogen can be used to maintain a low oxygen concentration inside a sealed bag or in anoxia chambers for dealing with insect infestation.[3]

The development of anoxic long-term storage environments can result in a reduction of oxidative and hydrolytic degradation effects. Anoxic storage, combined with new technology, can be used to control as well as monitor the effects of anoxic cases on specific artifacts, as compared with the control of other environmental parameters such as relative humidity, light, and pollution. An anoxic environment suitable for treatment of infested objects can be achieved in a variety of ways.

There are two basic approaches: static and dynamic. With the static procedure, which is the more common approach, objects are held under high-purity nitrogen or

1. Florin 1987, 199–205.
2. Postlethwaite 1987.
3. Hanolon 1993.

argon in a tightly sealed container with as little leakage of gas as possible. The container is purged of oxygen through a number of exchanges of high-purity nitrogen by using large quantities of an oxygen absorber, or through a combination of purging and absorption. With the alternate dynamic approach, an inert gas is continuously passed through the system during the treatment. Oxygen-free nitrogen or argon is used to flush all of the air out of the container by initially using a high purge rate, and once the oxygen concentration has fallen below 1000 ppm, the flow is reduced to that required level to maintain low oxygen level for the duration of treatment.

A number of early workers in the conservation of antiquities recognized the possibilities of these treatment methods and described and compared various approaches and systems, such as static, static-dynamic, and dynamic, in research papers. Hanlon et al. (1993, 387–96) and Daniel et al. (1993, 15–19) described the characteristics of each method. Koestler (1993, 94–96) used a dynamic system to treat a sixteenth-century Andrea del Sarto panel-painting that was infested with dry-wood termites. The panel was placed on a flat table and covered with a large sheet of barrier film taped to the surface of the table. This containment system was then flushed with humidified gas inserted through a port at one end and allowed to escape through another port at the far end. The treatment was performed successfully, but forty cylinders of gas were used over twenty days.

Koestler (1993, 94–96) described three static-dynamic treatments. These treatments used a containment chamber fabricated from a utility storage cart made of heavy gauge polyethylene, a Rentokil mini-fumigation bubble, and handmade pouches of a barrier film made with an ethylene-vinyl acetate copolymer. Treatments with the pouches combined the use of the nitrogen-purge and oxygen-scavenger techniques. Valentín (1993, 263–78) also evaluated the efficacy of the static-dynamic method in three different containment systems: plastic bags of low oxygen permeability; a tiny (80 cm^3), rigid vacuum chamber; and a 6.2 m^3 fumigation bubble.

The aim of this work is to illustrate the design of anoxic system in the storage areas and laboratories at both the Grand Egyptian Museum (GEM) and the National Museum of Civilization (NMEC) in Cairo.

1. *Care of Museum Collections*

Care is necessary if one is to keep objects with particular sensitivities (either cultural or biological) in both exhibition cases and storage facilities, since the risk of the loss in museum collections includes an accumulation of deterioration factors such as damp, insect attack, light, pollution, temperature and relative humidity, and microorganisms.[4] Risk management involves not only such aspects of collection preservation, but also the reduction of potential deterioration through human agents such as theft, fire, vandalism, and displacement and direct physical forces, which have historically

4. Burke 1996, 1–4.

contributed significantly in the loss of museum collections. Radiation with incorrect doses may also expose collections to further deterioration.[5] To conserve museum collections, anoxia and nitrogen systems have been used since they have many characteristics that qualify them as promising methods in conserving collections: these systems are simple, leave no hazardous residues, and are nontoxic.[6] The other advantage of the anoxic nitrogen system in conserving cultural heritage objects is that it does not cause color changes in treated painted objects.[7] Moreover, due to the selective effects of anoxic nitrogen systems on insects in a museum, they have the potential to eradicate insects at specific phases in their life cycle.[8]

2. *Experimentation*

2.1. Design of Mummy Storage Cabinets

Museum-quality storage equipment is usually constructed out of steel that has been powder-coated with an epoxy, acrylic, or polyester finish. Testing suggests that only the epoxy powder coating is durable. Anodized or powder-coated aluminum, although less common, is also an acceptable material for storage equipment. Older steel equipment was finished using a baked enamel coating. Because of the solvents used in the curing process, all coatings give off harmful gases until they are cured. Conservation of mummies requires that they be kept within well-sealed cabinets that create stable interior climates and provide buffers against temperature and relative humidity fluctuations, and also deter damage caused by light, dust, airborne pollution, and pest infestations. Such cabinets provide an extremely efficient "passive" way of housing collections and minimizing energy costs. Housing objects in a well-sealed, gas-inert cabinet is an effective way of creating a stable microclimate within a larger storage space that may be prone to relative humidity and temperature fluctuations.

Treating infested objects in a dynamic way with a flowing stream of nitrogen is convenient and effective in certain special or unique situations. This approach has been undertaken using small pouches, as well as larger chambers built around sizable or awkwardly proportioned objects. The dynamic mode has some special features, which are to be seen whenever this form of anoxia is used. When very dry nitrogen passes continuously over an object, water will be extracted from the object, and irreversible damage will occur. Equilibrium buffering will not take place, and humidification must be used. An exception to this may be the treatment of waterlogged objects where both anoxia and drying may be desired. In addition, oxygen absorbers are not employed in the dynamic mode; removal of oxygen is achieved entirely by purging.

5. Michalski 2004, 51–90.
6. Mekawa, Ankersmit, Neuhaus, Schellen, Beltran and Oersma 2007, 100–105.
7. Korenberg 2008, 49–58.
8. Katajisto 2004, 751–57.

2.2. Design of Nitrogen Systems for Mummies, Wood, and Archives

The design of the system should depend on the conservation of mummies collections, the state of mummies and surrounding air conditions, since mummies must be kept within a proper environment; air conditioning must be supplemented by HePFA filters, plus temperature and humidity controls (tables 1 and 2).

Through the design of the dynamic approach, nitrogen as an inert gas is continuously passed through the system during the treatment. The book-saver process uses a machine into which the bound books are placed along with petafluoropropane (HFC227), which contains a reagent that neutralizes the acidity without attacking the amount of the reagent in the contact ink. The amount of the reagent and the time during which the material and the reagent should be exposed to each other depends on the state of the material to be treated.

The concentration of nitrogen used must be at least 99.999%, the temperature must be at least 22°C, and testing of nitrogen generator system must have a capacity of 12–15 cubic meters per hour. Another important parameter to be considered is the level of relative humidity (RH) in the atmosphere of the bubble, although this figure does not influence the efficiency of insecticide treatment. The complete system for the carrying out of nitrogen treatment based on bubbles comprises a nitrogen generator and general control box, together with bubbles and bags.

2.3. Process Description

Ambient air is compressed in a lubricated, air-cooled compressor. Following the air buffer and water separator, this air enters the refrigeration dryer and filters for the removal of water and oils; the compressed air then flows through the carbon molecular sieve inside the absorber beds where oxygen is absorbed. During absorption in one bed, the second bed is regenerated by depressurization to atmospheric pressure. The absorption/desorption cycle is controlled by a fixed sequence of a low pressure controller (LP-C). Dust and microorganisms are stopped by the final filter.

Table 1. Technical principles in the design of an anoxic nitrogen system.

Item	**Technical Specifications**	
A. Compressor	111 m3/h equivalent to 89 Nm3/h, at 45°C, 10 bar, 15 kw, 400–3–50Hz	
B. Air Buffer	Capacity: 200 and liters	
C. Dryer	+ 22 Dew point + 3°C, Air cooled: the second dryer is used to cool the temperature and maintains performance in the Egyptian summer.	
D. Filters	1 water separator: WS 300 1 prefilter: G 200X Flow 200 Nm3/h Filtration: 1 micron maxi. (1mm) Oil: 0.5 mg/m3 at 21°C 1 Filter: G 200Y Flow 200 Nm3/h Filtration: 0.01 micron maxi. (1mm) Oil: 0.01 mg/m3 at 21°C 1 filter anti-dust : G 50Y Flow 50 Nm3/h to 7 bar Filtration: 0.01 micron maxi.	
E. Nitrogen Generator	Nitrogen flow Purity Pressure Dew point Oil residual Dust Compressed air need Minimum air pressure Maximum air pressure Temperature minimum Temperature maximum Voltage Power	12–15 Nm3/h 99.999999% 6.5 bar 40 °C <0.003 ppm 0.01 Micron 74 Nm3/h 9 bar 9 bar 5°C 35°C 230 V-1–50Hz 200 W

Table 2. Technical specifications for gas control (wood, mummies, and archives).

Units	Technical Specifications
Control Box, Humidifier, and Thermometer	• One per room • With 2 adjustments large flow flush of nitrogen (until to reach 450 ppm in the room). • Small flow for pressure maintaining (below 450 ppm) • Programming the desired relative humidity • Hygrometer to install in a room • Screen for displaying the relative humidity in the room. • Control of the injection of dry or wet nitrogen with adjustable contact • Water tank stainless steel • Thermometer and screen for displaying the temperature in the room.
General control box	• The central control box will directly analyze the level of oxygen in each room and decide if the room needs flushing or just needs to be maintained under pressure. • In the information about the oxygen the central control box. Information about moisture and temperature will be sent to the central control box. • All values, the rate of oxygen, humidity and temperature will be displayed and recorded continuously.
Security for people inside chamber of anoxia	• Measurement of low level of oxygen inside the room, the entrance door will be locked if level of oxygen is below 17%. • Sweeping by air before the entrance of peoples.
Bubbles, bags, and accessories	• The rooms and pockets to anoxia are made of special films. There are two types: transparent and nontransparent. • The heat seal requires a special tool, like heated spatula. • The bubbles and bags will be connected to the system of anoxia by PTFE hoses.
Kipping and wiring	• Piping of stainless steel pipes 20–26 mm • Electrical wiring to control the flow of nitrogen to the anoxia and quarantine room. Electrical wiring between anoxia and quarantine room to transfer the data of humidity and temperature.

2.4. Design of an Anoxia Chamber

A less expensive and more efficient solution is a standard container 20′ transformed into an air-tight space with carbon steel sheets welded inside and an air-tight door (table 3).

Table. 3. Technical principles in the design of an anoxia chamber.

Item	Technical Specifications
Anoxia chamber	• Valves for gas, valves for analyze, relief valve 1.2mbar, pressure control • Measurement of oxygen, moisture, temperature, recording of data, transfer of data to PC • Control of the injection of dry or wet nitrogen • Security for persons, measurement of low level of oxygen • Sweeping by air before the entrance of people • Exhaust of Nitrogen will have to be driven outside • Oxygen security level analyzer for the room outside • External dimensions: 6.1m L × 2.45m W × 2.6m H • Internal dimensions: 5.2m L × 2.3m W× 2.3m H • Door dimensions: 1.6m W × 1.8m H
Flexible anoxia bubbles	• They will be made with composite film (polyester/aluminium/polyethylen) and could be located in the entrance of "anoxia area" or in "multipurpose area." Bubbles and bags gas links can be made with flexible tubes and different kinds of connections. Several kits linking systems will be necessary for different kinds of treatments (one or more bags may be treated simultaneously). Smaller similar links are used for sampling and measuring internal values (02, RH, T°).
Compressor	• 25 kw 10 bar Flow 200 Nm3/h
Dryer	• Dew point +3°C • Air Cooled • Drying and refreshing compressed air from 60 to 45°C • For indoors installation: maximum temperature 25°C • (2 kw will be released in the room)
Air buffer	• Capacity: 750 Liters
Dryer	• Dew point +3°C • Air Cooled or Water cooled: refreshing air from 45°C to 30–32°C • NB: Water cooling will avoid to release 2 kw in the generator room • Water flow needed: 500L/h

Filters	• 1 water separator (eliminates liquid from compressed air) • 1 prefilter (eliminates droplets of oil) • Flow 500 Nm3/h • Filtration: maxi. (1mm) • Oil: 0.5 mg/m3 at 21°C • 1 Filter (eliminates aerosols of oil) • Flow 500 Nm3/h • Filtration: 0.01 micron maxi. (1mm) • Oil: 0.01 mg/m3 at 21°C • 1 filter anti dust (final filter) • Flow 50 Nrn3/h at 7 bar • Filtration: 0.01 micron maxi.	
Nitrogen generator	• Nitrogen flow • Purity • Pressure • Dew point • Oil residual • Dust • Compressed air need • Minimum air pressure • Maximum air pressure • Temperature minimum • Temperature maximum • Voltage • Power	25 Nm3/h 99.999999% 6.5 Bar 40 °C <0.003 ppm 0.01 Micron 74 Nm3/h 9 Bar 10 Bar 5°C 35°C 230 V-1–50Hz 200 W
Nitrogen buffer	Capacity 1000 Liters with back pressure regulator to obtain constant purity	
On line humidifier	Must be controlled by an hygrometer, it will deliver nitrogen with 100% moisture Automatic filling, stainless steel Must be connected on running water network Two separate gas piping must be installed from nitrogen generator to user rooms (anoxia chamber multipurpose area and wood workshop): one for dry nitrogen, the other for humidified nitrogen For multipurpose area and wood workshop a manual regulation will be made with a mixer tap and an electrovan will automatically regulate gas humidification for anoxia chamber.	
Oxygen trace analyzer	Oxygen trace analyzers differ from oxymeters by their high precision. Margin of error must be equal to or lower than 100ppm	

Safety oxymeter	Industrial legislation and labor laws impose a strict control of air quality (must stay > 17% O_2). During the treatment phase, anoxia area access must be controlled and dependent on the use of individual safety oxymeters. Humidity and temperature sensor. The same technical considerations may be applied to humidity and temperature sensors. • Detail screen • Optional central control box (right) and PC (on desk) • Humidifier

2.5. Description of the Process

Ambient air is compressed in a lubricated, air-cooled compressor; this air enters a separator and refrigeration dryer for removal of water. Compressed air is driven in a controlled temperature room (25°C) to an air buffer. It enters a second, water-cooled dryer, where its temperature is also decreased. A prefilter and a filter are used to remove oils. Compressed air flows through the carbon molecular sieve inside the absorber beds where oxygen is adsorbed. Nitrogen leaves the absorber beds, during the absorption in one bed, the second bed is regenerated by depressurization to atmospheric pressure. The adsorption/desorption cycle is controlled by a fixed sequence of a LP-C. Finally, dust and microorganisms are stopped by the final filter.

2.6. Monitoring System

A monitoring system is an essential part of anoxia device, and is composed of:

- An oxygen trace analyzer
- A humidity and temperature sensor (pressure for rigid chambers), at least one in the system.
- A data-logger, which measures and traces relative humidity, temperature, and oxygen concentration within the system. These components constitute a unit that may be movable, so that this system can be used for monitoring large bubbles outside of anoxia chamber area. Tile rigid chamber will need a fix regulation automaton (which measures, registers, and opens or closes gas supply). Bubbles and bags only need a movable traceability unit

2.7. Grand Egyptian Museum (GEM) Anoxia Apparatus

The anoxia apparatus is an automated piece of equipment that is used for the fumigation of biologically infested artifacts, in particular for insect infestations, where nitrogen is the preferable and cheapest gas, with no side effects on cultural heritage objects. The apparatus causes almost 100 percent insect mortality by decreasing the oxygen percentage down to 0.3 percent inside the chamber and replacing it with nitrogen gas as inert gas. The system consists of several units:

ADOX N_2 Unit. This unit is responsible for separating nitrogen gas from the air and repumping it again with maintenance of pressure inside the fumigation chamber during the process, and is considered the preferred and cheapest unit because it does not need any external nitrogen cylinders.

Technical specifications of the nitrogen chamber include nitrogen storage type SLE 36, which can hold thirty-six mummies. For lengthwise placement storage, it is divided into nine rows, each with boxes on tope of the other. Each box is airtight-welded, with a scuttle on two stable bands, with compressed lever locking. The silicon seal guarantees the airtight closing of the scuttles. Installation: nine rows will be connected in parallel as a single unit.

- Storage equipment: Thirty-six roll conveyor long, each roll conveyor with five numbers. Stainless steel rollers with plastic coating, one roller used as stopper.
- Mummy deposit: Thirty-six deposits made of stainless steel 1.4301, on runners with push handhold on face side, size 1900 L × 620 W × 70 H mm.
- Security: Each box with a pressure within the useable space and avoid raising over atmospheric pressure.
- Mounting sleeve for each box, to be connected to the nitrogen unite on site, air-tightened installed at the back of the devices.
- Technical datas: Materials, completely made out of stainless steel 1.4301, size of each box: 850mm W × 2100mm D × 550mm H
- Storage raw: 850mm W × 2100mm D × 2700mm H
- Complete storage raw: 7700mm W × 2100mm D × 2700mm H
- Scuttle: 36 scuttle, clear size 680mm W × 500mm H

Fumigation Chamber. This chamber is constructed to prevent the leakage of the nitrogen gas. It is equipped with a fan for optimizing the distribution of the air, and also it has holes for pumping the gas and others for air safety. The chamber contains sensors for periodically measuring temperature, relative humidity, nitrogen, and oxygen percentages. Finally, this chamber is provided with a tightly closed door.

Analyzer. Takes readings of temperature, relative humidity, nitrogen and oxygen percentages during the fumigation process. It must be calibrated twice yearly using an external nitrogen cylinder.

Humidifier Unit3. The humidifier unit adjusts the percentage of relative humidity during the fumigation process. It is provided with an external running water source that is responsible for the percentage of relative humidity inside the chamber as nitrogen gas is a dry gas.

3. *Discussion*

Our findings indicated that nitrogen and anoxia systems are effective against most insect and microorganisms colonizing cultural heritage objects, this in agreement with Morozkina and Kurakov,[9] who reported that nitrogen and anoxia systems are effective against *Fusarium*, *Chaetonium*, and *Trichoderma*, which are the most common generia deteriorating cultural heritage objects in addition to bacteria and actinomycetes.[10] Furthermore, the effect of anoxia is not limited to microorganisms, but this effect is extended to other insects infecting cultural heritage objects, since Bruchert *et al.*[11] illustrated the potent effect of anoxia and nitrogen systems in killing most insects infecting wood objects from Namibia.

Moreover, egg of insects were killed using nitrogen systems and anoxia; these results were confirmed by Katajisto,[12] who reported that nitrogen systems and anoxia killed eggs of most treated insects by desiccation.

We conclude that anoxia and nitrogen systems are effective in the preservation of wood, mummies, and archives against biological and insects attacks.

Part 2: Integrated Pest Management (IPM)

The most persistant causes of loss in museum collections is damage caused by insects, fungi, dust, and bacteria. The concept of integrated pest management (IPM) was developed during the 1950s and 1960s to address the agronomic problems caused by the use of broad-spectrum chemicals such as insecticide resistance, pest resurgence, and secondary pest outbreaks. IPM is an ecological approach to pest control, which requires selective agents that are effective on target-pest species, yet preserves natural enemies and retains their contribution to overall control. In the context of plant protection, bio-pesticides are a key component of integrated pest management programs,[13] but due to the problems imposed by insects in the field of museums, IPM aims to prevent pest problems from occurring, reducing the use of toxic materials that may adversely affect the environment and protecting materials from pests.[14]

The term "integrated" implies that numerous techniques or approaches are used to manage plants in the landscape as a balanced ecosystem. Pesticides are often used in IPM, but the emphasis is on keeping pests at low levels through the judicious use of other alternative pest-control strategies so that pesticides are used less often and the least toxic product is used. Rather than trying to eliminate all pests, a variety of control strategies are used to reduce pests to low, tolerable levels in order to maintain

9. Morozkina and Kurakov 2007, 544–49.
10. Valentin 1998, 17–29.
11. Bruchert et al. 2006, 161–93.
12. Katajisto 2004, 751–57.
13. Gui-Ming, Xiange-Yue, Lu-Quan 2001, 51–54.
14. Jessup 1997.

populations of natural enemies (beneficial organisms). The IPM differs from traditional pest control in that it employs a variety of control strategies rather than relying on a single pesticide strategy. These strategies include the use of biological control, resistant plant varieties, the use of biorational, low-toxicity pest control products, cultural control, proper plant selection for the site, mechanical and chemical controls, usually with two or more techniques employed at a time.[15]

Fumigants and other pesticides can cause long- and short-term health problems, ranging from nausea and headaches to respiratory problems. Many chemical treatments might not be harmful when initially used, but it is also known that many of the chemicals can damage the treated materials, and no chemical treatment provides a residual effect that will prevent reinfestation. Creating an anoxic microenvironment is remarkably simple and therefore anoxia is becoming the method of choice for treating infested objects in museums mainly because of its lack of toxicity to people and collections.[16] This reduces the costs of maintance and preservation of cultural heritage objects in the museums.[17]

Proteinaceous museum collection items, such as parchment, leather, and mummified tissues are highly susceptible to the growth of aerobic fungi and bacteria. Aerobic bacteria can damage both the surface and the layers of these materials, as do fungi with their blotches of white, green or dark-colored colonies. Some common aerobic microorganisms are: *Aspergillus niger, Aspergillus flavus, Penicillium commune, Actinomyces* sp. *Bacillus* sp. *Stroptomyces* sp. Anaerobic bacteria, instead, produce proteolyic enzymes, which cause collagen depolymerization and thus the loss of an object's strength and even its integrity. Anaerobic fungi are very infrequent in organic objects.

The integrated pest management plan includes monitoring and identification of the pest, inspection, habitat, modification, good sanitation, treatment, and evaluation.[18]

1. *Experimentation*

The implementation of IPM activities is divided into three steps:

(1) Identify insects that were found on infested objects at the GEM-Conservation Centre (GEM-CC) and the best method of treatment.

(2) Survey the kind and number of insects in the traps that are distributed on a monthly basis in laboratories and storage rooms in three stages:

   (a) Distribution (Traps – Maps).

   (b) Imaging and Identification (Imaging – Documentation – Isolation and Mounting).

   (c) Results (Monthly reports – Comparisons – Treatment).

15. Smith-Fiola 2007, 295–322.
16. Burke 1996.
17. Manachini, Billeci and Palla 2013.
18. Valentín 1993, 263–78.

(3) Determine suitable treatment method.

1.1. Strategy of IPM

(1) The conservation center is divided into three areas (A, B, and C) to make a super blocking for storage area C.
(2) The traps are distributed and collected monthly according to these areas.
(3) Sticky traps were used which is the most preferred to be used in museums.
(4) A map for each laboratory and storage room in the CC for easy monitoring, displaying the number and place of each trap.
(5) The number and place of traps are constant in each laboratory or storage room.
(6) Use of stereo microscopes with maximum magnification (90x) for imaging.
(7) Use of ethyl acetate for isolating insects and alcohol for preserving the insect body to make it flexible enough for easy mounting.
(8) Classifying identified insects that are dangerous (i.e. use objects as feeding material) and nondangerous insects.
(9) A monthly report contains a map for each area, data for each area, pictures of existing insects, and suitable treatment methods.

Comparisons had been made every three months but are now made yearly.

2. Results

The number of insects increased in summer months and reduced sharply in winter months. This is owing to the fact that insects hibernate in the winter months. Mating season for insects occurs in spring months (March, April, and May).

Our survey for insects causing deterioration among cultural heritage objects in GEM-CC indicated that the most common insects are:

Silver Fish (*Thermobia aegyptiaca*): Hazardous only during part of its lifecycle, it contributes to the deterioration of papyrus, paper, leather covers, and manuscripts.

Booklice (*Liposclis*): This insect eats carbohydrates, papyrus, the glue in books, and manuscript covers. The most common deterioration symptoms are irregular pores and deterioration in papers, papyrus, and books.

***Gebbium psylloides*:** Hazardous throughout its lifecycle. This insect is considered one of the most hazardous pests that infects both human and animal bodies, causing the deterioration of badly stored ancient textiles, especially associated with mummies.

German cockroach: Hazardous only during part of its lifecycle. Is characterized by a bad odor from gland-secretion. A pest for papyrus, books, and manuscripts, as it eats starch and the glue in books and manuscripts covers.

***Blatta orientalis*:** Hazardous only during part of its lifecycle. Found in hot areas, it eats decaying organic matter, causing deterioration of papyrus, books, manuscripts, and paper.

Larvae of Dermestidae Sp. (leather-skin beetle): Hazardous throughout its lifecycle. One of the main dangerous pests, infecting both human and animal remains, including bones and leather, and is a minor hazard to badly stored wool textiles, especially in conjunction with mummies (human and animal). It eats proteins.

3. *Discussion*

Current results show that most identified insects are resistant to most applied insecticides. This result was confirmed by Smith-Fiola,[19] since most insects are resistant to DDT (Dichloro diphenyl trichloroethane) so it was necessary to apply IPM. Our work focused on traping, map identification, and reporting identified insects collected from exhibition cases or from storage rooms.

References

BRUCHERT, V., B. CURRIE, R. PEARD, ET AL. 2006. "Biochemical and Physical Control on Shelf Anoxia and Water Column Hydrogen Sulphide in the Benguel Acoastal Upwell in Namibia." In Lev N. NERETIN (ed.), *Past and Present Water Column Anoxia*. Dordrecht: Springer, 161–93.

BURKE, J. 1996. "Anoxic Microenvironments: A Simple Guide," *SPNHC leaflets* 1, 1, 1–4.

DANIEL, V., G. HANLON, and S. MAEKAWA. 1993. "Eradication of Insect Pests in Museums Using Nitrogen," *WAAC Newsletter* 15.3, 15–19.

FLORIN, M.-L. 1987. "The Effect on Artifact Materials of the Fumigant Ethylene Oxide and Freezing Used in Insect Control," *ICOM, Committee for Conservation, 8th Triennial Meeting, Sydney, Australia, 6–11 September*. Sydney: ICOM Committee for Conservation, 199–208.

GUI-MING, L., Z. XIANG-YUE, and W. LU-QUAN. 2001. "The Use of Bacillus Thuringiensis on Forest Integrated Pest Management," *Journal of Forestry Research*, 12.1, 51–54.

HANLON, G., V. DANIEL, N. RAVENEL, and S. MAEKAWA. 1993. "Dynamic System for Nitrogen Anoxia of Large Museum Objects: A Pest Eradication Case Study." In K. TOISHI et al. (eds.), *Biodeterioration of Cultural Property 2: Proceedings of the 2nd International Conference on Biodeterioration of Cultural Property*. Tokyo: International Communications Specialists, 387–96.

JESSUP, W. 1997. *Intergrated Pest Management. AIC News* 22.3: 1–5.

KATAJISTO, T. 2004. "Effects of Anoxia and Hypoxia on the Dormancy and Survival of Substances of Eggs of *Acartia bifilosa* (Copepoda: Calanoida)," *Marine Biology* 145, 751–57.

KOESTLER, R. 1993. "Practical Application of Nitrogen and Argon Fumigation Procedures for Insect Control in Museum Objects." In K. TOISHI et al. (eds.), *Biodeterioration of Cultural Property 2: Proceedings of the 2nd International Conference on Biodeterioration of Cultural Property*. Tokyo: International Communications Specialists, 94–96.

KORENBERG, C. 2008. "The Photo-Ageing Behavior of Selected Watercolour Paints under Anoxic Conditions," *British Museum Technical Bulletin* 2, 49–58.

MANACHINI, B., N. BILLECI, and F. PALLA F. 2013. "Exotic Insect Pests: The Impact of the Red Palm Weevil on Natural and Cultural Heritage in Palermo (Italy)," *Journal of Cultural Heritage*, http://dx.doi.org/10.1016/j.culher.2012.11.028.

19. Smith-Fiola 2007, 295–322.

Mekawa, S., B. Ankersmit B., E. Neuhaus, et al. 2007. "Investigation into Impacts of Large Numbers of Visitors on the Collection Environment at Our Lord in the Attic, Museum Microclimates." In T. Padfield and K. Borchersen (eds.), *Contributions to the Copenhagen Conference 19–23 November 2007.* Copenhagen: The National Museum of Denmark, 100–105.

Michalski, S. 2004. "Care and Preservation of Collections." In P. Boylan (ed.), *Running a Museum: A Practical Handbook.* Paris: ICOM and UNESCO, 51– 90.

Morozkina, E. V., and A. V. Kurakov. 2007. "Dissimilatory Nitrate Reduction in Fungi under Conditions of Hypoxia and Anoxia: A Review." *Applied Biochemistry and Microbiology*, 43. 5, 544–49.

Postlethwaite, A. 1987. "Fumigation Choice, of Fumigant and Design of Facility." *ICOM, Committee for Conservation, 8th Triennial Meeting, Sydney, Australia, 6–11 September.* Sydney: ICOM Committee for Conservation, 1189–96.

Smith-Fiola, D. 2007. "Integrated Pest Management." In J. E. Kuser (ed.), *Urban and Community Forestry in the Northeast.* Dordrecht: Springer, 295–322.

Valentín, N. 1993. "Comparative Analysis of Insect Control by Nitrogen, Argon, and Carbon Dioxide in Museum, Archive, and Herbarium Collections," *International Biodeterioration and Biodegradation* 32, 263–78.

———. 1998. "Preservation of Historic Materials by Using Inert Gases for Biodeterioration Control." In S. Maekawa (ed.), *Oxygen-Free Museum Cases.* Los Angeles: The Getty Conservation Institute, 17–29.

The Papyrus Puzzle, or How to Unlock a Random Papyrus Collection?

Willem van Haarlem

Recently, the Allard Pierson Museum took over a somewhat neglected and hidden papyrus collection from the Special Collections Section of the Amsterdam University Library. The collection was assembled by the late professor of papyrology at the University of Amsterdam, Dr. P. J. Sijpesteijn. Over the course of many years, he purchased papyrus lots at various auctions. Together with complete Greek papyri, of which most are already published (fig. 1),[1] these lots often included as extras papyrus fragments in Coptic, Hieratic, and Demotic writing (fig. 2) as well, together with early Arabic texts on paper. Their size is varying from thumbnail to A4, and several hundreds in total. As an initial step, they have now been identified and catalogued, and every piece has been photographed as well. The next step was the conservation of these fragments. Some of them were loosely and simply kept in paper folders or envelopes that were not acid free (fig. 3), and thus were partly disintegrated into dust; others were kept between yellowing plexiglass frames, secured with deteriorating tape. The latter papyri were put in glass frames with new tape. The loose fragments were separated (sometimes intertwined in a complicated way) and then assembled in *Secol* covers, which are chemically neutral and acid free (fig. 4) and then collected in albums, stored in a climate-controlled environment. Finally, the more coherent texts should be made available for study and publication.

Even more recently, the papyrus collection of the Dortmond Museum of Writing has been disclosed in Amsterdam, with several dozen examples in Greek, Coptic, Hieratic, and Demotic as well. Although in a slightly better condition than the former one mentioned, this collection needs the same treatment. To the highlights belong some fragments of the Eighteenth Dynasty Book of the Dead owned by Amenhotep,[2] Overseer of the Sculptors of Amun (fig. 5). These are parts of a manuscript that is widely dispersed, mainly in London and Boston, and, as recently discovered, in Brisbane. Hopefully, this copy can once more be assembled in its entirety. Additionally,

1. Sijpesteijn 1980.
2. TM 133544 in the digital Book of the Dead archive at http://www.totenbuch.awk.nrw.de

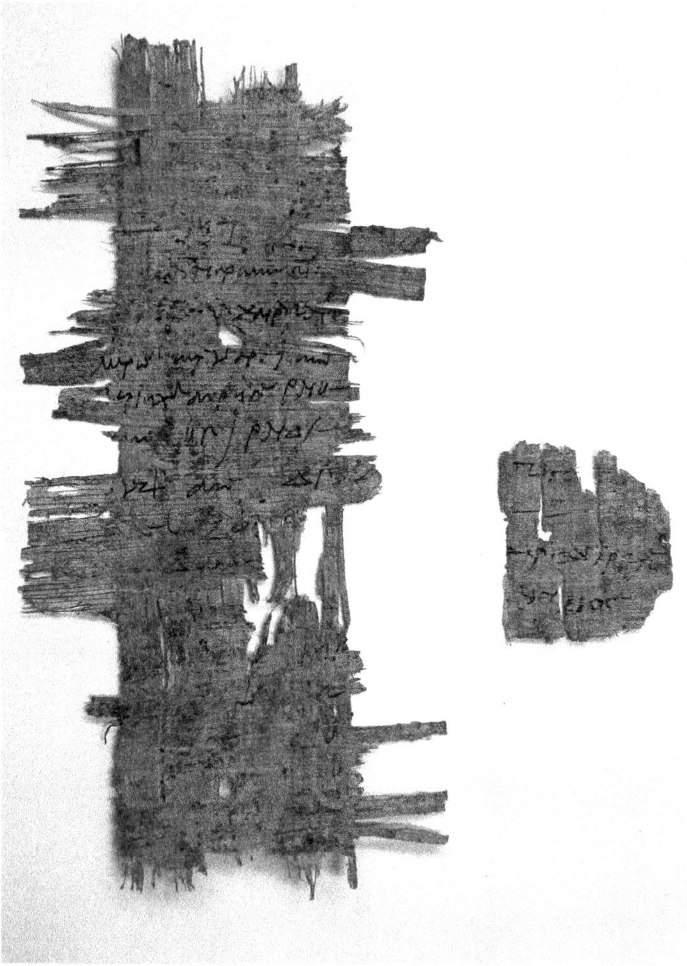

Fig. 1. One of the published Greek papyri. © Willem van Haarlem.

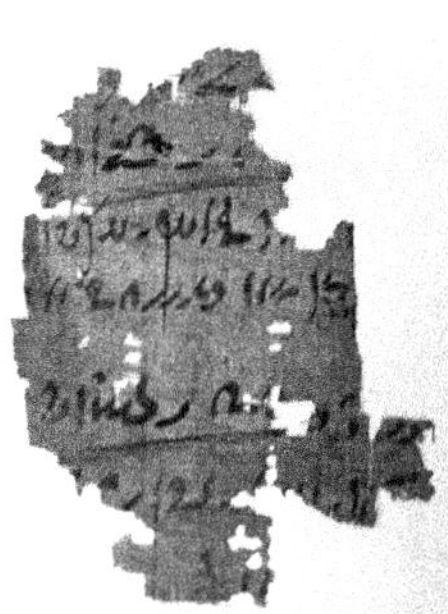

Fig. 2. A demotic fragment.
© Willem van Haarlem.

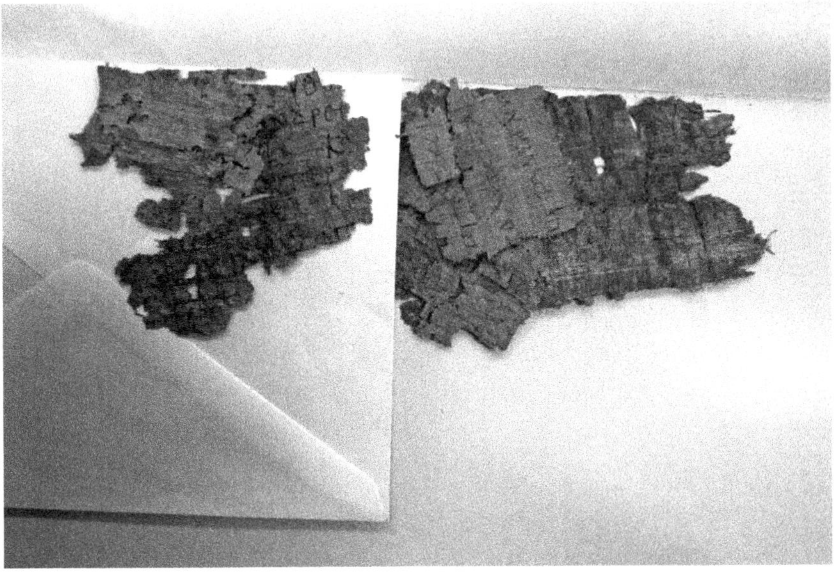

Fig. 3. An example of the state of the collection before conservation. © Willem van Haarlem.

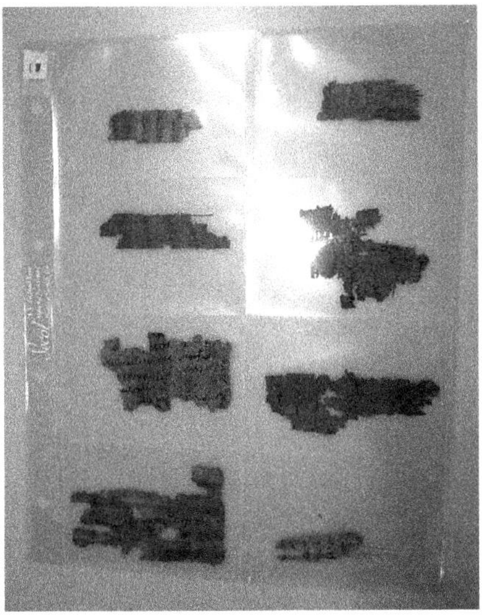

Fig. 4. The way of storing the fragments after conservation. © Willem van Haarlem.

Fig. 5. Fragment of the Book of the Dead of Amenhotep. © Willem van Haarlem.

the Egyptian objects (all inscribed) in this collection consist of shabtis, scarabs, stelae and a shabti box as well.

Reference

SIJPESTEIJN, P. J. 1980. *Die Amsterdamer Papyri (P. Amst. I)*. Zutphen: Terra.

Egyptology and Museum Education: The Budapest Program "On the Field of Osiris" as a Tool for Preserving Cultural Heritage

Hedvig Győry

The Hungarian program "On the Field of Osiris"[1] is a museum educational program in the Museum of Fine Arts, Budapest. The program is designed for children from ten to fourteen years old, working in teams in their own schools and sending the results of their work digitally. Through their activities, they not only learn much about ancient Egyptian culture, but also develop abilities and competencies, such as tolerance, appreciation of cultural heritage, and responsibility for it.

The Program Structure

The program is an e-learning course in the form of a complex competition, in which both Egyptological and educational aims are important. The 2011–2012 year's program was the fourth year the Museum of Fine Arts, Budapest organized it for children attending the fifth to eighth grades at middle school. They can enter the competition in teams with a maximum of ten children in September (fig. 1). It has three rounds plus a final, and is performed through the Internet.

Each round has the same structure. It starts with a story about children living in ancient Egypt. Their activities introduce the participants to life at that time, points to common and diverse features between modern and ancient ways of thinking, conditions and opportunities. In this particular story the setting was Deir el-Medina. The program was entitled "A guest is arriving." As the title suggests, an official guest was expected,[2] and the family of Nahtszu and Hnummose has to host him. So they prepared a place for him, bought a new sheet of linen, and made everything to accommo-

1. It can be found on the web through the homepage of the Museum (www.szepmuveszeti.hu) by clicking on „múzeumpedagógia," then on „vetélkedők," finally on „Ozirisz földjén."

2. This year, the story stopped unfinished, and was completed by the end of the fifth year's program. It is now openly available to view.

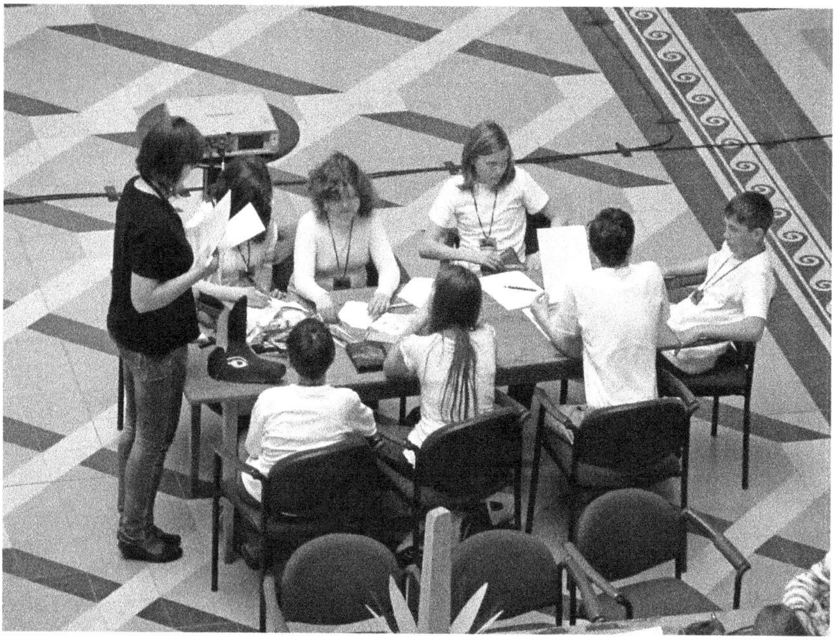

Fig. 1. The "Children of Egypt" team, Szatmárnémeti, at the final. © Hedvig Győry.

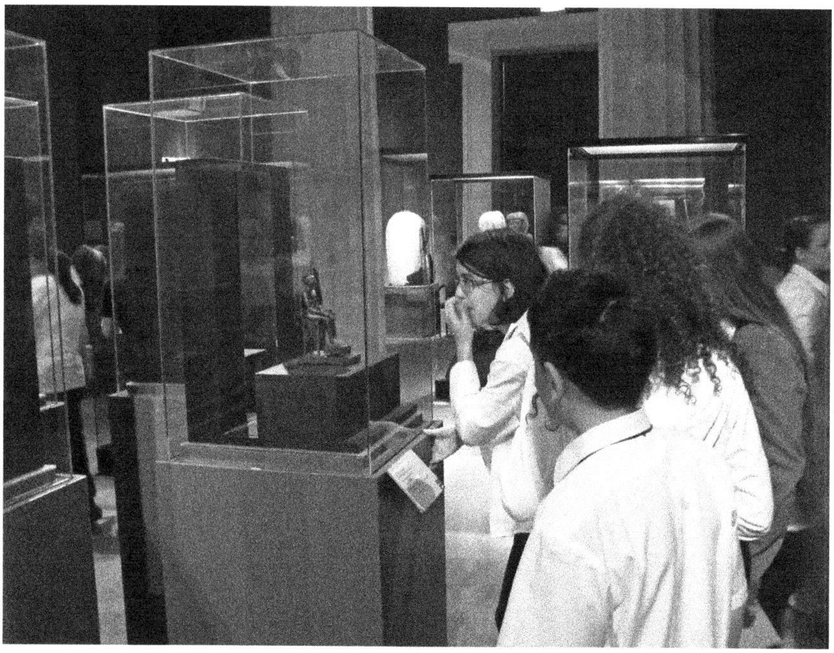

Fig. 2. Children in the museum-educational exhibition looking for their objects during the final. © Hedvig Győry.

date him suitably. Of course the children saw, heard, imagined, and did various things as an introduction to the competitors, among others, of the ancient textile industry, which was the main topic of the year's competition.

Although many elements are woven into the story, it can be read continuously. Missing knowledge, unknown expressions or interesting facts are added by links which leading to a "small encyclopedia" ("kislexikon") belonging to each round. To avoid repetitions, the titles in the previous small encyclopedias are collected in a common one, the letters of which are arranged into the shape of the *oudja* and *seneb* signs on the front page of the program.

After reading, the projects to complete are presented, each on a separate page. There are four of them. The first is a multiple-choice test. To find the right answers, the teams can look for data in the story and the encyclopedia where they can find the answers sometimes written out word by word, or sometimes to be deduced.

After this small review it is easier to start the next page. They were asked to imagine a given situation, somehow connected to the story, and formulate it. This time the first round is built on the instruction of Ptahhotep (given in Hungarian via link, translation by Vilmos Wessetzky) a lecture is given by the father to his sons about how they have to behave, especially when the distinguished guest is with them. The second time, the teams made a protocol for building a new tomb in the Valley of the Queens as the team personifies the leader of the right side working team in *Set-Maat*. The last unit had not finished the story, so the children had the possibility to finish it by finding why the guest had not arrived yet.

The arts and crafts, then the drawing project are the final tasks. Here a virtual Egyptian exhibition, which can be reached via a link, helps the teams to understand what objects looked like during pharaonic times. Here the children find three or four showcases from the permanent Egyptian exhibition 1996–2009 of the Museum of Fine Arts, Budapest (the new permanent exhibition is under construction; fig. 2). To make the page playful, the objects to find are concealed, opening in a new page when children click on the pictures of the linked objects within the display case photo. Descriptions and explanations are given with the image. As these aids were given in earlier years as well, several more display cases can be seen in the homepage arranged in an *ankh* sign on the front page.

In the first round, they can see fine clothes people wear as shown on a stele or a *broad*-collar on a mummy shroud in the collection of the Museum of Fine Arts. Moreover, to get more familiar with Egyptian textiles, this year's main theme, animal mummies also played a role. These are important pieces of information to help them complete the last project "festive attire for a festival in the village" (fig. 3). The second round asked the teams to plan a wall painting in a workers tomb, representing the owner offering to the goddess Meretseger (fig. 4). Of course her depictions appear among the objects shown in the virtual exhibition. Finally, the third unit asks for a picture in ancient Egyptian style about the favorite activity of the children themselves (fig. 5).

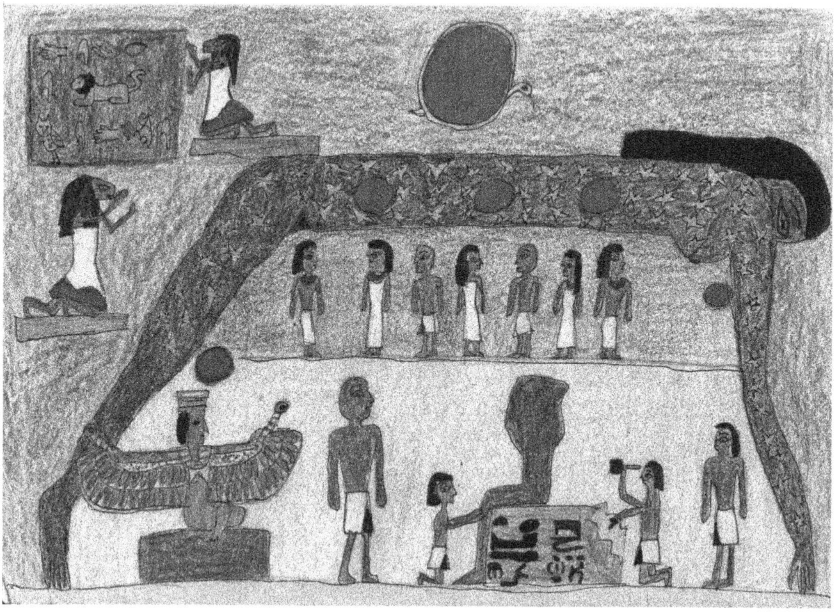

Fig. 3. The "Children of Anubis" team, Szederkény. Drawing for the first round. © Hedvig Győry.

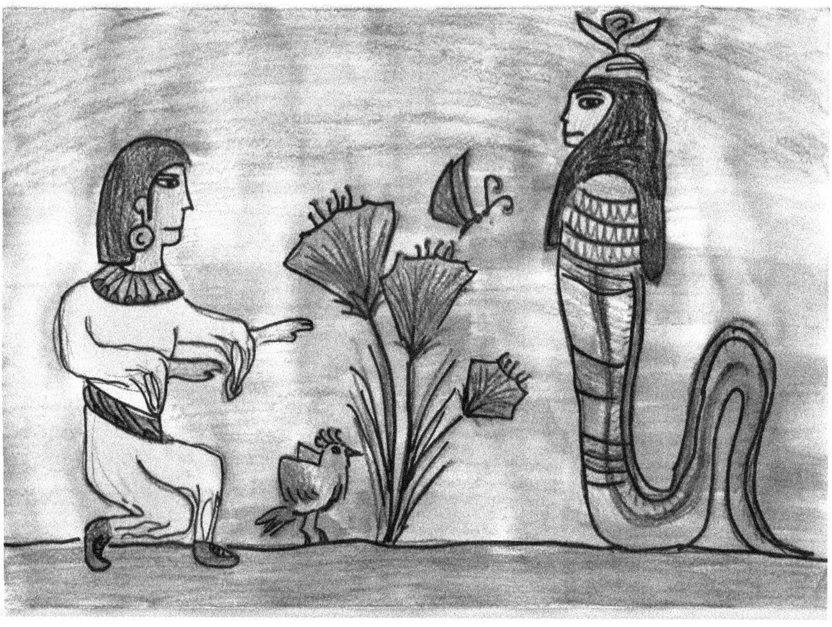

Fig. 4. The "Charm" team, Gödöllő. Drawing for the second round. © Hedvig Győry.

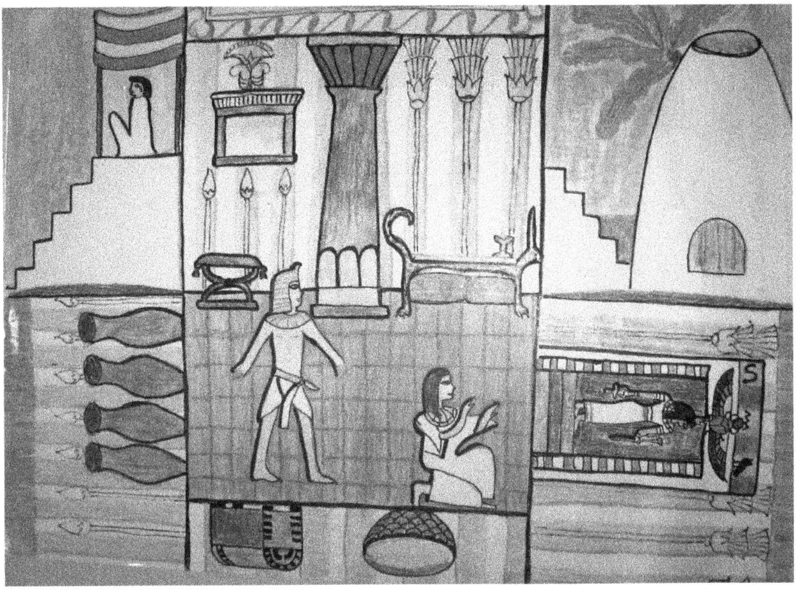

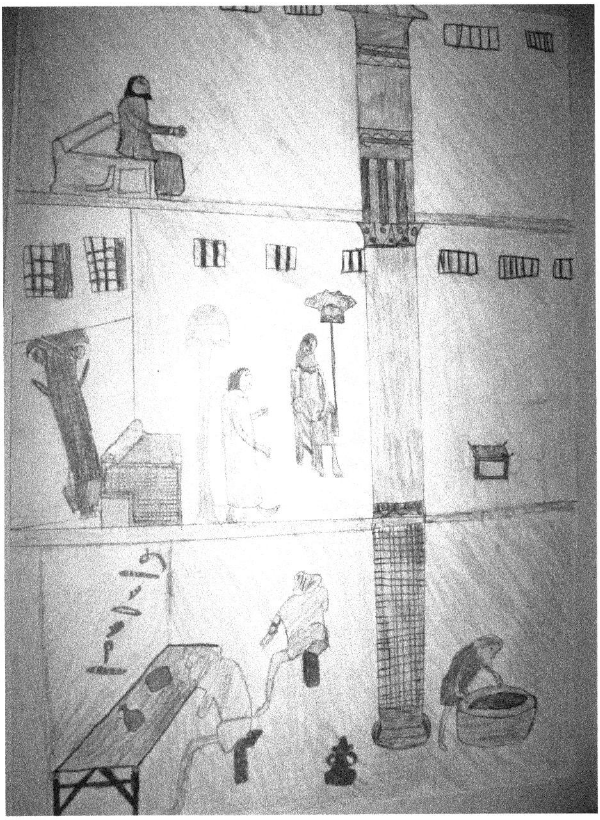

Fig. 5. The "Daughters of Isis" team, Ják. Two drawings for the third round. © Hedvig Győry.

In the arts and crafts projects, each team first prepared a horizontal ground loom and wove a simple bag on it (fig. 6). They could compare the material produced by them to those used by the ancient Egyptians. In the following round, they prepared a long girdle with a simple belt or strap loom made again by themselves. In the last round, the task was to decorate the girdle with amulet patterns at both ends (fig. 7). To get a large choice they were provided with the link to the *Global Egyptian Museum*, with 1,386 amulets from the Cairo Museum and other collections.

All the items prepared by the children remained with them; we need only the digital reproductions and the pictures taken from the craftworks and drawings. These are sent to us via e-mail. After having evaluated the entries, our committee opens the following round until they reach the final, where the best teams are invited to the Museum. Here they start the competition from zero; that is, only the entries on site count. The prizes for the best entries are given during an awards ceremony.

For the final, they were given homework, which was to make an amulet for each member of the team. The previous year, a pectoral was brought and the leader wore a special ancient Egyptian deity headdress (see, e.g., fig. 9). During the final, they were asked to explain what they brought with them and the committee appraised it. They were given a verbal task as well to prepare in advance at home. The previous year they wrote a hymn to an Egyptian deity, either Isis, Horus, Anubis, Hathor, Ra, or Nofertum. This time it was a five-minute scene with Nahtszu and Hnummose, the principle characters in the story. The act had a preparatory part, where the children explained how they planned the scene, and then came the pantomime of the work in a weaving workshop.

Two completely new tasks awaited them in the Museum. One was a multiple-choice test with questions concerning the Egyptological topics the children learnted during the program. The other work is always some drawing or painting in connection with the Egyptian collection. Two years ago the Museum had a temporary exhibition about the Mummy project. As last year no Egyptian exhibition was open, the Education Department organized with the Egyptian Department a "museum-educational" exhibition for the classes, and the competitors too advantage of it. This time the children explored the exhibition and created a poster for it. The details and title were up to them. The previous year they made a big drawing all together: each team got a piece of paper with a unit of the mythological papyrus of the Budapest collection. After finding the place of their unit in the whole composition, they painted it on a ten-meter-long textile strip (fig. 8).

How the Program Sensitizes Young People to Preserving Cultural Heritage

At first glance, this program seems to address exclusively ancient Egyptian culture. Indeed it says much about it, but it also has another side. When a museum educator works with children in a museum he/she always concentrates on the objects asking

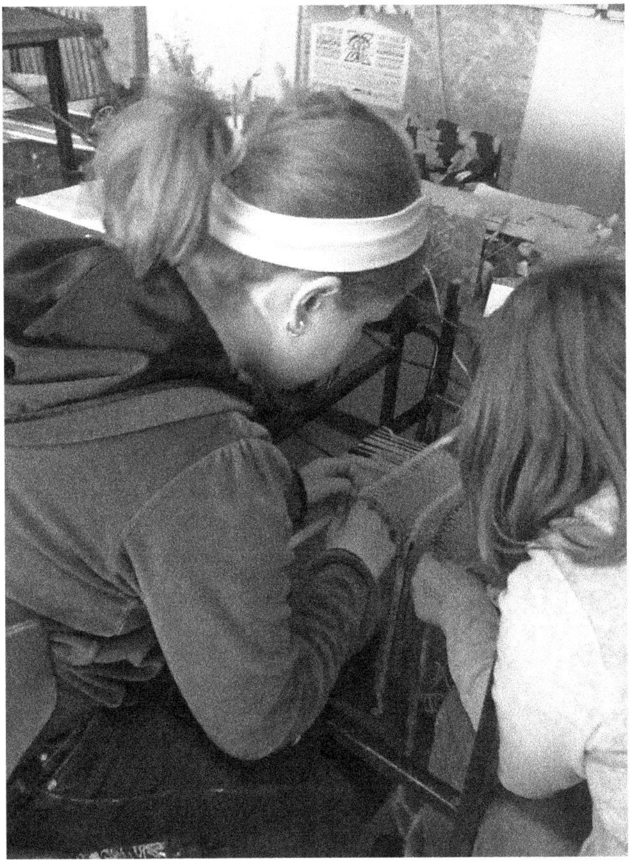

Fig. 6. The "Turquoise scarabs" team, Budapest. Weaving the satchel for the first round. © Hedvig Győry.

the questions, what are they?, how are they made?, what is their material?, what culture were they produced in?, who used them and how?, when were they used?, why were they used?, why people made them in the given shape?, in which situation was it fitting?, what is the significance?, what does it mean for us?, which other objects can we compare them to?, and how have they arrived to their present location? These are scholarly questions with appropriate answers. But are they really only scholarly questions? I think they are much more. Children can learn through them how to understand objects in general, and what Egyptian culture was like in particular. If it is made indirectly, via projects to complete, they become part of a person's life. Objects start to speak to people, to each one differently, according their previous experiences and knowledge. They act in different ways according to the socializations of groups, so it is very important in which directions the education offers the children to go.

The story in the "On the Field of Osiris" program is drawing the ancient Egyptian culture near to modern children. It gives a lively background to the objects and ideas characteristic at that time. Children can imagine themselves in the role of the characters there on one hand, and they preserve a cultural distance on the other. This time and space distance gives the possibility to stay objective, and consider the facts independently being in and out of the story at the same time. Similarities and diversities are striking, and ask for explanation and understanding. By this comparison, the cultural identity of the participants develops, and also the claim, at least to try, to understand why people have chosen such different ways to follow. This contrast urges them to think, to discuss the topic in the team, to find reasons and so develops the intellectual capability and empathy, and strengthens value judgment and tolerance for cultural diversity.

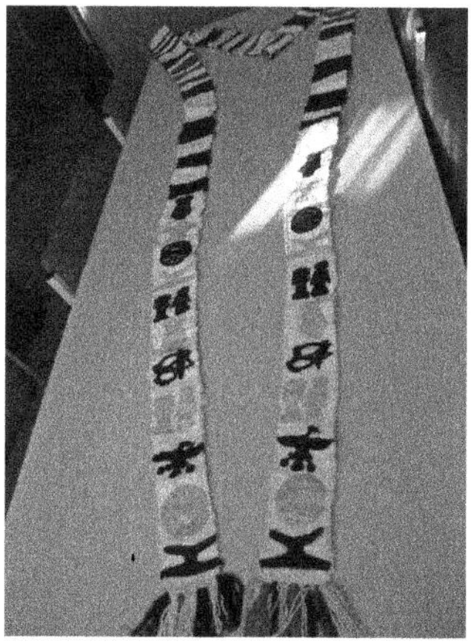

Fig. 7. The "Pleasure of the heart of Ra" team, Várpalota. Girdle woven and decorated with amuletic pattern for the third round. © Hedvig Győry.

To be able to create an original "Egyptian" work by writing, drawing, and preparing an object means collecting data concerning it, pondering them, and reflecting on the customs, abilities, organization of populations, and so on, of a given ancient society (fig. 9). Such activities bring with them, inevitably, a better understanding of this ancient culture, and the people living in it. If they read also from the extant texts, they even can "hear" their ideas. Beside the knowledge of data, however, personal experience is also very important. When people merely look at the objects, they easily underestimate the work involved in producing them; when they try to imitate the same objects, the approach to them changes drastically. By trial and error, new features appear, giving a more complete understanding of the objects, their producers, and the cultures that used them. At the same time, the children develop their mental and manual skills and learn where their limits in the various areas are.

As noted above, the program is designed for teams. In team work, people can stay passive or can work actively. The active participants admit the most impressions in their own world, but also passive participants can see many important elements, thinking them over and absorbing results that may activate them in various areas of their lives. Their personalities develop too, although more slowly because of the passivity. Trying new fields of activities, or imagining doing it, helps in self-recognition, which is important for each person. It helps build self-respect, without which the appreciation of other people and culture is unthinkable. Not valuing other people and their achievements leads to continuous fighting instead of living in peace. Thus

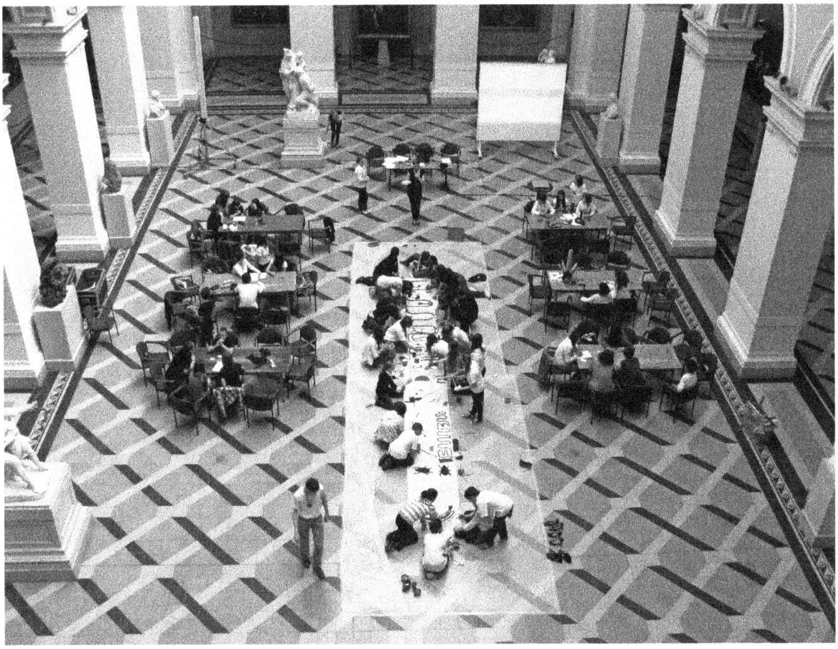

Fig. 8. The teams at work on the mythological papyrus. © Hedvig Győry.

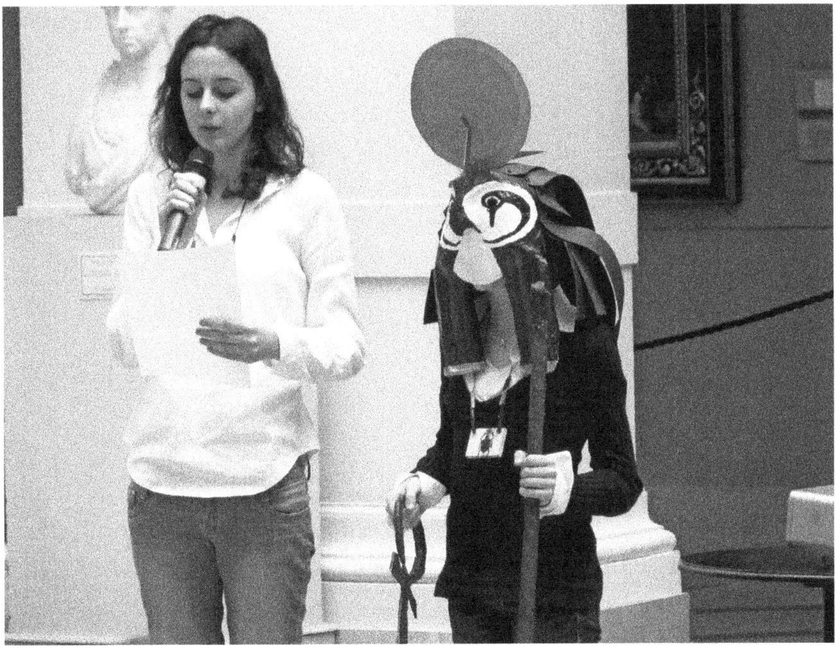

Fig. 9. Reading out the poem on Re composed at the final. © Hedvig Győry.

coming in closer contact in a positive way with the ancient Egyptian culture brings out a similar result as working in a group of people coming from different cultures. If the so-called contact-hypothesis is true, as experiments seem to back up, the better cultures understand each other, the better they find a common way to live together, develop tolerance, and appreciate each other and the material culture they created. The higher the level of education, the more people are receptive to universal cultural values, which include the responsibility felt for cultural heritage.

A Rescue from Oblivion

Paula Veiga

In 2006, while finishing my first masters in preclassical history and culture at the University of Lisbon, I was invited to be part of a team in Porto, in northern Portugal, to participate in the study of two Egyptian mummies in their collection.

I first saw the collection in 2005, and was amazed to discover that it included two Egyptian mummies; a male mummy with sarcophagus, and a female mummy in an advanced state of deterioration. This collection comprises 103 ancient Egyptian artifacts belonging to the University of Porto, including the female mummy, the object of this presentation, which is not exhibited in the new gallery, and which desperately awaits restoration.

Previously owned by the Egyptian Museum in Berlin,[1] this collection of ancient Egyptian artifacts was offered to Portugal in 1927as a gift to the Portuguese authorities after they returned a valuable collection of Assyrian artifacts to Germany. The *Cheruskia*, a 3,245-ton ship, arrived in Lisbon in 1914 en route between Iraq and Germany, carrying 448 crates of valuable Assyrian artifacts from pre-war German excavations.[2] The ship was interned in February 1916 (at British request), and then seized when Germany declared war on Portugal in March. The cargo was removed and stored; the ship was handed over to the British and sunk by a German submarine in 1918.

The collection offered to Portugal also included artifacts from Melanesia, now displayed in Portugal's Ethnology Museum. After World War I, not all were in favor of returning the artifacts to Germany. The British were interested in them, of course. A myriad of bureaucracy, documents, and contacts between Portugal, Germany, and the UK were generated during the years when the cargo was still in Portugal, and for some time after, as available in our archives; the details of the story are described in the catalogue produced for the Porto Egyptian Collection, at the University, where the Egyptian Gallery is located.

As no one in Portugal was qualified to identify or study the Assyrian artifacts, French specialists were invited to come and evaluate them.[3]

---

1. In the German documentation there was no mention of the Egyptian provenance of the items.
2. Die Ausgrabungen in Assur (1903–1914), Die Funde und ihre Odyssee, http://www.theologische-links.de/downloads/archaeologie/assur_andrae_funde.html.
3. Assyriologists Fancois Thureau-Dangin 1872 –1944 and Georges Contenau, 1877–1964.

After travelling from Iraq to Lisbon, the artifacts went to Porto. In 1921 the items were officially given to the University of Porto, arriving there in1922. After the return of the Assyrian artifacts to Germany, the gift collection of Egyptian artifacts was sent to Portugal in 1927[4] and it was divided in two sections;[5] one went to the Porto Faculty of Letters and, in 1940, it was moved to its present location, the Faculty of Sciences, more precisely the Anthropology Room.

In 1970, the collection was opened to the public. The collection had suffered relocation many times during which objects went missing with no accounting for what happened to them. Comparing the original German list and the existing collection, some artifacts are missing, including: a cartonnage coffin number 40 (perhaps belonging to the female mummy?); a calcite relief fragment Inv. ÄM 1135; seven scarabs numbers 3576, 3829, 3886, 3904, 4011, 5119, 5544; numerous amulets (*udjat* eye number 4270, heart 4761, *djed* pillar 6281, *uadj* papyrus 6467, Anubis 5543, Thot 5611, 5633, Ptah dwarf 5679, Bastet 5977, Isis with Horus child 8338); Padiamun officer statuette number 7736; and two wooden funerary ushabtys 8710. Other inconsistencies between the original list and the existing objects have been noted.

The other section of the Egyptian collection is housed in the Natural History Museum,[6] which was created in 1996. It includes several sections, among them the Mineralogy, Anthropology, Palaeontology, and Zoology Museums, which are presently closed for renovations after a fire in 2008.

The Two Mummies in the Egyptian Collection

Two human mummies, dated probably from the Late period or Greco-Roman period, came along with this gift collection. They are a male mummy, completely wrapped, and now displayed in the new exhibition gallery, and a female mummy, completely unwrapped. The female mummy's coffin is missing, although the coffin is mentioned on the original list, and it is identified by the same number 40. The male mummy's inventory number is 8504, and his coffin is number 8503.

Both mummies underwent an initial conservation procedure in 1981–1982, in Lisbon, at the Conservation Institute. The female mummy, in the midst of its' associated debris, is poorly displayed in a wooden box.[7] Here I will focuse on the deterioration of the female mummy.

At the time of these first preservation procedures, the female mummy was laid down on a straw mattress, much degraded from insect and rodent action; even a live mouse was found with it. New support to the head and major articulations was inserted after cleaning, and a new box was manufactured. The interior of the box was lined with Styrofoam, and protected with Melinex film. Plastic pouches were placed

4. Cunha 2006, 235.
5. Murta 2012, 832.
6. http://sigarra.up.pt/reitoria/pt/NOTICIAS_GERAL.VER_NOTICIA?P_NR=1283.
7. Murta 2012, 833.

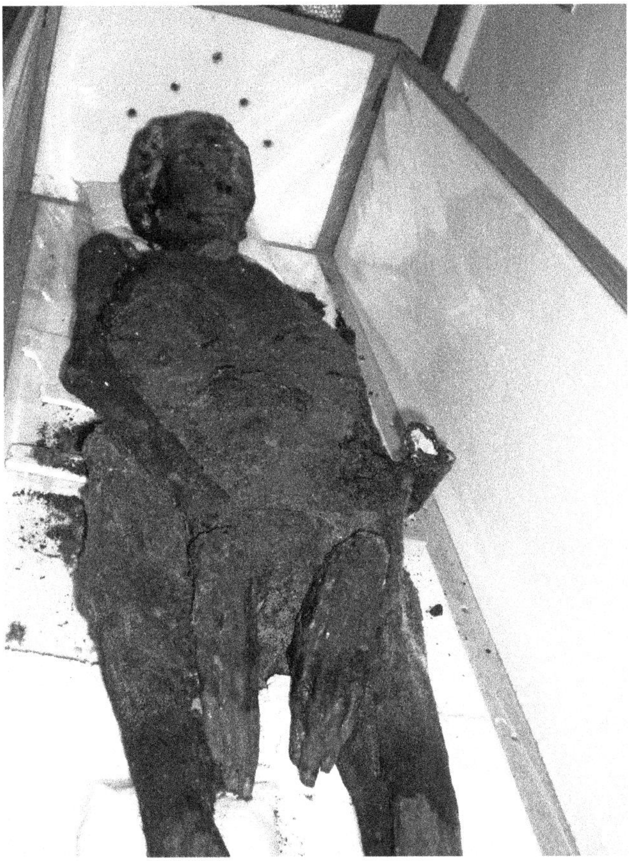

Fig. 1. Female mummy in advanced state of decomposition, mainly caused by fungi, needing urgent conservation. University of Porto. Inv. ÄM40/03 - FCP 41.01.100. © Paula Veiga.

in spaces, against sudden movement damage, as the mummy would have to travel back to Porto. Box and mummy were sterilized with ethylene oxide.[8]

The retrieval of data from the female mummy was completed on 23 February 2010 (figs. 1–3). I was present at this procedure and below I summarize my notes.

The testing was conducted at CUF Porto Institute,[9] with the assistance of a dental surgeon and a radiologist. Looking at the screens, our attention was drawn to the excessive wear and tear on her teeth. This is an ordinary finding in ancient Egyptian human remains, caused by the diet, outdoor activities, and the way they cooked food while they lived. She appeared to have the constitution of a young adult, but the teeth

8. Murta 2012, 833–4. Ethylene Oxide (EtO) sterilization is mainly used to sterilize products that cannot support conventional high temperature steam sterilization.

9. R. Fonte das Sete Bicas, 170,4460–188 Senhora da Hora, http://www.cufportoinstituto.pt/.

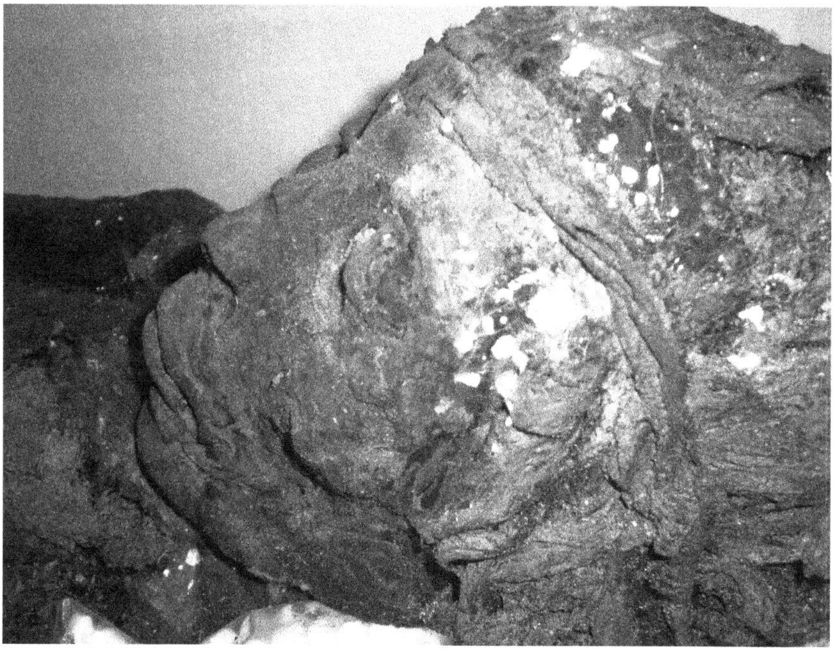

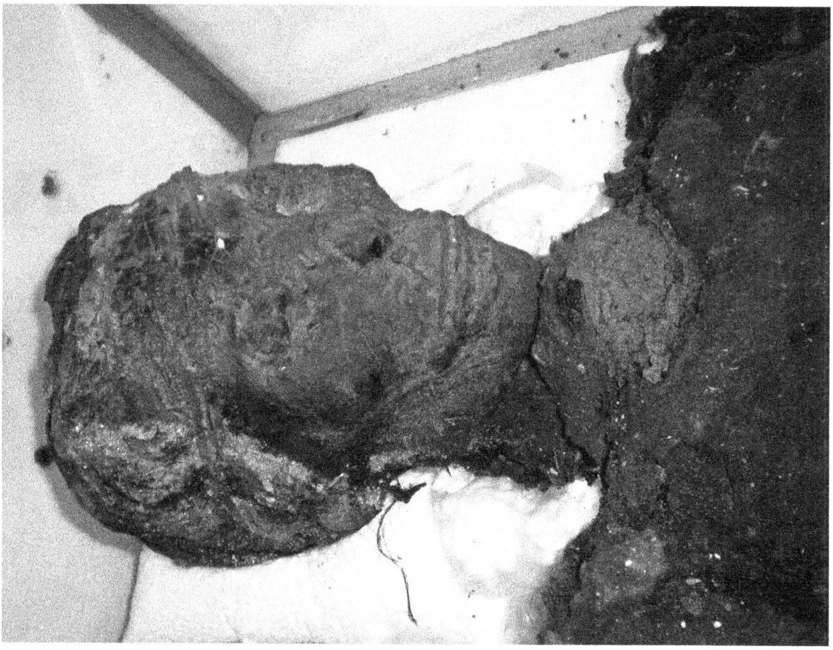

Figs. 2 and 3. Female mummy detail showing fungi activity. University of Porto. Inv. ÄM40/03 - FCP 41.01.100. Photos © Paula Veiga.

of someone at least ten years older. Looking at her body, the mummy also showed signs of stress marks on the atlas, and we discussed whether she might have carried weights on her head.

Our mummy did have evidence of trauma in the 5th and 6th cervical vertebrae, and three lumbar vertebrae showed trauma resulting from the impact of a perforating object and a cutting object. These injuries did not seem to have killed her, and were probably inflicted after her death. Any of the following might have caused the injury: a mummification error trying to cut the body to perform cleansing and filling actions; sometime after the burial, a robber looking for jewelry in the thoracic/pelvic areas, who tried to extract amulets and gemstones, piercing the body and causing the damage seen on the vertebrae; the body was mishandled while still in Egypt, perhaps while changing sarcophagi, or moving from the tomb to the market/seller/warehouse; the body was damaged in Germany while moving the mummy as she has no case and we are not sure how she arrived in Portugal, perhaps only in a simple wooden box.

To Conserve or Not to Conserve

In the museum gallery where the mummy was previously displayed, ideal conditions for its preservation were not met, thus it needed preservation procedures (done in 1981–1982). Its present location is a room serving as a provisional warehouse, with inadequate humidity, air circulation, and light levels. The mummy shares the space with other artifacts in conditions providing the perfect environment for fungal spores to proliferate. The damage can be seen with the naked eye.

Human remains have to be stored according to specified requirements. Certain techniques must be employed.[10] From my observations, conservation procedures are urgent. Dehumidifiers are essential to prevent the decay of mummy cases, as well as the human remains they contain. Those are not present in the room. Rebandaging or rewrapping is another option. But nothing has been done to restore and preserve this body.

The mummy is displayed in a physically correct position with minimum stress to its joints, but the supports are missing that would prolong its display life without damage. Foam beds, like the ones used for the Manchester Museum mummies are also recommended. Presently, the mummy is simply laid inside a box with some small pieces of Styrofoam known to have been placed there during the preservation procedures of 1981–82. Mortuary-type trolleys would be ideal to move around the mummy to store it in a more convenient place; the problem is that no other place exists.

Skulls and other body fragments must be supported and paper or other base tissue must be replaced periodically. In this case no supports are to be found accommodating this body, nor is any cover set over it to protect it from further damage and dirt.

10. David 1995.

Humidity must be controlled inside the case no higher than 25 percent. The required conditions are not observed in this room as it is simply an office room annex to the curator's office.

Nothing has been published yet because the university does not have funds to do it, nor has it allowed the Egyptologists who contributed to the project to publish their findings with another institution.

The Fire

Before the new gallery was organized in September 2011, and after the fire in May 2008, which caused some water damage,[11] the Egyptian collection was inadequately stored in a room next to the museum curator's office where the objects remained until my last visit. The items not chosen to be displayed in the new gallery are still in this room. I had the chance to see how the pieces were displayed in the new, but too small, exhibition gallery. A choice was made to display only the "good stuff"; most of the collection is still wrapped up in plastic and stored inappropriately.

The director of the Conservation Institute that did some work on the mummies in 1981–1982, told me at the 2010 Iberian Egyptology conference that they would conserve the objects for free again; it is just a question of protocols between the institutions. To my knowledge, no one from the University Museum showed any interest in contacting the conservators.

The new Egyptian gallery was opened last 22 September 2011 displaying a small number of the objects. Most of the collection is still in storage in the office room. The choice of artifacts was made according to their "sexiness." Objects needing restoration, such as the female mummy, were not chosen to be displayed.

The gallery is inadequate, in my opinion. An effort to conserve more objects and a different approach to the public should have been considered. I reiterate this as I heard some of the public visitors on the day of the opening complaining about the room being too small and too dark, to enable good object observation. I believe that the rest of the artifacts in the Egyptian collection are still packed and stashed in the office room and will not be displayed in the near future.[12]

The choice of artifacts to display was conducted in a nontransparent manner by the administration. The lack of interest by the university to sign protocols with other public entities reflects the general lack of interest of our public officials towards antiquities.

References

CUNHA M. J., and R. F. SOUSA. 2006. "A Colecção de Antiguidades Egípcias do Museu de História Natural da Universidade do Porto." *Revista da Faculdade de Letras*, Porto, III Série 7, 235–41.

11. News video about the fire: http://youtu.be/cBfJyKn-WMw.
12. I have written to the director of the museum and received no answer whatsoever.

David A. 1995. *Care and Conservation of Palaeontological Material*. Butterworth-Heinemann Series in Conservation & Museology. Boston: Butterworth-Heinemann.

Murta E. 2012. "Experiência de Egiptologia no Instituto de José de Figueiredo: sarcófago, múmias e máscaras." Pp. 831–40 in *Novos Trabalhos de Egiptologia Ibérica, IV Congresso Ibérico de Egiptologia*, II. Lisbon: Instituto Oriental. Centro de Historia da Faculdade de letras da universidade de Lisboa.

Veiga P. 2012. "Studying Mummies and Human Remains: Some Current Developments and Issues." *Journal of the Washington Academy of Sciences* Summer 2012, 1–22.

Graywacke: A Case Study for the Accurate Use of Appropriate Stone Terminology

Simone Burger Robin

The following article addresses the issue of the use of geological terminology for stone types and materials in the cataloging systems of museum collections, highlighting the problematic issue of the term graywacke.[1] This article is based on a presentation at the CIPEG conference in September 2012 addressing collections at risk. The question of appropriate cataloguing and labeling terminology in museums, catalogues and online publication of collections is still a concern in ancient Egyptian studies. It is a question that concerns the amount and dissemination of ancient Egyptian objects in museums and collections around the world. The case study of graywacke presented below underlines the problems with terminology in cataloging Egyptian, and for that matter all, antiquities. The variation in vocabulary regarding stone types is alarming at times, causing confusion, inaccurate statistics of objects and even hindering the potential of matching separated fragments. The case will be made that a more accurate assessment of materials and proper terminology should be put in place, taking the opportunity of updating information as more materials become accessible online.

When using published or online materials, there is a surprising lack of consistency with regard to the use of geological terms for stone types and materials. The specific case to be addressed here regards graywacke, but can be extended to other stone types and questions, such as calcite, marble, and the sometimes the slight variations between red and pink granite as well as black and gray granite.

Graywacke was quarried almost exclusively in the Wadi Hammamat in ancient Egypt. The stone was known as *becken* in ancient Egyptian.[2] Quarrying activity for graywacke in this area is documented through inscriptions in the quarry itself from

1. I would like to thank Professor Claire Derriks for the opportunity to give a presentation at the CIPEG meeting in September 2012. In addition, I would also like to offer thanks to Luc Delvaux of the Royal Museum of Art and History in Brussels for facilitating my study of MRAH Inv. E.6660 and offering helpful advice.

2. Andrew 1939, 153–90; Lucas 1939, 127–56; Shiah 1942, 189–205; De Putter and Karlshausen 1992, 87–88; Klemm and Klemm 2008, 297–314.

Dynasty 4 to 238 CE[3]. The quarries were likely exploited earlier than Dynasty 4. There are numerous Predynastic and Early Dynastic objects in graywacke that bear witness to the exploitation of these quarries earlier than the inscriptions attest. Graywacke was used in objects from ancient Egypt, from the palettes and vessels to statuary and architectural elements. It is sometimes abandoned as a stone choice during certain reigns and dynasties; while at other times used extensively and even exclusively for certain types of iconography.[4] The periodic use of this stone in ancient Egypt is a subject unto itself. It is fascinating to know and perhaps have a deeper understanding of why this relatively soft stone is used in some of the most important objects known from ancient Egypt.

In the literature, we find that there is a distinct confusion when reference is made to this stone. Terminology varies from siltstone to mudstone, schist, green schist, gray schist, slate, green, gray or black stone and on occasion simply hard stone.[5] Some of these terms are geologically incorrect, such as schist. Others, such as siltstone, are too broad and encompass other stone variations.[6] Terms such as green, gray, black or hard stone do not provide enough information. Thus, any black- or dark-colored, finely grained stone has the potential of being an object in graywacke. The subject at hand is not simply to use correct terminology for the sake of accuracy. The issue consists of having a clearer idea on the use of graywacke, the amounts of objects in this stone during certain periods in ancient Egypt and eventually bringing together, at least theoretically, objects that have been separated over time. The correct term in cataloging would provide information and data to bring about these possibilities.

An example that illustrates this topic is a fragment of a statue head in graywacke, measuring 13.5 cm in height, Musées royaux d'Art et d'Histoire, Bruxelles (MRAH) Inv. E.6660 (fig. 1).[7] The head is quite damaged and a large portion is missing. Yet, there are enough remaining details that offer quite a bit of information. The fragment consists of a royal head wearing the remains of a *nemes* headdress. The face is clearly Thutmoside, a term used for certain examples of statuary that date from the reign of Thutmose III and/or Hatshepsut through the end of Dynasty 26.[8] From the profile, there are the traces of a small portion of stone that extends from the top of

3. Klemm and Klemm 2008, 299.

4. For example, we find graywacke used exclusively for theophoric statue groups in Dynasty 20, from the reign of Ramesses IV through Ramesses XI.

5. The variations terminology can be found in online museum catalogues. First, by beginning with an object known to be graywacke, such as the triad of King Menkaura, the goddess Hathor and the deified Hare nome, Boston MFA Inv. 09.200 or Thutmose III striding from the Karnak Cachette, Luxor, Egyptian Museum Inv. J.2 (corresponding to Cairo CG 45054), and then continuing on to those objects that are likely to be graywacke.

6. Klemm and Klemm 2008, 299. Siltstone can also refer to olivine and breccia verde, for example.

7. Werbrouck 1934, pl. 18 ; Tefnin 1988, 48–49 ; Lefebvre and Van Rinsveld 1990, 126 ; *Global Egyptian Museum*, www.globalegyptianmuseum.org, international inventory number 07/003/1086 and MRAH Inv. E.6660. Listed as purchased in Paris in 1932 from the Pratt Collection.

8. Fazzini 1997, 114–15 ; Lurson 1998, 66–69 ; Russman 2005, 23.

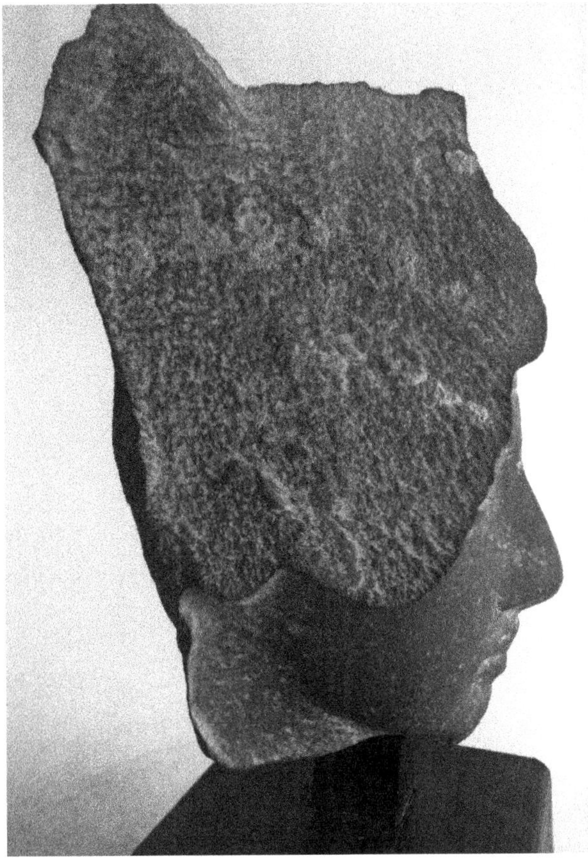

Fig. 1. Fragment of a statue head. Musées royaux d'Art et d'Histoire, Bruxelles. Inv. E.6660. © Simone Burger Robin.

the head. This detail is probably evidence of an additional crown, most likely a double crown.[9] The proper left side of the face has a more complete eye area, consisting of an almond-shaped eye with a dipped inner canthus. There is a heavy upper eye lid line and kohl line. This kohl line extends outwards to the break line. The eyebrow, which is modeled and outlined by a thinly inscribed line follows the natural curve of the brown and then slants downwards to parallel the cosmetic line. The nose has a smoothly rounded tip, and the cheeks are rather full. The mouth consists of an upper and lower lip, outlined with a lip line and having a marked philtrum. A portion of the *uraeus* is still visible, consisting of a trace of the frontal mass of the head of the snake and a horizontal looping detail. The *nemes* is striated with lines etched into the stone surface somewhat crudely. The striation contrasts with general technical quality of the treatment of the face. The bans of the striation form a pattern of one thicker band and one thinner band.

Not every king or reign appears to have used graywacke. The use or not of

9. I would like to thank Luc Delvaux for pointing out this important detail.

graywacke does not necessarily signal a prohibition to using this stone, but probably reflects contemporary tastes and availability of certain stone types in different periods and reigns. Thus, the question regarding the original owner of MRAH Inv. E.6660 depends on assessing which king used graywacke as a statue material, favored Thutmoside features and was portrayed with a *nemes* and double crown. Once these three elements have been established, the list of potential identities narrows significantly to Ramesses II, Ramesses IV, Ramesses VI, and Ramesses IX.

Of the early and later Ramesside kings listed above, all four used graywacke in their royal statuary. Three out of the four, Ramesses II, Ramesses IV, and Ramesses IX, used Thutmoside traits, and two out of the four, Ramesses II and Ramesses VI, used a double crown in his imagery. Thus, the one king who used all three elements that we find on the fragment in Brussels is Ramesses II.[10]

The use of proper geological terminology is of great importance when searching for comparative examples. The standardized use of graywacke as a stone choice quickly becomes an issue. There are numerous catalogues in print and online where the variation in terminology regarding this stone choice is alarming. Much of this confusion can be traced to the original catalogue, when and where stone choice was not always a central issue. However, with time and conversion to online accessibility, mistakes and misnomers have yet to be corrected and changed. Modern cataloguing methodology stresses minute accuracy. The relative general inconsistency is surprising and potentially time consuming and expensive to remedy. However, it is not impossible or insurmountable as a problem, especially with electronic resources. When looking for potential comparative materials to MRAH Inv. E.6660, the search must be extended well beyond graywacke and encompass all the stone types described above as well as extending it as far as gray and black granites. The search, as a result, unnecessarily goes from very large to massive.

Initially, the fragment had the potential to date from any king from Thutmose III/ Hatshepsut through the end of Dynasty 26. The treatment and shape of the eyes does not have much in common with other examples of Thutmose III graywacke statuary. Based upon comparisons, this fragment cannot date to the reign of Thutmose III. There are few if any documented graywacke statues that date to the reign of Hatshepsut, and this eliminating Hatshepsut as a potential date. Through stylistic analysis, the understanding of New Kingdom iconography and the known use of graywacke as a stone choice, the most likely candidates for dating can be narrowed down to the reigns of Ramesses II through the end of Dynasty 20. Initially, this fragment had the

10. There is a smaller, additional detail concerning the looping of the body of the uraeus. This, too, appears to be an element that could aid in identification. On MRAH Inv. E.6660, there is a small section of the looping body of the uraeus to the proper left side of this element. We find this iconographic detail in the statues of Ramesses II and Ramesses VI. We do not see it on Ramesses IV statues. However, there are less than a handful of Ramesses IV and Ramesses IX heads that are known today. There are simply not enough examples to determine if this uraeus detail is a defining element of Ramesses IV and Ramesses IX iconography.

potential to date to the reign of Ramesses IV, which would have increased the number of known Ramesses IV heads in graywacke significantly. However, after comparing this fragment example to works that date from the reigns of Ramesses IV and VI, it is clear that this fragment head does not date to either reign. Small details such as the treatment of the cosmetic eyebrow and looping of the proper left side of the *uraeus* do not match with examples of late Ramesside statuary. Furthermore, Ramesses VI is not a possible identification for the Brussels fragment. There are known graywacke statues that date to his reign, and he is shown in a *nemes* and double-crown.[11] However, they do not demonstrate a strong Thutmoside stylistic tendency. As a result, Ramesses VI appears not to be a possible date for the Brussels fragment.

The last Ramesside king who has graywacke statuary is Ramesses IX. There is one graywacke statuette showing the king prostrate.[12] There are only four known examples of Ramesses IX statuary, none of which demonstrate any shared stylistic traits or iconographic affinities with the Brussels fragment. Ramesses IX, thus, does not seem to be a likely date for MRAH Inv. E.6660.

Thus, once the list of potential owners for MRAH Inv. E.6660 has been limited to Ramesses II, the question must be asked as to whether or not there are any known comparable statues or fragments that compare to the Brussels fragment. With graywacke as a key element, the following statues in Cairo were identified as either being comparable or even potential mates to the fragment: JE 37980, CG 42140, CG 42141, CG 42144, and CG 45028. All of these statues are moderately scaled, graywacke of Ramesses II and originate from Karnak. They offer a rich trove of comparative materials for MRAH Inv. E.6660. They share similarities such as rather moderate dimensions, with JE 37980 and JE 45028, standing or seated fragments not surpassing 78 cm in height. There are differences in the details of their iconography and manufacture. They do not appear to be the work of one craftsman, artisan, or perhaps workshop. They all demonstrate clear Thutmoside traits: the rounded face, the curved nose and in some cases the treatment of the eye area.

These statues have been the subject of certain studies, as they are referred to in passing in several important articles. In particular, JE 45028 was discussed by Hourig Sourouzian in an article discussing *raccords*.[13] However, there has never been a specific study of this group of statues, to which we may add MRAH Inv. E.6660, based on stone type, dimension, treatment of the eye area, as well as the *nemes*. On the *nemes*,

11. Legrain 1906, 19–20, pl. XVI; Seele 1960, 200–201; Monnet 1963, 220–26; Kitchen 1969–1983, 286 (line 15)–287 (line 7); Murnane 1971–1972, 129–30; Wente 1973, 230–32; Kitchen 1982, 124 (as Ramesses V); Bryan 1987, 16 (attributed to Ramesses VI); Mysliwiec 1992, 98; Dodson 1997, 36 (as Ramesses V) ; Sist 1997, 186; Dodson and Hilton 2004, 189; Coulon and Jambon, Cachette de Karnak 2012: http://www.ifao.egnet.net/bases/cachette/?id=262.

12. Matthiew 1930, 31–32; Aldred 1955, 3–8; Vandier 1958, 631; Swann Hall 1968, 168; Kitchen VI, 1969–1983, 449, 10–15; Grimal 1986, 160; Fazzini 1994, 114; Malek 2012, 74 (listed as probably from Heliopolis).

13. Sourouzian 1998, 287–88.

which included the head band along the forehead, the striations include a pattern of one thicker band alternating with one thinner band. The bands are scratched or etched into the stone surface, as opposed to sanded, flattened strips alternating with more highly polished raised areas. The remains of the proper left *uraeus* loop are all still visible.

There are three statues from the Karnak Cachette that date to the time of Ramesses II that today are headless, namely, JE 37980, CG 42140 and JE 45028, and are potential candidates for a match or *raccord*. Statue CG 42140 offers an interesting possibility.[14] This statue fragment resembles quite closely in its iconography the well-known image of Ramesses II now in Turin (Turin 1380): the proper right-hand holding of the *hequa* scepter, with the left hand resting on the knee, the pleated ceremonial robe, and sandals on the feet. However, there is one major difference in the headdress. The Turin example wears the blue crown whereas here Ramesses II clearly has the proper left lappet of a *nemes* flap. The question one might pose is do we have other examples of the combination of a double-crown with the *hequa* and pleated robe. In 1995, Suzanne Bickel discussed this type of iconography in an article concerning a Late period royal statue and created a list of this type of seated statue with *hequa*.[15] There are no known examples that wear a double crown in her list. Thus, it would be tempting to match the MRAH Inv. E.6660 with this statue, but more iconographic study needs to be done.

Another potential match is JE 37980.[16] The break lines on this statue are temptingly close to the break lines on MRAH Inv. E.6660. However, as much as one would have liked to match these based upon the similarity of the shape of the break area to the form of the Brussels fragment, the statue clearly does not have the remains of a double crown. In addition, the height of the statue—27 cm—is too small for the 13.5 cm high fragment to fit.

A third possibility is JE 45028, which may be the best potential match.[17] Once again we find Ramesses II, this time in a striding position, wearing sandals, holding a scepter in his proper right hand. We see the clear remains of a *nemes* head dress. The upper portion of the head is missing. The proportions are correct. The head fragment matches the overall size of the statue. However, there is one troubling aspect: MRAH Inv. E.6660 has the remains of what looks to be a double-crown element, or an additional extension of the *nemes*. Would a combination of long ceremonial robe, scepter, striding statue have a double crown? There are innovations in royal iconography during the reign of Ramesses II, although not much has of yet been published. What

14. Kitchen VI, 1969–1979, 586; Chevereau 1994, 10; Sourouzian 1994, 503 and Coulon and Jambon, Cachette de Karnak: http://www.ifao.egnet.net/bases/cachette/?id=25.

15. Bickel 1995, 93–102.

16. Verbovsek 2002, 345 and Coulon and Jambon 2012, Cachette de Karnak: http://www.ifao.egnet.net/bases/cachette/?id=492.

17. Sourouzian 2002, 407 and Coulon and Jambon, 2012, http://www.ifao.egnet.net/bases/cachette/?id=1214.

might be a possibility is that the upper, broken extension of MRAH Inv. E.6660 was not a double crown but perhaps the base of a different type of headdress extension.

MRAH Inv. E.6660 might have also come from a now lost graywacke statue of Ramesses II that may have had a more tradition double-crown iconographic combination of elements. However, without any additional evidence, this remains speculation. With the amount of statues that compare to the Brussels fragment, Ramesses II appears to be the only possible date for this object. In addition, since the other known examples of small to moderately-sized Ramesses II graywacke statuary all come from Karnak Temple, we may also conclude that the fragment too may have likely originated from that site.

The study of MRAH Inv. E.6660 brings to light the problems associated with the use of inaccurate terminology in cataloging. A variety of names used for the same stone coming from the same quarry area makes the subject unnecessarily complicated. Moreover, it also points to an underlying problem of a lack of precision in many published and online museum catalogues and other publications. The confusion this produces impedes the goal of creating precise cataloguing structures as well as opportunities for new *raccords* or matches. As extensive as the problem is today, it is one that can be improved with some effort, particularly as institutions take advantage of the changeover to electronic cataloging resources.

References

ALDRED, A. 1955. "A Statue of King Neferkare' Ramesses IX." *JEA* 41, 3–8.

ANDREW, G. 1939. "The Greywackes of the Eastern Desert of Egypt." *BIE* 21, 153–90.

BICKEL, S. 1995. "La statue d'un roi Psammétique reconstituée." *BIFAO* 95, 93–102.

BRYAN, B. M. 1987. "Portrait Sculpture of Thutmose IV." *JARCE* 24, 3–20.

CHEVEREAU, P. M. 1994. *Prosopographie des cadres militaires égyptiens du Nouvel Empire*. Antony, France: P.-M. Chevereau.

COULON, L. and E. JAMBON. 2012. *Cachette de Karnak*, http://www.ifao.egnet.net.

DODSON, A. 1997. "The Sons of Ramesses III." *KMT* 8.1, 29–43.

DODSON, A. and HILTON D. 2004. *The Complete Royal Families of Ancient Egypt*. London: Thames & Hudson.

FAZZINI, R. 1994. "Several Objects and Some Aspects of the Art of the Third Intermediate Period." Pp. 113–37 in E. GORING, N. REEVES, and J. RUFFLE (eds.), *Chief of Seers, Egyptian Studies in Memory of Cyril Aldred*. London: Kegan Paul International.

GRIMAL, N. 1986. *Les termes de la propagande royale égyptienne, de la XIXe Dynastie à la conquête d'Alexandre*. Mémoires de l'Académie des Inscriptions et Belles-Lettres, Nouvelle Série 6. Paris: de Boccard.

KITCHEN, K. A. 1969–1983. *Ramesside Inscriptions*, vol. 6. Oxford: British Museum Press.

KITCHEN, K. A. 1982. "The Twentieth Dynasty Revisited." *JEA* 68, 116–25.

KLEMM, R., and D. KLEMM. 2008. *Stones and Quarries in Ancient Egypt*. London: Blackwell.

LEFEBVRE, F., and B. VAN RINSVELD. 1990. *L'Égypte: Des Pharaons aux Coptes*. Brussels: Service éducatif, Musées royaux d'art et d'histoire.

LEGRAIN, G. 1906. *Statues et statuettes des rois et particuliers*. Catalogue de Musée du Caire 2. Cairo: Imprimerie de l'Institut français d'archéologie orientale..

LUCAS, A. R. 1938. "The Ancient Egyptian bekhenstone." *ASAE* 38, 127–56.

LURSON, B. 1998. "Les gestes de culte dans les statuaires royales égyptiennes et mésopotamiennes (fin IIIe – fin IIe millénaires): éléments d'une étude comparée." Pp. 57–76 in C. CANNUYER, J. RIES, and A. VON TONGERLOO (eds.), *Les voyages dans les civilisations orientales*. Acta Orientalia Belgica 11. Brussels: Société belge d'études orientales.

MALEK, J. 2012. *Topographical Bibliography of Ancient Egyptian Hieroglyphic Texts, Statues, Reliefs and Paintings VIII: Objects of Provenance Not Known*, Oxford: Griffith Institute, Ashmolean Museum.

MATTHIEW, M. 1930. "A Note on the Coronation Rites in Ancient Egypt." *JEA* 16, 31–32.

MONNET, J. 1963. "Remarques sur la famille et les successions de Ramsès III." *BIFAO* 63, 209–36.

MURNANE, Jr. W. J. 1971–1972. "The 'King Ramesses' of the Medinet Habu Procession of Princes." *JARCE* 9, 121–31.

MYSLIWIEC, K. 1992. "Une statue groupe en haut-relief de Ramsès IV." Pp. 89–100 in J. OSSING and E. K. NIELSEN (eds.), *The Heritage of Ancient Egypt, Studies in Honour of Erik Iversen*. Copenhagen: Carsten Niebuhr Institute.

DE PUTTER, T., and C. KARLSHAUSEN. 1992. *Les pierres utilisées dans la sculpture et l'architecture de l'Égypte pharaonique. Guide pratique illustré*, Brussels (*Connaissance de l'Égypte Ancien*). Brussels: Connaissance de l'Egypte.

RUSSMANN, E. R. 2005. "Art in Transition, the Rise of the Eighteenth Dynasty and the Emergence of the Thutmoside Style in Sculpture and Relief." Pp. 23–27 in C. ROEHRIG, R. DREYFUS, and C. HELLER (eds.), *Hatshepsut, from Queen to Pharaoh*. New York: Metropolitan Museum of Art.

SEELE, K. C. 1960. "Ramesses VI and the Medinet Procession of the Princes." *JNES* 19, 184–204.

SHIAH, N. 1942. "Some remarks on the bekenstone." *ASAE* 41, 189–205.

SIST, L. 1997. "Riflessi sociali nella statuaria ramesside." Pp. 172–93 in Anonymous (ed.), *L'Impero ramesside, Convegno internazionale in onore di Sergio Donadoni*. Rome: Dip. de Scienze Storiche Archeologiche e Antropologiche dell'Antichita.

SOUROUZIAN, H. 1994. "Inventaire iconographique des statues en manteau jubilaire de l'Époque thinite jusqu'à leur disparition sous Amenhotep III." Pp. 499–530 in C. BERGER, G. CLERC and N. GRIMAL (eds.), *Hommages à Jean Leclant*. Vol. 1: *Études pharaoniques*. Bibliothèque d'étude 106. Cairo: Institut français d'archéologie orientale.

———. 1998. "RACCORDS RAMESSIDES." *MDAIK* 54, 279–92.

———. 2002. "Conservation of Statuary." Pp. 39–41 in Z. HAWASS and L. BROCK (eds.), *Egyptology at the Dawn of the Twenty-First Century: Proceedings of the Eighth International Congress of Egyptologists, Cairo, 2000*, vol. 3. Cairo and New York: American University in Cairo Press.

SWANN HALL, E. 1968. "Some Ancient Egyptian Sculpture in British Collections." *Apollo* 87 (73), 160–69.

TEFNIN, R. 1988. *Sculptuur van het Oude Egypte: Statues et statuettes de l'Ancienne Égypte*, Brussels: Musées royaux d'art et d'histoire.

VANDIER, J. 1958. *Manuel d'archéologie égyptienne*. Vol. 3: *Les grandes époques, La statuaire*, Paris: Picard.

VERBOVSEK, A. 2002. "Motiv und Typus der sogenannten Hyksosmonumente: ein neuer methodischer Ansatz zur Untersuchung altägyptischer Rundbilder." *SAK* 30, 305–50.

WENTE, E. F. 1973. "A Prince's Tomb in the Valley of the Kings." *JNES* 32, 223–34.

WERBROUCK, M. 1934. *Musées Royaux d'Art et d'Histoire, Bruxelles, Département égyptien, Album*. Brussels: Musées royaux d'art et d'histoire.

II. Collections, History, and Renovation

Sarah Belzoni and Her Mummy: Notes on the Early History of the Egyptian Collection in Brussels

Eugène Warmenbol

Giovanni Battista Belzoni and his wife[1] Sarah stayed in Egypt for four years, from 1815 to 1819, and his feats became legendary during his lifetime. He opened the Second Pyramid at Giza and the rock-hewn temple of Abu Simbel; he found the royal tombs of Ay, Ramesses I, and Sethy I in the Biban el-Melek. This last discovery, especially, as the king's alabaster sarcophagus was still in it's place, reached and fascinated the larger public, much in the same fashion as the discovery of Tutankhamun's tomb made Howard Carter famous.[2]

On Giovanni Belzoni's return, he published, in 1820, his *Narrative of the Operations and Recent Discoveries within the Pyramids, Temples, Tombs, and Excavations, in Egypt and Nubia*, which is (in the manner of the time) as much a travelogue as an excavation report, and he exhibited, in 1821, in the Piccadilly "Egyptian Hall," a commercial exhibition hall, with an Egyptian-style façade,[3] a plaster reproduction of part of Seti's tomb, based on wax casts made there, together with a complete scale reproduction of the tomb, composed of watercolor paintings on a cloth backing. His book was translated into French as early as 1821, and published as *Voyages, recherches et*

A first version of this paper (in French) appeared online after the *Encounters with Ancient Egypt* at the Institute of Archaeology, University College London. The text was read on the 18th of December 2000 during the session Perspectives on Ancient Egypt since Napoleon. A second version (also in French) was published as chapter 9, entitled "Sarah Belzoni et sa momie" in Warmenbol 2012, 217–40 (with nine illustrations). Since then, we have learned a lot about Sarah and her husband through fruitful contacts with John J. Taylor and Anna Baghiani of the Société Jersiaise in Jersey, and, in the aftermath of the 29th CIPEG Annual Meeting in Brussels, with Beatrix Gessler-Löhr (Heidelberg) and, especially, Marco Zatterin (Brussels), who has published an important monograph on Gianbattista Belzoni and who is a major collector of "Belzoniana." Aidan Dodson (Bristol) read our manuscript and weeded it out.

1. One of our correspondents in Jersey, John Taylor, recently discovered a document dated 1804 and signed Giovanni Bolzon in which he declares his intention to marry Sarah Parker-Brown. "Bolzon" is the original, Venetian, spelling of Giovanni's name, which he Italianized to "Belzoni" early in his life.
2. As stated by Christophe 1979, 6. Gessler-Löhr 2013 recently showed he is not, strictly speaking, the discoverer of the tomb.
3. See Werner 2003, 82–86, 100–104.

découvertes en Egypte et en Nubie; the exhibition was shown in Paris, at the Boulevard des Italiens at the end of 1822, and remained there until the end of 1824.[4]

The "strong man Egyptologist," however, died of dysentery early in December 1823, on his way to Timbuktu, looking for the sources of the Niger, those of the Nile remaining elusive.

We will not attempt here to add to the biography or bibliography of Giovanni Belzoni (1778–1823) himself, which is already very rich,[5] but will look at those of his wife Sarah Parker-Brown[6] (1783–1870), who was also a remarkable figure. She lived in Brussels from 1833 to 1857, and this was of some consequence to the collections des Musées Royaux d'Art et d'Histoire, which acquired their first mummy through her.

The Padua Giant

The popularity of the "Padua giant," a nickname the Venetian adventurer owed to his tall stature, can be measured, among other things, by the fact that his "adventures" had already been romanticized in a booklet for youngsters in 1821. This is entitled *Fruits of Enterprize Exhibited in the Travels of Belzoni in Egypt and Nubia; Interspersed with the Observations of a Mother to Her Children,*[7] wherein his "enterprise," so typical of Georgian Britain, is given as an example to follow (fig. 1). A French translation, *L'Egypte et la Nubie ou curiosités de ces pays, tirées du voyage de Belzoni (traduit de l'anglais par M. ***, et orné de jolies gravures)*, appeared in 1823.[8] In the Netherlands, the weekly *La Récompense*, aimed at a youthful readership, published a life of Belzoni in 1829,[9] following a version for adults published two years earlier in *Le Courrier des Pays Bas*, which is quite lauditory.[10] The life of Giovanni Belzoni is described as "one of the most useful for the progress of sciences,"[11] and our fearless explorer is deemed

4. For a view of the "Egyptian Hall" and it's interior: Curl 1994, figs. 110–111; for the exhibition "à gauche des Bains Chinois," in Paris: Humbert 1998, 116–17. See, mainly, Pearce 2000, 109–25.

5. There are quite a few: Clair 1957 ; Disher 1957; Mayes 1959; or, more recently Zatterin 2000; Hume 2012. See also Fagan 1975, 95–248 (Part Two: The Greatest Plunderer of Them All; Manley and Ree 2001, 82–99; and Siliotti 2001. An exhibition was organised in 2007 at the Museo Civico Archeologico in Bologna: "Giovanni Battista Belzoni. Un Indiana Jones alla riscoperta dell'Egitto."

6. We know her real name thanks to the document referred to in note 1.

7. The author is Lucy Sarah Atkins, later Atkins-Wilson (1801–1863), who published at least one other book for children before her twenty-first birthday, *The India Cabinet Opened: In Which Many Natural Curiosities Are Rendered a Source of Amusement to Young Minds, by the Explanations of a Mother.* She will eventually have nine children herself.

8. Christophe 1979, 6.

9. *La Récompense*, nos. 10, 12 et 14, 8th of March, 22d of March, and 5th of April 1829; quoted by Battistini 1935–1936, 7.

10. *Le Courrier des Pays Bas*, no. 213, Wednesday 1st of August 1827; quoted by Battistini 1935–1936, 7–8. It appears that Sarah Belzoni arrived in Brussels shortly before this publication (see further on).

11. "Une des plus utiles au progrès des sciences."

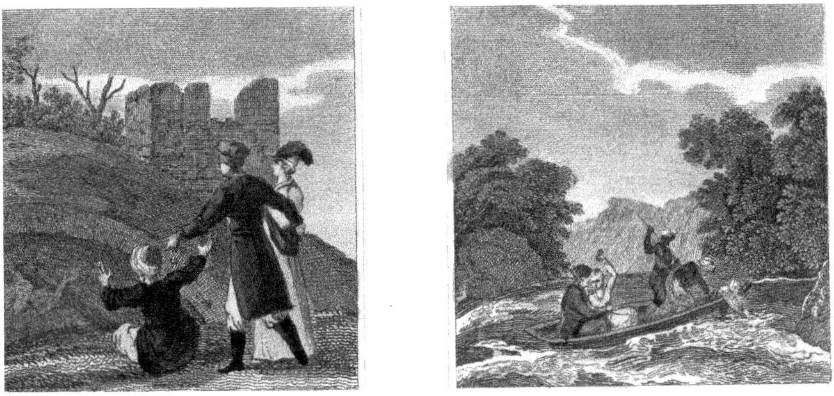

Fig. 1. "Madame Belzoni," as imagined in *L'Égypte et la Nubie ou curiosités de ces pays, tirées du voyage de Belzoni*, Paris, 1823, opposite p. 18.

to have proven "what perseverance can do to a man strongly organized, to help him overcome the obstacles to the success of his research."[12] He is a model for all explorers.

Giovanni Belzoni was assuredly better known in the 1820s and 1830s, in Belgium, than, for example, the Tuscan Egyptologist Ippolito Rosellini, who was indeed a less flamboyant figure, and he had an admirer there, a self-declared "intimate friend" named Martialis Reghellini de Schio (1763(?)–1855). He was a compatriot (Schio is also in the Veneto) and was also a freemason.[13] Reghellini probably met Belzoni in London, when he had his exhibition running. The latter too was a freemason, a Royal Arch member of the School of Plato Chapter in Cambridge, and was received among the "Masonic Knights Templar" in Norwich in 1821. He appears to have been introduced (parrainé) by the Reverend George Adam Browne, a man close to Augustus Frederick, Duke of Sussex, the sixth son of George III and Grand Master of the United Grand Lodge of England from 1813 to 1843.[14] Giovanni Belzoni dedicates his *Hieroglyphics Found in the Tomb of Psammis Discovered by G. Belzoni*, published in 1822, to the Duke. It may be noted that one of the six silver medals struck by the city of Padua in the honor of Belzoni after his donation to the city of two statues representing the goddess Sekhmet was given to "His Royal Highness the Duke of

12. "Ce que [peut] la persévérance dans un homme fortement organisé, pour vaincre les obstacles qui s'opposent au succès de ses recherches." *Le Courrier des Pays Bas*, no. 213, Wednesday the 1st of August 1827, 3.

13. It is very improbable that Belzoni was introduced into Masonry in Egypt. The "Société Secrète Egyptienne," which went back to Bonaparte's military campaigns, kept very strong links with France. The "Grand Cophte" or "Vénérable" of the Alexandria lodge was (in 1818) his archrival Bernardino Drovetti, consul-general of France from 1811 to 1814 and from 1820 to 1829. See Galtier 1989, 150–151. About Drovetti, see Ridley 1998.

14. Hamill and Mollier 2003, 212 (without ref.). More about his Grand-Mastership is to be found on the website www.masoniclibrary.org.au

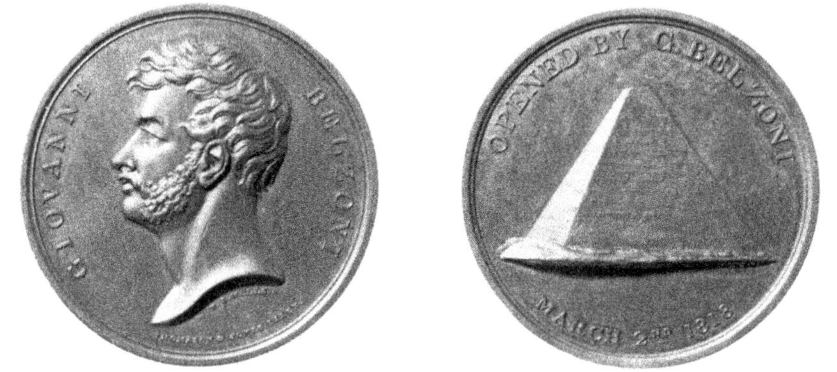

Fig. 2. Bronze medal commemorating the opening of Chephren's pyramid by Giovanni Belzoni. British Museum, Coins and Medals CM 1947,0607.220, © Trustees of the British Museum.

Sussex" (fig. 2). He was also the active chairman of the Society of Arts from 1816, and Reghellini may have met him in this context.[15]

Reghellini de Schio

Martialis Reghellini arrived in Brussels around 1822, but little is known about his life. The few facts we do have, are mostly to be found in the books he wrote. He seems to have known (well?) prince Eugène de Beauharnais (1781–1824), Viceroy of Italy and Grand Master of the Italian Grand Orient and Suprême Conseil,[16] but also Bonaparte's aide de camp during the Egyptian campaign, whom Reghellini met after Bonaparte's downfall, while in voluntary (?) exile in Munich,[17] trying to get his paintings out of (Austrian) Italy. He indeed arrived in the Low Countries with an art collection, including twenty-four paintings from the duke of Mantua's gallery, with the intention of selling them to king William, "with whom he was dealing [...] since a long while."[18] An etching after a painting once in his collection bears an inscription saying it came "from the famous collection of the Duke of Mantua, who got it from Giulio Romano" and was then (about 1826) "in the collection of Reghellini de

15. Disher 1957, 165 and p. 92 (pl.); Mayes 1959, 268 and 318, n. 9. The Duke allegedly reached the 90th and highest degree of the "Rite de Misraïm": *Annales chronologiques, littéraires et historiques de la maçonnerie des Pays-Bas*. VI. Années 1826–1828, Bruxelles, 1828, 236. Regarding the statues of Sekhmet in Padua, see Jaeger 1996, 192 and n. 26.

16. For his sumptuous Egyptianizing mansion in Paris, see Humbert 1998, 98–100; and Hammadi and Dumont 1988, 91–93.

17. See Bartier 1981, 206.

18. "Avec qui il est en marché [...] depuis longtemps." Bartier 1981, 219. The interesting story of the collection's acquisition is in *Catalogue de tableaux précieux formant la collection de M. Reghellini de Schio, précédé d'une Notice historique sur l'arrivée de ces tableaux dans le Royaume des Pays-Bas*, Brussels, 1826. Among other collections mentioned: Correr (Venice), Giustiniani (Vicenza), Raspi (Venice) etc.

Schio."[19] Wherever he got his collection, it is also stated Reghellini also sold at least five paintings in England, which he visited three times just to do that, before the end of 1828. He most probably met the Duke of Sussex during these trips, at the Society of Arts[20] but, considering the date of the last trip, it was not then that he could have met Giovanni Belzoni, who had died five years earlier.

Martialis Reghellini became a member of the *Vrais Amis de l'Union*, a Brussels lodge, in November 1825 and thus published his works on freemasonry, to which we have already referred, after this date.

Giovanni Belzoni was by then considered an authority on ancient Egypt, and Reghellini was looking for sources on Egyptian religion, as he wanted to show that Freemasonry is "the outcome of Egyptian, Jewish and Christian religion." His three volumes on the subject are dense and confusing[21]. Belzoni's *Narrative* was actually the only modern work he consulted about ancient Egypt, a fact that no doubt contributed to enhance his reputation among Martialis Reghellini's readers. They probably took relish, as he did, in the discovery by Belzoni of bull's bones in Khaefre's sarcophagus: "if such a discovery had been made by the Holy Helen or at the time of the Crusades, priests or relics-dealers would have made up a legend, and we would have ended up with a Holy Apis, who would have his churches, his monks and his virgins."[22] Martialis Reghellini left the *Vrais Amis de l'Union* in 1840, perhaps turning to *Les Amis du Progrès*, where he might have asked for affiliation.

Sarah Belzoni in Brussels

We do not know if the friendship between Giovanni Belzoni and Martialis Reghellini might explain the former's widow arriving in Brussels, as early as 1827, if not earlier,[23] when it is still a city of the United Kingdom of the Netherlands. Whatever the truth

19. "Provient de la fameuse collection du Duc de Mantoue qui le tenait de Jules Romain." Walek 1991, 201 and notes. This is all about the famous "Czartoryski youth," once held to be a self-portrait by Raphael. The inscription is signed by the etcher Pieter De Vlaminck and the addressee is his master Joseph Odevaere. This is assuredly the painting mentioned by the *Messager des Sciences et des Arts* de 1826, 417. The Messager reports on Reghellini de Schio's intention "de vendre à Guillaume Ier le portrait de Raphaël." The work was actually included in the above mentioned public sale (Catalogue..., no. 30) and it's importance is much stressed in the catalogue. One wonders when, where and how the Czartoryski family, who gave it's present name to the painting, comes into the picture!

20. Bartier 1981, 219. Reghellini de Schio knew Morison de Greenfield, who belonged to the house of the duke of Sussex, and who was a key figure of the "Rite de Misraïm." See Bartier 1981, 217, n. 89. We do not know if Reghellini was also a member.

21. Reghellini de Schio 1829. Another massive work was published in 1825.

22. "Si pareille découverte eût été faite par Ste. Hélène ou au temps des croisades, les prêtres et les marchands de reliques auraient inventé une légende, nous aurions un St. Apis et il aurait lui-même ses églises, ses moines et ses vierges." Reghellini de Schio 1829, 42–43.

23. A brief note in the April 26th, 1827 issue of *Poulson's American Daily Advertiser* (Philadelphia) comments that a subscription is underway for the support of Sarah Belzoni "widow of the celebrated traveller" and "partner in the arduous undertakings of her husband, who is now living in Brussels." See www.sil.si.edu/ondisplay/nile-notes/explore-01.htm.

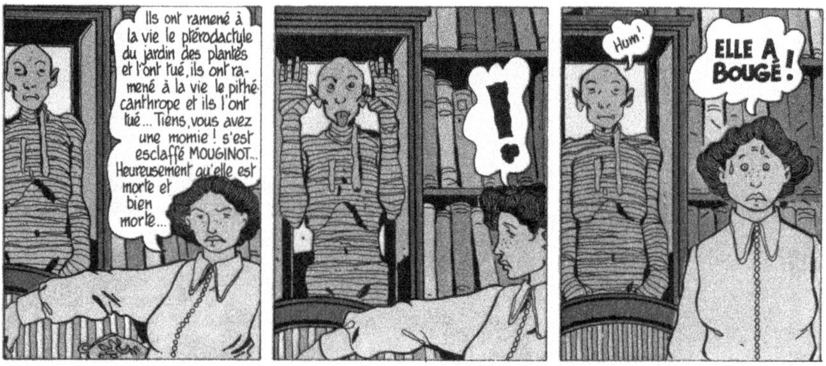

Fig. 3. Adèle Blanc-Sec and her mummy. Tardi 1978, 9.

is, the English-born Sarah Parker-Brown[24] had settled in Ixelles, "at the gates of Brussels" by that date, with a great number of drawings, but also some antiquities in her luggage (fig. 3).

"Madame Belzoni's creditors," writes Pryse Lockhart Gordon,[25] who visited her in Brussels about 1828, "with a liberality highly creditable to them, bestowed a pittance on her, which enables her to exist in a country where provisions are cheap. She occupies a small apartment, which is her museum and dormitory. In one corner is a mummy, in another an African mackaw, and an Angola cat, her *compagnon de voyage* for fifteen years. Fragments of skulls, skeletons of rare animals and various other articles of great interest to her, are carefully preserved, because they were collected by her dear departed friend (i.e. Giovanni Belzoni). She has not thrown off her weeds, and seldom stirs beyond the threshold." ... "She still talks of making a pilgrimage to Africa to visit her husband's tomb!" ... "She has lately published a prospectus of a work she has been long meditating – a series of lithographic prints, representing the figures and hieroglyphs on the celebrated tomb (i.e., of Sethy I)" (see appendix 1).

Another visitor, the Irish novelist Sydney Owenson (1783–1859), better known as Lady Morgan, found her, in 1833[26] "occupying a little back room, on the second floor of a small house in the dreary suburb of the *glacis*. Her only window commanded a view of the red-tiled roofs of the city of Brussels; and beyond, an illimitable prospect of its environs. The disconsolate companion of the most heroic of all modern travellers was still in faded weeds, and intently occupied in reading from a very fine folio Bible. A large coffin, covered with hieroglyphs, stood open and upright before her; - it contained the most perfect mummy perhaps in existence. The walls and floors of her little room were covered with fragments, drawings, and objects of Egyptian

24. According to the document mentioned in note 1, she was Sarah Parker-Brown and not Sarah Bane or Sarah Banne, as written down by a Belgian civil servant in 1857, probably after mishearing "Brown."
25. Gordon 1830, 405.
26. The text is a letter dated October 20th, 1833, originally published in *Athaenaeum*, no. 312.

antiquity.... She said she wanted nothing but the means of leaving Europe, and laying herself down in the tomb 'under the shade of the avasma' at Gato" (Giovanni's, in Gwato, Benin). "I endeavoured to bring Mrs. Belzoni to the point," Lady Morgan adds, "as to what could be done to save her declining years from actual want. She put into my hands the prospectus of an intended publication, by subscription, of a series of lithographic views of the model of the Egyptian tomb which Belzoni discovered in the Valley of Baban-el-Mallok, near Thebes, in 1818[27] (see appendix 1); and pointed to the mummy, which is of the third or highest class, viz. a priestess; it is extremely valuable, from its rarity and high state of preservation."

We will return to the mummy (fig. 4), which got quite some attention from the daily press, a mummy being a rare and precious commodity.[28] It was there described as "perfectly preserved" and, "according to Herodot's description of the different ways of embalming," must have belonged to a "person of distinction."[29] One of the newspapers states that "Mrs. Belzoni's sojourn in Belgium is an opportunity [...] to remind the general public of the services rendered by her husband to science through his travels and discoveries."[30]

We know that Sarah stayed in Brussels until 1857 at least, thereafter to go to Jersey, where she died in 1870. She obviously had a strong hope to get to Africa before the end of 1834, when she gave her antiquities, and her mummy, in custody to the "Musée de Bruxelles,"[31] which would become the "Musée d'Armes Anciennes, d'Armures, d'Objets d'Art et de Numismatique" (the core of the present Royal Museum of Art and History), opened in August 1835.[32]

Sarah Belzoni may have come to Belgium to benefit from the special conditions offered by Belgian printers, who were not too careful then about copyright infringement,[33] but the fact she remained in Brussels for twenty-five years probably means she was in dire straits and simply could not afford to move. What is known, however, is that a new edition of the *Narrative of the operations and recent discoveries within the pyramids, temples, tombs and excavations in Egypt and Nubia* appeared

27. She evidently refers to Belzoni 1828.

28. *L'Emancipation*, 4th year, no. 157, 6th of June 1833; and *Le Belge*, no. 157, 6th of June 1833. The former of these newspapers publishes a new biography of Giovanni Belzoni two days later. The paper makes it very well understood some of his finds are with his widow and are for sale. Articles quoted by Battistini 1935–1936, 9 and n. 1. Sarah Belzoni and her mummy make us think of the cartoon character Adèle Blanc-Sec and her mummified friend (Tardi 1978, *passim*; see fig. 3 here).

29. *L'Émancipation*, 4e année, no. 157, 6th of June 1833, 2.

30. On "Sarah senza Giovanni," see Zatterin 2000, 261–70.

31. *Journal de la Belgique. Pièces officielles. Nouvelles diverses*, no. 309, Wednesday the 5th of November 1834, 2. The very same text is to be found in *Le Courrier belge*, no. 312, Saturday the 8th of November 1834, 2.

32. *Le Courrier belge*, no. 312, Saturday the 8th of November 1834; *Courrier de la Meuse*, no. 263, 6th of November 1834; et *Journal de Belgique. Pièces officielles. Nouvelles diverses*, no. 309, Wednesday the 5th of November 1834; quoted by Battistini 1935–1936, 9 and n. 2.

33. This mainly concerns books originally printed in France: Dopp 1932 (*non vidi*).

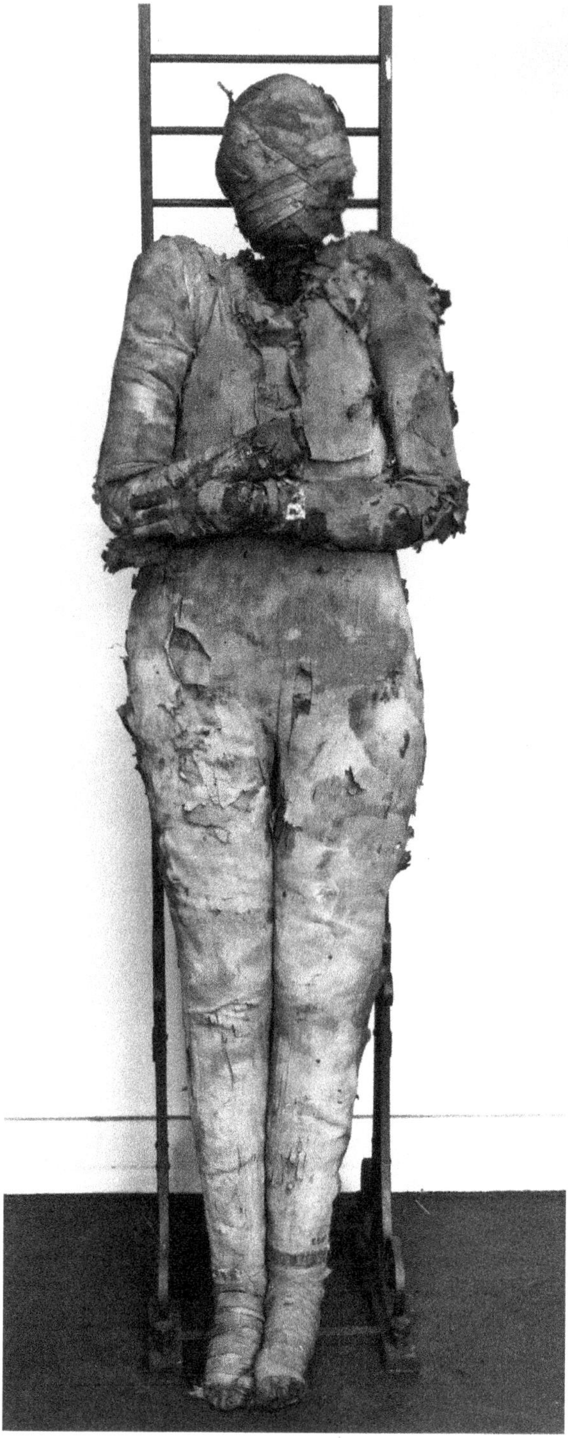

Fig. 4. "Butehamun's mummy," photographed before its autopsy in 1941. © Institut Royal du Patrimoine Artistique, Brussels.

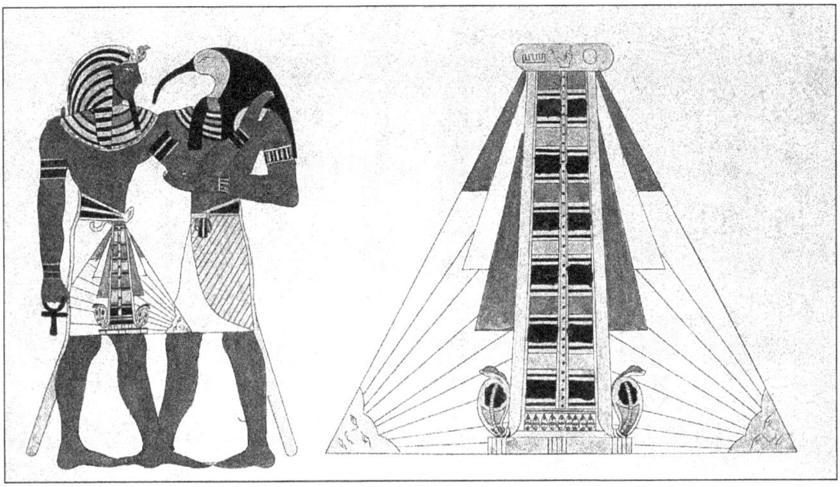

Fig. 5. "The Royal Egyptian Masonic Apron," according to Giovanni and Sarah Belzoni. Archives de l'Académie royale de Belgique, Bruxelles, dossier 346.

in Brussels in 1835, edited by H. Rémy, "imprimeur du Roi."[34] But Sarah Belzoni was obviously not making ends meet, probably selling some antiquities to private collectors, while also soliciting some public attention. She thus turned to the venerable Académie royale des Sciences et Belles-Lettres in 1841 or 1842.

Sarah Belzoni at the Academy

At the end of 1841 or at the very beginning of 1842, Sarah Belzoni turned to Adolphe Quetelet, Secrétaire perpetual of the Académie royale des Sciences et Belles-Lettres, and sent him three texts in English, the first one just "Dedicated to the Masonic Brethren universally," the second one entitled "The Royal Egyptian Masonic Aprons," the third one "The Tomb of Pharaoh Ousirei, King of Egypt in the Val Beban el Mallok, Thebes, Upper Egypt, from historical records sixteen hundred years before Christ." All three of them are dated 1841 and have been calligraphed by another hand, a colored illustration being provided with one of them showing what Giovanni or Sarah herself deemed to be a masonic apron as seen in Sethy's tomb[35] (fig. 5).

34. *Egypte* 1995, 26, no. 24; and Bruwier 1998, 20 and note 24, refer to a copy then in the possession of Florimond Lamy, with a handwritten statement, in French, by Sarah Belzoni: "La sousignée [*sic*] déclare avoir publié l'ouvrage de son mari, dont elle est en partie l'auteur, Bruxelles, le 28 août 1835.... Mrs. Belzoni's account of the women of Egypt, Nubia, and Syria" is to be found p. 409 to p. 444 of the Belgian edition."
35. "Un tablier emblématique employé dans les mystères égyptiens," *Bulletin de l'Académie royale des Sciences et Belles-Lettres de Bruxelles*, IX, 1ère partie, 1842, 2. She calls Sethy "Ousirei," which was the reading of his name by J.-F. Champollion. Th. Young's reading was "Psammuthis": these were the early days of Egyptology! The three texts and the illustration are also to be found in Weisse 1880, 36–43, after identical originals written for Sarah Belzoni in 1843 (see below). The illustration is also to be found in van de Sande 1995, 27.

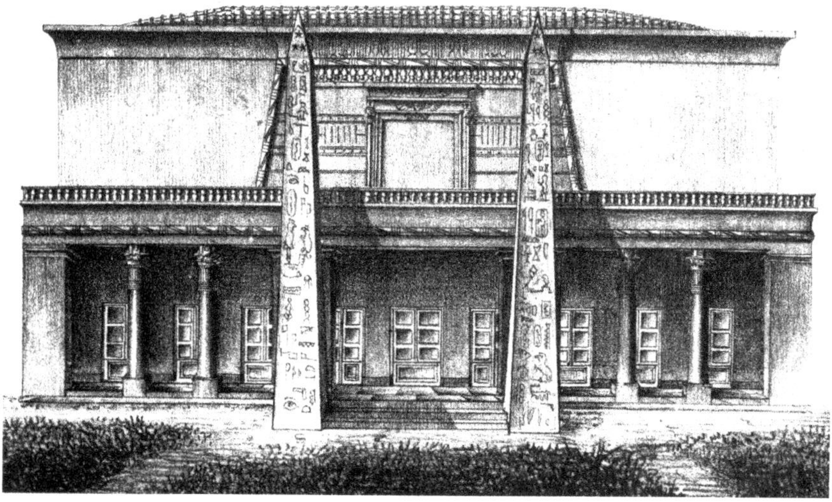

Fig. 6. An early example of an Egyptianizing masonic temple: *La Parfaite Union et Saint-Jean du Désert réunis*, in Valenciennes, France (1841). Hamill and Mollier 2003.

A letter in her own handwriting accompanied these papers (fig. 6), which reads as follows:

> Sir, In taking the liberty of sending the accompanying rough sketch to you, I beg to observe that I have no pretentions whichever to be considered an authoress but, anxious to elucidate a few points on the drawings of the last tomb discovered by my husband the late traveller in which free masonry is predominant. The aprons were exclusively royal and masonry of a much more exalted character and very different to modern masonry was combined with the arts and science in general. The aprons I have had embroidered for his Royal Highness the Duke of Sussex, and will be sent to England in a few weeks. If you wish to see them I shall have great pleasure in showing them to you.[36]

The Academy had not previously shown much interest for Egypt or Egyptian antiquities, although the Minister of Interior had solicited the Academy's opinion regarding the matters that could be investigated by Edouard Blondeel de Cuelebrouck. He had been Consul-General for Belgium in Alexandria since 14 September 1838[37] and had informed the Minister "that he might have some time to spend on scientific investigations,"[38] asking for some directions from the government. He actually left Cairo on 19 June 1840, and did not return until 10 October 1842, searching for a po-

36. Archives de l'Académie royale de Belgique, dossier 346. Anna Baghiani has been searching for these aprons, but she has found no trace of them as yet. She also double-checked my reading of the letter.
37. He had actually been there since the 4th of May 1838.
38. "Qu'il lui serait possible de disposer de quelque temps pour se livrer à des recherches scientifiques."

tential colony for Belgium somewhere in the general area of Ethiopia and Somalia.[39] Thus, more or less a year after Blondeel's offer, during the Academy's meeting of the 7th of August 1841, the Ministry announced that "in accordance with its instructions, M. Zizinia, consul in Alexandria, M. Blondeel being absent, undertook to collect information about the population of Egypt."[40] Over a year later, during the meeting of 3 December 1842, the Ministry finally deposited "a manuscript by M. Zizinia, Consul in Alexandria, answering the scientific questions regarding Egypt formulated by the Academy."[41] Neither the questions nor the answers were published by the Academy, which says much about the true degree of interest in Egypt among the academicians.[42]

Accordingly, Sarah Belzoni was discussed during the Academy's meeting of 15 January 1842; the astronomer Adolphe Quetelet, another "friend" of Martialis Reghellini,[43] was by then the Secrétaire perpétuel. A few months later, Joseph Roulez, who was teaching Roman history at the Ghent University, and had probably been present at the meeting, complained in a letter to Conrade Leemans, director of the Dutch National Museum of Antiquities, about "the opposition of the Academy" towards his offer to acquire antiquities "to form the core of a museum in the capital."[44] At the same time, however, and to his own surprise, he had to admit the sudden interest of at least Adolphe Quetelet for these matters: "While I gave a paper on some fragments of antique sculpture I had discovered reused in a private house in Arlon,"[45] he writes, "M. Quetelet suddenly took a great fancy for antiquities and proposed the creation of a special commission for those of the kingdom. As the proposition came from an astronomer, it was taken seriously and a commission was formed, composed of seven or eight members of the Academy, among whom I know no other archaeologist than myself."[46]

39. Duchesne 1953, 100–179. See also Archives de l'Académie royale de Belgique, dossier 10334.

40. "Conformément à ses désirs, M. Zizinia, consul à Alexandrie, s'est occupé, en l'absence de M. Blondeel, de rassembler des renseignements sur la population de l'Egypte." Concerning Zizinia, see Warmenbol 2012 b, 32–33; regarding this piece of "intelligence," see Archives de l'Académie royale de Belgique, dossier 10339.

41. "Un mémoire manuscrit de M. Zizinia, consul à Alexandrie, sur les questions scientifiques que l'académie avait formulées relativement à l'Égypte."

42. *Bulletin de l'Académie royale des Sciences et Belles-Lettres de Bruxelles*, VII, 1ère partie, 1840, 120; Idem, VIII, 2ème partie, 1841, 58; Idem, IX, 2ème partie, 1842, 482. The referees reporting on Zizinia's study were Cornelissen, Thiry and Marchal. The latter would publish a "Notice sur les relations commerciales des Flamands avec le port d'Alexandrie d'Egypte, avant la découverte du Cap de Bonne-Espérance," in *Bulletin de l'Académie royale des Sciences et Belles-Lettres* XI, 1ère partie, 1844, 153–76, which is supposedly an annex to his report on Zizinia's work. See also Archives de l'Académie royale de Belgique, dossier 4958.

43. Reghellini de Schio 1829, III, 54. The description of the mummy published by Capart 1935, 113, is dated the 29th of June 1842.

44. "Pour en former le noyau d'un musée dans la capitale."

45. Roulez 1842, 350–52.

46. "Alors que je donnais une notice succinte de quelques morceaux de sculpture que j'avais trouvés dans une maison particulière à Arlon, M. Quetelet s'éprend tout d'un coup d'une belle passion pour les antiquités et propose la création d'une commission spéciale pour celles du royaume. Pour cette fois la proposition venait d'un astronome, elle a été prise en considération et l'on a formé une commission qui se compose de sept à huit membres de l'Académie, parmi lesquels je ne connais d'autre archéologue que moi...." Archives

Sarah Belzoni sent the same text about "The Royal Egyptian Masonic Aprons" and "The Tomb of Pharaoh Ousirei, King of Egypt etc." to the Grand Orient of the Netherlands in 1844, which decided to print and publish them, and to one or another Masonic authority in England, where they where published in 1861 under the general title "Mrs. Belzoni on Freemasonry in Egypt"[47] which tends to show this was "her thing."

Sarah Belzoni in the Museum

In May 1847, Sarah Belzoni finally sold the star-piece of her collection, the mummy mentioned above (the subject of a poem by Horace Smith, published in 1825: see appendix 2). It has been found, or has been associated since its discovery, with the inner coffin[48] of Butehamun, head of the workers of the Theban necropolis early in the Twenty-First Dynasty, but it can not be his body, as the wrappings are clearly of a later date.[49] It was, nevertheless, important as the first mummy to enter a Belgian public collection, soon to be followed by a child's mummy, presented by Amédée de Beauffort (1806–1858).[50] The mummy was exhibited for some years at the Palais de l'Industrie, an early predecessor of the Musées Royaux d'Art et d'Histoire, and was sold to the Government precisely when the collections were moved to the Porte de Hal. Antoine Schayes became curator of this Musée Royal d'Artillerie, d'Armures et d'Antiquités in March 1847, shortly after becoming a member of the Classe des Lettres of the Royal Academy. The man was very well introduced in the world of dealers and sales rooms, "where his flair allowed him some happy buys, not just for himself, but also for his friends."[51] He also collected Egyptian antiquities (see further, below).

Baudouin van de Walle has suggested that "humanitarian," rather than scientific, considerations drove the acquisition of the mummy, given Sarah Belzoni's situation at the time. It may, however, actually have been the only way to settle the ownership of a popular exhibit! Sarah Belzoni hoped to get two thousand francs for her mummy, but

---

of the Rijksmuseum van Oudheden in Leiden: Files 19.5.1/1–18. See also (A. Quetelet), Séance du 8 octobre, *Bulletin de l'Académie royale des Sciences et Belles-Lettres de Bruxelles* IX, 2ème partie, 1842, 352–53; et (A. Quetelet), Séance du 5 novembre, ibid., 361.

47. Hamill and Mollier 2003, 212–13.

48. Other coffins of Butehamun are in the Museo Egizio, Turin (2236–37): Davies 1997, 52–53, 56; Verhoeven and Vassilika 2010.

49. The mummy is Musées royaux d'Art et d'Histoire, Bruxelles, Inv. E.5288. See Jonckheere 1942; and, recently, Francot et al., 1999, 10–12, no. 7. See also Limme 1989, 107. The coffin is Musées royaux d'Art et d'Histoire, Bruxelles, Inv. E.5299. See Niwinski 1988, 112, no. 47; and, recently Verhoeven and Vassilika 2010. See also Niwinski 2008, 253 and nn. 32 and 33. A classic work on Butehamun in Brussels is Harris 1960.

50. Musées royaux d'Art et d'Histoire, Bruxelles, Inv. E.1184; Schayes 1854, no. 1; Limme 1980, 42; Francot et al., 1999, 5–7, no. 4. Amédée de Beauffort was "inspecteur général des beaux-arts, des lettres et des sciences" and first director of the Museum, in 1835. See Bruwier 1998, 31–33 (and notes) about him.

51. "Où son flair lui permettait de faire d'heureux coups, non seulement pour lui-même, mais pour ses amis." Hymans 1911–1913, col. 619.

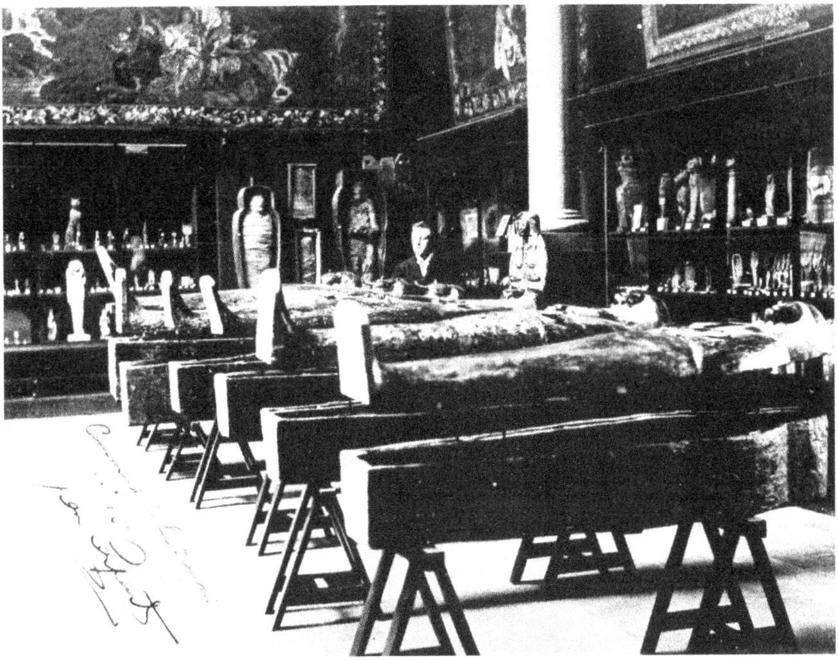

Fig. 7. The Egyptian collection, shown with by Jean Capart in 1897 ("Comme je l'ai trouvée"). Sarah Belzoni's mummy is well visible in the background, just next to Jean Capart. Van de Walle, Limme, and De Meulenaere 1980, fig. 2.

in the end only got four hundred. Jean Capart took the view that this was a considerable amount of money for the period; on the other hand, it was only a fifth of what the owner was hoping for: perhaps a kind of state subsidy to the poor widow, but certainly not a testimony to the government's generosity (fig. 7).[52]

The right hand of the mummy was missing (everything is missing now, save the head, after Frans Joncheere's destructive autopsy), retained by Sarah Belzoni and a few years later given to John Adam Weisse. "Among other pleasant recollections of this energetic lady," he writes (see also below), "I cannot help mentioning the delicate manner in which she presented to me the right hand of a mummy now in the Brussels Museum, minus the hand. It is considered as the hand of an Egyptian queen."[53] We have no idea were this hand could be now.

"All the older natives of Brussels remember the museum at the Porte de Hal, where they went on Sundays with the whole of the family," reminisces Jean Capart, "to see the stuffed horses, souvenirs of the "Joyeuse Entrée" of Albert and Isabella and

52. Capart 1935, 111–13; van de Walle 1980, 11–12.

53. Weisse 1880, 63; Jonckheere 1942, 10. Regarding the obession with mummys' hands and feet, see Warmenbol 1997.

the ethnographic collections [featuring a mummy acquired from Belzoni's widow], crammed into the attic of the old fortress." He thus stresses the popularity of the "object" with the general public, but also says something about the fascination he himself had for it. According to Capart, this was probably the first mummy he ever saw: it might have helped him, very early on, in deciding his career.[54] It is pleasing to think that the rather austere Capart can thus be considered as, in a way, indebted to the flamboyant Belzoni.

Sarah in Brussels, Still

A late(r) testimony of Sarah's presence in Brussels, is that of John Adam Weisse, who "lived in "Madame Belzoni's" house, and became her medical adviser," to his own testimony. He states that "in 1851 or 1852 Parliament voted to "Madame Belzoni" an annual pension of one hundred pound sterling [...]," adding: "The good lady needed this help very much, for she told me she had passed twenty-two years in Brussels,[55] during which she had repeatedly petitioned Parliament for a pension, in consideration of her husband's services." Some of Giovanni Belzoni's manuscripts, or at least copies of those presented to the Acadamy about 1842, fell into the hands of this John Adam Weisse. The latter texts are to be found in *The Obelisk and Freemasonry, according to the Discoveries of Belzoni and Commander Gorringe*, published in 1880.[56] John Adam Weisse was a medical man, but with a strong taste for mysticism, which Sarah Belzoni probably shared.

We can imagine that this kind of work reflects the less "grounded" conversations a Belzoni, a Reghellini, or masons of their kind might have had (and certainly still have!) as members of the Rite de Misraïm, the Rite de Memphis, or another of that fashion. "In all masonic rites," Reghellini wrote, "the format of the Egyptian mysteries, was preserved. The trials and the teaching are the same, the goal and end are the same."[57]

Sarah Belzoni moved in 1857 from the Glacis de Waterloo (now Boulevard de Waterloo) to the rue du Cerf (now rue du Grand Cerf, next to the Parc d'Egmont),

54. "Tous les vieux Bruxellois se souviennent [du] musée de la Porte de Hal, où ils allaient en famille - le dimanche voir les chevaux empaillés, souvenirs de la Joyeuse Entrée d'Albert et Isabelle, les séries ethnographiques [parmi lesquelles se voyait une momie acquise de la veuve de Belzoni], installées dans les combles de la vieille forteresse." Capart 1936, 52. See also his Introduction to Jonckheere 1942, 5: "Je crois bien que la momie dont il est question est la toute première que j'ai vue et elle me fut montrée par mon père, lorsque j'étais enfant, au troisième étage de la porte de Hal ... Malgré toutes [mes] relations plus récentes dans le monde des momies, je n'ai jamais perdu de vue ma première."

55. Weisse 1880, 64–65. He met her in 1849: twenty-two years take us back to 1827...

56. Weisse 1880, 36–38 for "Dedicated to the Masonic Bretheren universally," 39–40 for "The Royal Egyptian Masonic Aprons" and p. 40–43 for "The Tomb of Pharaoh Ousirei, King of Egypt etc." Some uncritical comments are in Tompkins 1981, 339; see also Mayes 1959, 295, and Hamill and Mollier 2003, 212–13. See also n. 37 above.

57. "Dans tous les rites maçonniques, on a conservé les formalités des épreuves des mystères égyptiens: l'enseignement est le même, le résultat auquel on prétend est le même...." Reghellini de Schio 1825, 7.

which are quite close to one another. She was then living on the pension the British government had finally allowed her, from 1851 onwards.[58] John Adam Weisse is probably referring to these new premises when he testifies to the fact that "to support herself she hired a large house, and underlet the best parts of it"; this means, most probably, that the pension saved her. When he met her, she was still living "on the upper floor of a house near the *Boulevard de Waterloo*" and her "only society were two small Italian greyhounds, the most intelligent animals I ever saw."[59] The Angola cat must have died.

She left the Belgian capital shortly after that (but perhaps not before the 1860s), to settle in Jersey. She would die there on 12 January 1870 at eighty-seven years old, living on her pension. She was buried at the Mont à l'Abbé cemetery in Saint-Helier, where her tombstone has recently been rediscovered and restored (fig. 8).[60] Her goddaughter Selina Belzoni Tucker inherited her meagre estate. Selina Belzoni Tucker was at that time living in Cheltenham,[61] but she had previously worked as a governess in Brussels and (by 1851) in London. She died in Weston-super-Mare, near Bristol, in 1889. The last remains of the Belzoni collection (watercolors of the Sethy I tomb, some small antiquities, plus a sketch-book of Giovanni and a notebook of Sarah's) being given to Bristol City Museum by her cousin in 1900.[62]

Martialis Reghellini died in a home in 1853, without ever getting a pension from the Belgian government, but having been helped by Eugène Defacqz, Grand Maître National du Grand Orient de Belgique from 1842 to 1852, and Louis de Potter, a notorious republican close to the Italian "Carbonari."[63]

Antoine Schayes in the Museum

Apart from the mummy and coffin of Butehamun, no more than a dozen other Egyptian objects appear in the first catalogue of the Musée royal d'Armures, d'Antiquités et d'Ethnologie, written by A.-G.-B. Schayes.[64] Most of them had been given to the Museum, including four ushabti donated in 1844 M. Bové, who is most probably an heir of Nicolas Bové (1802–1842), a "naturalist-traveller" who lived in Egypt from 1829 to 1832.[65] The most beautiful, in alabaster, belongs to a priest called Menkheper,

58. Battistini 1935–1936, 11; Taylor 2011.
59. Weisse 1880, 65.
60. Baghiani and Taylor 2012 ; Dodson and Baghiani 2012.
61. Jersey Archive, D/Y/A/35/8. With special thanks to Stuart Nicolle. See also Clayton 1998, 47, wondering who might have been the Frederick William Collard, "Belzoni's descendant," who gave the golden medal Belzoni was wearing around his neck (see n. 13) to the Department of Coins and Medals of the British Museum. Certainly no one bearing the name "Collard" seems to appear in Selina Belzoni Tucker's family tree, insofar as it can be reconstructed from public documents.
62. Dodson and Baghiani 2013.
63. See Bartier 1981.
64. Schayes 1854, 77–78. See also van de Walle 1980, 11–12 and *passim*.
65. He was born in the Grand-Duchy of Luxemburg. See Koltz 1869, 202–206. He was "director of cultures" in Cairo under Ibrahim Pasha.

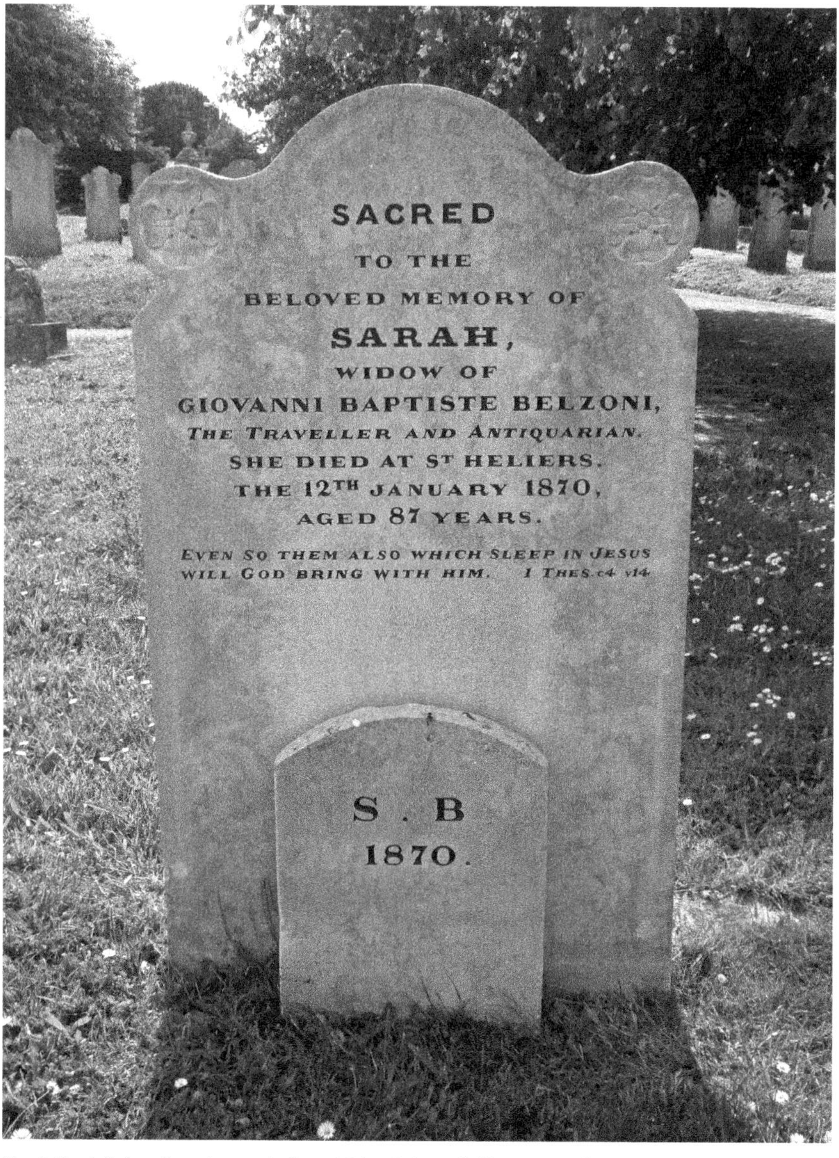

Fig. 8. Sarah Belzoni's tombstone in Saint-Helier (Mont à l'Abbé cemetery). © Aidan Dodson.

dating to the end of the Eighteenth Dynasty, who is not, however, to be identified with the grand-priest of Ptah under Amenhotep III (fig. 9).[66] One of the faience ush-

66. Musées royaux d'Art et d'Histoire, Bruxelles, Inv. E.5578; Schayes 1854, no. 9; Limme 1980, 47, B 29; *Du Nil* 1991, no. 197; Delvaux 1993, 143, no. 14. We express our thanks to Beatrix Gessler-Löhr (Heidel-

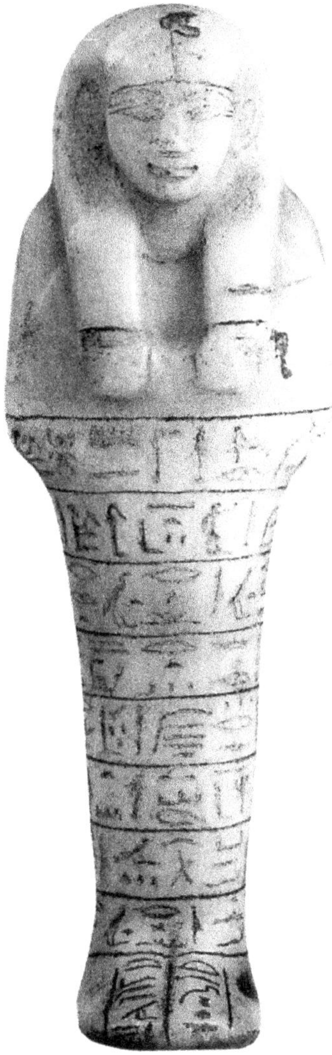

Fig. 9. Ushabti bearing the name of Menkheper. Bruxelles. Inv. E.5578. © Musées royaux d'Art et d'Histoire, Bruxelles.

abtis in the same collection comes from the tomb of one Horudja, also represented in the Rijksmuseum van Oudheden in Leiden.[67] The single funerary cone given by M. Bové, bears the name of Hor, priest of Amun and Montu and those of King Usermaatre-meryamun Sheshonq (VI).[68]

The canopic jar from this first collection was also donated in 1844, but this time by one François Auguste Van Hamme (1789–after 1857), about whom we know very little.[69] He was from Bruges and might thus have known Charles Bogaerts or Jean-Baptiste De Lescluze, both from Bruges and dealers in Egyptian antiquities.[70] The jar comes from the tomb of Horemheb, son of Shepensopdet, of the Twentieth-Sixth Dynasty, another canopic jar of whom ended up in the collections of the Metropolitan Museum of New York.[71]

The wooden stele of Paarkha (fig. 10), stuccoed and painted, of Ptolemaic date, was in fact the first Egyptian object bought for the Museum, also in 1844. It was acquired during the public sale of the Van Huerne collection, though we see no good reason for the museum to have done so. Some Roman antiquities of local provenance were bought at the same sale, and might explain why A.G.B. Schayes was

berg) for her information on the high priests of Ptah in Memphis and the reference to Raedler 2011, who discusses the Eighteenth Dynasty high priests in particular.

67. Musées royaux d'Art et d'Histoire, Bruxelles, Inv. E.5567; Schayes 1854, no. 10; Limme 1980, 47. See also Schneider 1977, 2:189–90.

68. Musées royaux d'Art et d'Histoire, Bruxelles, Inv. E.3990; Schayes 1854, no. 11; Limme 1980, 55. See also De Garis Davies and Macadam 1957, nos. 25–26.

69. www.genealogieonline.nl/fr/genealogie-peeters-rouneau.

70. Warmenbol 2012 a, 147–72.

71. Musées royaux d'Art et d'Histoire, Bruxelles, Inv. E.5897; Schayes 1854, no. 7; Limme 1980, 43 and fig. 9; Delvaux 1993, 146, no. 38.

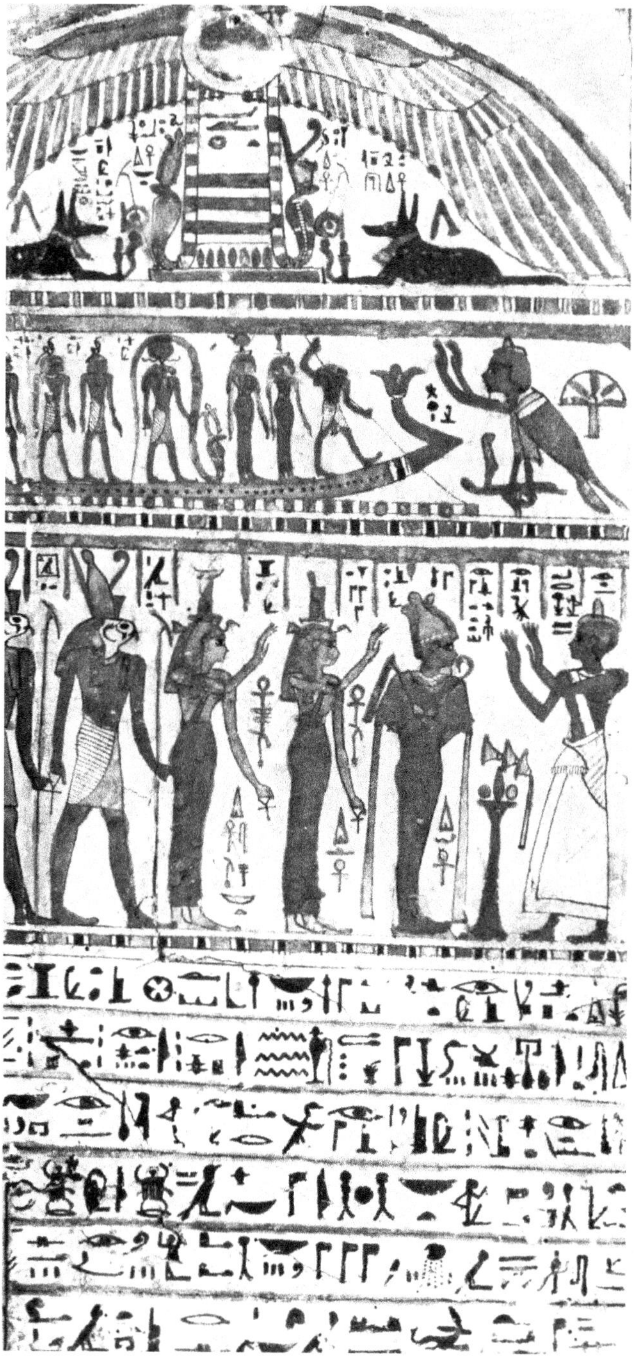

Fig. 10. Detail of the stela of Paarkha. Musées royaux d'Art et d'Histoire, Bruxelles. Inv. E.8396. © Musées royaux d'Art et d'Histoire, Bruxelles.

present.[72] According to the catalogue, the painting was "extremely well preserved," which might have made it attractive, perhaps more so than the four other stele for sale, three of them in limestone. We do not know where Van Huerne bought his antiquities, though he had a couple of mosaics apparently bought in Rome.[73] Joseph Van Huerne (1753–1844) was also from Bruges and might also have been acquainted with Charles Bogaerts or Jean-Baptiste De Lescluze.

We are also at a loss to explain the acquisition of two cat's sarcophagi, that were already part of the Musée royal d'Armures, d'Antiquités et d'Ethnologie when its first catalogue was published.[74] They were bought in 1850, that is, by A.-G.-B. Schayes, from a M. Zitelli, who is most probably Italian, but that is almost as far as we can get.[75]

Conclusion

It is quite obvious there was no policy in Belgium in the middle of the nineteenth century regarding the acquisition of Egyptian antiquities. A.-G.-B. Schayes made his own collection, and it is far more important than the one of which he was the custodian. When this was sold in December 1859, at the Grand Place in Brussels, the Belgian government, quite significantly, does not buy a single piece. There were ninety-five lots, that is, 199 objects to be had. The curator of the future Musées royaux d'Art et d'Histoire, in other words, had a personal collection that, quantity-wise at least, was more important than those of the two earliest major *mecenae*, Gustave Hagemans[76] and Emile de Meester de Ravestein.

We find it strange, on the other hand, that A.-G.-B. Schayes apparently did not consider a donation (perhaps death came too quickly), while his friend Gustave Hagemans already did so at this very time. He was an Italy at the time of the auction, which explains how Albert d'Otreppe de Bouvette and Emile de Meester de Ravestein got all the best pieces, including all the coffins. These were sold during the 1857 auction of Giovanni Anastasi's collection, where A.-G.-B. Schayes, again, must

72. Musées royaux d'Art et d'Histoire, Bruxelles, Inv. E.8396; Schayes 1854, no. 3; Limme 1980, 45 and fig. 10; De Meulenaere, Limme and Quaegebeur 1985, 75. See also De Loë 1937, 119.

73. *Catalogue des collections de tableaux, dessins, gravures, antiquités, curiosités et objets d'histoire naturelle, formant le Cabinet Van Huerne, dont la vente se fera à Bruges, en la maison mortuaire, le 21 octobre 1844*, Ghent, 1844. The Egyptian antiquities are to be found on pages 119–20 (nos. 683 à 721, the stele under no. 716), and the mosaics as well (nos. 725–726). An illustrated copy of the catalogue is at the Bibliothèque royale in Brussels (Ms. 21.681), but it does not show the Egyptian objects.

74. Musées royaux d'Art et d'Histoire, Bruxelles, Inv. E.7071 and Inv. E.7072; Schayes 1854, nos. 4 et 5; Limme 1980, 42–43. To our knowledge, these coffins have never been illustrated? Recent research by Isabelle Therasse suggests Emile de Meester de Ravestein actually bought them (most probably in Rome) from Signore Zitelli.

75. We are aware of the existence of a Miocene predecessor to our modern cats, called Felis zitelli, but have no idea if this might be significant in this context.

76. Warmenbol 2008; 2012a, 333.

have been personally present.[77] It is only after the donation of the d'Otreppe and de Meester collections,[78] the former in 1865 and 1873 to the Musée Curtius in Liège, the latter in 1884 to the Musées royaux d'Art et d'Histoire, that these coffins will become public property. A Late period stele mentioning a Bakmeher, probably from Aswan,[79] preceded them, as did two statuettes, one of unknown provenance, dating to the Middle Kingdom and in granite, the other from Athribis, of the Late period and in limestone,[80] and a large Late period (?) bronze situla, all bought in May 1860 from a man called Thirot.[81]

It is rather curious that these objects were bought by the Museum from Thirot, as all four of them appeared at auction twice shortly before, once in Paris (Anastasi) and once in Brussels (Schayes). The Belgian government had no policy as far as the acquisition of antiquities is concerned, and, moreover, had missed some golden opportunities to buy good quality at a good price.[82]

The objects bought from Thirot are in fact almost the only ones to enter the Brussels collection—apart from the very important Hagemans donation—between the publication of the catalogue written by Antoine Schayes in 1859, and the one written by Théodore Juste in 1864.

One object, however, deserves a special mention, namely, a gilded bronze Osiris from the "Cabinet de Crassier." It was given to the Brussels museum by Louis M.-G. de Crassier (1772–1851), who was public prosecutor in Malines and Brussels, but also secretary general of the Ministry of Justice. As a member of the Institut Archéologique Liégeois, he probably met other erudites, such as Gustave Hagemans and Albert d'Otreppe de Bouvette. He was the great-grandson of Guillaume de Crassier (1662–1751), a well-known antiquarian and a correspondent of dom

77. *Catalogue d'une superbe collection d'antiquités égyptiennes, romaines, gallo-romaines, étrusques, … provenant de feu M. A.-G.-B. Schayes, dont la vente … aura lieu …, à Bruxelles, le Mardi 6 Décembre 1859 et 2 jours suivants*, Brussels, 1859. About these coffins, see a remarkable piece of sleuthing: De Meulenaere 1980, 75–80. See also Hellinckx 2006; and Warmenbol 2006, 103–11. A.-G.-B. Schayes was a bibliophile and the owner of quite a few "classics": della Valle, Dapper, Lucas, De Bruyn, Le Mascrier, Pococke, Niebuhr, Savary, Denon. *Catalogue de la Bibliothèque de M. A.-G.-B. Schayes, dont la vente aura lieu … le lundi 9 mai 1859 et jours suivants*, Brussels, 1859, *passim*.

78. E. de Meester de Ravestein, as Luc Limme pointed out, never mentions A.-G.-B. Schayes.

79. Musées royaux d'Art et d'Histoire, Bruxelles, Inv. E.5287; Juste 1864, B 26; Limme 1980, 45. Voir aussi Limme 1979, no. 18.

80. Musées royaux d'Art et d'Histoire, Bruxelles, Inv. E.789 and E.3405; Juste 1864, C 55 et C 56; Limme 1989, 108; 1980, 52–53. See also, for the first piece, Balty 1998, 18; and for the second, Vernus 1978, 73–74 (document 77).

81. Musées royaux d'Art et d'Histoire, Bruxelles, Inv. E.6722; Juste 1864; D 59; Limme, 1980, 56.

82. We do not know either what became of the two mummies in the Van Parijs collection, sold in October 1853, in Brussels since the beginning of the nineteenth century, as the man died in 1829. The catalogue of this collection, written by A.-G.-B. Schayes also mentions an Osiris and an Harpokrates in bronze. See *Catalogue d'une belle et riche collection d'objets d'art et de haute curiosité, tels que antiquités égyptiennes, grecques et romaines … composant le Cabinet de feu M. Van Parijs, amateur, dont la vente publique aura lieu, par suite du décès de Mme. Ve. Van Parijs, le lundi 3, le mardi 4, le mercredi 5 octobre 1853 et jours suivants … à Bruxelles*, Brussels, 1853, nos. 1–4, 86–87 and 767.

Bernard de Montfaucon. The latter will illustrate several pieces of his collection in *L'Antiquité expliquée;* the Osiris was probably part of this late-seventeenth or early eighteenth-century collection.[83]

Quantitatively, the Egyptian collection of what are now the Musées royaux d'Art et d'Histoire does not take precedence over the collection in Liège (more or less "stable" since 1873) and the one in Antwerp (more or less "stable" since 1879), before the Emile de Meester de Ravestein donation, in 1884, with its one hundred and fifty objects, including coffins and canopics, most of them bought in Italy.[84]

Appendix 1. The text of a prospectus announcing a publication of lithographs planned by Sarah Belzoni (1828)

Dessins du tombeau égyptien découvert par Belzoni (Prospectus)[85]

Madame Belzoni se propose de publier par le moyen de la lithographie, l'ensemble des bas-reliefs et des hiéroglyphes sculptés sur les parois du tombeau royal égyptien découvert en 1818, près de Thèbes par feu M. G. Belzoni (fig. 11).

Les frais d'un ouvrage d'une aussi vaste étendu rendent indipensable de s'assurer de 200 souscripteurs au moins, avant d'entamer l'entreprise. La liste des souscripteurs, parmi lesquels Madame Belzoni compte déjà des noms très-distingués, sera publiée avec l'ouvrage.

Cet ouvrage formera un atlas de 80 planches au moins. Il paraîtra par livraisons de 8 planches, grand format ; il y aura de 12 à 14 livraisons, à raisons de 25 francs chaque, non coloriée, et 36 francs coloriée, payables par livraison, à fur et à mesure qu'elles seront remises.

Les 10 planches relatives à ce tombeau qui ont déjà été publiées dans l'atlas qui fait partie du *Voyage de M. Belzoni,* seront données de nouveau à leurs places respectives : elles seront livrées *gratis* aux souscripteurs du présent ouvrage.

La sollicitude que M. Belzoni manifesta constamment pour conserver ce précieux manuscrit à la science, détermine Madame Belzoni à entreprendre ce travail, malgré les peines morales et physiques qui l'accablent, et les nombreuses difficultés contre lesquelles elle a eu à lutter depuis la mort de son mari. Elle se repose avec confiance sur les sentimens et l'encouragement des amis des sciences pour lui faciliter les moyens d'atteindre un but si désirable.

Les recherches récentes et profondes de plusieurs savans ont déjà dévoilé à l'Europe quelques-uns des secrets mystiques de la mythologie égyptienne. On peut

83. The object is unfortunately lost, or at least not identifiable. Juste 1864, C 16; Limme 1980, 50 and n. 52. About Guillaume de Crassier, see Helbig 1873 a, coll. 487–490 ; and Capitaine 1854, 347–424. About his son, see Helbig 1873 b, coll. 490–493.

84. Van de Walle, Limme and De Meulenaere 1980, 57–73 et 75–80; van de Walle 1985, 149–55. The latter dates the donation to 1874. See also Evers 2008, 259–78.

85. We reproduce the text included in Champollion-Figeac et al., 1830, 423–24; see also Belzoni 1828 (*non vidi*), in-8° (14 pp.) probably published in Paris rather than London.

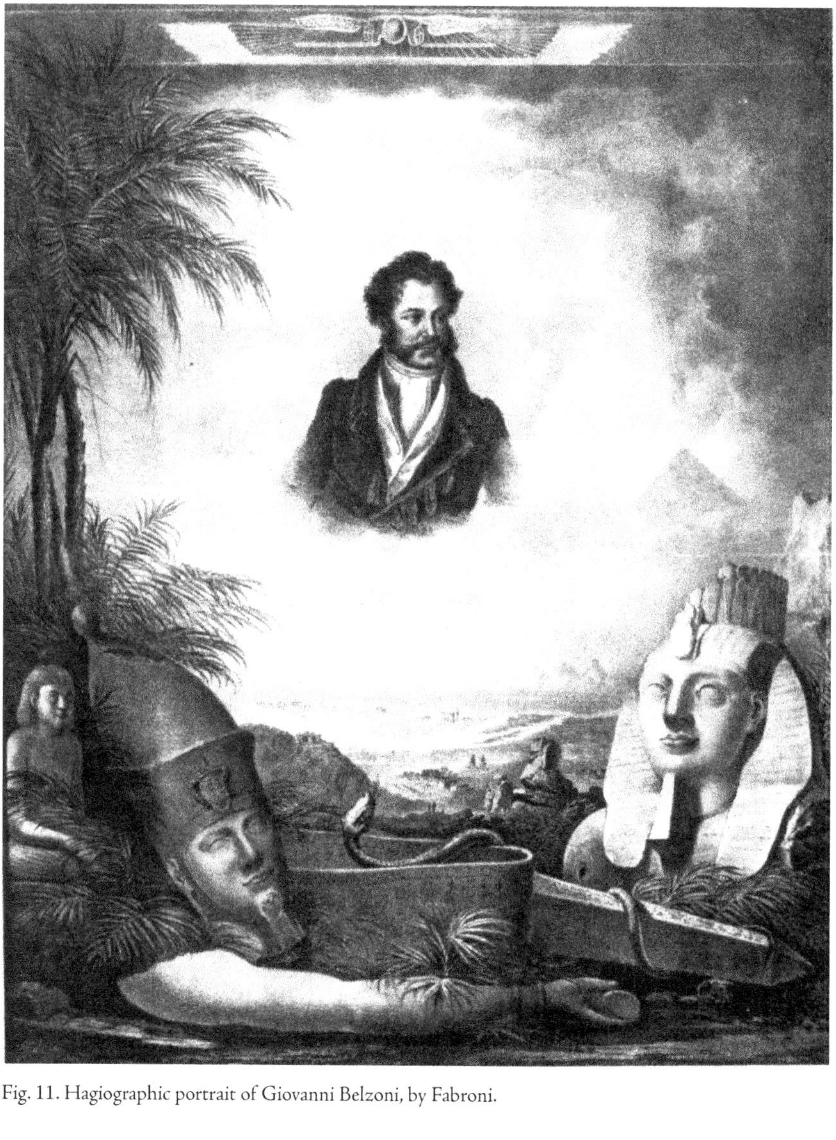

Fig. 11. Hagiographic portrait of Giovanni Belzoni, by Fabroni.

donc se flatter de voir bientôt un heureux résultat de leur persévérance et de leurs tentatives, maintenant qu'on est en possession de la clef de ces hiéroglyphes, restée impénétrable jusqu'à présent.

Les dernières découvertes, surtout de M. Champollion le jeune, relativement à la mythologie égyptienne, rendent ce tombeau l'un des plus intéressans qui existent, puisqu'il est un des plus complets (fig. 12). Aussi est-il le seul monument qui a été entièrement copié jusqu'à l'époque du voyage de Belzoni. On peut souscrire chez MM. Firmin Didot, imprimeurs-libraires, rue Jacob, no. 24, à Paris.

Appendix 2. Address to the mummy at Belzoni's exhibition, by Horace Smith (1825)[86]

And thou hast walk'd about (how strange a story !)
In Thebes's streets three thousand years ago,
When the Memnonium was in all its glory,
And Time had not begun to overthrow
Those temples, palaces, and piles stupendous,
Of which the very ruins are tremendous.

Speak ! for thou long enough hast acted Dummy,
Thou hast a tongue come let us hear its tune ;
Thou'rt standing on thy legs, above-ground, Mummy !
Revisiting the glimpses of the moon,
Not like thin ghosts or disembodied creatures,
But with thy bones and flesh, and limbs and features.

Tell us – for doubtless thou canst recollect,
To whom should we assign the Sphinx's fame?
Was Cheops or Cephrenes architect
Of either Pyramid that bears his name ?
Is Pompey's Pillar really a misnomer ?
Had Thebes a hundred gates, as sung by Homer ?

Perhaps thou wert a Mason, and forbidden
By oath to tell the mysteries of thy trade, -
Then say what secret melody was hidden
In Memnon's statue which at sunrise play'd ?
Perhaps thou wert a Priest - if so, my struggles
Are vain, for priestcraft never owns its juggles.

Perchance that very hand, now pinion'd flat,
Has hob-a-nobb'd with Pharaoh, glass to glass ;
Or dropped a halfpenny in Homer's hat,
Or doff' d thine own to let Queen Dido pass ;
Or held, by Solomon's own invitation,
A torch at the great Temple's dedication.

I need not ask thee if that hand, when arm'd,
Has any Roman soldier maul'd and knuckled,
For thou wert dead, and buried, and embalm'd,

86. We made use of an 1896 edition (www.unz.org/Pub/WarnerCharles-1896v41–16789).

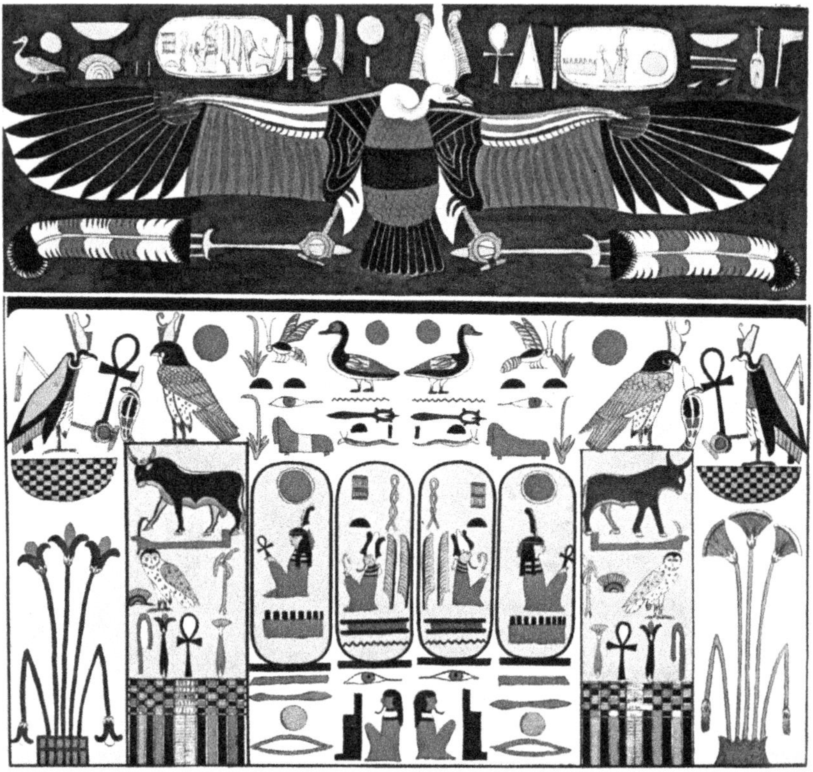

Fig. 12. "From the Tombs of the Kings at Thebes," one of the magnificent colored lithographs published by Giovanni Battista Belzoni in 1820.

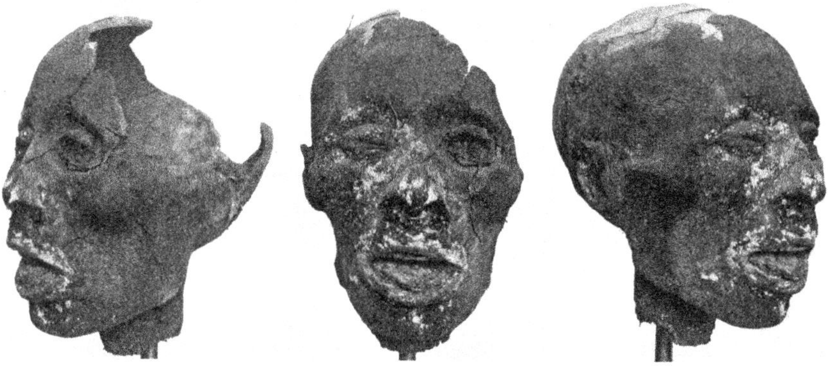

Fig. 13. The head of "Butehamun's mummy," clearly showing his "wither'd tongue." Jonckheere 1942, fig. 35.

Ere Romulus and Remus had been suckled : -
Antiquity appears to have begun
Long after thy primeval race was run.

Thou couldst develope, if that wither'd tongue (fig. 13)
Might tell us what those sightless orbs have seen,
How the world look'd when it was fresh and young,
And the great deluge still had left it green -
Or was it then so old that History's pages
Contain' d no record of its early ages ?

Still silent? incommunicative elf
Art sworn to secrecy ? then keep thy vows ;
But prythee tell us something of thyself -
Reveal the secrets of thy prison house :
Since in the world of spirits thou hast slumber'd,
What hast thou seen - what strange adventures number'd ?

Since first thy form was in this box extended,
We have, above-ground, seen some strange mutations ;
The Roman empire has begun and ended,
New worlds have risen we have lost old nations,
And countless kings have into dust been humbled,
While not a fragment of thy flesh has crumbled.

Didst thou not hear the pother o'er thy head,
    When the great Persian conqueror, Cambyses,
Marched armies o'er thy tomb with thundering tread, -
    O'erthrew Osiris, Orus, Amis, Isis ;
And shook the pyramids with fear and wonder,
When the gigantic Memnon fell asunder ?

If the tomb's secrets may not be confessed,
    The nature of thy private life unfold :
A heart has throbbed beneath that leathern breast,
    And tears adown that dusty cheek have rolled ;
Have children climbed those knees, and kissed that face ?
What was thy name and station, age and race ?

Statue of flesh, – immortal of the dead !
    Imperishable type of evanescence !

Posthumous man, - who quit'st thy narrow bed,
And standest undecayed within our presence !
Thou wilt hear nothing till the judgment morning,
When the great trump shall thrill thee with its warning.

Why should this worthless tegument endure,
If its undying guest be lost forever ?
O, let us keep the soul embalmed and pure
In living virtue, that when both must sever,
Although corruption may our frame consume,
The immortal spirit in the skies may bloom !

References

ATKINS WILSON, L. S. 1821. *Fruits of Enterprize exhibited in the Travels of Belzoni in Egypt and Nubia; interspersed with the Observations of a Mother to her Children*, London.

BAGHIANI, A., and J. TAYLOR. 2012. "Sarah Belzoni's Grave and Tombstone," *Egyptian Archaeology: The Bulletin of the Egypt Exploration Society* 40, 36.

BALTY, J.-Ch. et al. 1988. *Musées Royaux d'Art et d'Histoire, Bruxelles. Antiquité*. Brussels: Crédit Communal.

BARTIER, J. 1981. "Francs-maçons italiens et français à Bruxelles à l'époque du roi Guillaume d'après des documents inédits." Pp. 203–24 in *Laïcité et franc-maçonnerie. Etudes rassemblées et publiées par Guy Cambier*. Brussels: Presses de l'Université libre de Bruxelles.

BATTISTINI, M. 1935–1936. "La fama di Giovanbattista Belzoni nel Belgio." *Atti della Regia Accademia di Scienze, Lettere ed Arti in Padova* 52, 5–11.

BELZONI, S. 1828. *Prospectus. Madame Belzoni se propose de publier une Série de Lithographies d'après des dessins originaux et inédits, du modèle de la Tombe Égyptienne qui fut découverte dans la vallée de Baban-el-Malook, près de Thèbes, Haute Égypte, dans l'année 1818, par Giovanni Batista Belzoni, mort à Gato, dans le Royaume de Bénin, le 3 décembre sur sa route pour Houssa et Timbuctoo*. Paris: Firmin Didot.

BRUWIER, M.-C. 1998. "J.-J. Rifaud en Belgique." Pp. 17–34 in *L'Égypte au regard de J.-J. Rifaud, 1786–1852. Lithographies conservées dans les collections de la Société royale d'Archéologie, d'Histoire et de Folklore de Nivelles et du Brabant wallon*. Nivelles: Société Royale d'Archéologie, d'Histoire et de Folklore de Nivelles et du Brabant wallon.

CAPART, J. 1935. "Le cercueil et la momie de Boutehamon," *Bulletin des Musées Royaux d'Art et d'Histoire*, 3ème série 7, 111–13.

———. 1936. *Le Temple des Muses*. Brussels: Musées royaux d'Art et d'Histoire.

CAPITAINE, U. 1854. "Analectes. Correspondance de Bernard de Montfaucon, Bénédictin avec le baron G. de Crassier, archéologue liégeois," *Bulletin de l'Institut Archéologique Liégeois* 2, 347–424.

CHAMPOLLION-FIGEAC, J.-J., et al. (eds.). 1830. "Archéologie, numismatique. 267. Dessins du tombeau égyptien découvert par Belzoni (*Prospectus*)," *Bulletin des sciences historiques. Antiquités. Philologie* 14, 423–24.

CHRISTOPHE, L.-A. (ed.). 1979. G. *Belzoni, Voyages en Égypte et en Nubie*. Paris: Pygmalion/Gérard Watelet.

CLAIR, C. 1957. *Strong Man Egyptologist*. London: Oldbourne.

Clayton, P. A. 1998. "A Pioneer Egyptologist : Giovanni Baptista Belzoni, 1778–1823." Pp. 41–50 in P. Starkey and J. Starkey (eds.), *Travellers in Egypt*. London: Taris Parke.

Curl, J. 1994. *Egyptomania: The Egyptian Revival: A Recurring Theme in the History of Taste*. Manchester, UK: Manchester University Press.

Davies, B. G. 1997. "Too Many Butehamuns? Additional Observations on Their Identity," *Studien zur Altägyptischen Kultur* 24, 49–68.

De Garis Davies, N., and M. F. L. Macadam. 1957. *A Corpus of Inscribed Egyptian Funerary Cones*. Oxford: Griffith Institute.

de Loë, Baron A. 1937. *Belgique ancienne. Catalogue descriptif et raisonné. III: La période romaine*. Brussels: Vromant.

Delvaux, L. et al. 1993. "Collection d'antiques." In Dierkens A. and J.-M. Duvosquel (eds.), *Henri-Joseph Redouté et l'Expédition de Bonaparte en Égypte*. Brussels: Crédit Communal, 141–49.

De Meulenaere, H. 1980. "Une histoire mystérieuse de cercueils." In B. van de Walle, L. Limme, and H. De Meulenaere, *La collection égyptienne: Les étapes marquantes de son développement*. Brussels: Musées royaux d'Art et d'Histoire, 75–80.

De Meulenaere, H., L. Limme, and J. Quaegebeur. 1985. *Peter Munro, Die spätägyptischen Totenstelen. Index et addenda*. Brussels: Musées royaux d'Art et d'Histoire.

Disher, M. D. 1957. *Pharao's Fool*. London: Heinemann.

Dodson, A., and A. Baghiani. 2013. "Restoration of the Headstone of Sarah Belzoni in the Mont à l'Abbé Cemetery, St Helier, Jersey," *ASTENE Bulletin* 55, 14.

Dopp, H. 1932. *La contrefaçon des livres français en Belgique de 1815 à 1852*, Recueil de Travaux publiés par les Membres des Conférences d'Histoire et de Philologie de l'Université de Louvain. Louvain: Librairie Universitaire.

Duchesne, A. 1953. *A la recherche d'une colonie belge. Le consul Blondeel en Abyssinie (1840–1842). Contribution à l'histoire précoloniale de la Belgique*. Institut Royal Colonial Belge. Section des Sciences morales et politiques. Mémoires. Collection in 8°. Série historique. Tome XXX, fasc. 3. Brussels: Académie Royale des Sciences d'Outre-Mer.

Du Nil à l'Escaut. 1991. Brussels: Blondé Artprinting.

Égypte et regards occidentaux. 1995. Mariemont: Musée Royal de Mariemont.

Evers, C. 2008. "Emile de Meester de Ravestein, diplomate et archéologue." Pp. 259–78 in A. Tsingarida and A. Verbanck-Pierard (eds.), *L'Antiquité au service de la Modernité ? La réception de l'Antiquité classique en Belgique au XIXe siècle. Actes du Colloque international organisé du 27 au 29 avril 2005 à l'Université libre de Bruxelles et au Musée royal de Mariemont*. Brussels: Le Livre Timperman.

Fagan, B. M. 1975. *The Rape of the Nile: Tomb Robbers, Tourists, and Archaeologists in Egypt*. London: Macdonald & Jane's.

Folsom, Ch. 1834. *The Select Journal of Foreign Periodical Litterature*: Boston: Bowen.

Francot, C., L. Limme, F. Van Els, M.-P. Van Lathem, and B. Van Rinsveld. 1999. *Les momies égyptiennes des Musées royaux d'Art et d'Histoire et leur étude radiographique*. Turnhout: Brepols and Musées royaux d'Art et d'Histoire.

Galtier, G. 1989. *Maçonnerie égyptienne, Rose-Croix et Néo-chevalerie. Les fils de Cagliostro*. Paris: Rocher.

Gessler-Löhr, B. 2012. "Who Discovered "Belzoni's Tomb'? A Glimpse behind the Scenes of Early Exploration and the Antiquities Trade." Pp. 101–23 in *Talking along the Nile: Ippolito Rosellini, Travelers and Scholars of the Late 19th Century in Egypt. University of Pisa, June 14–16th 2012*. Pisa: Pisa University Press.

Hamill, J., and P. Mollier. 2003. "Rebuilding the Sanctuaries of Memphis: Egypt in Masonic Iconography and Architecture." Pp. 207–20 in J.-M. Humbert and C. Price (eds.),

Imhotep Today: Egyptianizing Architecture. London: UCL Press.

HAMMADI, R., and M.-J. DUMONT. 1988. *Paris Arabesques. Architectures et décors arabes et orientalisants à Paris*. Paris: Koehler.

HARRIS, J. R. 1960. "A propos de la prétendue momie du scribe royal Boutehamon." *CdE* 35, nos. 69–70, 89–91.

HELBIG, H. 1873a. "Crassier (Guillaume-Paschal, baron de)." In *Biographie nationale*, IV. Brussels: Académie royale des Sciences, des Lettres et des Beaux-Arts de Belgique, cols. 487–490.

———. 1873b. "Crassier (Louis-Marie-Guillaume-Joseph, baron de)." In *Biographie nationale* IV. Brussels: Académie royale des Sciences, des Lettres et des Beaux-Arts de Belgique, cols. 490–493.

HELLINCKX, B.-R. 2006. "Cercueils et cartonnages." In E. WARMENBOL (ed.), *La Caravane du Caire. L'Égypte sur d'autres rives*. Louvain-la-Neuve: Versant Sud/La Renaissance du Livre, 205–22.

HUMBERT, J.-M. 1998, *L'Égypte à Paris*. Paris: Action artistique de la Ville de Paris.

HUME, I. N. 2012. *Belzoni: The Giant Archaeologists Love to Hate*. Charlottesville: University of Virginia Press.

HYMANS, H. 1911–1913. "Schayes (Antoine-Guillaume-Bernard)." In *Biographie Nationale* XXI. Brussels: Académie Royale des Sciences, des Lettres et des Beaux-Arts de Belgique, cols. 604–626.

JAEGER, B. 1996. "Le café Pedrocchi de Padoue et la "modification du regard" porté sur l'Égypte ancienne en Italie au XIXe siècle." Pp. 189–225 in J.-M. HUMBERT (ed.), *L'Égyptomanie à l'épreuve de l'archéologie. Actes du colloque international organisé au musée du Louvre par le Service culturel les 8 et 9 avril 1994*. Paris: Musée du Louvre; Brussels: Editions du Gram.

JONCKHEERE, F. 1942. *Autour de l'autopsie d'une momie: le scribe royal Boutehamon*. Brussels: Fondation Egyptologique Reine Elisabeth.

JUSTE, Th. 1864. *Catalogue des collections composant le Musée Royal d'Antiquités, d'Armures et d'Artillerie (Bruxelles), précédé d'une notice historique*. Brussels: Bruylant-Christophe.

KOLTZ, J. P. J. 1869. "Notice sur Nicolas Bové, naturaliste-voyageur," *Bulletin de la Société Royale de Botanique de Belgique* 8.2, 202–6.

LIMME, L. 1979, *Stèles égyptiennes*. Guides du département égyptien 4. Brussels: Musées royaux d'Art et d'Histoire.

———. 1980. "L'accroissement de la collection jusqu'en 1884." In B. VAN DE WALLE, L. LIMME, and H. DE MEULENAERE, *La collection égyptienne: Les étapes marquantes de son développement*. Brussels: Musées royaux d'Art et d'Histoire, 39–73.

———. 1989. "La collection égyptienne des M.R.A.H. Notes additionnelles sur les étapes marquantes de son développement." *CdE* 20, nos. 127–128, 98–110.

LOCKHART, G. P. 1830. *Personal memoirs ; or, Reminescences of men and manners at home and abroad, during the last half century. With occasional sketches of the author's life*, II. London: Henry Colburn and Richard Bentley.

MANLEY, D., and P. RÉE. 2001. *Henry Salt. Artist, Traveler, Diplomat, Egyptologist*. London: Libri.

MAYES, S. 1959. *The Great Belzoni*. London: Putnam.

NIWINSKI, A. 1988. *21st Dynasty Coffins from Thebes*. Mainz: von Zabern.

———. 2006. "The *Book of the Dead* on the Coffins of the 21st Dynasty." In B. BACKES, I. MUNRO, and S. STÖHR (eds.), *Totenbuch-Forschungen. Gesammelte Beiträge des 2. Internationalen Totenbuch-Symposiums* 2005. Studien zum Altägyptische Totenbuch 11. Wiesbaden: Harrassowitz, 245–64.

Pearce, S. M. 2000. "Giovanni Battista Belzoni's Exhibition of the Reconstructed Tomb of Pharaoh Seti I in 1821," *Journal of the History of Collections* 12, 109–125.

Raedler, C. 2011. "Prestige, Role and Performance." Pp. 135–54 in R. Gundlach and K. Spence (eds.), *Palace and Temple. Architecture – Decoration – Ritual. 5th Symposium on Egyptian Royal Ideology. Cambridge, July, 16th–17th 2007*. Wiesbaden: Harrassowitz.

Regellini de Schio, M. 1825. *Esprit du dogme de la Franche-Maçonnerie. Recherche sur son origine et celle de ses différens rites, compris celui du Carbonarisme*. Brussels: Tarlier.

———. 1829. *La Maçonnerie considérée comme le résultat des religions égyptienne, juive et chrétienne*. Brussels: Tarlier.

Ridley, R. T. 1998. *Napoleon's Proconsul in Egypt: The Life and Times of Bernardino Drovetti*. London: Rubicon.

Roulez, J. 1842. "Note sur quelques antiquités romaines d'Arlon," *Bulletin de l'Académie royale des Sciences et Belles-Lettres de Bruxelles* 9, 2ème partie, 350–52.

Schayes, A. G. B. 1854. *Catalogue et description du Musée royal d'Armures, d'Antiquités et d'Ethnologie*. Brussels: Weissenbruch.

Schneider, H. D. 1977. *Shabtis: An Introduction to the History of Ancient Egyptian Funerary Statuettes, with a Catalogue of the Collection of Shabtis in the National Museum of Antiquities at Leiden*. Leiden: Rijksmuseum van Oudheden.

Siliotti, A. (ed.) 2001. *Belzoni's Travels: Narrative of the Operations and Research Discoveries in Egypt and Nubia*. London: British Museum Press.

Tardi, J. 1978. *Momies en folie*. Tournai: Casterman.

Taylor, J. 2011. "Egypt in Jersey," *Ancient Egypt* 11.6, 38–41.

Tompkins, P. 1981. *The Magic of Obelisks*. New York: Harper & Row.

van de Sande, A. 1995. *Vrijmetselarij in de Lage Landen. Een mysterieuze broederschap zonder geheimen*, Zutphen: Walburg Pers.

van de Walle, B. 1980. "La collection égyptienne depuis ses origines jusqu'à la mort de Jean Capart." Pp. 7–37 in B. van de Walle, L. Limme, and H. De Meulenaere, *La collection égyptienne: Les étapes marquantes de son développement*. Brussels: Musées royaux d'Art et d'Histoire.

———. 1985. "Emile de Meester de Ravestein (1813–1889)." Pp. 149–55 in *Liber Memorialis, 1835–1885*. Brussels: Musées royaux d'Art et d'Histoire.

van de Walle, B., L. Limme, and H. De Meulenaere. 1980. *La collection égyptienne. Les étapes marquantes de son développement*. Brussels: Musées royaux d'Art et d'Histoire.

Verhoeven, U. and E. Vassilika. 2010. "Ein Nekropolenschreiber am Ende des Neuen Reiches + Katalog 54." In *Ägyptens Schätze entdecken: Meisterwerke aus dem Ägyptischen Museum Turin*. Munich: Prestel, 182–87.

Vernus, P. 1978. *Athribis: Textes et documents relatifs à la géographie, aux cultes, et à l'histoire d'une ville du delta égyptien à l'époque pharaonique*. BdE 74. Cairo: Institut Français d'Archéologie Orientale.

Walek, J. 1991. "The Czartoryski "Portrait of a Youth" by Raphael," *Artibus et historiae* 12, no. 24, 201–24.

Warmenbol, E. 1997. "Un pied serre-papier." In *Les amours d'une princesse égyptienne: Le Roman de la Momie*. Namur: Abbaye St-Gérard de Brogne, 66–70.

———. 2006. "Les antiquités égyptiennes d'Albert d'Otreppe de Bouvette. L'archéologie des nations et l'archéologie des provinces." In E. Warmenbol, *La Caravane du Caire: L'Égypte sur d'autres rives*. Louvain-la-Neuve: Versant Sud/La renaissance du Livre, 103–11.

———. 2008. "Gustave Hagemans et son cabinet d'amateur." Pp. 223–58 in A. Tsingarida and A. Verbanck-Pierard (eds.), *L'Antiquité au service de la Modernité ? La réception de l'Antiquité classique en Belgique au XIXe siècle. Actes du Colloque international organisé du 27 au 29 avril 2005 à l'Université libre de Bruxelles et au Musée royal de Mariemont.* Brussels: Le Livre Timperman.

———. 2012a. *Le lotus et l'oignon: Égyptologie et égyptomanie en Belgique au XIXe siècle.* Brussels: Le Livre Timperman.

———. 2012b. *L'Égypte vue par Florent Mols et Jacob Jacobs (1838–1839): L'orientalisme en Belgique.* Brussels: Racine.

WEISSE, J. A. 1880. *The Obelisk and Freemasonry, according to the discoveries of Belzoni and Commander Gorringe. Also Egyptian symbols compared with those discovered in American Mounds*, New York.

WERNER, A. 2003. "Egypt in London: Public and Private Displays in the 19th Century Metropolis." In J.-M. HUMBERT and C. PRICE (eds.), *Imhotep Today: Egyptanizing Architecture.* London: UCL Press, 75–104.

ZATTERIN, M. 2000. *Il Gigante del Nilo: Storia e avventure del Grande Belzoni, l'uomo che svelò i misteri dell'Egitto dei faraoni.* Milan: Arnoldo Mondadori.

Aegyptiaca Incognita: The Birth, Development, and Use of University Collections with Ancient Egyptian Objects in Northwest Europe in the Nineteenth and Twentieth Centuries

Ben van den Bercken

In 2005 Mrs. Martha Lourenço, who is now active in the UMAC-branch of ICOM, wrote her dissertation on university collections and university museums.[1] Her goals were to gather existing knowledge about these collections and to underline their importance for society in general. One of her conclusions was that more research needs to be done on the origins and development of this particular type of collection as this information will be valuable when facing future dilemmas and developments of these collections. We also need to look back to look forward.

Thus, the following study is subdivided into several sections that deal with specific points to understand the development of university collections with *aegyptiaca*, spanning the nineteenth and twentieth centuries, and their relation with the development of the disciplines Egyptology and archaeology. The first section concerns the historical foundation and development of these collections in order to understand their sociohistorical background before we can look at the key issues of this study. We will see that the development of the first university collections with *aegyptiaca* in Northwest Europe started before 1800 (§1). The second part of this study addresses the development of the first university collections with *aegyptiaca* as they formed the prelude to the development of the nineteenth century collections (§2). The third step

I would like to thank Dr. Mirjam Hoijtink from the University of Amsterdam and Prof. Dr. Olaf Kaper from the University of Leiden for their guidance in this MA-thesis. I would like to thank Dr. Dietrich Raue and Dr. Stephen Quirke for their help in accessing the archives of the Ägyptologisches Museum Georg Steindorff and the Petrie Museum of Egyptian Archaeology. I would also like to thank Prof. Dr. Claire Derriks and Dr. Luc Delvaux for providing me the opportunity to publish this paper and hence contribute to renewed attention for university collections, and finally thank Prof. Dr. Claire Derriks and Dr. Simone Burger for their advice on the manuscript text.

1. Lourenço, 2005.

is to investigate the factors that played a role in the birth and development of the Egyptian collections at northwestern European universities in the nineteenth and twentieth centuries (§3). The fourth step (§4) was to survey the major turning points in the development of archaeology and Egyptology during this same time period and their influence on ancient Egyptian collections.

The third and fourth steps also made possible a new chronological framework for the development and founding of new collections in northwestern Europe in the nineteenth and twentieth centuries and their historiographies. The third and fourth steps are discussed in this new framework in paragraphs 3.1 to 3.3. After addressing these questions, it becomes possible to analyze the relationship between the development of the collections of the Ägyptologisches Museum Georg Steindorff of the University of Leipzig and the Petrie Museum of Egyptian Archaeology at University College London and the disciplines of Egyptology and archaeology (§4), leading to some interesting conclusions (§5).

1. University Collections and Museums: A Short Biography

The development of the university museum and university collection is best illustrated by the overview given by Lourenço and Boylan.[2] According to Lourenço, university collections can be grouped into "teaching collections," "study collections," and "research collections."[3] University museums developed out of the so-called "teaching museums," best exemplified by the *Museion* in Alexandria, the Athenian *Lyceum* and Plato's *Akademia.*[4] The birth of the university in the twelfth century is often regarded as a logical consequence of the interaction between medieval Eastern and Byzantine knowledge institutions and monasteries.[5]

With a more critical perspective on the "lectio-disputatio"-model at the end of the medieval period, several "teaching collections" emerged.[6] By the sixteenth century, universities started to integrate into territorial states due to the diminishing influence of emperors and popes, and the curriculum was thus geared to more local needs. This

2. For the development of university museums and collections, see Lourenço 2005; Boylan 1999, Warhurst 1984, and De Clercq and Lourenço 2003. For the development of the university, see Zonta 2002, De Ridder-Symoens 1992, De Ridder-Symoens 1996, Rüegg 2004 and Rüegg 2010.

3. Lourenço 2005, 82.

4. Lourenço 2005, 50–51; Boylan 1999, 43. There are even earlier examples, but with these recreational status functions might have played a more important role, e.g., in Egypt and China.

5. See also North 1992, 338. See Zonta 2002, 26–30. The monasteries might even have been the predecessors of the colleges where academics lived and learned together. The initially strong link between church and university might originate from there. For the more rational world view, see Zonta 2002, 27 and 30.

6. One would hold an argument (lectio) in which the validity of the assertions was based on the quotation of authorities in the field of the matter discussed. After this followed the (disputatio). An interesting later example of a teaching collection was the collection at the University of Göttingen used by Christian Gottlob Heyne (1729–1812) to introduce archaeology as a science at the university using "aanschouwelijk onderwijs" (education based on perception, Hoijtink 2009, 24–27).

was the beginning of the end of "universitas," the boundlessness of the universities.[7] Antedating this development the number of universities increased.[8] Under the influence of Francis Bacon and Andreas Vesalius, "study collections" already emerged during the Renaissance. These collections, often of natural history or anatomy, emerged in England and spread to the east and south.[9]

Empiricism supported the need for new observations and hence material for study.[10] In the eighteenth century the so-called "research collections" emerged out of the need to create a corpus for comparison to use as a foundation for valid hypotheses and interpretations in an increasing taxonomical approach. Description, comparison, and classification were the keywords. The exploitation of teaching collections for students and researchers brought about the need to display and exhibit in teaching museums.[11] The "university museum" as we know it, came into being in 1683 when the Ashmolean Museum opened its doors in Oxford and became a model for similar institutions. For the first time, the functions of teaching, research, and exhibition fused and an infrastructure was formed (study rooms, class rooms, exhibition rooms, and library all in one institute).[12]

The development of the teaching collections, research collections, teaching museums and university museums in the nineteenth and twentieth centuries are closely related to the development of the universities of which they were part. During the first half of the nineteenth century, there were three university models. The first was the medieval model, which still existed in conservative England in the beginning of the nineteenth century. This model was based on the "*trivium-quadrivium*-system," a two-phase system (respectively three and four years study), after which the successful graduate was ready for a job as a clergyman or state official.[13]

The second model is the Napoleonic model, which aimed at establishing a new institution to erase the *Ancien Regime*. Though the university was not accessible for everyone, classes became more specialized and the curriculum was based on the needs of the young Republic.[14] The goal was to teach a new class of state officials to create

7. The universitas points to the role of universities in the 13th century. Universitas means that the university was not so much an educational institute belonging to a city or diocese, but served a greater ("international," "universal") ideal: the gathering and teaching of knowledge (Zonta 2002, 27–28).

8. The universities spread among others to the east, to Russia, see Zonta 2002, 34–35.

9. This led to the birth of anatomical theaters in among others Padua and Leiden (for the latter see Van Berkel 2005, 137).

10. Frijhoff 1996, 46.

11. Lourenço 2005, 54. Lourenço mentions as examples the hortus botanicus, the anatomical museum in Leiden and Pisa, and the university library of Altdorf (Nuremberg). In other cases this could also be private teaching museums like the collection of the physician Frederik Ruysch in Amsterdam, see http://ruysch.dpc.uba.uva.nl/cgi/t/text/text-idx?page=ruysch-les;c=ruysch;cc=ruysch;lang=nl.

12. Later on the Conservatoire des Arts et Métiers in Paris fulfilled a similar function, see Lourenço 2005, 66.

13. In this education the emphasis was on the study of the seven arts: grammar, rhetoric, dialectic, math, geometry, music and astronomy. See also Charle 2004, 53.

14. Charle 2004, 44–45.

stability and harmonization in the education system with a new ideology and the suppression of intellectual opposition. A clear division between the faculties emerged.

The third model, the Prussian, or Humboldt university, model (as opposed the Napoleonic model) and was first applied in Berlin in 1810. Wilhelm von Humboldt (1767–1835) stressed the importance of professors conducting research, as this research and its results could be immediately used in the education of their students. Practice of science was more important than the training of students for a specific profession. Philosophy became an essential element, and students were taught to work in an interdisciplinary fashion, putting their research in perspective.[15] From World War II onwards, we have seen a hybrid system in which the Prussian (*"Interesse-Student"*) and the Napoleonic model (*"Brotstudent"*) have been mixed, depending upon trends, societal changes and the influence of globalization.[16]

From 1800 to 1930, most university museums came into being.[17] In this period, specialized museum institutions were formed, focusing on archaeology, ethnology, natural history, art history and collections related to these fields.[18] At this time, these collections were used by Prussian universities as research collections and in England (e.g., Cambridge, Oxford, Glasgow, London, and Manchester) for teaching and (inter)national research.[19]

Beyond being a tool for education and research, a collection was also perceived as a tool of prestige for the university and its educational mission. Moreover, the university collection played an important role of preserving environmental and cultural heritages. Universities were major components in this role until the 1960s when independent specialized institutions took over this mission.[20] From 1990 onwards, a number of inventory initiatives have emerged as a response to have an overview of different university collections and their states of preservation. This has created awareness of the need to search for ways to preserve these collections for the future.[21]

15. Charle 2004, 48.

16. Charle 2004, 57–61. For the globalization see Rüegg 2010, 38. For the Napoleonic model and the university for the masses, see Neave 2010, 54.

17. Lourenço 2005, 68 and 372–74.

18. Boylan 2000, 47. In the Ashmolean this happened in 1860 when among others the collection of natural history was transferred to the University Museum of Natural History, see Whitehouse 2009, xii. A similar process can be seen in the "Leidse kwestie." In this case disposal of university collections to the government ("rijksmusea") enabled the museums to obtain more funding for the collections. In Leiden this shaped the more specialized institutes of the National Museum of Antiquities (1867), the National Museum of Ethnology (1837) and the National Museum of Natural History (1822), see Hoijtink 2009, 170.

19. Warhurst 1984, 76–77.

20. Warhurst 1984, 77.

21. In the Netherlands a good attempt to make an inventory of these collections was published in the report "Om het academisch erfgoed," 1996. A solution that has been applied nowadays is the integration of different sorts of collections like the collections of antiquities and rare books of the University of Amsterdam in 2008 (the Allard Pierson Museum and the Bijzondere Collecties).

2. *The First University* Aegyptiaca *Collections*

After the introduction of Christianity as a main religion of the Roman Empire in the fourth century AD, ancient Egyptian culture was first suppressed and then slowly forgotten. Despite the isolation of Egypt from the West after the conquest of the country by the Arabs in AD 641, Egyptian objects found their way into western collections.[22] *Aegyptiaca* that were moved to the West during the Roman and Byzantine periods became the object of study.[23] The best-known example is that of the Jesuit Athanasius Kircher (1602–1680). During his stay in Rome, Kircher focused principally on deciphering hieroglyphs. His work led to some interesting new perspectives, but it did not result in the decoding of ancient Egyptian. However, Kircher's work reflected his access to Arabic sources and *aegyptiaca* brought to Europe by travellers.

Another phenomenon came in of anatomical and natural history interest in ancient Egyptian mummies. These often ended up in anatomical cabinets like that brought together by Otto Heurnius as discussed below.[24] However, the interest in Coptic Egypt seems to have been more intense than pharaonic Egypt. In the first half of the nineteenth century Egyptologists principally collected Coptic writings. Coptic language was, next to classical languages, the basis for the development of Egyptology at the universities.

One of the earliest university *aegyptiaca* collections was that of the Hogeschool Leiden (later Leiden University). In Leiden, the anatomy professor Otto Heurnius (1577–1652) started collecting *aegyptiaca* from an interest in anatomy around 1620. Along with mummies, objects of daily life were also collected.[25] Later on these objects would become part of Casper Reuvens's (1793–1835) "Archeologisch Kabinet" and more recently, forming an integral part of the National Museum of Antiquities in Leiden.

A second, early collection can be found in Uppsala, Sweden, dating from the seventeenth century. In 1694, the art cabinet of the Augsburg king Charles XI was donated to the University of Uppsala. It contained, among other objects, a *shabti*,

22. An often heard argument that during the Islamic period there was little attention for the pharaonic past is not true and based on a hiatus that was kept up by the West. Muslim scholars also studied ancient Egypt. A recent treatment of this subject can be found in El-Daly 2005, 1–8.

23. Ancient Egyptian objects left Egypt during the Roman and Byzantine periods as war spoils and souvenirs, e.g., the large obelisks and naophore statues. Sometimes they even were a source of inspiration, e.g., in the villa of Hadrian in Tivoli where also imported objects have been found; see, e.g., the Vatican Museum website: http://mv.vatican.va/3_EN/pages/MEZ/MEZ_Sala05.html (consulted on 24–3–2011) and the Ägyptisches museum in Munich, http://www.aegyptisches-museum-muenchen.de/de/index.htm (consulted on 29–3–2011).

24. In fact the collection of Heurnius is regarded by Lourenço's typology as one of the first "teaching collections." The collection brought together by Heurnius for the Hogeschool Leiden was a shared responsibility of the Dutch state and the Hogeschool Leiden from 1818 onwards. In 1863 the collection became part of the National Museum of Antiquities in Leiden and in 1971 it was officially separated from Leiden University, Hoijtink 2009, 57 and 170–71.

25. See Van Berkel 2005, 139.

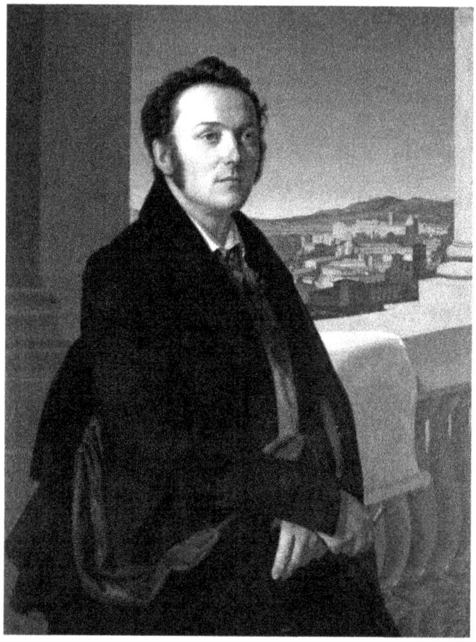

Fig. 1. Gustave Seyffarth, one of the earliest professors in Egyptology at the University of Leipzig. © Ägyptologisches Museum Georg Steindorff, University of Leipzig.

a fragment of mummy wrappings, and a scarab.[26] The French traveller Aubry de la Montraye mentioned the presence of a mummy in the anatomical classroom around 1715–1720.[27] It is interesting that here also there is another direct link between anatomical education and *aegyptiaca*. Based upon the seemingly direct relationship between anatomy and *aegyptiaca*, we might conclude that university *aegyptiaca* collections in general emerged as a by-product of the study of anatomy, or that this science gave a strong impulse to the development of these collections.

3. *The Collections and Their Context in the Nineteenth and Twentieth Centuries in Northwestern Europe*

As discussed above, a comparison between the development of the *aegyptiaca* collections and that of the study of archaeology and Egyptology in nineteenth- and twentieth-century northwestern Europe makes it possible to identify three periods of development in the collections.

3.1. Period 1820–1890: Pioneering

The first "Egyptologists" were scholars employed at an university, who often had a background in classical languages. Such is the case with Gustave Seyffarth (1796–1885, fig. 1), who started the Egyptian collection in Leipzig around 1842 and used

26. Betz 2005, 11–12.

27. See Betz 2005, 12 for this mummy. This mummy was mentioned before in 1704.

it in his classes.[28] Other universities also had collections that were however not used in education and thus were "dormant" (e.g., in Oxford, Cambridge, Manchester, and Gent).[29] In the first half of the nineteenth century, research into ancient Egyptian languages and culture was revolutionary as positions at universities were created for it from this time onwards (Jean-François Champollion[1790–1832] being the first). This led to the takeover of the research functions of the *academies* by the universities.[30]

After an energetic start to a university-level Egyptology, the political instability caused by the Napoleonic wars engendered a period of stagnation from 1830 to 1870. Moreover, the presence and growth of national collections, such as the Louvre and Neues Museum, made university *aegyptiaca* collections somewhat redundant. Yet, at the same time, Egyptology started to become an established scientific discipline because of the work of pioneers like Karl Lepsius (1810–1884), Charles Lenormant (1802–1859), and Emmanuel De Rougé (1811–1872).

From 1870 onwards, a second wave started in Egyptology of education and collection building, with the appointment as professor of Georg Ebers (1837–1875), Johannes Dümichen (1833–1894), and Heinrich Brugsch (1827–1894). Ebers trained the next generation of Egyptologists at the universities of Jena and Leipzig, many of whom went on to establish new professorships elsewhere (e.g., Alfred Wiedemann (1856–1936) and Adolf Erman (1854–1937).[31] Ebers was also occupied with writing novels about ancient Egypt for the general public, encouraging the growing interest in *Egyptomania* in the second half of the nineteenth century, and inspiring future students like his successor at the University of Leipzig, Georg Steindorff (1861–1951; fig. 2).[32] Ebers also gave lectures and opened up the university collection to the general public.[33]

It is remarkable that other university collections were only emerging in the 1880s (e.g., in Uppsala and Lyon) after the establishment of the first Egyptological libraries and seminar spaces from 1874 onwards. The preoccupation with classical heritage and the appropriation of it, mainly in England and France, played a role in this. Important linguistic publications date from this period, most specifically Ermans's hieroglyphic grammars (1883 and 1894) and the division of the hieroglyphic language into multiple phases. The composition of university collections mirrors this development. For example, in Leipzig in this period most of the objects collected were inscribed. In the first half of the nineteenth century rivalry, among the empires and early states played a role in the emergence of Egyptology as a science.

28. Blumenthal 1981, 3–7.

29. "Dormant collections" are collections that existed earlier but did not play an active role in Egyptological education, study, or presentation purposes.

30. Leezenberg and De Vries 2001, 228–29.

31. Blumenthal 1981, 11–12.

32. Blumenthal 1981, 12.

33. Blumenthal 1981, 13 and Fischer-Elfert and Seyfried 2009, 328.

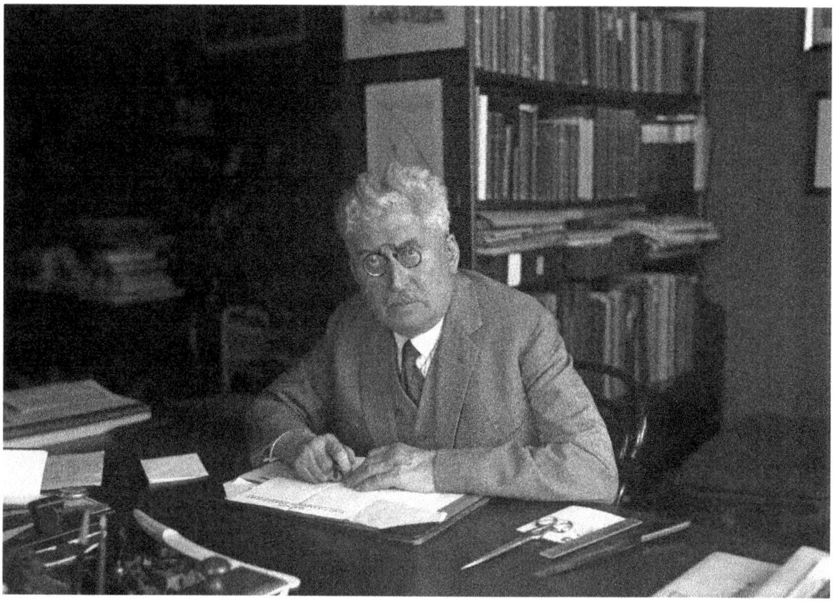

Fig. 2. Georg Steindorff, working at the University of Leipzig in 1931. © Ägyptologisches Museum Georg Steindorff, University of Leipzig.

During the years 1880–1890, students of the first generation of professors in Egyptology became professors themselves at other universities and started university *aegyptiaca* collections for educational purposes. In Lyon (1886), Strasbourg (1888), Uppsala (1889), and Bonn (1891), new collections were started and dormant collections were put to use.

3.2. Period 1890–1939: Gathering

The next, third generation of professors focused on a new perspective in the study of ancient Egypt, namely, archaeology. This increasing importance of material culture, due to developments in archaeology in Europe and the Near East, was supported by the work of William Flinders Petrie (1853–1942; fig. 3). He created a favorable climate for the rapid growth of existing university collections and university positions.[34] Petrie also generated an awareness of the use of these collections in understanding ancient Egyptian culture and "the ancient Egyptian," paralleling the "*verstehende*" humanities method of Wilhelm Dilthey (1833–1911).[35]

Petrie developed a method and vision at University College London in the beginning of the 1890s. He used his own collection that later became the UCL collection as

34. Janssen 1992, 1–26.
35. Leezenberg and De Vries 2001, 138–40.

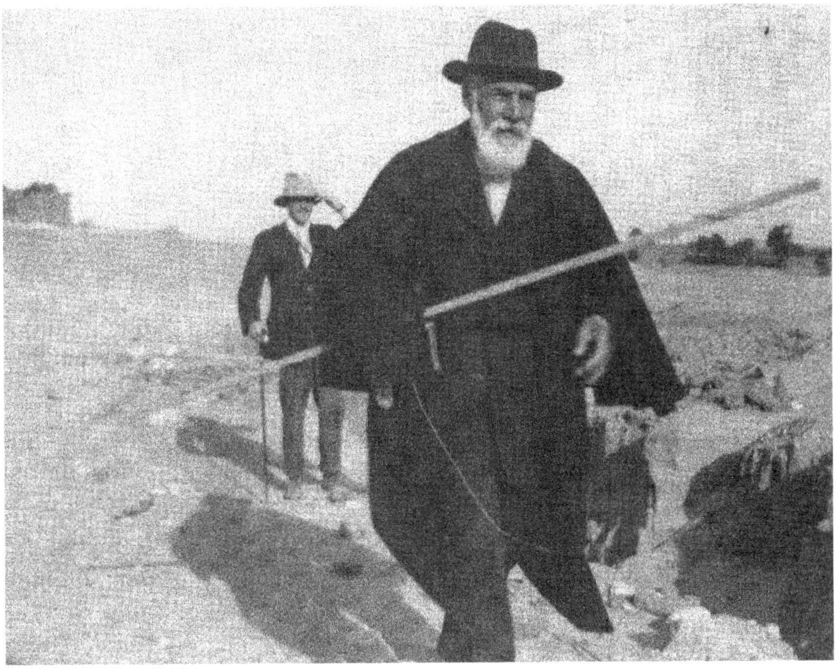

Fig. 3. William Matthew Flinders Petrie, working at Abydos in 1922. © Petrie Museum of Egyptian Archaeology, University College London.

an aid in education.[36] Steindorff did the same in Leipzig.[37] Differences in collection-based education were apparent, as the objects found in excavation under Petrie from Kahun and Amarna focused on ancient Egyptian daily life, while Steindorff's statuary and relief material from Gizeh focused on Egyptian art (fig. 4).

In the period 1890–1914 universities profited from a favorable excavation climate in Egypt and obtained finds from, for example, the British School of Archaeology in Egypt, the Egypt Exploration Fund and Manchester Egyptian Association. Both Petrie and Steindorff relied heavily on private sponsors, industrials, businesspeople, and royalty, who were fascinated by ancient Egypt which now emerged from behind the Ottoman veil.[38] University collections profited greatly from this interest and fascination, especially in Liverpool, Uppsala, Manchester, Tübingen, Cambridge, Bonn, Heidelberg, and, at a later stage, Lyon. New collections were established in Groningen, Amsterdam, Utrecht, and Lille. This process was temporarily halted by World War I.

36. The Edwards professorship was created after the will and inheritance of Amelia Edwards who felt sympathetic to Egyptology and Petrie; see Janssen 1992, 1–4; Rees 1998; and Moon 2006.
37. Blumenthal 1981, 15–31, esp. 17.
38. See also Petrie's inaugural lecture in Janssen 1992, appendix 2.

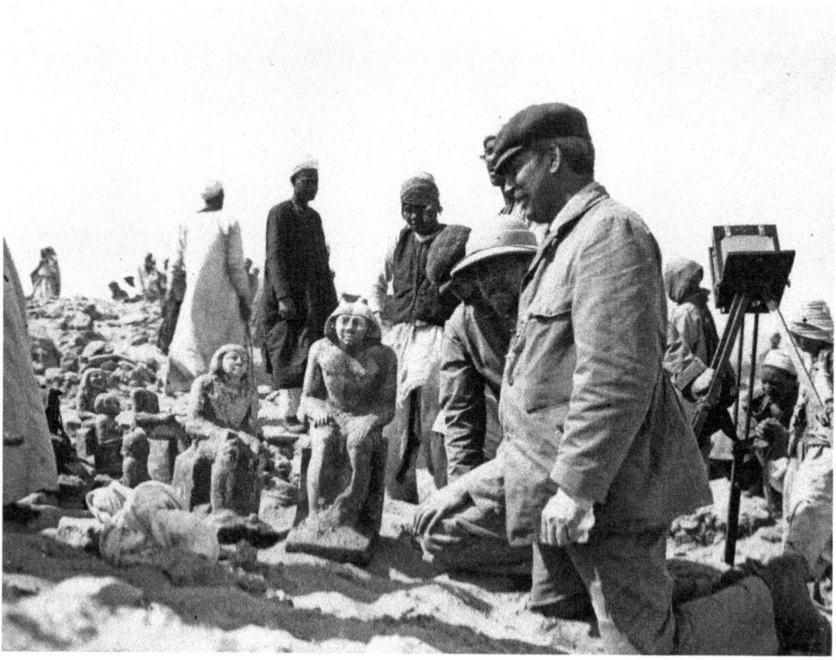

Fig. 4. Georg Steindorff working at the excavations in Gizeh in 1905, uncovering a statuary ensemble of the official Djascha. © Ägyptologisches Museum Georg Steindorff, University of Leipzig.

Both Petrie and Steindorff understood the crucial essence of public support for the university collection and their fieldwork. This translated itself in public lectures and classes, but also by the accessibility of the collection to the general public (e.g., by Petrie in 1915).[39] Steindorff gave public tours through the collection in Leipzig, showing his latest finds (fig. 5), but also wrote in the local newspaper about his travels and work in Egypt (fig. 6). Both Petrie and Steindorff were convinced that the original should be used in university classes, such as Petries's class: "Stone and Metal Vases" and "Objects of Daily Life," and Steindorff's class on "Erklärung der Denkmäler der ägyptologischen Sammlung."[40] Petrie published many of his findings and materials in a series of publications from 1914 onwards. Steindorff only published marginally on the university collection. This difference might be due to their activities. Steindorff focused on education and the popularizing of ancient Egypt, while Petrie excavated in Egypt for three-quarters of the year.

The years 1900–1939 witnessed the spectacular growth of university collections with objects from ancient Egyptian daily life. We also find an essential difference between earlier and later parts of these same collections as that the later entries had a

39. Janssen 1992, 18–19.

40. Respectively Janssen 1992, 9–10 and Blumenthal 1981, 26–27.

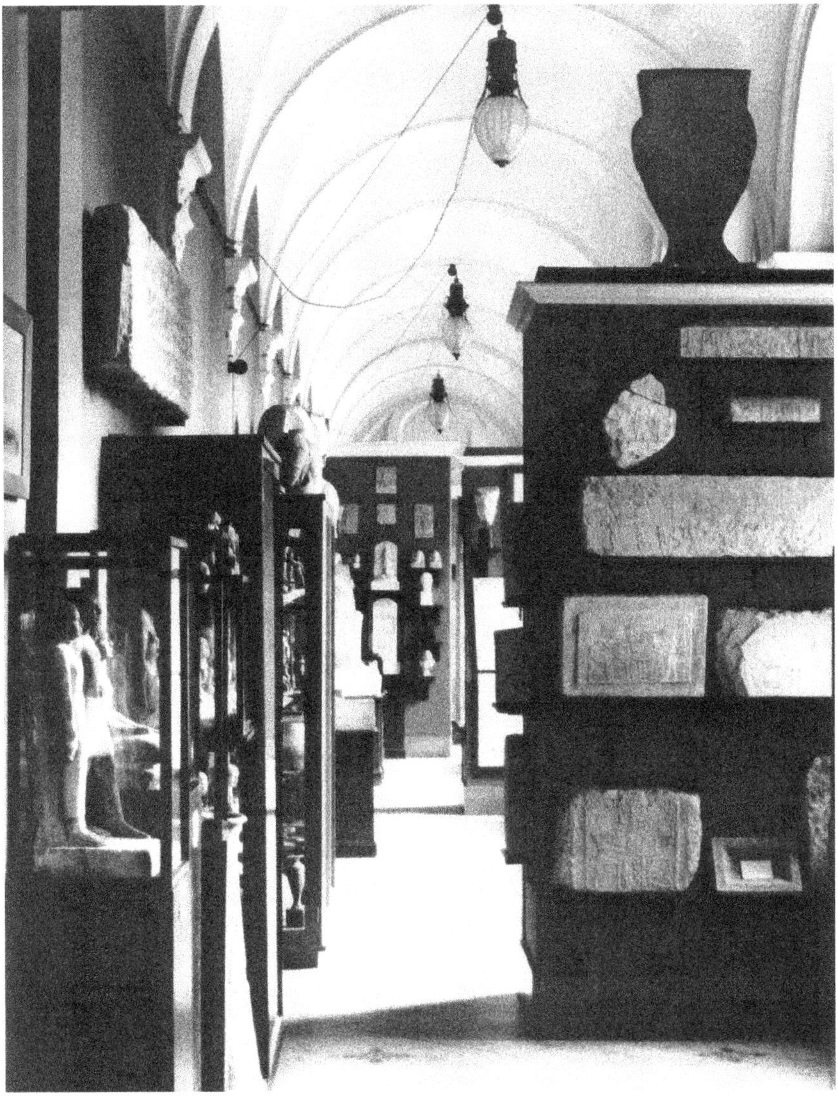

Fig. 5. View of one of the first displays of the *aegyptiaca* of the Ägyptologisches Museum Georg Steindorff (display before 1914). © Ägyptologisches Museum, Georg Steindorff, University of Leipzig.

more-properly recorded archaeological context and relative date, thanks to Petrie's sequence dating (fig. 7).

The next generation of Egyptologists and archaeologists focused more on the cultural and linguistic components of ancient Egyptian culture and less on excavation. This was the end of the strong growth of the university *aegyptiaca* collections. From the beginning of the twentieth century until World War II, displayed *aegyptiaca* were

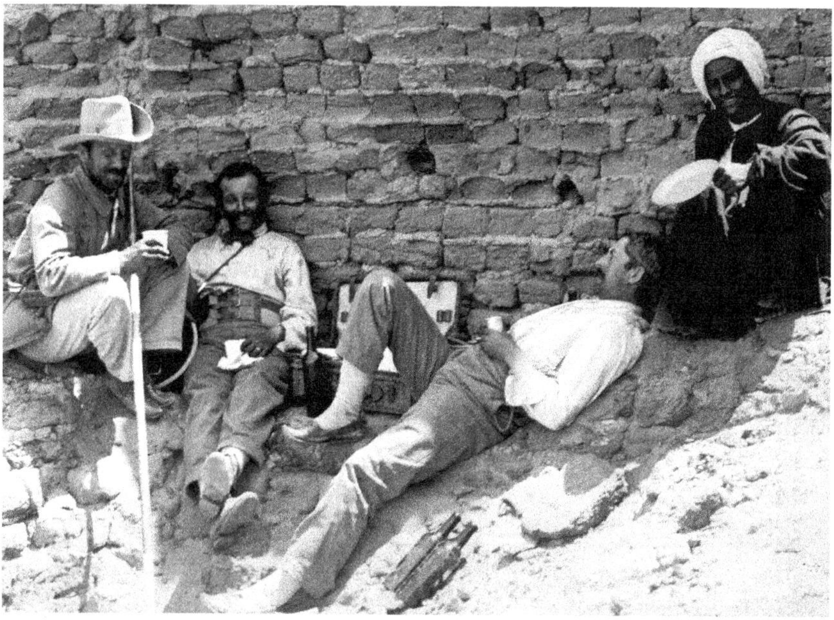

Fig. 6. A hard-earned lunch break from the archaeological work at Mirgissa. From left to right Heinrich Schäfer, Ludwig Borchardt, Georg Steindorff, and a local worker. © Ägyptologisches Museum Georg Steindorff, University of Leipzig.

increasingly regarded aesthetically as opposed to the *en masse* presentation. This esthetic development process was especially visible in Germany. However, in London, at UCL, this collided with every one of the principles of Petrie's, who argued vehemently to counter this phenomenon.[41]

3.3. Period 1945–2000: Processors

World War II saw a halt in Egyptological education and the deterioration and partial destruction of some university collections especially in Germany (e.g., Göttingen and Bonn). After World War II the collections only became available after a period of time, and the focus was henceforth more on the collections themselves. This was also possibly a result of the unstable relationship of revolutionary Egypt with European and North American excavation projects that only resumed after 1952.

During the period between 1945–1970, there was a strong structuralist emphasis in Leipzig. In Walther Wolf's *Wesen and Wert der Ägyptologie*, Egyptology itself was questioned. The emphasis on culture, which was so characteristic for the first part of the twentieth century until the end of the National Socialist regime in 1945, was

41. For the process of aesthetical development see Konijn 2005, 417. For Petrie's reaction on this process see Janssen 1992, 40.

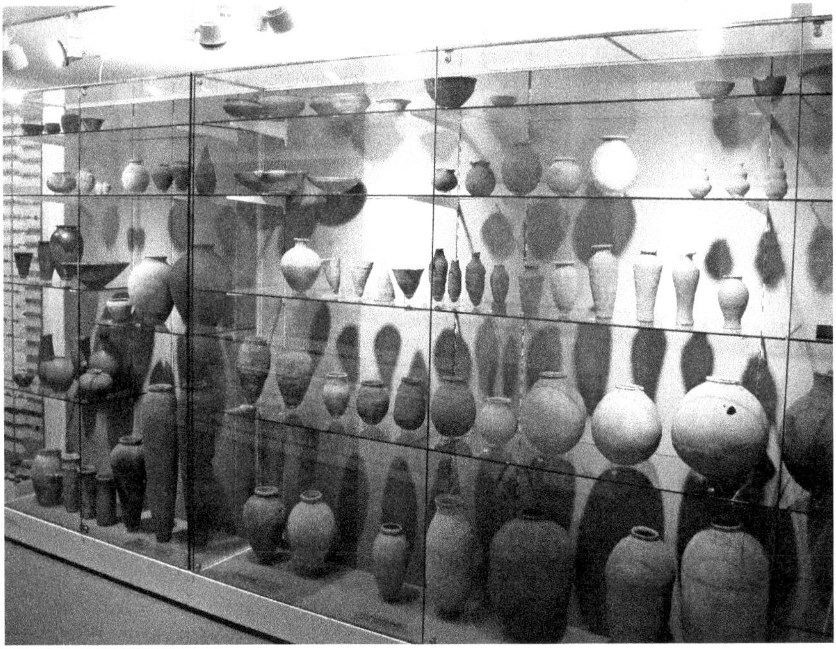

Fig. 7. Display case with a chronological overview of the pottery in the collection of the Ägyptologisches Museum Georg Steindorff. © Ägyptologisches Museum Georg Steindorff, University of Leipzig.

abandoned (the so called "Kossinna-Syndrom" coined by Smolla).[42] Siegfried Morenz (1914–1970) continued Wolf's path with his "Strukturforschung" focus on Coptic Egypt, Egyptian religion, and intercultural change and perception history.[43] His educational emphasis also attracted students of history, philosophy, and theology. The use of assistants enabled larger classes. But the strict DDR regime complicated both education and collection expansion. The collection was even closed to the general public for some time. Morenz's vision was continued by Elke Blumenthal. While at the same time, the collection entered the public domain, which generated more public support (fig. 8). Frequent, temporary exhibitions and a permanent display in 1976 opened up the collection to the public. This again necessitated research and systematic cataloguing of the collection which really becomes visible in the 1980s and 1990s.

At University College London, Jaroslav Černý focused on linguistics, art, architecture, and religion due to the inaccessibility of the collection after World War II.[44] After the appointment of Walter Emery at UCL in 1951, the collection resurfaced from the cellars and was fully used in education.[45] Students of Emery again had the

42. See Härke 1991, 206 and Smolla 1980.
43. Fischer-Elfert and Seyfried 2009, 340; Blumenthal 1981, 37.
44. Janssen 1992, 54–63.
45. Janssen 1992, 70–85.

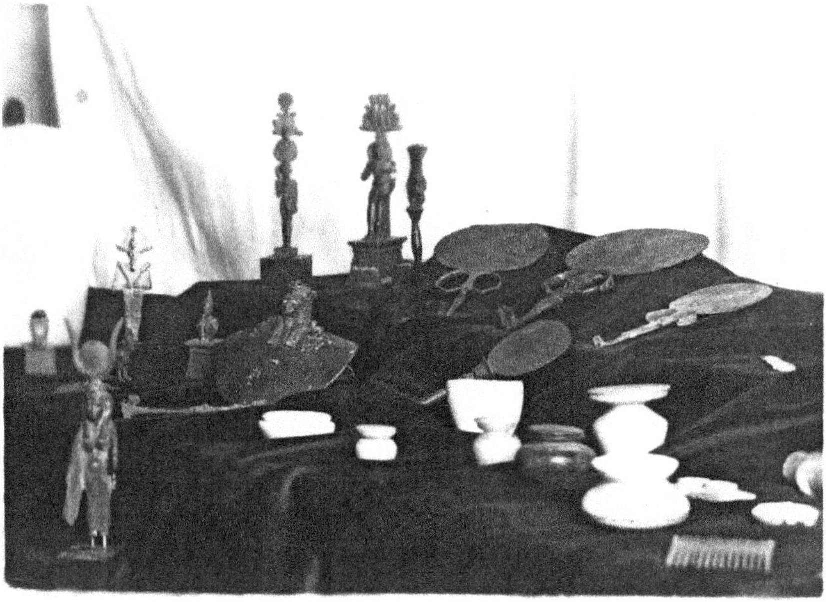

Fig. 8. One of the first exhibitions of the collections from the Ägyptologisches Museum Georg Steindorff after the Second World War. © Ägyptologisches Museum Georg Steindorff, University of Leipzig.

possibility to train themselves in fieldwork as in Petrie's day and small amounts of objects started arriving again at UCL. Emery's successors Harry Smith and Geoffrey Martin continued Emery's multidisciplinary study of ancient Egyptian culture including the study of Coptic and Demotic.[46] Students worked with the collection during classes and were trained to look carefully at objects. Inventory and cataloguing projects initiated a period of increased publication from 1970 onwards. The museum remained opened but started to use temporary exhibitions only at a relatively late date (after 2000). Since 1915, the breadth and diversity of the Petrie Museum has it a collection of infinite possibilities (fig. 9).

Though collection and education in Leipzig became relatively stagnant, elsewhere the 1960s and 1970s were a prosperous period for universities and their excavations in Egypt, for example, the work of Fritz Hintze (1915–1993) of the Seminar of the Humboldt University, Säve-Söderbergh of the Victoriamuseum, and Jean Leclant of the University of Strasbourg. This period also saw the transformation of university collection from only being used for education and research (e.g., Groningen, Gent, Lyon, and Durham) to museums.

Since the 1980s, the growth of university *aegyptiaca* collections in northwestern Europe have started to diminish while its public display has been increasing rapidly.

46. Janssen 1992, 86.

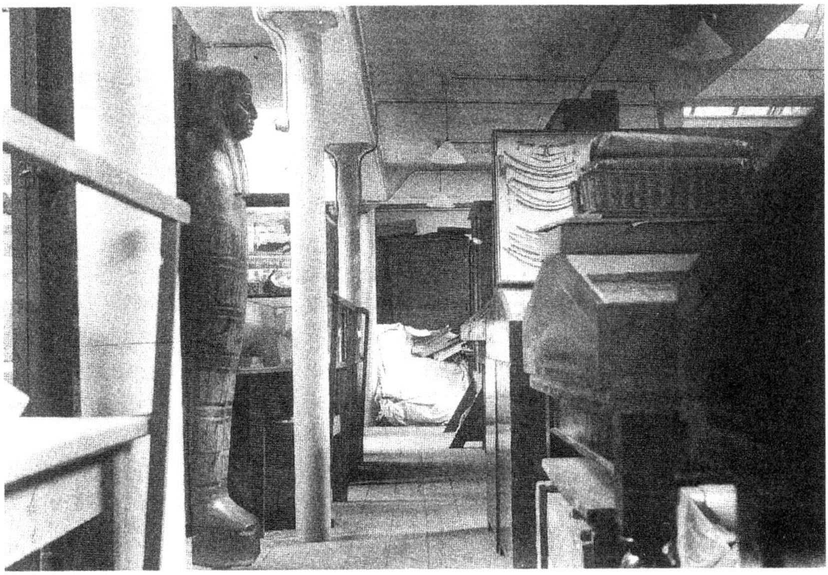

Fig. 9. View on the tightly packed Petrie Collection rooms. © Petrie Museum of Egyptian Archaeology, University College London.

An example of this trend is the Allard Pierson Museum in Amsterdam. It has become increasingly more open to the public since 1965.The same phenomenon can be seen at university museums in Gent (since 1963), Swansea (1976), and Trier (1982). Commercialization has also become a factor, and the need for public support has developed into one of the most important goals for university collections and museums.

4. *The Relationship between Discipline and Collection: The Collections in Leipzig and London*

The disciplines of Egyptian archaeology and Egyptology were formed by a research community, a physical dataset, and a theoretical framework. Both disciplines study ancient Egyptian culture. This study involves fieldwork, the processing of data, publication, the study of material from collections, the study of literature, linguistic research, and, more recently, the study of the disciplines themselves. A university *aegyptiaca* collection should thus be a logically coherent corpus of objects. It enables *"aanschouwelijk onderwijs"* of ancient Egypt (education by looking at the object), and is a source and laboratory for research-oriented education and research by specialists. The fact that it is a university collection underlines its relation and accessibility to the university curriculum.

From the abovementioned characterization it becomes clear that there is a relationship between the collections and the disciplines of archaeology and Egyptology.

Can the collections be considered separate from the disciplines of archaeology and Egyptology? Though there is a relationship, there should be little problem in looking at the collection from a theoretical perspective other than archaeology or Egyptology.[47] Furthermore, the disciplines Egyptology and archaeology are not exclusively concerned with the education of the next generation of researchers. This task falls to the university. Thus, we can speak of two different entities. The relationship between the collections and disciplines can best be seen as a relation of exchange, for example, the exchange of new insights, "personnel," material, and knowledge of ancient Egypt in general. The collections are at the same time the vanguard and ambassador of Egyptian archaeology and Egyptology in the university community. Products of education and research move in and between the disciplines and the collections in both directions.

Keeping this in mind there are some remarks that can be made about the relationship between the collections of our two cases study, the Ägyptologisches Museum Georg Steindorff in Leipzig and the Petrie Museum of Egyptian Archaeology in London, and the development of Egyptology and archaeology. Both the objects in the collections of Leipzig and London do not seem to have played a role in Adolf Ermans scientific work in distinguishing separate phases in the hieroglyphic script (among others in Middle and Late Egyptian). Erman only refers to Ebers" publication of the Papyrus Ebers in the *Belegstellen* of his grammar, while he further refers to objects and sources in other collections, for example, in Cairo, British Museum, Louvre, Berlin, Turin, and Leiden.[48] Steindorff and Brugsch also do not seem to have used the university collections for their work on the Coptic and demotic grammars.

Petrie designed his sequence dating on the basis of the UCL ceramic collection. This system was revised later by Petrie using the same collection and later Werner Kaiser further refined the system using the UCL collection.[49] Though the Petrie Museum contains an interesting collection of ceramics, it did not play a role in the design for the "Vienna System" used for the creation of a "fabric corpus" for ceramic typology. The Fitzwilliam Museum contributed to this system.[50] More recently in the last few decades, a "low" and "high-tech analysis," consisting of a microscopic provenance study for Near Eastern ceramics has also now been used for ancient Egyptian artifacts by Leiden University. However, university collections have not played a role in this ceramic analysis.

A more accurate approach to recording the provenance and dating of objects came about from the methods employed as early as Auguste Mariette (1821–1881) and then followed by Petrie (fig. 10). As a result, relatively early on, the collection of the UCL was more properly documented, as are many of the collections to which Petrie donated excavation material. In addition, the materials at the University of Leipzig,

47. The way in which the collection of the Petrie Museum was used in the light of "eugenics" in the temporary exhibition "Typecast: Flinders Petrie en Francis Galton" is interesting.

48. For the "Belegstellen" see Ermans grammar of 1928.

49. Drower 1985, 251–52; Kaiser 1956, 93.

50. For the Vienna System see Aston 1996, 1–9, for the Fitzwilliam see Arnold and Bourriau 1993, 168.

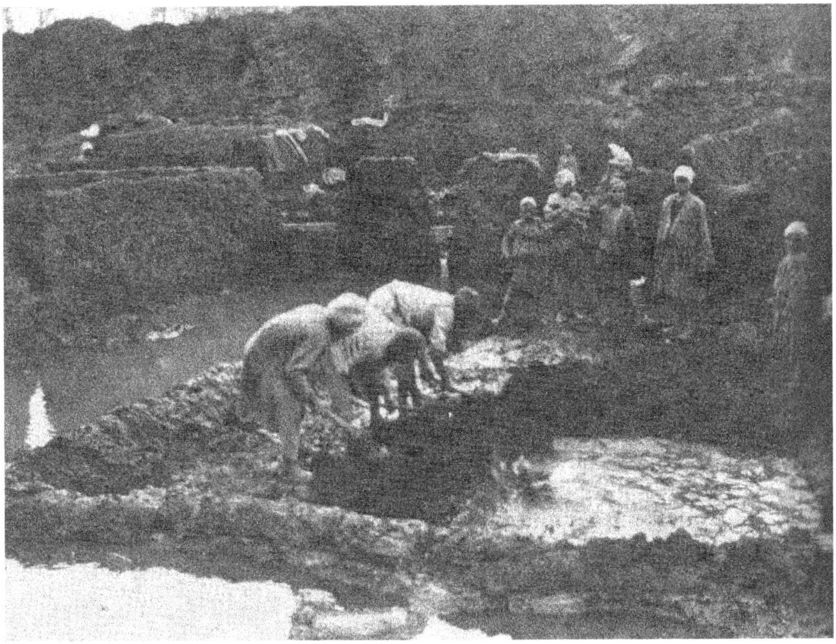

Fig. 10. Petrie's excavation work at the Ptah temple at ancient Memphis in 1910. Working systematically in squares made it possible better to assign a provenance to the objects. © Petrie Museum of Egyptian Archaeology, University College London.

originating from the excavations conducted by Steindorff are also well documented and catalogued. However, the information or "biography" (fig. 11), on objects in university collection contrasts with the lack of information on objects found in the larger, national collections. These objects were often pulled from the sand by agents of the consuls in Egypt in the early nineteenth century and then were sold on to museums. Because the recording of the context of the objects became more common practice at the end of the nineteenth century, we see that in general the relatively late university collections have better object biographies compared to objects in the larger national collections.

The development of the collections of Leipzig and London was greatly influenced by an increased interest in objects of daily life. In London this category is ubiquitous and published by Petrie.[51] In the Leipzig collection, we find large assemblages of grave goods among which pottery, cosmetic objects and jewellery still ordered systematically.[52]

The university collections also played a role in the analysis of Egyptian art. A number of important works by Steindorff, Wolf, and Schäfer each use *aegyptiaca* from

51. Petrie 1927.
52. Steindorff 1937, 114, pl. 59.

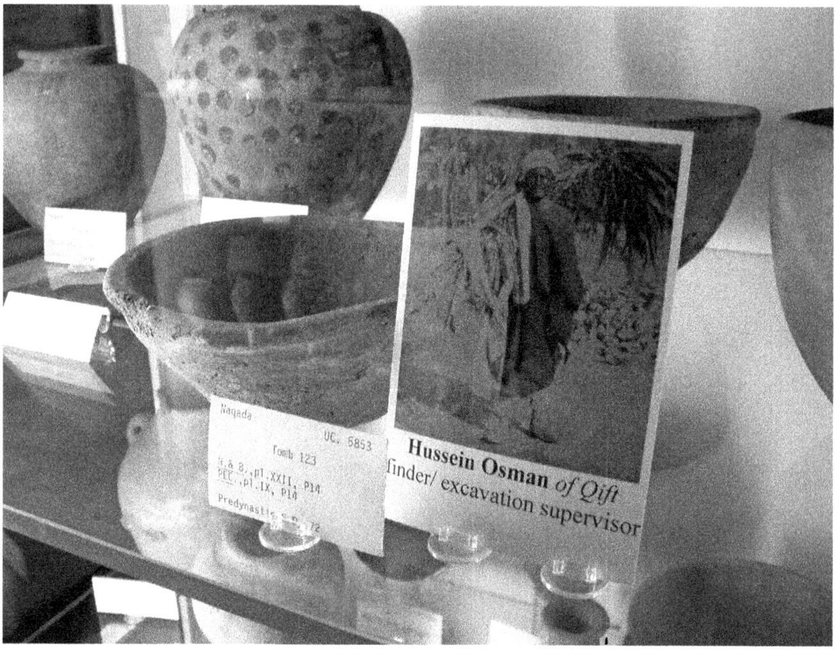

Fig. 11. Example of a better-understood object biography: pots and bowls from Naqqada, presently on display in the Petrie Museum of Egyptian Archaeology (UCL), together with a photograph of Mr. Hussein Osman who found the objects during Petrie's excavations. © Petrie Museum of Egyptian Archaeology, University College London.

the collections of Leipzig, Cambridge, Oxford, and Heidelberg. Some of these publications that are used up until today make use of objects from these collections to illustrate the development of Egyptian Art.[53] This to us is an indication that the university collections at the time of writing of these important works were well known and contained objects important enough to analyse Egyptian art.

A final element that deserves attention is the treatment of human remains or mummies. In the 1990s, the realization emerged that we should treat these remains with respect.[54] This has led to a more respectful presentation of the royal mummies in the Egyptian Museum in Cairo. Mummies or mummy parts can often be found in university collections. In Leipzig, the exhibiting of unwrapped mummies stopped in 1993. The museum in Leipzig was one of the first museums to do this. The unwrapped mummies were removed from display, and only wrapped mummies are now exhibited (fig. 12). In London, such issues were addressed, but the momentum to remove unwrapped mummy parts has yet to see the light of day.[55] This ethical question also has repercus-

53. See for example Schäfer 2002, 379 no. 56 and p. 388 nos. 4 and 6.

54. See for example Kåks 1998, 10–11.

55. There is still a mummified head in the permanent exhibition.

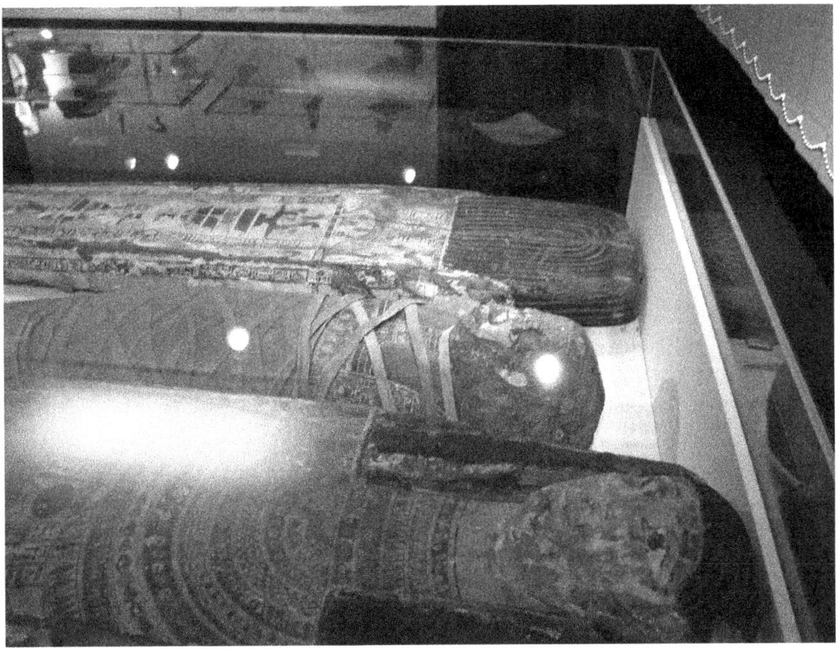

Fig. 12. Detail of the mummy room in the Ägyptologisches Museum Georg Steindorff. Mummies are displayed (wrapped) together with their coffins. © Ägyptologisches Museum Georg Steindorff, University of Leipzig.

sions for the mummy(parts) found in excavations. The respect for these remains has augmented and more and more often these remains are now reburied.

University collections appear to have influenced archaeology and Egyptology minimally at best. Yet, the impact of these collection was formative. The strongest examples of this influence and impact are relative dating through definable sequences and the discourse on the ethical display of mummy (parts) and their treatment in general. The relationship between university collections and academic disciplines is a dynamic that can be reflected in the changing interest for linguistics and archaeology, and the development of new dating techniques that expands the potential for university collections to contribute in a significant way to the study of archaeology and Egyptology. The importance of these collections for archaeology and Egyptology cannot be underestimated and varies with evolving research interests. This is a process that will continue.

5. *Concluding Remarks*

Although it is difficult to address comprehensively the relationship between the development of the collections and the development of the scientific disciplines as has been attempted in section 4, the focus on the collections at the universities of Leipzig and London (section 5) has given us a glimpse into this bond. On one side, developments in Egyptology and archaeology did have influence on university *aegyptiaca* collections. The two most important developments were: 1) contextual excavation (Petrie) and 2) the separation of the hieroglyphic language in phases (Erman). On the other side, influence of the collections on the development of Egyptology and archaeology was minimal though strong and for the time being lasting. The two most important developments were: 1) relative dating by sequences (Petrie) and 2) the ethical discourse on displaying unwrapped mummies and mummy parts.

The factors that played a role in the birth and development of these university collections of *aegyptiaca* can be characterized as follows: first we have seen that in European capitals with large national collections of *aegyptiaca*, there were no university *aegyptiaca* collections until midway through the nineteenth century. The city of Berlin exemplifies this. The presence of these large national collections made the necessity of a university collection superfluous, such as Champollion and Lepsius who used the national collections in education.

Second, the background in classical studies of scholars like Seyffarth seems to have attributed to the development of the collections. Seyffarth had the opportunity to do research into Egyptian antiquity in conjunction with his duties as professor in classics, which linked the emerging discipline of Egyptology to the university curricula. The influence of the Humboldt University model, in which research-based education was the norm, is reflected in this approach, namely, using objects to support "*aanschouwelijk onderwijs*" or looking at and investigating the objects during classes. At this early stage, university *aegyptiaca* collections became an important component of a university education.

A third factor in the development of these collections from the end of the nineteenth century onwards was the imperial aspiration of the modern European states. At the end of the nineteenth century and leading up to World War I, these imperial aspirations combined with the financial means of industrialists, prominent business people and royalty, created the right environment for the birth and development of university *aegyptiaca* collections.

From the present state of this research, two other observations can be made. First, the development of university collections is generally to be placed in the 1880s and 1890s, fifty years later than that of large national collections such as the Rijksmuseum van Oudheden, the Altes- en Neues Museum, the Musée Charles X and others. It would be interesting to see if this trend was not limited to northwestern Europe but also occurred in other regions. The second observation shows us that the development of university collections in the nineteenth and twentieth centuries in northwestern Europe can be divided into three periods: the "period of the pioneers" 1820–1890, the "period of the gatherers" 1890–1939, and the "period of the processors" 1945–2000. This division fits the developments of the collections at the universities of Leipzig and London, as well as at other universities, including Bonn, Uppsala, Liverpool, and Lyon.

This research is still in its infancy and the matter is far larger than can be addressed in this essay. Developments in southern and eastern Europe and other regions, as well as the periods prior to the nineteenth century have been purposely left unaddressed. However, this research has uncovered a framework for the developments in the nineteenth and twentieth centuries. It has addressed factors that played a role in this development, and this thesis is demonstrated in the relationships and exchanges between numerous collections and the people responsible for their development and use. This work is only a modest first step in the investigation of the birth and development of university *aegyptiaca* collections, a direction of research that is *as important* for present day university collections of *aegyptiaca* as is the investigation of future perspectives and developments of these collections.

Bibliography

Arnold, D., and J. Bourriau (eds.). 1993. *An Introduction to Ancient Egyptian Pottery. Fascicle 2*, Mainz: von Zabern.

Aston, D. A. 1996. *Egyptian Pottery of the Late New Kingdom and Third Intermediate Period (Twelfth–Seventh centuries BC): Tentative Footsteps in a Forbidding Terrain*. Studien zur Archäologie und Geschichte Altägyptens 13. Heidelberg: Heidelberger Orientverlag.

Bercken, B. van den. 2011. *Aegyptiaca incognita. Universitaire collecties Oudegyptische objecten: hun ontstaan, ontwikkeling en gebruik in Noordwest-Europa in de 19de en 20ste eeuw.* MA-thesis University of Amsterdam.

Van Berkel, K. 2005. "Institutionele verzamelingen in de tijd van de wetenschappelijk revolutie (1600–1750)." In E. Bergvelt, D. J. Meijers, and M. Rijnders (eds.), *Kabinetten, galerijen en musea: Het verzamelen en presenteren van naturalia en kunst van 1500 tot heden*. Zwolle: Waanders.

Betz, R. 2005. "The Victoria Museum of Egyptian Antiquities at Uppsala University. Past, Present and Future." *Palarch* 2.3, 11–20.

Blumenthal, E. 1981. *Altes Ägypten in Leipzig*. Leipzig: Leipziger Universitätsverlag.

Boylan, P. J. 1999. "Universities and Museums: Past, Present and Future," *Museum Management and Curatorship* 18.1, 43–56.

Charle, C. 2004. "Patterns." In W. Rüegg (ed.). *A History of the University in Europe*. Vol. 3: *Universities in the Nineteenth and Early Twentieth Centuries*. Cambridge: Cambridge University Press, 33–80.

Davies, N. 1996. *Europe: A History*. London: Pimlico.

De Clercq, S. W. G., and M. C. Lourenço. 2003. "A Globe Is Just Another Tool: Understanding the Role of Objects in University Collections." *ICOFOM Study Series* 11/2003, http://www.museum.or.jp/icom/studse.html.

De Ridder-Symoens, H. (ed.) 1992. *A History of the University in Europe*. Vol. 1: *Universities in the Middle Ages*. Cambridge: Cambridge University Press.

———. 1996. *A History of the University in Europe*. Vol. 2: *Universities in Early Modern Europe (1500–1800)*. Cambridge: Cambridge University Press.

Drower, M. S. 1985. *Flinders Petrie: A Life in Archaeology*, London: Gollancz.

EL-DALY, O. 2005. *Egyptology, the Missing Millennium: Ancient Egypt in Medieval Arabic Writings*. London: University College London.

FISCHER-ELFERT, H., and F. SEYFRIED. 2009."Ägyptologie." In U. VON HEHL, U. JOHN, and M. RUDERSDORF (eds.), *Geschichte der Universität Leipzig 1409–2009. Fakultäten, Institute, Zentrale Einrichtungen, 4, 1. Halbband*. Leipzig: Leipziger Universitätsverlag.

FRIJHOFF, W. 1996. "Patterns." In H. DE RIDDER-SYMOENS (ed.). *A History of the University in Europe*. Vol. 2: *Universities in Early Modern Europe (1500–1800)*. Cambridge: Cambridge University Press, 43–110.

GREENE, K. 2002. *Archaeology: An Introduction*. 4th ed. London: Routledge.

HÄRKE, H. 1991. "All Quiet on the Western Front? Paradigms, Methods and Approaches in West German Archaeology." Pp. 187–222 in I. HODDER (ed.), *Archaeological Theory in Europe: The Last Three Decades*. London: Routledge.

HOIJTINK, M. H. E. 2009. *Caspar J.C. Reuvens en de musea van oudheden in Europa (1800–1840)*, http://dare.uva.nl/document/131132.

JANSSEN, R. M. 1992. *The First Hundred Years: Egyptology at the University College London 1892–1992*. London: University College London.

KAISER, W. 1956. "Stand und Probleme der Ägyptischen Vorgeschichtsforschung," *Zeitschrift für Ägyptische Sprache* 81, 87–109.

KÅKS, P. 1998. "Human Remains and Material of Ritual Significance," *ICOM Newsletter 1998 Special issue*, 10–11.

KONIJN, F. 2005. "Presentatie in kunstmusea na de Tweede Wereldoorlog." Pp. 415–52 in E. BERGVELT, D. J. MEIJER, and M. RIJNDERS (eds.). *Kabinetten, galerijen en musea. Het verzamelen en presenteren van naturalia en kunst van 1500 tot heden*. Zwolle: Waanders.

LEEZENBERG, M., and G. DE VRIES. 2001. *Wetenschapsfilosofie voor geesteswetenschappen*. Amsterdam: Amsterdam University Press.

LOURENÇO, M. C. 2005. Between Two Worlds: The Distinct Nature and Contemporary Significance of University Museums and Collections in Europe, http://webpages.fc.ul.pt/~mcLourenço/

MOON, B. 2006. *More Usefully Employed: Amelia B. Edwards, Writer, Traveler and Campaigner for Ancient Egypt*. London: Egypt Exploration Society.

NEAVE, G. 2010. "Grundlagen." In W. RÜEGG (ed.). *Geschichte der Universität in Europa*. Band 4: *Vom Zweiten Weltkrieg bis zum Ende des 20. Jahrhunderts*. Munich: Beck, 47–75.

NORTH, J. 1992. "The quadrivium." Pp. 337–59 in H. DE RIDDER-SYMOENS (ed.), *A History of the University in Europe*. Vol. 1: *Universities in the Middle Ages*. Cambridge: Cambridge University Press.

PETRIE, W. M. F. 1927. *Objects of Daily Use, with over 1800 Figures from University College, London*. London: British School of Archaeology in Egypt.

REES, J. 1998. *Amelia Edwards: Traveller, Novelist and Egyptologist*. London: Rubicon.

RÜEGG, W. (ed.) 2004. *A History of the University in Europe*. Vol. 3: *Universities in the Nineteenth and Early Twentieth Centuries*. Cambridge: Cambridge University Press.

———. 2010. *Geschichte der Universität in Europa*. Bd. 4:. *Vom Zweiten Weltkrieg bis zum Ende des 20. Jahrhunderts*, Munich: Beck.

SCHÄFER, W. 2002. *Principles of Egyptian Art*. Oxford: Clarendon.

SMOLLA, G. 1980. "Das 'Kossinna-Syndrom,'" *Fundberichte aus Hessen* 19/20, 1–9.

STEINDORFF, G. 1937. *Aniba II*. Glückstadt: Service des antiquités de l'Égypte.

WARHURST, A. 1984. "University Museums," in: THOMPSON J. M. A. (ed.), *Manual of Curatorship: A Guide to Museum Practice*. London, 93–100.

WHITEHOUSE, H. 2009, *Ancient Egypt and Nubia in the Ashmolean Museum*. Oxford: The Ashmolean Museum.

Zonta, C. A. 2002. "The History of European Universities: Overview and Background." In N. Sanz and S. Bergan (eds.), *The Heritage of European Universities*. Strasbourg: Council of Europe Publications, 25–38.

Highlighting the Camillo Leone Egyptian Collection

SABINA MALGORA

This article is dedicated to dott.ssa Anna Rosso, museum curator for thirty-five years, now retired. Her skill, competence, enthusiasm, and passion, and her unwavering smile in the face of difficulty, impressed me. I was honored to study the Camillo Leone Egyptian Collection under her direction several years ago. At the same time, this article is dedicated to Amedeo Corio, President of the Fondazione Istituto di Belle Arti, who has devoted his career to making the museum ever more active.

The Camillo Leone Museum is an archaeological and historical museum, located in the historic centre of Vercelli. This town is the capital of the province of Vercelli,[1] part of the Piedmont Region, in northwest Italy. Vercelli, an important agricultural and commercial center, leads in the European rice market as the site of the biggest Rice Stock Exchange and the Rice Cultivation Development Station. The town center occupies the area of a second-century BC fortified roman camp. Pliny the Elder (*HN* 3.17) refers to the town as "Vercellae Libicorum ex Salyis ortae."

Remarkable among the town's rich monuments is the church of Sant Andrea, a medieval masterpiece in romanesque-gothic style. In addition to the University, Vercelli boasts an important Music Academy with international renown. There are two museums in Vercelli: the Camillo Leone Museum, located in two ancient buildings, Casa Alciati and Palazzo Langosco, under the direction of the Fondazione Istituto di Belle Arti (Foundation of the Fine Arts Institute),[2] and the Francesco Borgogna Museum, an art gallery.[3] The latter, with its magnificent collection of Renaissance paintings, is the second-most-important art gallery of the Piedmont Region after the Sabauda Gallery in Turin.

The Francesco Borgogna Museum opened to the public in 1908 following the bequest of the lawyer Antonio Borgogna (1822–1906), a cultural traveller and fine-arts connoisseur. This beautiful neoclassical building was his home and now displays

1. Faccio-Chicco-Viola 1933; Viale 1939; Viale 1971; Sommo 1982; Rosso et al. 1984.
2. Faccio-Mella 1910; Viale 1934; Schiolla 1980; Corio 1990; Rosso 1996, 2004, 2007; www.museoleone.it.
3. Viale 1969; Lacchia 2001; Schiavi 2001; Berardi 1996; Lacchia 1996–97; Berardi 1985; www.museoborgogna.it.

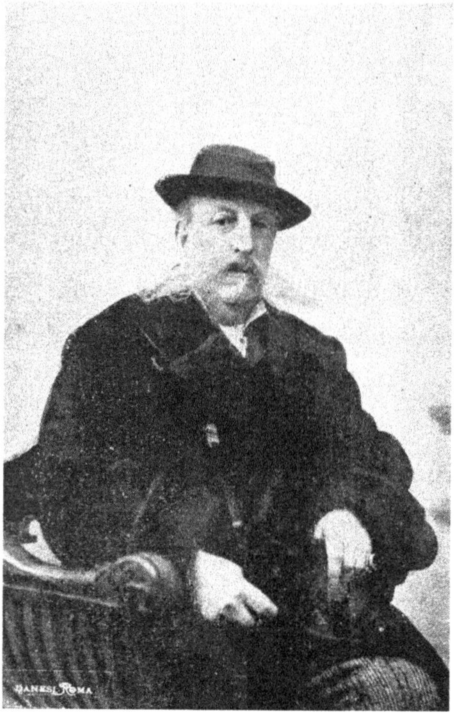

Fig. 1. Camillo Leone 1830–1907. © Museo Camillo Leone.

more than eight hundred objects on three floors. Visitors can admire the Borgogna collections of paintings, sculptures, ceramics, furniture, and objects from the fifteenth to nineteenth centuries, arranged as in a home. The building also contains numerous Renaissance altar pieces and detached wall frescoes coming from the Fine Arts Institute and churches.

The Camillo Leone Museum is named for the notary Camillo Leone (fig. 1),[4] who was born in Vercelli on December 17, 1830 into a local wealthy middle class family. After completing his legal degree, he became a notary but did not spend much time in the office. At the death of his father, he inherited a considerable fortune, enabling him to devote his life to the study of history, and to the collecting of antiques.

In 1874, Leone became a member of the Fine Arts Institute, the most important cultural institution of the town. It was created for the town craftsmen who could use it to better themselves and to improve their work quality. The Institute was also involved in collecting paintings of the local pictorial school. Today, the Institute is still active and operates the school and the museum.

In 1877, Leone became a member of the Lombard Historical Society, and in 1880 he was appointed a member of the Vercelli Archaeological Committee. In 1884, he was also a City Councillor, with the task of collecting antiques to preserve the artistic heritage of the town, thus enhancing his personal collections. In 1889, he became a member and later president of the Turin Archaeological and Fine Arts Society. He often went to the capital of the Piedmont region to participate in the activities of scholars and intellectuals, while at the same time he was looking after his antiques collections.

Leone died in 1907, leaving all his fortune and collections to the Fine Arts Institute. His last will and testament contained only one clause: to set up a Museum, a goal he worked towards his entire life. He spent his time, energy, and wealth so that

4. Baldissone 2007; Rosso 2007.

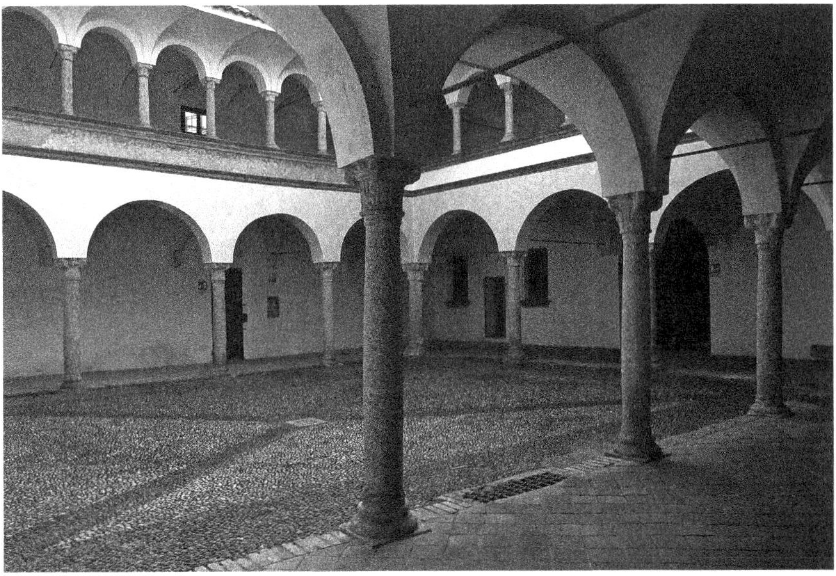

Fig. 2. Casa Alciati courtyard. © Museo Camillo Leone.

everything should remain at the disposal of the town and of future generations. The museum preserves clear evidence of his activity as a scholar entirely dedicated to the collection of historical artifacts.[5]

The museum first opened to the public with a small exhibition in 1910, but the official opening did not occur until 1922. The objects were installed in the rooms of his house, the Palazzo Langosco. The year 1931 was crucial for the museum, when Vittorio Viale, Director of the Turin Municipal Museums, was appointed by Carlo Verzone, president of the Fine Arts Institute, to the directorship of the two Vercelli museums, the Leone and the Borgogna. Vittorio Viale's first duty was to rearrange the collections. He decided to redistribute the collections of the two museums, moving objects, furniture, and paintings from one to the other. The Leone became an archaeological and ancient art Museum; the Borgogna a gallery.

In 1934, the Leone museum was enlarged by the acquisition of the Alciati Building, a noble family house dated to the fifteenth–sixteenth centuries, recently restored. In 1939, Vittorio Viale organized an exhibition for the visit to the town of the Prime Minister Benito Mussolini: "Vercelli from the Roman Period to Fascism."[6] The necessary building works were done by Augusto Cavallari Murat (1911–1989), a well-known civil engineer and Professor of Architecture at Turin University. The two

5. Rosso 2007, 69, 76.
6. Viale 1939.

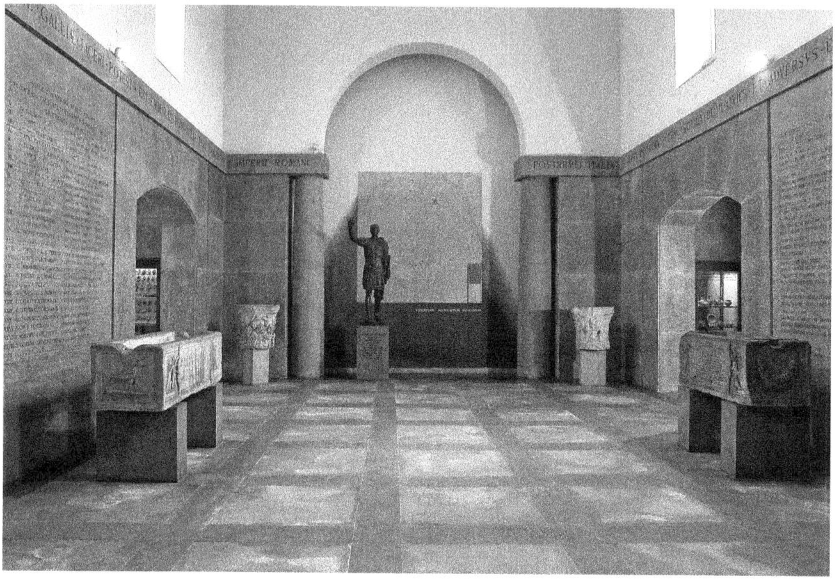

Fig. 3. The Roman Basilica room of the Camillo Leone Museum. © Museo Camillo Leone.

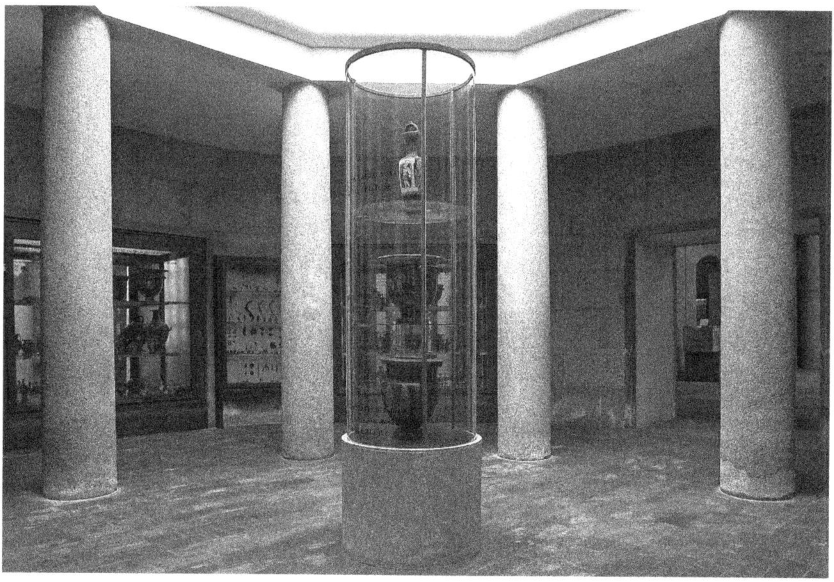

Fig. 4. The Colonnade Room. © Museo Camillo Leone.

ancient buildings were linked by a wide and complex corridor, almost giving to the museum the appearance that we see today.

The museum plan is made to reconstruct the history of the city chronologically, moving from prehistory through the nineteenth century. The first part of the museum is located in the Alciati Building, with the entrance in the sixteenth century courtyard (fig. 2). From this courtyard, the visitor will reach a second but smaller courtyard with jars and sarcophagi of the Roman Era. There one finds the entrance to the first room dedicated to prehistory. The second room contains Greek pottery from the South of Italy, Gnathian pottery, some red figure vases,[7] the Egyptian collection, Etruscan buccheri, pottery from Cyprus, and Hellenic and Roman bronzes. The third room is dedicated to the Roman period and it is built in the form of a Roman basilica, containing objects discovered in Vercelli and in its territory organized by materials: glass, marble, pottery, bronze (fig. 3). The next room is dedicated to Roman epigraphs, and another room to the Medieval period. The remains of the ancient basilica of St. Mary the Great, rebuilt in the twelfth century and destroyed in 1777 occupy one of the rooms. Lastly is the room with Incunabula and books made in the sixteenth century numbering fourteen hundred volumes.[8] The last three rooms on the ground floor of the Alciati building show several Risorgimento events. These include the revolts of 1821 through the wars of 1849 and 1859, underlining the flooding of the land outside Vercelli to stop the Austrian army advance.

The second part of the Museum is the Langosco building adorned with an elegant staircase. Visitors may admire, in its rooms, jewel cases dating from the twelfth through the eighteenth centuries made in Venice, Limoges and Sicily, seventeenth-century portraits from Piedmont and Flanders, sixteenth-century paintings of the local school, seventeenth-century decorations, sixteenth- and seventeenth-century faience, and eighteenth-century garments and decorations.[9]

The Egyptian collection is located in the second room (fig. 4), called the Colonnade Room, in showcase number 56. The room is very evocative, with its octagonal form, the natural light coming from a skylight, and the columns that create a deambulacrum in front of the showcases. The room is dedicated to Greek pottery coming from the south of Italy, Etruscan pottery, Hellenic ex-votos representing anatomical parts, Gnathian pottery (third–second centuries BC) and Apulian vases with red figures (fourth century BC). In the centre of the room, inside a cylindrical showcase, are the most important pieces: a crater with red figures, a lekithos, and a large Apulian crater.

The Egyptian collection was catalogued, but not published, by Vittorio Viale in the 1930s. His records are collected in the museum, but not exhibited. The objects were put in the showcases in 1939 and never moved. Most of the objects were fixed (especially some amulets) against the wall, with glue or, in some cases, even stuck from rust. Some items were lent to the "Ur Sunu" exhibition, in 2008, organized by Sabina

7. Cambitoglou-Harari 1997.
8. Misiti-Rosso 1998; Misiti 1999.
9. Casati-Migliorini 2001.

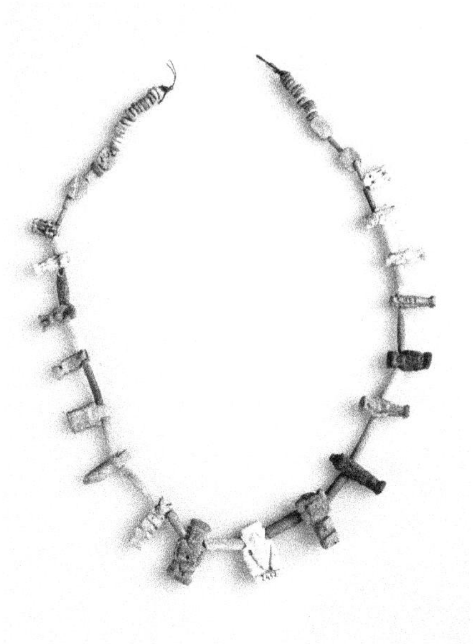

Fig. 5. Neckless with beads and amulets. Inv. 2252/ 943. © Francesca Brambilla and Serena Serrani.

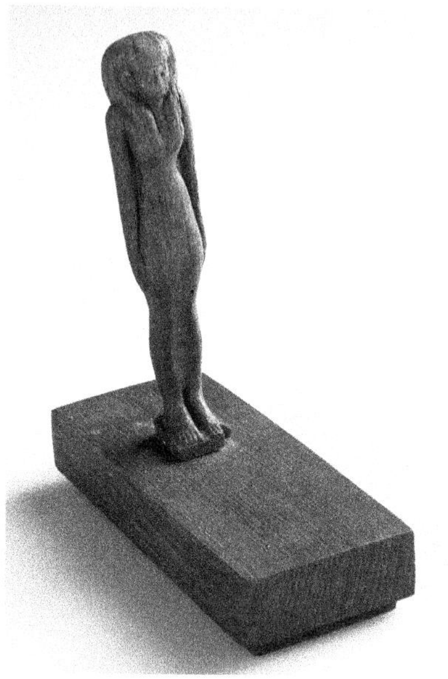

Fig. 6. Wooden female statuette. Inv. 2411/ 905. © Francesca Brambilla and Serena Serrani.

Malgora[10] in Casale Monferrato, and to the "Egitto Nascosto" exhibition in 2009 with Silvia Einaudi[11] as curator, in Pinerolo.

In the autumn of 2011, thanks to *VercelliViva*,[12] a cultural association sponsored by the Piedmont Region, a catalogue was published. All objects have been removed, cleaned, and reinstalled in a similar fashion to the outline of 1934, as suggested by the Soprintendenza.

The Egyptian collection is composed of two groups of artifacts, one from the notary Camillo Leone and the other from the lawyer Antonio Borgogna. These Egyptian antiquities bring us to the beginning of Italian and European collecting in the nineteenth century, although the two collections show different taste and mood.

Most antiquities collections are direct expressions of nineteenth-century taste, and of the maniacal interest in the Egyptian world, a consequence of the romantic appeal of the famous "Grand Tours," which drove many people to collect strange, ancient or just exotic objects, and to display them in their houses. Later on, fortunately, many families took the decision to share with the public the possibility to enjoy the

10. Malgora 2008.
11. Einaudi 2009.
12. www.vercelliviva.org. The key person of VercelliViva is the Prof. Mariella Gallo Ferraris, president at the time of the editing of the catalogue, but always and deeply involved in every project of the association. To this Lady go my esteem and consideration, without her efforts the catalogue would never be published.

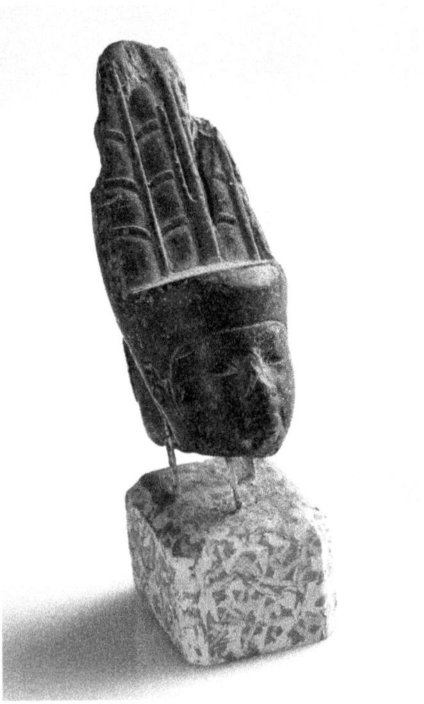

Fig. 7. Head of a black basalt statuette representing the god Amon. Inv. 2279/825. © Francesca Brambilla and Serena Serrani.

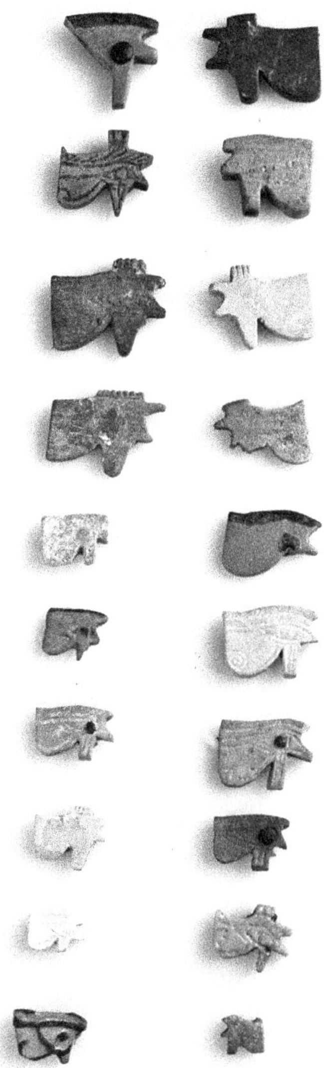

Fig. 8. *Udjat* eyes amulets. © Francesca Brambilla and Serena Serrani.

beauty of the collections by donating them to a museum, institution, or a town council.

Mr. Leone, additionally, gave value to an object not only considering its beauty, the skill of its creator, and the obvious function, but also, and even more so, looking at its meaning to better understand the history. People should collect objects because they are historical memories. He wanted his collections to be appreciated by the community. This Egyptian collection is highly valued, not only thanks to the quantity of the artifacts but also to their quality. They have been a part of the town history and have been an example for other collectors, assuring the collection's influence in the future. The approach of Mr. Leone to the antiquities is unusually modern for the time in which he lived.

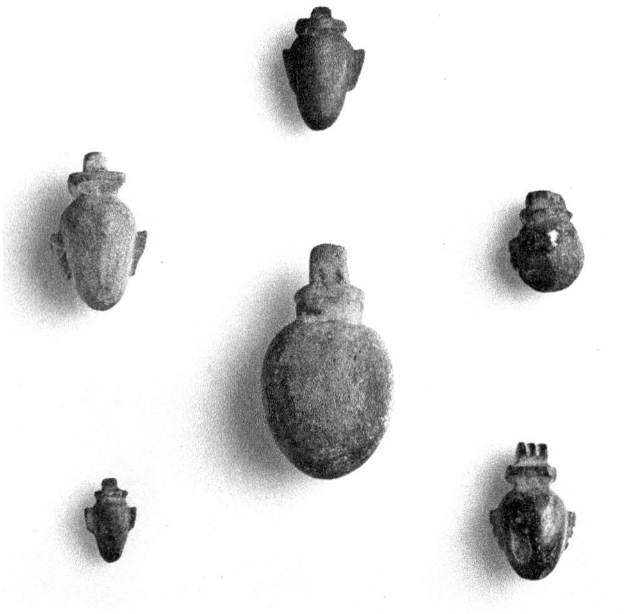

Fig. 9. Heart Amulets. Inv. 2398/839–2303/84. © Francesca Brambilla and Serena Serrani.

The Egyptian collection of the lawyer Antonio Borgogna consists of the objects he purchased during his visit to Egypt in 1893. It is supplemented with descriptions and photos of Egypt, showing a magic moment when the most important monuments had finally been cleaned out from the sand.

The objects were displayed in his house,[13] in the so-called Arabian Hall, this installation never having been recorded with an image. The collection moved to the Leone museum in 1931. The Borgogna collection expresses his romantic feeling, his fine taste, and his love for the exotic. The Borgogna approach is very different from that of Mr. Leone. In fact, Mr. Borgogna only later considered the possibility of displaying his objects to the public.

There are a variety of two-hundred small-scale objects of different materials, like wood, alabaster, faience, and hard stones. Most are funerary objects of unknown provenance having been purchased from antique dealers who did not have any information regarding the discovery site. The collection contains seventy amulets, twenty scarabs, thirty-seven shabtis, some wooden and some made of faience. Personal ornaments include twelve necklaces with faience and hard stones beads, and amulets, most of which were assembled in modern times (fig. 5). Other objects include cartonnage fragments with a female goddess (Inv. 2242/799); three wooden statuettes representing Sokar in the form of a falcon (Inv. 2255/806–2258/808); a wooden female statuette (Inv. 2411/905, fig. 6) dated to the Third Intermediate period, measuring 10.11

13. Lacchia 2001; Lacchia-Rosso 2011.

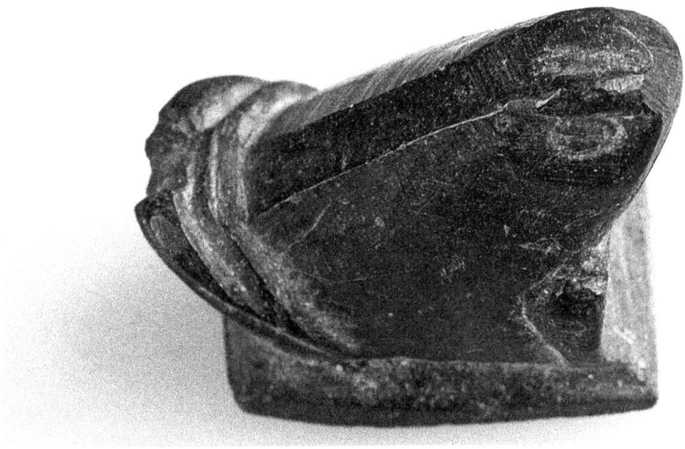

Fig. 10. Amulet representing a frog. Inv. 2319/854. © Francesca Brambilla and Serena Serrani.

cm; a small black pottery vase (Inv. 2401/899); an alabaster vase (Inv. 2402/900); a wooden statuette representing Isis feeding her son Horus (Inv. 2240/798); a head of a black basalt statuette representing the god Amon (Inv. 2279/825) (fig. 7) dated to the New Kingdom–Late periods, measuring 5.48 cm; and some mummy fragments including a small crocodile mummy.

The types of amulets are:[14] *udjat* eyes (fig. 8); *djed* pillar; *wadj* sceptre; *sma*; two fingers; solar disk; hearts (Inv. 2398/839–2303/843; fig. 9); tools like *pesesh-kef*; two feathers; head rests; divinities like Bes, Anubis, Tauret and Thot; animals like a bee and a frog (Inv. 2319/854) (fig. 10). The frog is a beloved animal, because in the Vercelli area, due to the rice cultivation and the massive presence of water, frogs are numerous and are an important part of the diet. There is even a festival dedicated to the frogs.

Some items were not correctly classified by Vittorio Viale between 1931 and 1939. Examples are items (Inv. 2312/848–2316/852)[15] classified as head rests instead of stands for bronze vases of the Imperial Roman period (fig. 11).

The scarabs, dated from the Twelfth Dynasty to the Late period, are made of faience and stone, especially basalt.[16] The largest scarab is winged (Inv. 2385/891), made of faience, datable to the Late period, measuring 16.5 cm long and 7 cm wide. The wings are different; probably one is the original and the other from an associated find (fig. 12).[17]

14. Malgora 2011, 30–42; for a general view see Ferrari 1996; Andrews 1994.
15. Malgora 2011, 40.
16. Malgora 2011, 43–46; for general view: Newberry 1979; Martin 1985.
17. Malgora 2011, 43–46.

One of the most impressive objects is the wooden headrest (Inv. 2399/898), dated to the Middle-New Kingdom, provenance unknown (fig. 13). Equally remarkable is the wooden throwing stick (Inv. 2378/824), dated to the New Kingdom.[18] Two other items are fascinating, but dubious: a wooden statuette of the *ba* bird (Inv. 2281/827) and a wooden statuette representing Ptah-Sokar-Osiris (Inv. 2249/800).

In the "toilette objects" section, it is worth mentioning the two kohl tubes, one in alabaster with its lid (Inv. 2403/901) (fig. 14), and one in dark green diorite with a removable lid (Inv. 2404/902) (fig. 15) dated to the New Kingdom. There is also a special light blue/green faience kohl tube in the shape of the god Bes (Inv. 2263/812) (fig. 16) dated to the Late period;[19] the wooden comb (Inv. 2398/897) dated to the New Kingdom; and also a wooden cosmetic spoon in shape of a snake (Inv. 2298/895).[20]

Unfortunately, in the category of human remains, there are only mummy fragments: four mummy hands,

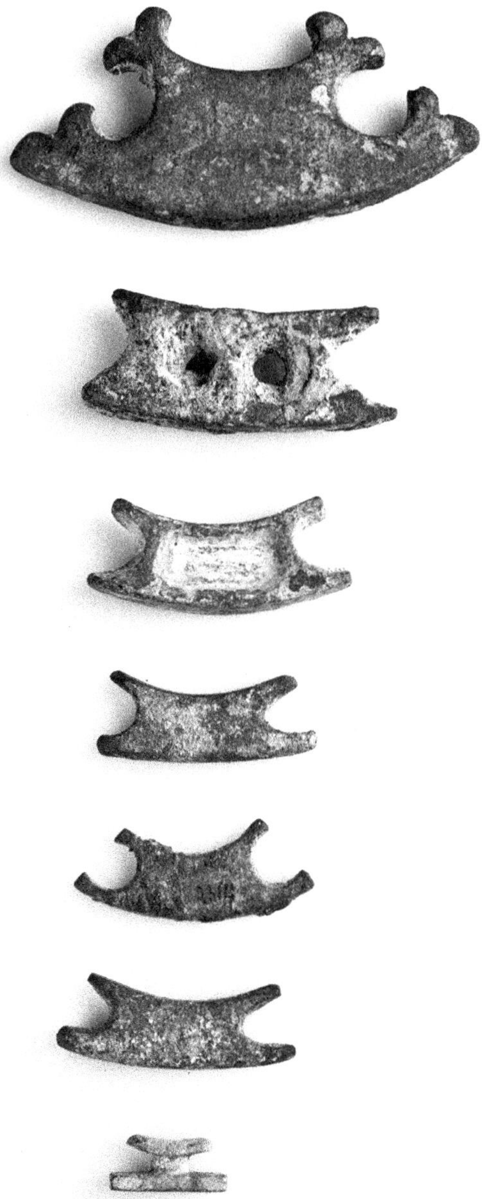

Fig. 11. Stands for bronze vases of the Imperial Roman period. Inv. 2312/848–2316/852, and the headrest amulet, Inv. 2318/853. © Francesca Brambilla e Serena Serrani.

18. Malgora 2011, 24–25.
19. Malgora 2008, 188–89; Einaudi 2009, 161–62; Malgora 2011, 74–75.
20. Einaudi 2009, 164; Malgora 2011, 73.

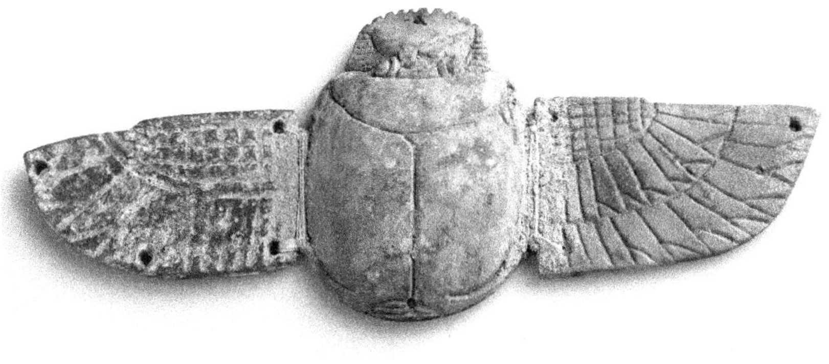

Fig. 12. The winged scarab. Inv. 2385/891. © Francesca Brambilla and Serena Serrani.

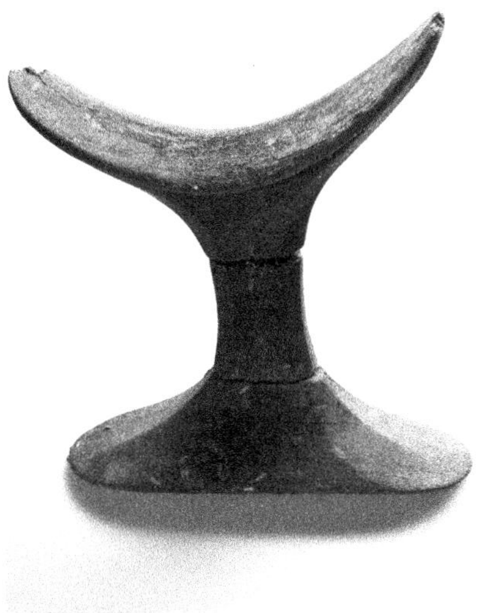

Fig. 13. Wooden headrest. Inv. 2399/898. © Francesca Brambilla and Serena Serrani.

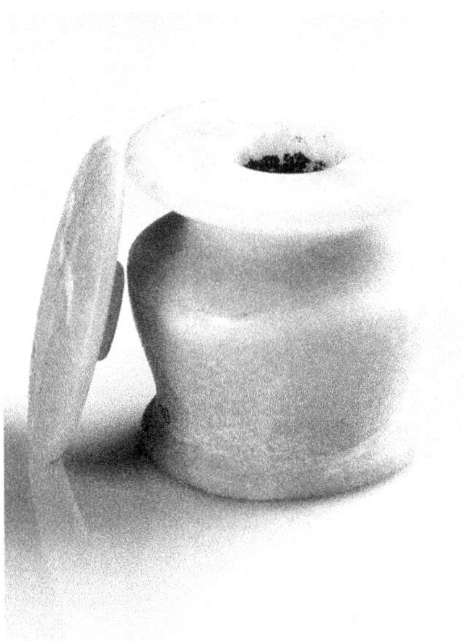

Fig. 14. Alabaster kohl vase with lid. Inv. 2403/901. © Francesca Brambilla and Serena Serrani.

unwrapped (Inv. 2287/832, 2288/4622, 2289/4623, 2290/4624).[21] The one exhibited to the public is well preserved, with some amulets adhered to the resins on the skin (fig. 17). The only complete mummies of the collection were two large crocodiles from the Borgogna collection, but were lost before moving the Borgogna Collection to the Leone Museum.[22] There are four small well preserved crocodile mummies,

21. Malgora 2011, 79.

22. Personal communication of the President of the Foundation of the Fine Arts Institute, who remem-

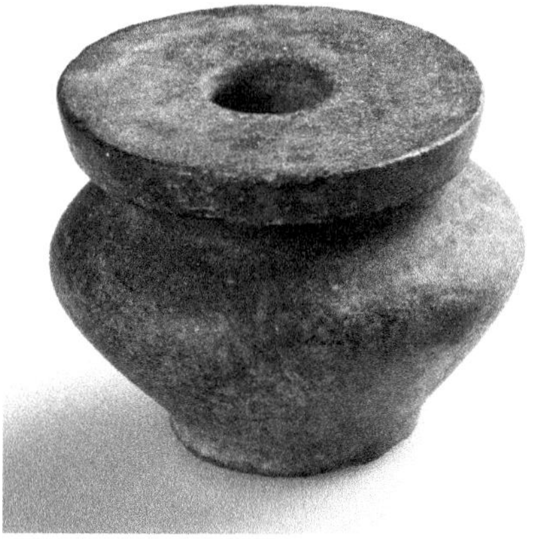

Fig. 15. Dark green diorite kohl vase with a removable lip. Inv. 2404/902. © Francesca Brambilla and Serena Serrani.

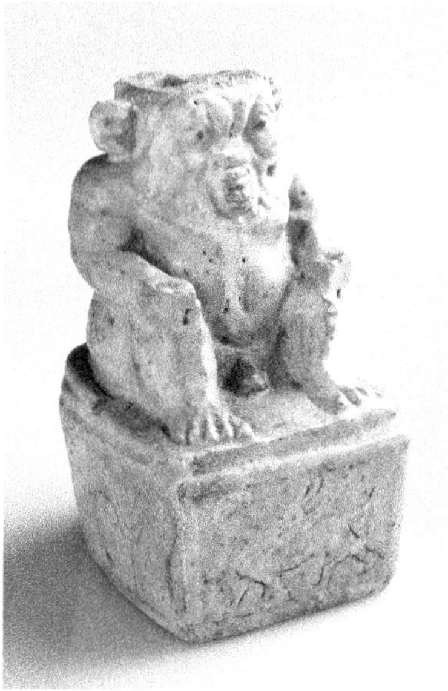

Fig. 16. Light blue/green faience kohl vase in the shape of the god Bes. Inv. 2263/812. © Francesca Brambilla and Serena Serrani.

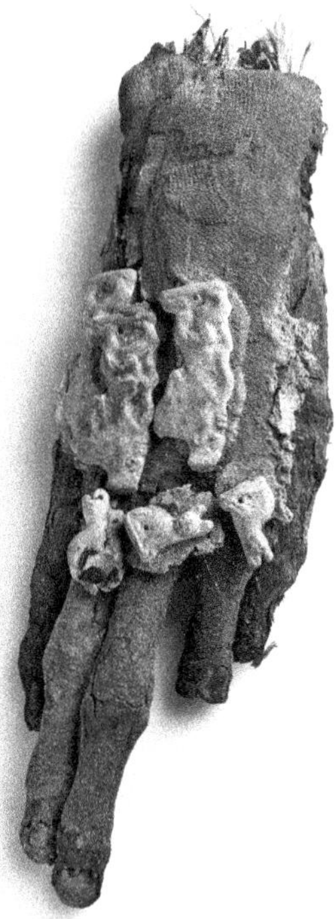

Fig. 17. Hand of a mummy with amulets. Inv. 2287/832. © Francesca Brambilla and Serena Serrani.

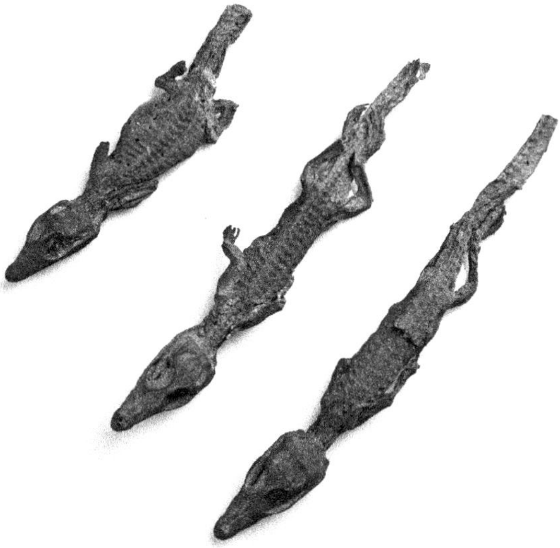

Fig. 18. Three small crocodile mummies. © Francesca Brambilla and Serena Serrani.

three of them displayed to the joy of the young visitors[23] (Inv. 2291/833–2294/836) (fig. 18).

There are some interesting pieces among the shabtis that were analysed by the shabti specialist, Niek De Haan.[24] There are three shabtis for Wahibraemachet (Inv. 2412/906), dated to the Late period, Twenty-Sixth Dynasty, ca. 570–525 BC, made of faience, possibly blue/green glaze turned gray, measuring 11.37, 11.2, and 11.35 cm, provenance unknown (fig. 19). They are mummiform, with faces of mediocre shape, tripartite wig, and divine beard. The arms are crossed right over left on the chest, the left hand holding a pick, the right hand a hoe, and the cord of a basket is suspended behind the left shoulder. It has a trapezoidal base with a back pillar containing one vertical column of incised inscription. The translation is: "The illuminated one, the Osiris, Wahibraemakhet, true of voice."

The shabti of Psamtek (Inv. 2421/914) is dated to the Late period, Twenty-Sixth–early Twenty-Seventh Dynasties, ca. 570–525 BC,[25] made of blue/green faience, measuring 18 cm (fig. 20). It is mummiform, with a beautifully shaped face, tripartite wig, divine beard, arms crossed right over left on the chest; the left hand holds

bers to having seen them in the Arabic Hall of the Franscesco Borgogna's House, before the dismantling.

23. Malgora 2011, 76–78.

24. De Haan and Malgora 2011, 47–60. The following text on the description of the shabtis was kindly provided by Niek de Haan. The study of the shabtis would not have been possible without the work of Niekh De Haan. For a general view see Schögl 1986; Schneider 1977.

25. De Haan 2013.

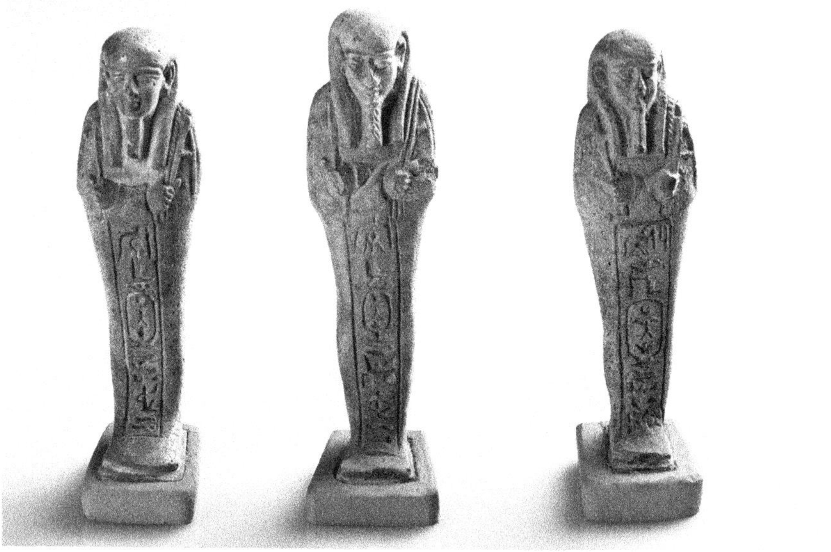

Fig. 19. Three shabties for Wahibraemachet. Inv. 2412/906. © Francesca Brambilla and Serena Serrani.

a pick, the right a hoe, and the cord of a basket which is suspended behind the left shoulder. It has a trapezoidal base with a back pillar containing nine horizontal lines of incised inscription. The translation is: *The illuminated one, the Osiris, the overseer of the scribes of the royal meals, Psamtek, son of Meryneith, he speaks: O shabti* (chapter six follows). The shabtis of Psamtek son of Meryneith are well represented in many museums and private collections. He was buried near the causeway of the pyramid of Unas at Saqqara, in the vicinity of the monastery of Apa Jeremias. His tomb was discovered by Mariette in 1860. Psamtek was a minister under pharaoh Petubastis III.

The shabti for Nesiwab(?)amenra (Inv. 2425/918) is dated to the Third Intermediate period (Twenty-First Dynasty, ca. 1080–945 BC). It is made of blue glaze faience, details in black, measuring 8.99 cm, provenance unknown (fig. 21). It is mummiform, with mediocre face, tripartite wig with *seshed* headband, arms crossed left over right on the chest, each hand holds a hoe, with a basket on the back. The text is: *The Osiris, Nesiwabamenra.* There are no other examples of the shabtis of this owner known. Perhaps the title of the owner was Wab-priest of the temple of Amun-Ra at Thebes, similar to the *Wab*-priest Amenhotep who was buried at Deir el-Bahri in Cache 2. The inscriptions for Amenhotep show the double use of the name of the owner and the title of the owner. Therefore, it could well be that the owner was also a Wab-priest.

The shabti for Nesikhonsu(pa)khered (Inv. 2427/920) is dated to the Third Intermediate period, Twenty-First Dynasty, ca. 1080–945 BC. It is made of blue glazed

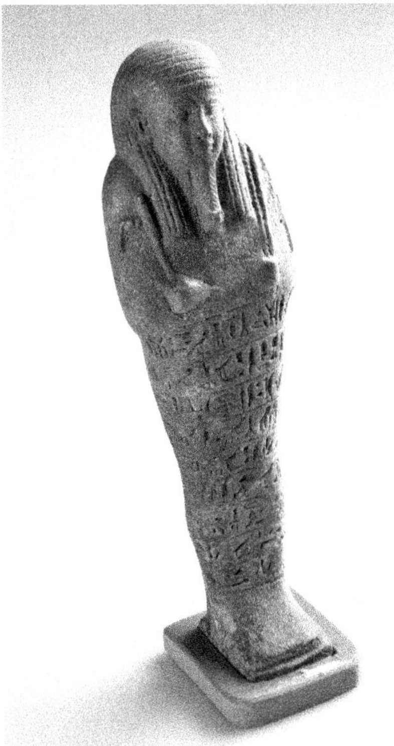

Fig. 20. The shabty of Psamtek. Inv. 2421/914. © Francesca Brambilla and Serena Serrani.

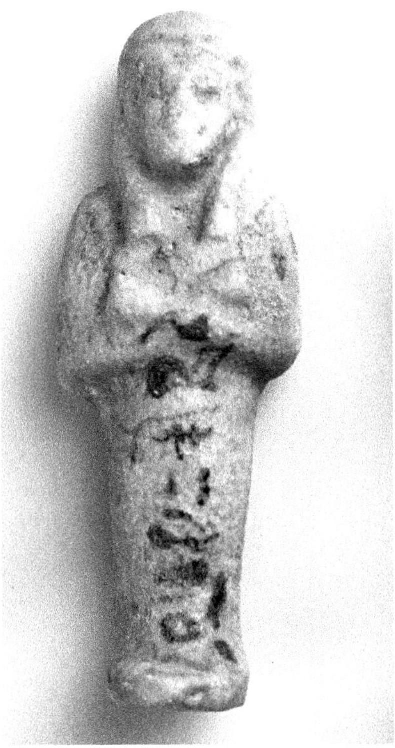

Fig. 21. The shabti for Nesiwab(?)amenra. Inv. 2425/918. © Francesca Brambilla and Serena Serrani.

faience with details in black, measuring 9.30 cm, provenance unknown (fig. 22). It is mummiform, with a poorly shaped face, tripartite wig with *seshed* headband, arms crossed left over right on the chest, each hand holds a hoe, with a basket on the back. The text says *The Osiris, Nesi-Konsu-(pa)-Khered.* There are two series of shabti gangs know for Nesikhonsu(pa)khered, but they appear to be for two different individuals. Group one is in Cambridge, Fitzwilliam Museum: E.146a-p.1891 (16 spec.); Copenhagen, National Museet: A.A.a.111; London, Petrie Museum: UC40340; and Brooklyn, Brooklyn Museum: 16.375–76. Group two is in Vienna, Kunsthistorisches Museum: 1686a/25. The provenance of this example is unknown.

One of the oldest shabtis (Inv. 2431/924) in this collection is made of wood with traces of bitumen, dated to the New Kingdom, Eighteenth to Twentieth Dynasties (ca. 1350 to 1200 BC), measuring 18 cm, provenance unknown. It is mummiform, with a well-shaped face, plain tripartite wig, hands not indicated, thus it can no longer be seen whether the hands held two hoes. It is uninscribed. This item attests that, in some cases, shabtis were covered in black varnish. The wooden shabtis were originally

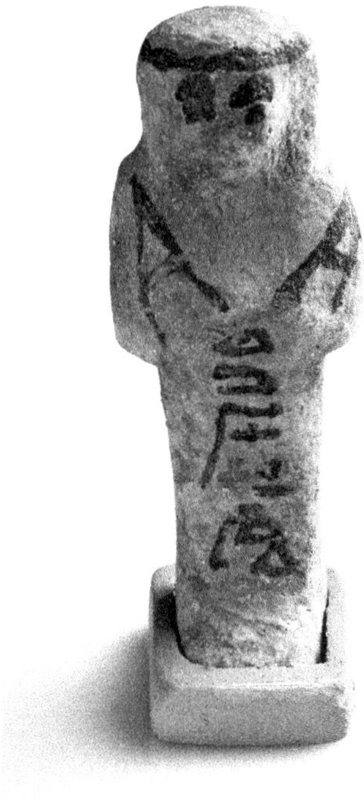

Fig. 22. The shabti for Nesikhonsu(pa)khered, Inv. 2427/920. © Francesca Brambilla and Serena Serrani.

fully covered in black varnish for multiple reasons. Black was associated with Osiris by the ancient Egyptians. All wanted to be associated with Osiris in death, thus they covered some of these wooden shabtis in black varnish, the examples for Seti I being the best known. However, the other, more practical reason was that the varnish protected the wood from rotting and woodworms, thus maintaining their function in the afterlife. This example is very similar in appearance to the next shabti (Inv. 2447), presumably originating from the same workshop and perhaps for the same owner (fig. 23).

This wooden shabti (Inv. 2447/938) shows traces of original paint, blue on the wig and yellow on the front, but the text is lost (fig. 23). It can be dated to the New Kingdom (Eighteenth–Twentieth Dynasties, ca. 1350 to 1200 BC; provenance unknown) and measures 19 cm It is mummiform, with a simple modelled face, duplex wig, hands crossed, arms indicated. It can no longer be seen whether the hands held two hoes as the hands are no longer indicated. It was most likely originally inscribed in a single column on the front of the piece.

Another interesting wooden shabti (Inv. 2447/938) with painted stucco is dated to the New Kingdom, Nineteenth Dynasty ca. 1200 BC, measuring 24 cm, provenance unknown (fig. 23). It is mummiform, with a roughly modelled face, plain tripartite wig, hands crossed on the chest, each holding a hoe, two water pots and a seed pack are indicated on the back as well as a mummy cloth. A single column of painted hieroglyphs is applied on the front. The text translates: *The Illuminated one, the Osiris* (the rest illegible). The water pots indicated on the back of the shabti are typical for the Nineteenth Dynasty.[26] Similar shabtis can be found in Naples, Florence, Vienna, and the British Museum.

There is a shabti of the overseer type (Inv. 2443/934), dated to the Third Intermediate period, Twenty-First–Twenty-Fifth Dynasties, ca. 1080–656 BC, made of blue-glazed faience, details originally in black, measuring 7.16 cm, provenance

26. Stewart 1995.

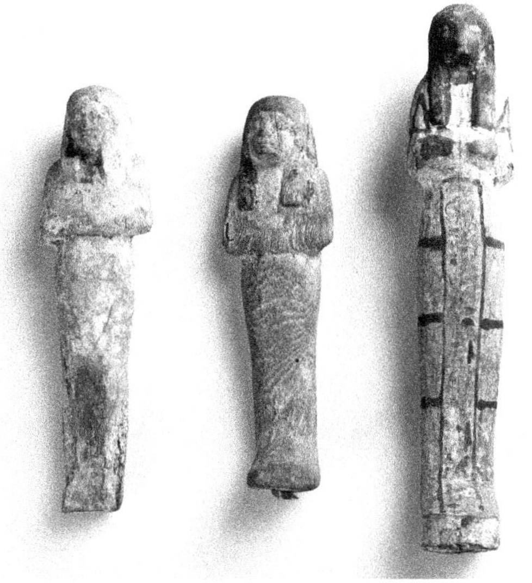

Fig. 23. Shabtis. Inv. 2447/938, 2431/924, 2432/925. © Francesca Brambilla and Serena Serrani.

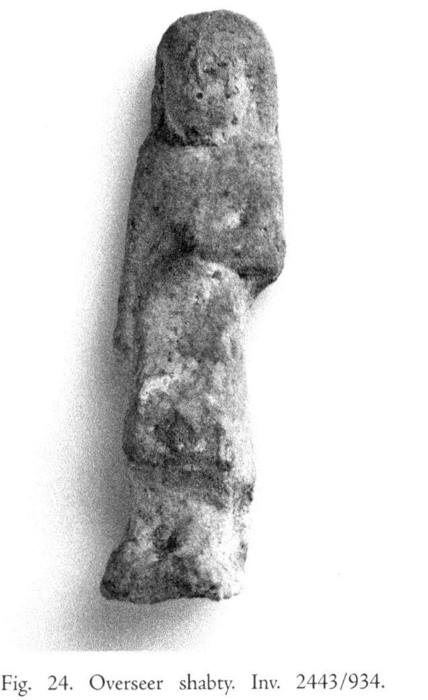

Fig. 24. Overseer shabty. Inv. 2443/934. © Francesca Brambilla and Serena Serrani.

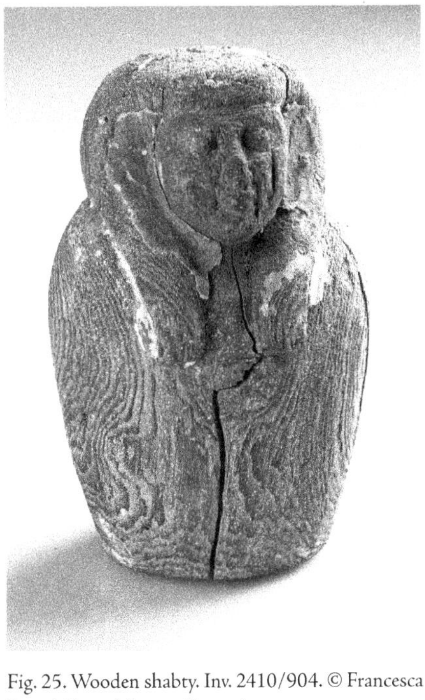

Fig. 25. Wooden shabty. Inv. 2410/904. © Francesca Brambilla and Serena Serrani.

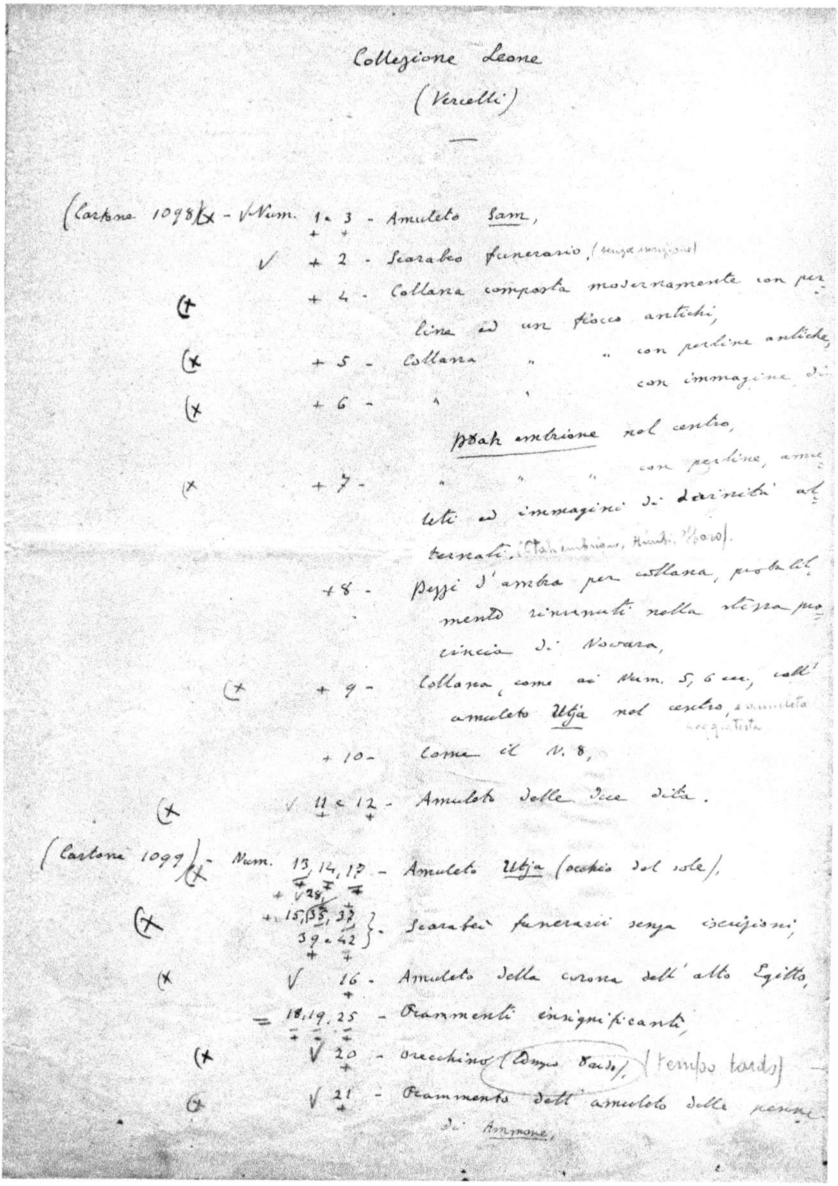
Collezione Leone
(Vercelli)

(Cartone 1098) - Num. 1 e 3 - Amuleto Sam,
+ 2 - Scarabeo funerario, (senza iscrizione)
+ 4 - Collana composta modernamente con perline ed un fiocco antichi;
+ 5 - Collana " con perline antiche,
+ 6 - " con immagine di Ptah embrione nel centro,
+ 7 - " con perline, amuleti ed immagini di divinità alternati, (Ptah embrione, Horus, Thoeris).
+ 8 - Pezzi d'ambra per collana, probabilmente rinvenuti nella stessa provincia di Novara,
+ 9 - Collana, come ai Num. 5, 6 ecc., coll'amuleto Ucja nel centro,
+ 10 - Come il N. 8,
11 e 12 - Amuleto delle due dita.
(Cartone 1099) - Num. 13, 14, 17 - Amuleto Ucja (occhio del sole),
15, 35, 37, 39 e 42 - Scarabei funerarii senza iscrizioni;
16 - Amuleto della corona dell'alto Egitto,
18, 19, 25 - Frammenti insignificanti,
20 - Orecchino (tempo tardo)
21 - Frammento dell'amuleto delle penne di Ammone,

Fig. 26. Ernesto Schiaparelli manuscript, first page, with title. © Museo Camillo Leone.

unknown (fig. 24). The face is poorly shaped, with plain wig, right arm stretched to the right side possibly holding a whip, left arm bent on the chest, presumably holding a whip, wearing a long skirt, legs and feet indicated. Unfortunately the glyphs can no longer be read, making identifying the owner very difficult. A comparable shabti is

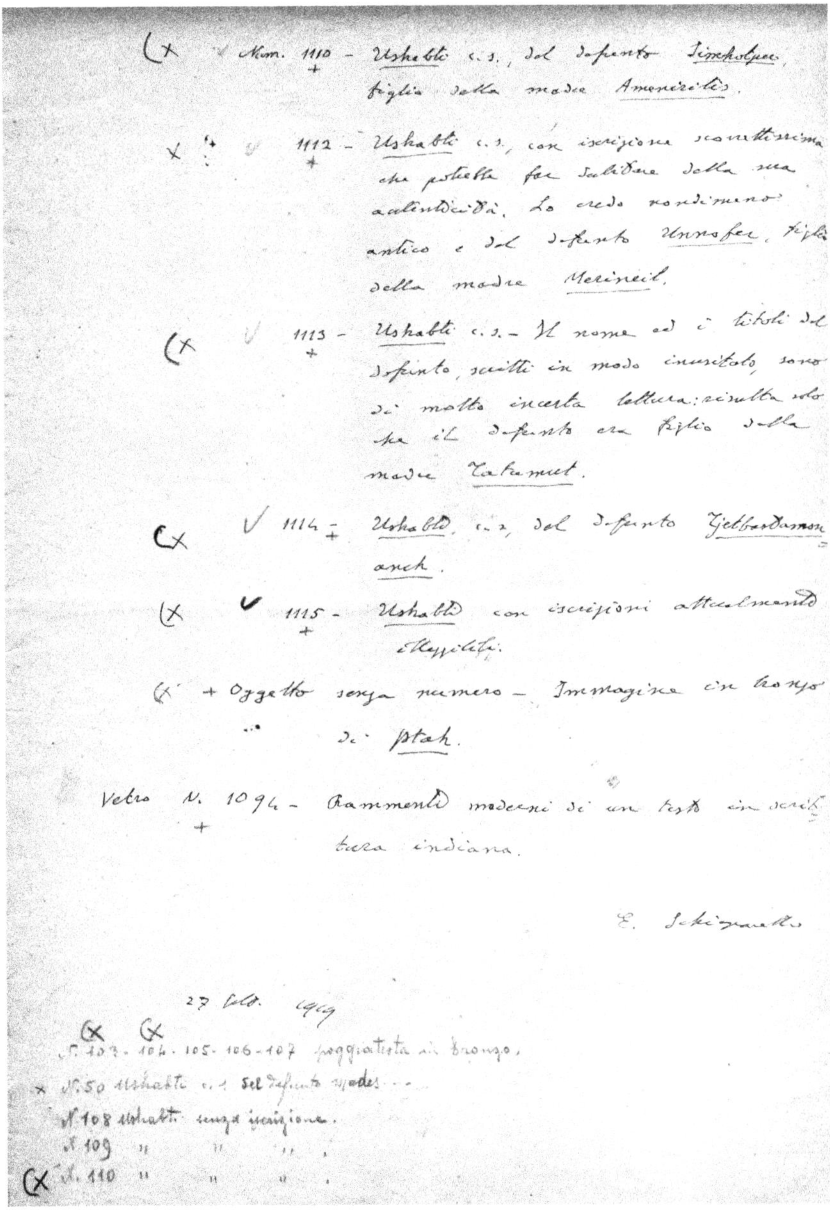

Num. 1110 – Ushabti c.s., del defunto Timeholpue, figlio della madre Ameneiritis.

1112 – Ushabti c.s., con iscrizione scorrettissima che potrebbe far dubitare della sua autenticità. Lo credo nondimeno antico e del defunto Unnofer, figlio della madre Merineit.

1113 – Ushabti c.s. – Il nome ed i titoli del defunto, scritti in modo inusitato, sono di molto incerta lettura: risulta solo che il defunto era figlio della madre Takamut.

1114 – Ushabti c.s., del defunto Tjetbastamon-ankh.

1115 – Ushabti con iscrizioni attualmente illeggibili.

+ Oggetto senza numero – Immagine in bronzo di Ptah.

Vetro N. 1094 – Frammenti moderni di un testo in scrittura indiana.

E. Schiaparelli

27 feb. 1909

N. 103 - 104 - 105 - 106 - 107 poggiatesta di bronzo.
N. 50 Ushabti c.s. del defunto [illegible] ...
N. 108 Ushabti senza iscrizione.
N. 109 " " " .
N. 110 " " " .

Fig. 27. Ernesto Schiaparelli manuscript, last page with date and signature. © Museo Camillo Leone.

known for Amenemhat of the Twenty-Second Dynasty, Leiden AF 126a, published in Schneider, 1977, 2: 140–41, pl. 117.

A curious case is the wooden shabti (Inv. 2443/934), with traces of plaster, dated to the New Kingdom (Eighteenth to Twentieth Dynasties, ca. 1350 to 1200 BC, provenance unknown), measuring 11.93 cm (fig. 25). It is mummiform, with a well-shaped face and plain tripartite wig. The hands are not indicated. It can no longer be seen if the hands held two hoes as the fragment is of the upper half only. The text is not preserved. The shabti was carefully cut in two parts. In fact, it can stand properly. It appears to be a shabti from the New Kingdom.

There are some dubious objects, probably fakes made in the nineteenth century. These include nine scarabs that are not exhibited to the public, a wooden statuette representing a scribe (Inv. 2283/829), a statuette representing a nobleman (Inv. 2284/830), and a wooden model of a papyrus boat (Inv. 2379/890).[27]

Some objects are not exhibited, due to the bad state of preservation and the lack of money for restoration. The most important is a mummy mask made of cartonnage, dated to the Third Intermediate period or Late period, probably Twenty-Fifth Dynasty (Inv. 2286/1895).[28]

During the time of the study of the objects, the curator of the Museum, dott.ssa Anna Rossi, found an important document concerning the collection. It is a signed manuscript of Ernesto Schiaparelli, with the date 27 February 1919. At that time he was Soprintendente of the Piedmont Region and Vallée d'Aoste Antiquities, professor of Egyptology at the University of Turin, and director of the Egyptian Museum in Turin. The manuscript is a list of the Egyptian objects of the Camillo Leone collection, sent to him by Vittorio Viale for a quick analysis of the objects. Every item is simply listed with description, material, measurements, and date. Two pages of the manuscript, the first with the title (fig. 26) and the last with the date and signature (fig. 27) were scanned to become the background of the cover of the catalogue with the image of the shabti of Psamtek.[29]

References

ANDREWS, C. A. R. 1994. *Amulets of Ancient Egypt*. London: British School of Archaeology in Egypt.

BALDISSONE, G. 2007. *Camillo Leone: Una vita da museo. Memorie 1876–1901*. Novara: Interlinea.

BERARDI, L. 1985. *Il Civico Museo Borgogna, Vercelli*. Milan: Garolla.

BERARDI, L. 1996. "Vercelli. Museo Francesco Borgogna." In G. C. SCHIOLLA (ed.), "... Quei leggierissimi tocchi di penna o matita..." *Le collezioni di disegni in Piemonte*. Milan: Charta.

27. Malgora 2011, 24, 28–29.

28. Malgora 2001, 27.

29. Acknowledgments: VercelliViva, its president, Mariella Gallo Ferraris and the cda, Luigi Corradino, Rosa Berzero, Andreina Fumagalli, Gabriella Maglione, for supporting the catalogne and for their friendship; the Piedmont Region for supporting the catalogue; the museum staff: Luca Brusotto, Federica Bertoni, Ricccardo Rossi, Antonella Picco e Mariangela Dovi for the kind assistance and help. The director of the Francesco Borgogna Museum, Cinzia Lacchia, for revising the part concerning the museum. The President, Amedeo Corio and the Curator, Anna Rosso, for their revision and suggestions.

Cambitoglou, A., and H. Harari. 1997. *The Italiote Red-Figured Vases in the Museum Camillo Leone at Vercelli.* Rome: L'ERMA di Bretschneider.

Casati-Migliorini, P. 2001. "Raccolte ceramiche nei musei minori italiani. La collezione di maioliche e porcellane del Museo Leone di Vercelli," *Ceramic Antica* 11, 30–43.

Corio A. 1990. *L'istituto di Belle Arti di Vercelli tra '800 e '900.* Vercelli: Cassa di Risparmio di Vercelli.

De Haan, N. 2013. *Psamtek Son of Mery-Neith.* Voorhout: Shabti Collections Publications.

Einaudi S. 2009. *Egitto Nascosto, Collezioni e Collezionisti dei Musei Piemontesi (Castello di Pinerolo 21 marzo–5 luglio 2009).* Milan: Silvana.

Faccio G. C., and F. Arboreo Mella. 1910. *Museo Camillo Leone: Vercelli. Illustrazioni e Cataloghi.* Vercelli: Tipo-Litografia Gallardi Ugo.

Faccio G., C. Chicco, and F. Viola. 1933. *Vecchia Vercelli.* Vercelli: Viola.

Ferrari D. 1996. *Gli amuleti dell'antico Egitto.* Bologna: Imola, La Mandragora.

Lacchia C. 2001. "La storia del Museo." In C. Lacchia and A. Schiavi (eds.), *Museo Borgogna. Storia e Collezioni.* Cologno Monzese: Silvia.

———. 1997. I rapporti internazionali di Antonio Borgogna per l'acquisto delle opere della sua collezione, Tesi di laurea in Storia dell'Arte Moderna, relatore Prof.ssa M. Di Macco, Università degli Studi di Torino, Seconda facoltà di Lettere e Filosofia, sede di Vercelli, A.A.

Malgora S. 2008. *Ur Sunu. Grandi Dottori dell'Antico Egitto.* Vercelli: Saviolo.

———. 2011. *La collezione egizia del Museo Camillo Leone.* Novara: Interlinea.

Martin G. T. 1985. *Scarabs, Cylinders and Other Ancient Egyptian Seals.* Warminster: Aris & Phillips.

Misiti, C., and A. Rosso. 1998. *Il Museo e la Biblioteca di Camillo Leone*, in: *The International Association of Bibliophily Colloquium 1998 (Torino 27 settembre-1 ottobre)*, vol. 3, 29–38.

———. 1999." Camillo Leone e la sua"diletta raccolta di libri" , in: *Bibliofilia subalpina*, Quaderno 199, Torino: Centro Studi Piemontesi, 123–44.

Newberry, P. E. 1979. *Ancient Egyptian Scarabs: An Introduction to Egyptian Seals and Signed Rings.* London 1906, repr. Chicago: Ares.

Nicholson P., and A. Rosso. 1996. "Vercelli, Istituto di Belle Arti e Museo Leone." In G. C. Schiolla (ed.), "*... Quei leggierissimi tocchi di penna o matita...*" *Le collezioni di disegni in Piemonte.* Milano: Charta, 214–16.

Rosso, A. 2003–4. "Museo Camillo Leone di Vercelli. Collezione Leone e Poma Borgogna." Pp. 103–5 in F. Gandolfo and L. Lenti (eds.), *Gioielli. Collezioni etnografiche subalpine Catalogo della mostra, Valenza-Rivoli. Valenza, Centro comunale di cultura.* Rivoli: Casa del Conte Verde.

———. 2007. "Il Museo del notaio Camillo Leone." In G. Baldissone (ed.), *Camillo Leone: Una vita da museo, Memorie 1876–1901*, Novara: Interlinea, 68–95.

——— (ed.). 2008. *Guida al Museo Camillo Leone.* Vercelli: Whitelight.

Rosso, A. et al. 1984. *Storia, epigrafia, archeologia a Vercelli nell'Ottocento, Guida alla mostra, Vercelli - Museo Leone 5–20 Ottobre 1984.* Vercelli: Cassa di Risparmio di Vercelli.

Schögl, H. A. 1986, *"Uschebti," LÄ* 6:896–99.

Schneider, H. D. 1977. *Shabtis*, I–III, National Museum of Antiquities, Leiden: Rijksmuseum van Oudheden.

Sciolla, G. C. 1980. "Atlante dei Musei piemontesi. Il Museo Leone di Vercelli," *Cronache Economiche* 4, 3–14.

Schiavi, A. 2001. "Le collezioni del Museo." In C. Lacchia and A. Schiavi (eds.), *Museo Borgogna. Storia e Collezioni.* Cologno Monzese: Silvia.

Sommo, G. 1982. *Vercelli e la memoria dell'antico.* Vercelli: Gruppo Archeologico Vercellese.

STEWART, H. M. 1995. *Egyptian Shabtis*. Princes Risborough: Shire.

VIALE, V. 1934. *Guida ai Musei Leone e Borgogna di Vercelli*. Vercelli: Tip. F. Chiais.

———. 1939. *Vercelli e la sua provincia dalla romanità al fascismo. Mostra di storia, di arte, di economia. Guida-itinerario*. Vercelli.

———. 1969. *Il Civico Museo Borgogna. I dipinti: catalogo*. Cinisello Balsamo: A. Pizzi.

———. 1971. *Vercelli e il Vercellese nell'antichità*. Vercelli: Cassa di Risparmio.

The New Installation of the Egyptian and Nubian Rooms in the Museo Arqueológico Nacional (National Archaeological Museum), Madrid, Spain

M. Carmen Pérez-Die and Esther Pons Mellado

The National Archaeological Museum in Madrid is currently undergoing complete renovation, both of the building itself and of the permanent exhibition rooms (fig. 1).[1] In 2010 the Department of Egyptian Antiquities designed a large-scale museographic project that has not been completely implemented. In 2011, the rooms allocated by the Spanish Ministry of Educación, Cultura y Deporte to Egypt and Nubia in the new distribution plan are smaller than before, and there was not any room specifically devoted to Nubian archaeology.[2] The actual number of square meters is less than in the old layout, even though the Egyptian and Nubian Rooms have received the greatest number of visitors over recent years. In our opinion, in this Ministry's design project, there are also too many architectural features of the rooms themselves, which hinder the free flow of visitors and the full appreciation of the items on display (fig. 2). In view of the above and as required by the Ministry, the Egyptian Department has had to alter the 2010 design project and exhibition layout and to prepare a new one. In 2012 the title of the new exhibition became The Nile: Egypt and Nubia.

The central theme of the whole exhibition is therefore the River Nile. To explain certain themes, we have sometimes exhibited Egyptian and Nubian artifacts together, although we are conscious that these cultures are contextually very different from each other, and we have emphasized this difference, above all in terms of the chronology. We have attempted to demonstrate the similarities and points of contact between Egypt and Nubia, and also the contrasts, thus presenting a dialogue between the two cultures.

1. The last permanent exhibition was open in 1980 under the supervision of M. Almagro and M. C. Pérez-Die.
2. Architect: Juan Pablo Frade, in collaboration with EMPTY and Acciona.

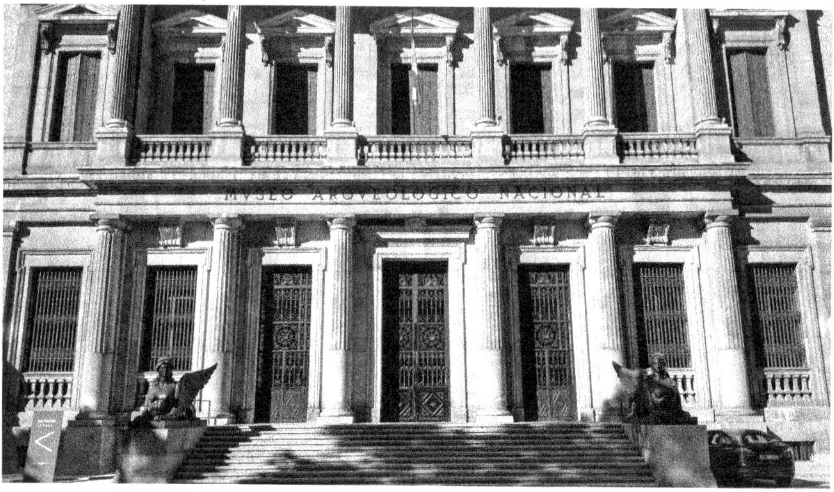

Fig. 1. Museo Arqueológico Nacional. Madrid. © Carmen Pérez-Die.

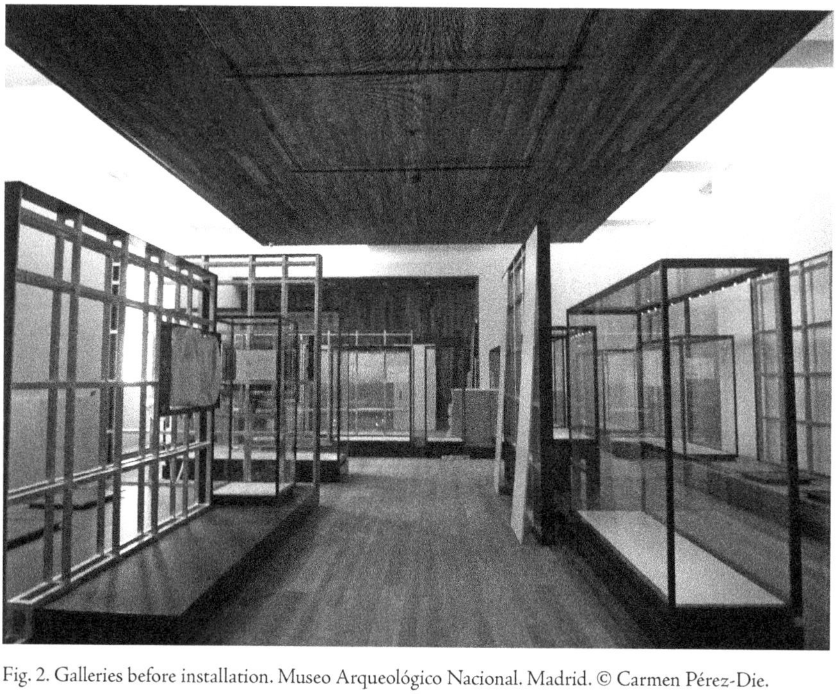

Fig. 2. Galleries before installation. Museo Arqueológico Nacional. Madrid. © Carmen Pérez-Die.

Another aspect that has been considered is the different readings that a single artifact may have. In the exhibition rooms the display cases and texts have accompanying line drawings and watercolors illustrating the exhibition theme (fig. 3).

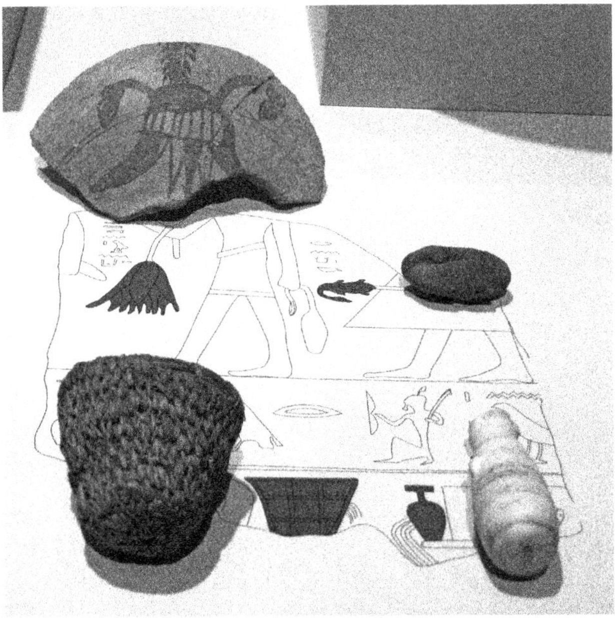

Fig. 3. Drawings and watercolors illustrating the exhibition theme. © Carmen Pérez-Die.

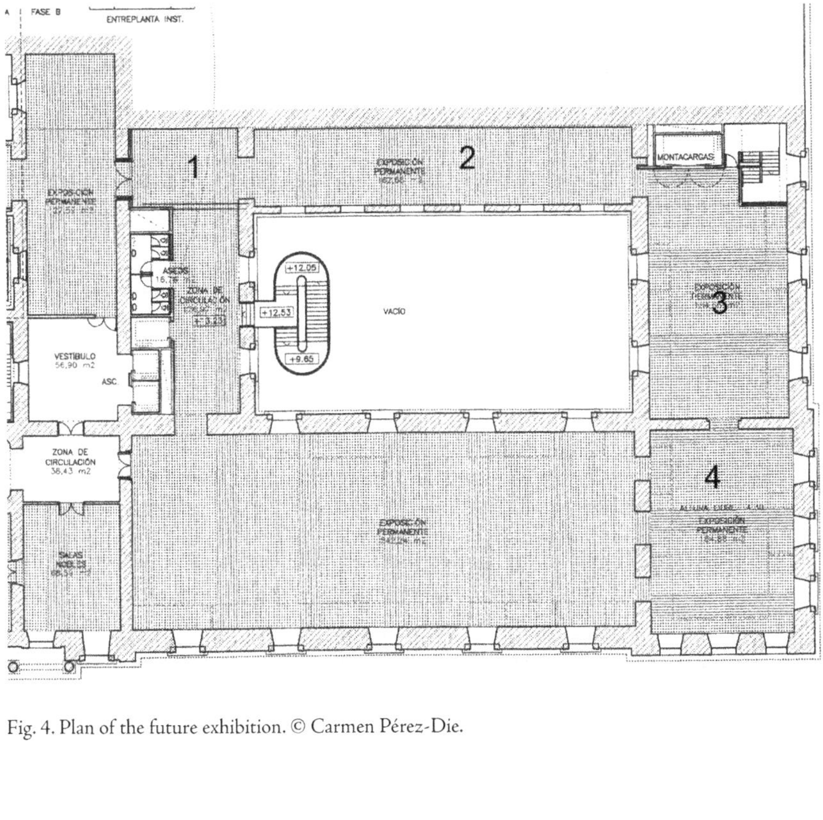

Fig. 4. Plan of the future exhibition. © Carmen Pérez-Die.

Under the main headings Environment, People, Society, Beliefs, and the Funerary World (as will be seen below), objects are displayed from the cultures of Egypt and Nubia, but with each object retaining all its individuality, context, and chronology (fig. 4).

Room 1 exhibits the results of the archaeological missions in Egypt and Nubia. The museum has been involved in two important archaeological activities: the campaign in Nubia in relation to the building of the Aswan Dam, and the excavation in Heracleopolis Magna, which is still underway. Room 2 is devoted to items related to the Nile and the life of the people on the banks of the river in both Egypt and in Nubia: the landscape, flora and fauna, the people represented by their society, royalty, daily life, products, and so on. Room 3 is divided into two parts. On the left are exhibited the Nubian antiquities corresponding to religion and the funerary world. The rest of this room is devoted to Egypt, specifically to religion and the afterlife. Finally, the Egyptian antiquities occupy the whole of Room 4 displaying items found in the necropolis and other objects related to the resurrection of the dead.

In visual terms, two different colors were chosen for the room signs and object labels: yellow for Egypt and brown for Nubia (fig. 5). The color-coded signs and labels show the provenance and chronology, and provide a description.

Room 1

As already mentioned above, the two display cases in this room show the results of the excavations in Egypt and Nubia carried out by the National Archaeological Museum, with objects, photos, drawings, publications, and more. Our intention is to change the objects and the documents on display at regular intervals, especially those from Heracleopolis Magna, as the Museum is currently excavating this site. Information on the results of each campaign will be made available here (fig. 6).

Room 2

The first part includes maps, an introduction to the history of Egypt and Nubia and a comparative chronology of the two cultures. The room will contain two other maps, the first of them concerning the territory and history of Egypt. In the text we explain the differences between the valley and the deserts, and the division of territory into *nomes* (fig. 7). The periods of Egyptian history—Old, Middle, and New Kingdoms, Late period, Greco-Roman period, which alternated with eras of fragmentation known as Intermediate periods—are also defined.

The other map shows the territory and the history of Nubia. It demonstrates how Nubia was divided into two regions: Lower Nubia or Wawat, and Upper Nubia or the Land of Kush. A series of independent cultures (A and C-Groups) flourished here, and later became independent kingdoms, such as Kerma and Kush.

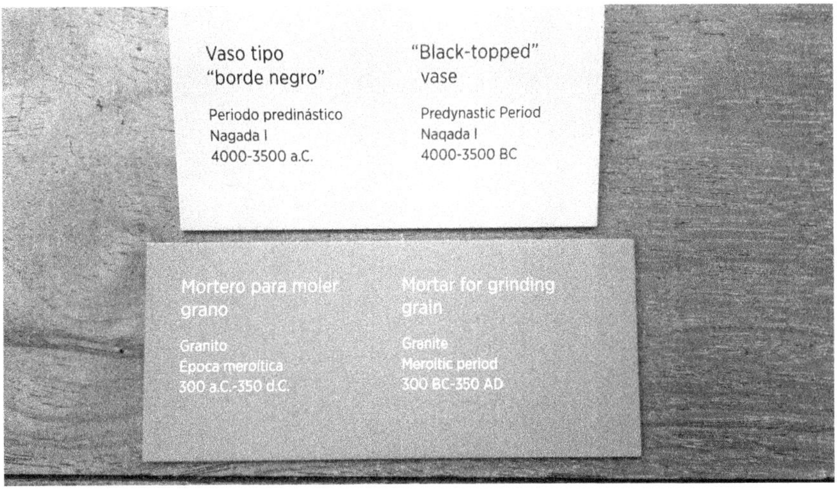

Fig. 5. Signs and labels for Egypt and Nubia. © Carmen Pérez-Die.

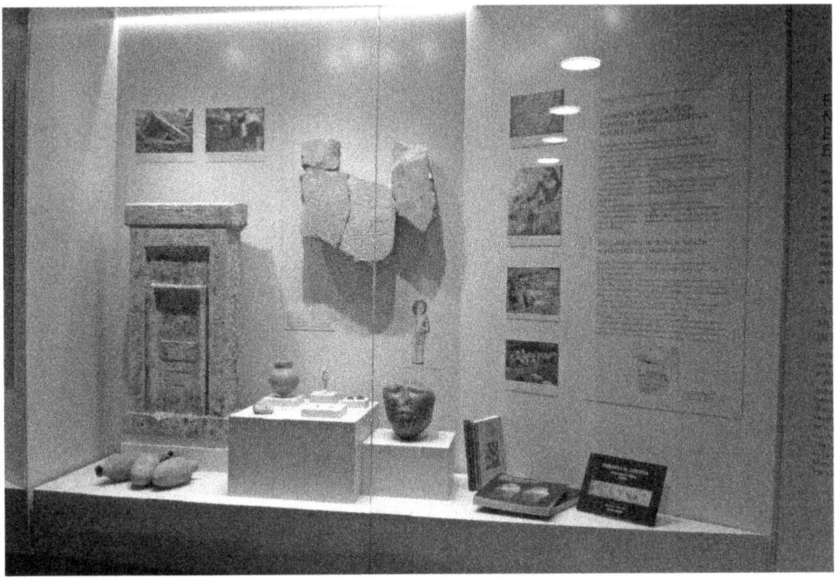

Fig. 6. Showcase illustrating the archaeological mission in Heracleopolis Magna. © Carmen Pérez-Die.

All this historical and chronological information is followed by the exhibits. Our aim is to offer the visitor a journey along the Nile, in order to understand something of the landscape, the Egyptians and Nubians who lived beside the river, and their heritage. Along the upper part of the wall there is a backlit canvas with a large watercolor representing the Nile from the Mediterranean to beyond Khartoum, marking the main cities, monuments and deities. Below, there is a large display case (fig. 8).

EGIPTO: TERRITORIO E HISTORIA

EGYPT: TERRITORY AND HISTORY

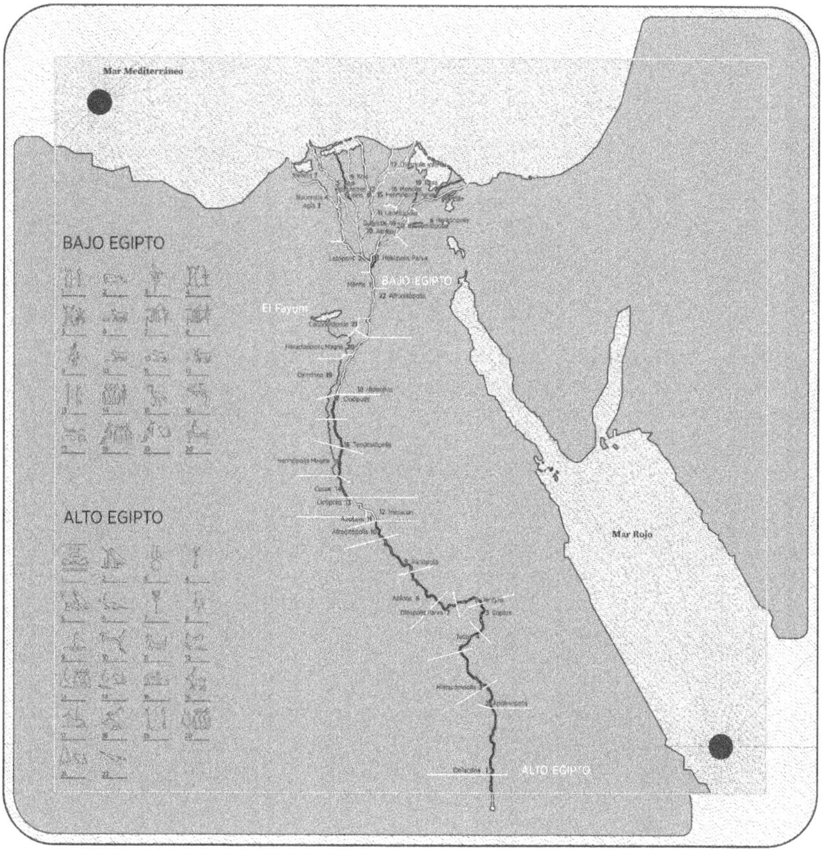

Fig. 7. Map of Egypt. © Carmen Pérez-Die.

The Nile is presented as the "River of Life" for those who inhabited its banks, but it also facilitated travel and trade between the Nubian south and the Egyptian north, and served as a link between the Mediterranean world and sub-Saharan Africa. Nubians and Egyptians have always been connected by this great waterway. From Khartoum to Aswan, the Nile flows through the birthplace of the Nubian or Kushite civilisation, and from Aswan to the Mediterranean it continues through the land of the pharaohs.

The river and its banks, teeming with many different animals, like frogs, fish, and crocodiles, supplied the people with food, and, by means of artificial canals, abundant

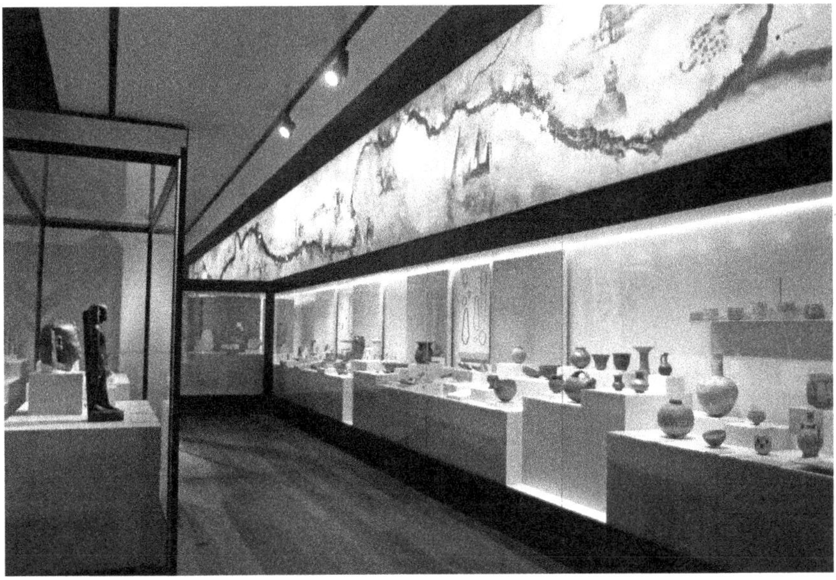

Fig. 8. View of the exhibition gallery. © Carmen Pérez-Die.

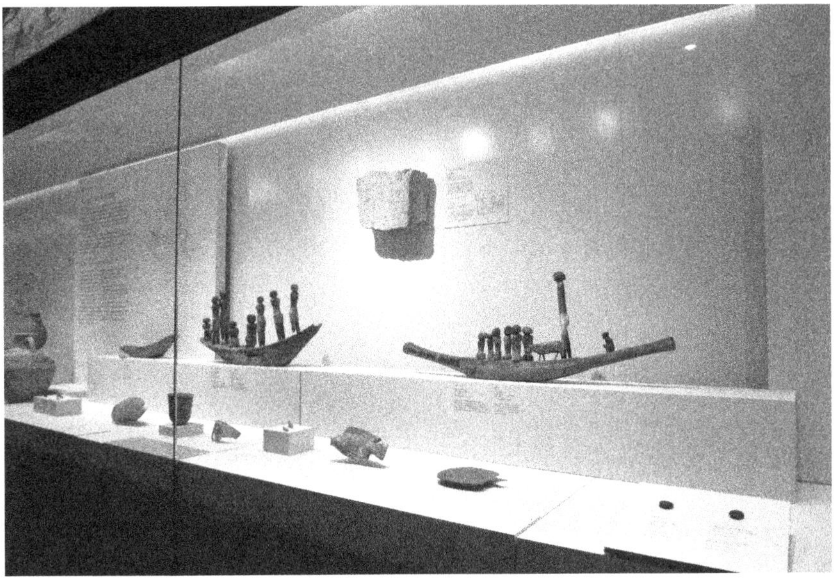

Fig. 9. Nilotic live. © Carmen Pérez-Die.

water was made available for irrigation, domestic use, and human and animal consumption (fig. 9).

Many plants are associated with Egyptian culture, such as papyrus, lotus, and palm. Some animals were a part of everyday life, such as birds, insects, dogs, cats, bovids, horses, and dromedaries while others roamed freely across the desert, like oryxes, antelopes and jackals. Lions, monkeys, hippopotamuses, ostriches, giraffes, and other animals only found in the heart of Africa today inhabited Egypt and Nubia in ancient times.

The Population. Two display cases show the iconography of inhabitants of Egypt and Nubia and their representations in art. When depicting people in drawings or reliefs, Egyptian artists combined frontal and side views. In sculpture the faces usually have regular features, bodies were realistically rendered, and careful attention was paid to the details of the garments. Classical sources refer to the Nubians as "Ethiopians" (men of burnt faces). They are depicted as having dark complexions, thick lips, curly hair and slightly bulging eyes, although facial features were occasionally stylized.

The Languages and Writing in the Nile Valley. From Egypt we present the three different writing systems: Hieroglyphic, Hieratic, and Demotic. A wealth of documents in Greek, Coptic, and Arabic produced in Egypt in Late Antiquity and the medieval period are also exhibited. In ancient Sudan, the Nubians used Egyptian hieroglyphs until the second century BC when examples of Meroitic writing began to appear. Later, the Greek, Coptic, Old Nubian, and Arabic languages were introduced and continued to be spoken in the region for centuries.

Egyptian and Nubian Society. Egyptian society was highly stratified. At the top was the pharaoh, who embodied the omnipotence of the state, followed by his highest-ranking subordinates.

In Nubia, the royal family played an important role. The Kushite sovereigns imitated the iconography and attire of their Egyptian counterparts. Starting in the second century BC, Nubian queens, called *candace*, ruled as independent sovereigns. Skilled archers, warriors, priests, and herders inhabited those distant Nubian territories.

The Egyptian pharaohs are represented in sculptures including the statue of Nectanebo I, the stela of Seankhiptah, shabtis and scarabs with royal names, statues and coins of the Ptolemaic kings. Also on display here is the *quaternion* of Augustus, a unique coin commemorating the conquest of Egypt.

Daily Life and Crafts in Egypt. The upper classes dressed elegantly for ceremonies, with wigs of flowers, but in everyday life they wore simple linen tunics, skirts, and sandals. Combs were made of bone or wood, and mirrors were made of a metal that, when highly polished, reflected as well as glass. The ancient Egyptians went barefoot or used homemade footwear. The ritual sandals they used for religious ceremonies consisted of a sole with straps that wrapped around the foot.

Alabaster vessels were used to store perfumes, ointments, and *kohl*. Egyptian elites wore magnificent pieces of gold and silver jewellery, typical of a rich and varied popular goldsmith tradition, which contrasted with those of inferior quality worn by lower-ranking people.

Egyptian craftsmen were experts at modelling pottery, carving alabaster, making faience, glass, cloth, and basketwork. They also mastered other disciplines such as metalwork, painting, and sculpture.

Vessels of pottery and alabaster were used in the world of the living as containers for storing grain and liquids, and in the world of the dead as part of the burial offerings. Pottery is shown in chronological order.

Objects made of faience and Egyptian blue were highly prized, both for their color, which was close to that of semiprecious stones like turquoise and lapis lazuli, and their significance as symbols of regeneration and life.

The clothing fabrics produced by the Copts constitute an exceptional legacy. Cloth was generally woven using the tapestry technique from materials such as linen and wool with thread of silk, cotton, and even hemp. They were decorated with bright colors and a wide variety of geometric and plant motifs as well as zoomorphic and anthropomorphic figures.

Daily Life and Crafts in Nubia. A variety of artifacts used in the home and daily life such as cooking utensils, oil lamps, and loom weights have been found in Nubian tombs and towns. Nubia had excellent archers who put their skill to good use as members of the army. Nubian warriors were buried with their weapons and other objects such as thumb rings, quivers, and metal arrows.

The Nubians, like the Egyptians, paid careful attention to their personal appearance, which advertised their social status. They painted their eyes, dressed and adorned their hair, and donned pieces of jewelry like necklaces, earrings, bracelets, and metal bands worn on the arm or, occasionally, the ankle.

Faience and glass were made in Nubia, although it is sometimes hard to distinguish between native and imported products. The most important innovation was the appearance of blown glass in the first century BC.

Nubian Pottery is presented by chronology: "A-Group" and "C-Group" Cultures, Kerma Culture, Meroitic, X-Group, and Medieval Pottery.

Room 3

The Egyptian pantheon is presented in a display case exhibiting the "triads" and the principal deities: Isis, Osiris, Ptah, Neith, Apis, Min, Sekhmet, Bastet, among others. Some Egyptian deities appeared in the form of animals, adopting their attributes and conveying their mysterious and unfathomable nature. They were embalmed and placed in cemeteries. Ibises, crocodiles, and falcons have been found in tombs, many in their own coffins, or their organs have been placed in canopic jars, as in the case of the Mnevis bull that is kept in the National Archaeological Museum.

The Temple, the Priesthood and the Rituals. The priesthood was the social class associated with the temples. There were also priestesses who participated in ceremonies by playing music, singing, and shaking the sistrums during the frequent rituals. Water taken from the sacred lake was placed in *hes*-vases or *situlas* and used for libations with mythical connotations.

The rest of Room 3 displays objects related to the funerary world in Egypt and Nubia, with those from Nubia on the left, and from Egypt on the right. Nubian or

Kushite Tombs have two kinds of structures. The first, typical of the "C-Group" of Kerma and of the post-Meroitic period, consists of a tumulus sometimes surrounded by *bucranea* (bovine skulls) that covered the grave. The second type of royal tomb, influenced by neighboring Egypt, has a steep pyramid as a superstructure. These royal graves have been found in El Kurru, Nuri, and Meroe.

The exhibits from Nubia include two models of tombs and one "*ba*" statue and some objects found in burials in Nubia by the Spanish Mission during the rescue campaign in the region from 1961 to 1965.

The Funerary World and the Afterlife in Egypt. Some objects found at the First Intermediate period/early Middle Kingdom necropolis of Heracleopolis Magna, introduce the visitors to the Egyptians tomb. First we present the false doors and the offering tables. On the west wall of the chapel there was a false door separating the world of the living from the world of the dead. The funerary meal was depicted on the central panel, while the door jambs and lintels were inscribed with the invocation of the offering and the name and title of the owner. The offering tables were placed in front of these false doors where relatives could gather around them and recite the inscribed formula so that the deceased could partake of the goods mentioned.

Along with the false doors and tables of offerings there can be seen here a fragment of the wall of the tomb of Neferkhau and Satbahetep. At the top is a menu with the list of food. In the top register the funerary priests are shown performing the rituals: opening the deceased's mouth to allow him to recover his vital functions, pouring libations, burning incense, and reading texts. Below them the bearers are bringing the offerings to the tables (not preserved) of Neferkhau and Satbahetep (fig. 10).

Room 4

In a fourth room, two mummies are on display, one of which belongs to Nespamedu, a 55-year-old adult male wrapped in a shroud and covered by five gilded cartonnage cases. The conservation-restoration of the mummy of Nespamedu has been a multidisciplinary project. Although addressed as a single process, experts from different fields have participated in the intervention. The first step was to eradicate insects and disinfect the mummy using inert gases, and then to remove the cartonnage cases covering it. After analyzing the constituent materials and the mummification process using techniques such as X-ray, scanning electron microscope, gas chromatography, and infrared spectroscopy, the next step was to clean the mummy, remove deformations, reinforce the structure, and consolidate the textile elements. The final step was to reintegrate volume and color losses. All of these actions were carried out according to international criteria of minimal intervention and respect for the original. The mummy was often covered with a net made of tubular faience beads. A heart scarab was placed on the chest and around it the figures of the Four Sons of Horus.

In the center of the last room we present a replica of a burial chamber. This replica, made with artifacts from different places and periods, shows what a burial cham-

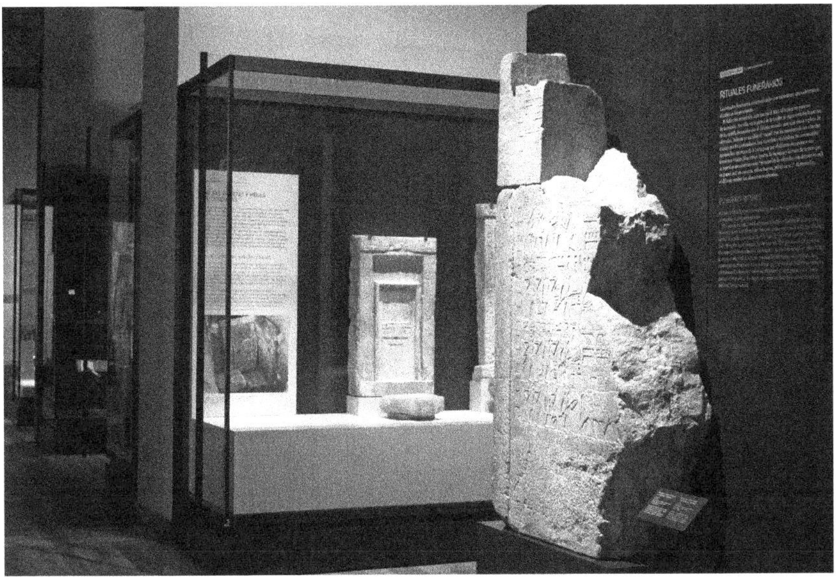

Fig. 10. Funerary rituals. False door from the tomb of Neferkhau and Satbahetep. © Carmen Pérez-Die.

ber from the Twenty-First or Twenty-Second Dynasty (1076–730 BC) might have looked like. It contained the coffin of a singer of Amun, surrounded by canopic jars, necklaces, alabaster vases, and shabtis placed inside a box belonging to Nesytanebtawy, a priestess mistress of the house, singer of Amun. The reproduction mummy inside the coffin was made at the museum in the early twentieth century.

Around the burial chamber we can see the wooden masks. During the Late period and the Graeco-Roman period, masks consisting of several layers of heavily pressed linen and stucco, or a coat of gold leaf, were placed on the head. Plaster was another material used to make masks, and black and white stones were embedded into the eyes to imitate the eyeballs and iris.

The types of anthropomorphic coffins and the decoration on them varied from one period to another. They were made of polychrome wood, and might have very elaborate decorations, all of them were characterized by a predominance of religious images and invocations of the funerary deities.

Funerary figurines include shabtis from different periods, a shabti box from Deir el-Medina, figures of the god Sokaris, a viscera box, and more.

The survival of the dead is presented in the last part of this room represented by the journey during the twelve hours of the night, accompanying the god Re in his boat and his rebirth at the dawn of the new day.

The coffin of Ankhefenkhonsu is decorated with texts from the short version of the *Amduat* showing the deceased's *akh* in Re's boat as it arrives at the threshold of the infernal abode, where he continues his journey, guided by genies and gods who lead him to the throne of the great god Osiris. At the end of the night, the god Re-Khepri, in the form of a scarab, "rises into the day" at sunrise, accompanied by the dead person, and rows through the sky in the sun boat. The twenty-four hour cycle starts again, ensuring the survival of the gods and of the dead for all eternity.

Interactive and multimedia productions and autoguides are available to complete the collection.

References

Almagro M., and M. C. Pérez-Die. 1980. "Les nouvelles salles d'archéologie égyptienne au Musée Archéologique National de Madrid: Aspects techniques et pedagogiques." *Göttinger Miszellen* 51, 9–17.

Alvarez-Ossorio, F. . *Una visita al Museo Arqueologico Nacional.* Madrid: Museo Arqueológico Nacional, 31–39.

———. 1929. "Museo Arqueológico Nacional, Guia de la Sección Primera." *IV Congreso Internacional de Arqueología,* 14–15.

Pérez-Die, M. C. 1979. "La collection égyptienne du Musée Archéologique National de Madrid, Espagne." Pp. 515–18 in *Acts of First International Congres of Egyptology, Octobre 2–10, 1976.* Schriften zur Geschichte und Kultur des Alten Orients 14. Berlin: Akademie Verlag.

———. 1985. *Guía didáctica del Museo Arqueológico Nacional. Egipto.* Madrid. Ministerio de Cultura.

———. 1991. "Egipto y Próximo Oriente." In *Guia del Museo Arqueológico Nacional,* Madrid: Ministerio de Cultura, 90–112.

———. 1992. "Historia de la coleccion egipcia del Museo Arqueológico Nacional," *Aygyptiaca Complutense* 1, 17–26.

Pérez-Die, M. C., S. Zurinaga, and J. Córdoba. 2008. *Egipto, Nubia y Oriente Próximo: Colecciones del Museo Arqueológico Nacional.* Madrid: Ministerio de Cultura.

The Ancient Egyptian Collections in Croatia and the Project Croato-Aegyptica Electronica

MLADEN TOMORAD

Approximately four to five thousand Egyptian artifacts usually dated as late as the eighth century AD, are housed in institutional and private collections in Croatia. Most of the artifacts are housed in archaeological museums (at least 3,264), in regional and town museums (at least 573), in lapidariums and in situ (11), and in other cultural institutions (3; table 1). At least five hundred other artifacts are housed in known private collections in Croatia.

Egyptian antiquities in Croatian institutional and private collections consist mostly of various types of smaller objects such as scarabs, amulets, shabtis, tablets made of different materials, jewelry, fertility symbols, and statuettes of deities as well as footwear, various vessels and canopic jars, animal images, and male and female statues. Within this vast number of objects, larger groups can be identified, like statues of gods (primarily Osiris and Isis) made of different materials, various wooden and stone stelae with inscriptions and paintings of mostly a funerary character, inscriptions on papyrus and linen, and Books of the Dead. The sarcophagi for the burial of human and animal remains of different material, mummies, and mummy wrappings form a group in their own right.[1] Thirteen complete or fragmentary sphinxes from Diocletian's palace in Split (fig. 1), originally from the ancient Egyptian temple complex of Karnak, are also worth mentioning.[2] In various regions of Croatia, the great number of artifacts related to the diffusion of Egyptian cults during the Graeco-Roman period can be found. In Zadar, Pula, and on the island of Veliki Brijun a monolithic stone block with the protome of a Jupiter-Ammon head can be seen.[3] In the Lapidarium of the Archaeological Museum in Zagreb, are several fragments of the cornice of a funerary stele with a pair of lions and a head of Serapis (from Petrovci and Srijemska Mitrovica), along with the nice statues related with the cult of Isis from Nin, Srijemska Mitrovica, and Sisak.[4] The collection of Ptolemaic coinage and coinage from the Ro-

1. Tomorad 2003a, 31–80; 2005; 2006a, 6–37; forthcoming.
2. Selem 1970; 1997, 97–106; Tomorad 2003a, 55; 2006a, 24, 30–31; forthcoming.
3. Tomorad 2003, 48–49, 52; 2005, 16–17, 20; 2006a, 24–25, 28; forthcoming.
4. Tomorad 2003a, 41–42; 2005, 7, 16–17, 20; 2006a, 10; forthcoming.

Table 1. Egyptian collections in museum institutions in Croatia

Egyptian collection in museum institutions	# of artifacts
The Archaeological Museum, Zagreb	2958
The Mimara Museum, Zagreb	502
The Archaeological Museum, Dubrovnik	191
The Archaeological Museum, Split	131 (139)[a]
The Archaeological Museum of Istria, Pula	39
The Museum of Slavonia, Osijek	19
The Archaeological Museum, Zadar	16
The Collection of the St. Euphemia monastery, Kampor - Rab	10–21?[b]
The Museum of Contemporary Art, Zagreb	11
The Museum of the City of Varaždin, Varaždin	7
Diocletian Palace, Split	5+2?
The Archaeological Collection of the Franciscan Monastery, Sinj	6
Department for history of building and architecture, Split	3
The Franciscan monastery - The Archaeological collection, Košljun (Krk)	10[c]
Museum of the city of Šibenik, Šibenik	3
Lapidarium on the Island of Veliki Brijun	1
Lapidarium, Novigrad (Istria)	1
Museo del territorio parentino, Poreč	1
Lapidarium of the City museum of Senj, Senj	1
The Archaeological Collection and Lapidarium of Grga Novak, Hvar	1
Museum "Narona," Vid near Metković	1
The Collection of "Narodno sveučilište," Imotski	1
The Museum of the City of Požega, Požega	1
The Museum of the City of Koprivnica, Koprivnica	1
The Museum of the City of Križevci, Križevci	1
The Museum of the City of Zagreb, Zagreb	1
The Museum Bostan, Bostan	1
The Museum of the City of Pregrada "dr. Zlatko Dragutin Tudjina," Pregrada	1
Totals 1	3,929–3,962?
The Ptolemaic coinage in other museums in Croatia	ca. 140
Totals 2	ca. 4069

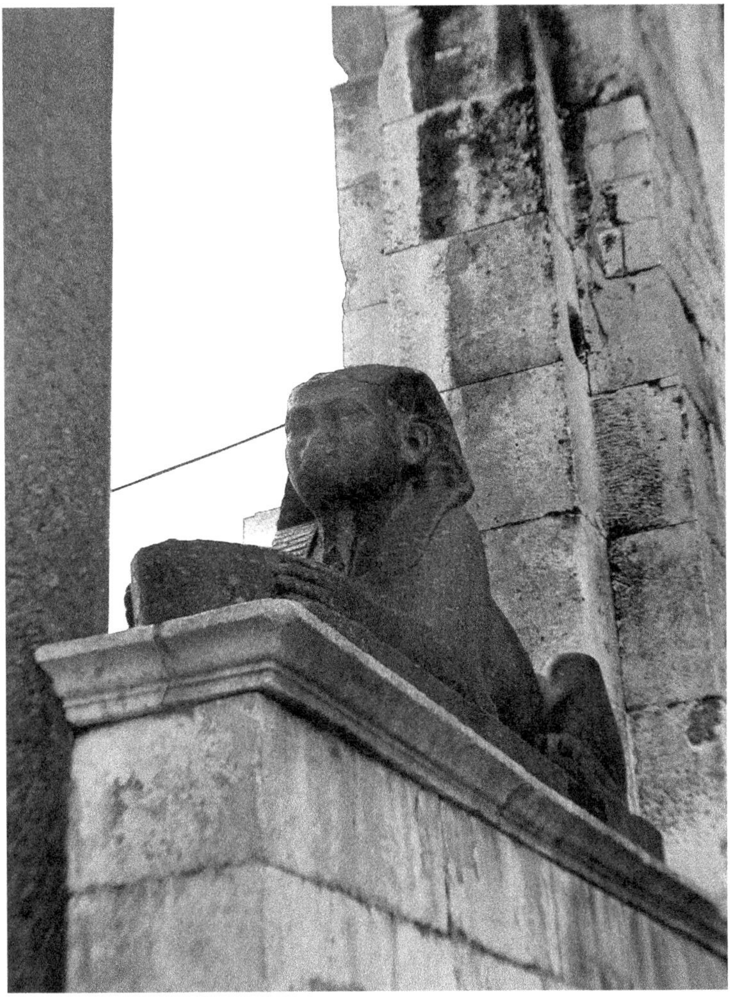

Fig. 1. A sphinx of the ruler of the early Eighteenth Dynasty (Thuthmose I or Thutmose III). From Thebes, fifteenth century BC, in situ in the peristyle of the Diocletian palace in Split where it was brought in the late third–early fourth century CE. © Mladen Tomorad.

Notes to Table 1

[a] The smaller number is related to the artifacts that were surely in the museum in the end of May 2013. The bigger number refer to the items that supposed to be in the museum, eight artifacts seem to be lost or misplaced.

[b] This collection is not analyzed and published. I saw it almost ten years ago but in that time it could not be examined and fully analysed.

[c] I found out about the existence of this collection in the end of May 2013. The Franciscan monastery at the island Košljun currently house these Egyptian artifacts: shabti, pseudo-shabti, three scarabs and five amulets of cats. These items were discovered at the Hellenistic necropolis in the ancient city Curicum, modern city Krk.

man imperial Alexandrian mint (dated from emperor Augustus to Constantine I) is also associated with ancient Egypt. These coinage collections are today part of the very large Numismatic Department of the Archaeological Museum in Zagreb,[5] but such collections also exist in the Archaeological Museum in Split, the Archaeological Museum of Istria in Pula, and in the museums of the cities Rijeka and Senj.[6] Glass and faience collections can also be found in the Museum Mimara in Zagreb (fig. 2).[7]

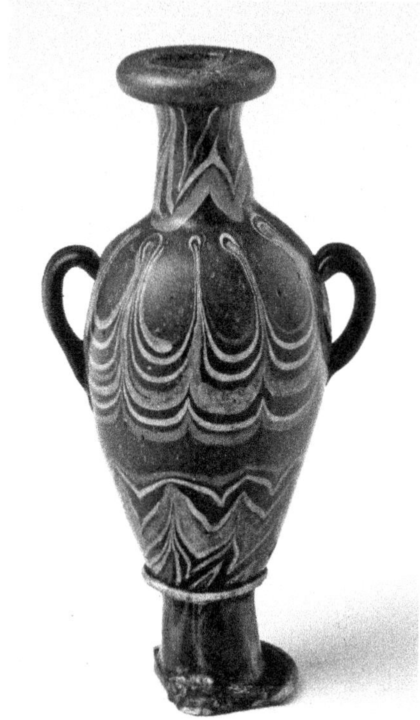

Fig. 2. Amphoriskos. Fourteenth century BC. The Glass collection, Museum Mimara. Inv. ATM 1335. © Museum Mimara, Zagreb.

The numismatic collection of the Alexandrian mint from the Roman Emporer (from Augustus to Constantine I) is very large. This collection contains the images of various Roman emperors and their co-rulers.[8]

The Egyptian antiquities in the Croatian institutional and private collections consist of (1) material acquired from abroad through intermediaries or donations; and (2) material associated with ancient Egyptian cults from various provinces of the Roman Empire. Such artifacts were acquired by Croatian museums or private collectors mostly through archaeological excavations, or in some cases by purchase. The material from this second category presents problems, especially in the second half of the nineteenth century when they were commonly considered to be fakes. Fortunately, recently it has been mostly established that such artifacts originated in ancient Rome, and now these antiquities are considered to be genuine.[9]

The ancient Egyptian antiquities from the known institutional and private collections have rarely been fully systemized and analyzed according to commonly used

5. Tomorad 2003a, 42–48; 2005, 7–11; 2006, 12–16; forthcoming.

6. These coins were discovered during the archaeological excavations in the nineteenth and twentieth centuries in Croatia, Bosnia, and Herzegovina, Istra, in Senj, along the coast of Dalmatia and at the islands of Korčula, Hvar, and Vis. The number of these coins is really hard to determine. It seems there are at least two hundred coins in the institutions mentioned above, but the exact number is uncertain.

7. Ratković–Bukovčan 2001; Tomorad 2003a, 67–69; 2005, 12–13; 2006, 18; forthcoming.

8. Tomorad 2005, 9–11; 2006, 14–16; forthcoming.

9. Tomorad 2006b; forthcoming.

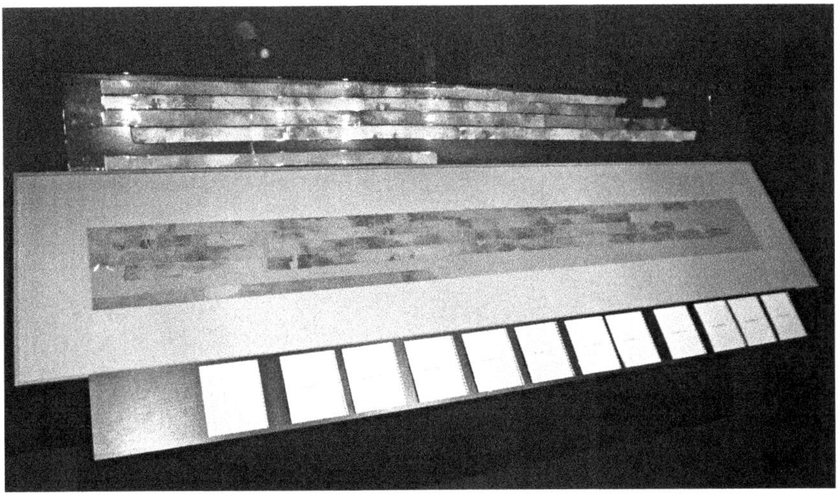

Fig. 3. Liber linteus zagrabiensis, linen wrappings of the Egyptian mummy of Nesi-hensu. Fourth century BC. The Archaeological museum in Zagreb. Inv. 665. © Archaeological Museum, Zagreb, Filip Beusan.

typologies or according to their function. At the present time, we can divide all known collections into two major groups:

(1) The institutional collections, which have been systematically analyzed, presented, and published in exhibition catalogues and scientific periodicals. These are mostly the collections of the Archaeological Museum in Zagreb and the Archaeological Museum in Split. For the Egyptian collection of the Archaeological Museum in Zagreb there are several catalogues: a very old catalogue by Š. Ljubić,[10] a catalogue in French by J. Monnet Saleh,[11] and the new Croatian/English catalogue published by I. Uranić.[12] Many specialized exhibition catalogues[13] or specialized publications[14] were also published during the twentieth century. Egyptian artifacts housed in the Archaeological Museum in Split have been presented and published mostly in Bullettino di archeologia e storia Dalmata (Split [Spalato], 1878–1918) and Vjesnik za arheologiju i historiju dalmatinsku (Split, 1919–present day), but also in books.[15] The Egyptian antiquities included in the Ante Topić Mimara museum in Zagreb are published in several museum catalogues, a small catalogue about the glass collection,[16] and in articles and books by M.

10. Ljubić 1871, 1889a, 1889b.
11. Monnet Saleh 1970.
12. Uranić 2009.
13. Gorenc 1979; Rendić–Miočević 1982; Rendić–Miočević 1993; Uranić 1996, 1999, 2003, 2005, 2012.
14. Brunšmid 1904, 1905, 1907, 1914; Rendić–Miočević 1986.
15. Selem 1997; Tomorad 2003a, 52–55.
16. Ratković–Bukovčan 2001.

Tomorad.[17] The large collection in the Archaeological Museums in Dubrovnik[18] and Pula[19] have only recently been partly analyzed and published. The minor collections in the museums have mostly been examined during the last decade[20] with the exception of the collection of the Franciscan monastery in Sinj,[21] the Archeological museum in Zadar,[22] the Museum of Slavonia in Osijek,[23] and the important collection in the Museum of Varaždin, which has only recently has been systematically analyzed.[24] The important position Croatia has in the world of ancient history and Egyptology is mostly due to the large and valuable collection in the Archaeological Museum in Zagreb that includes a world rarity, the so-called "Zagreb Egyptian mummy with the linen book (Liber linteus Zagrabiensis)" (fig. 3).[25]

(2) The collections in institutions and in private collections that are not on display and are previously uknown and unpublished. Their number is still unknown. It is necessary to establish how many artifacts are kept in regional museums and to determine their origin, their authenticity, date, and cultural and historical value. It is often very hard to say how the artifacts found their way to these institutions, mostly because valuable documentation about the purchase, donations, or excavations has not survived. The private collections form a special group. They are almost completely unknown to the scientific public. The genesis and the number of the artifacts kept in such collections in uncertain and mostly unknown.

The Archaeological Museum in Zagreb

The Archaeological Museum in Zagreb is the only museum in Croatia that has systematically collected and presented ancient Egyptian antiquities since the middle of the nineteenth century. By systematic preservation, and the presentation of the Egyptian collection through permanent exhibitions and many part-time temporary exhibitions, the Archaeological Museum in Zagreb has become one of the most important institutions in Croatia which constantly gives the general public and scholars diverse information about the culture and history of ancient Egypt.

17. Tomorad 2003a, 63–69; 2005, 11–13; 2006a, 16–18; 2009a, 541–44; forthcoming.

18. Uranić 2002; Menalo 2003; Tomorad 2003a, 56–63; 2005, 13–16; 2006, 19–21; forthcoming.

19. Jurkić-Girardi 2001, 5–17; Džin 2001, 18–21; Uranić 2001, 22–28; Tomorad 2003a, 48–51; 2006a, 24–25; 2007a; forthcoming.

20. Tomorad 2003a, 63–64, 69–70, 73–79; 2006b, 26–37; forthcoming.

21. Cambi 1971; Selem 1979; 1997, 93–95; Tomorad 2001; 2003a, 75–76; 2004a; 2005, 22; 2006a, 31; 2006b, 287–288; 2011; forthcoming.

22. Giunio 2002, 29–37; Tomorad 2003a, 51–52; 2005, 20; 2006a, 27–28; forthcoming

23. Selem 1972, 38–40; Selem 1980, 20–23; 1997; Filipović 1997; Tomorad 2003a, 73–74; 2005, 21; 2006a, 29; forthcoming.

24. Tomorad 2002; 2009a, 539–41; forthcoming; Tomorad and Uranić 2006.

25. Rendić–Miočević 1986; 1993; Tomorad 2003a, 31–48, 81–89; 2003b; forthcoming; Uranić 2005, 49–51; 2009, 107–12.

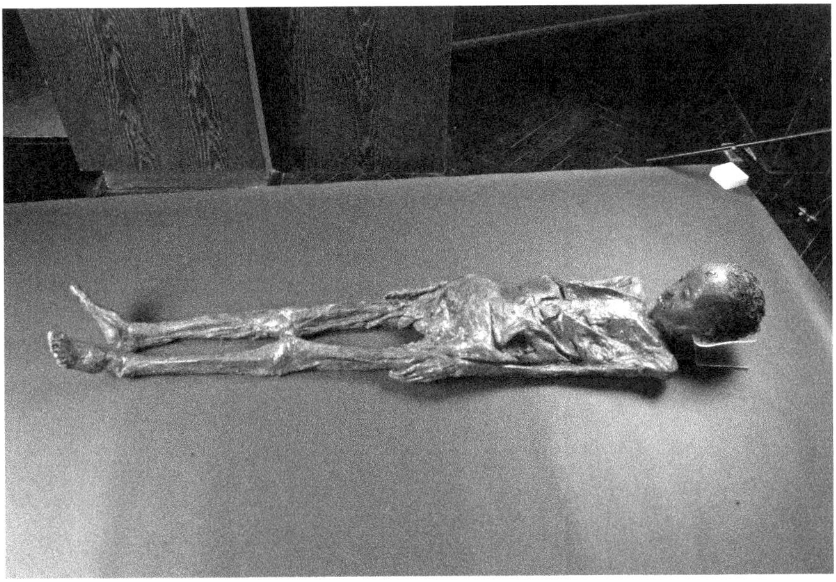

Fig. 4. The Mummy of Nesi-hensu. Fourth century BC. The Archaeological Museum in Zagreb. Inv. 664. © Archaeological Museum, Zagreb, Filip Beusan.

The Egyptian Department

The Egyptian collection in the former National Museum of Croatia and today's Archaeological Museum in Zagreb has been formed through different sources during its 150 years of existence. The so-called Zagreb mummy and its wrappings[26] were part of the first Egyptian artifacts in the collection (fig. 4). They were brought to the museum on 5 August 1862[27] during the time of the curator Mijat Sabljar (Dubica, 1790–Zagreb, 1865).[28] Thanks to the bishop Josip Juraj Strossmayer and Franjo Rački, historian, politician, and at that time the president of the ex-Yugoslav Academy of Science and Art, the collection was augmented in 1868 with a large collection of Egyptian antiquities from the private collection of baron Franz Koller (Mnichovo Hradište, 1767–Naples, 1826) which was purchased earlier that year from the heirs of Baron Koller.[29] Up to the present day, this formerly private collection formed in the early nineteenth century was the backbone of the Egyptian department. During the 150 years of its existence, its holdings were increased many times, mostly through small donations from local citizens, a single donation from the Egyptian government

26. The Archaeology museum in Zagreb, Inv. 664–665.
27. Tomorad 2003a, 83; 2003b.
28. Tomorad 2003a, 31.
29. Mirnik and Uranić 1999; Tomorad 2003a, 31, 33.

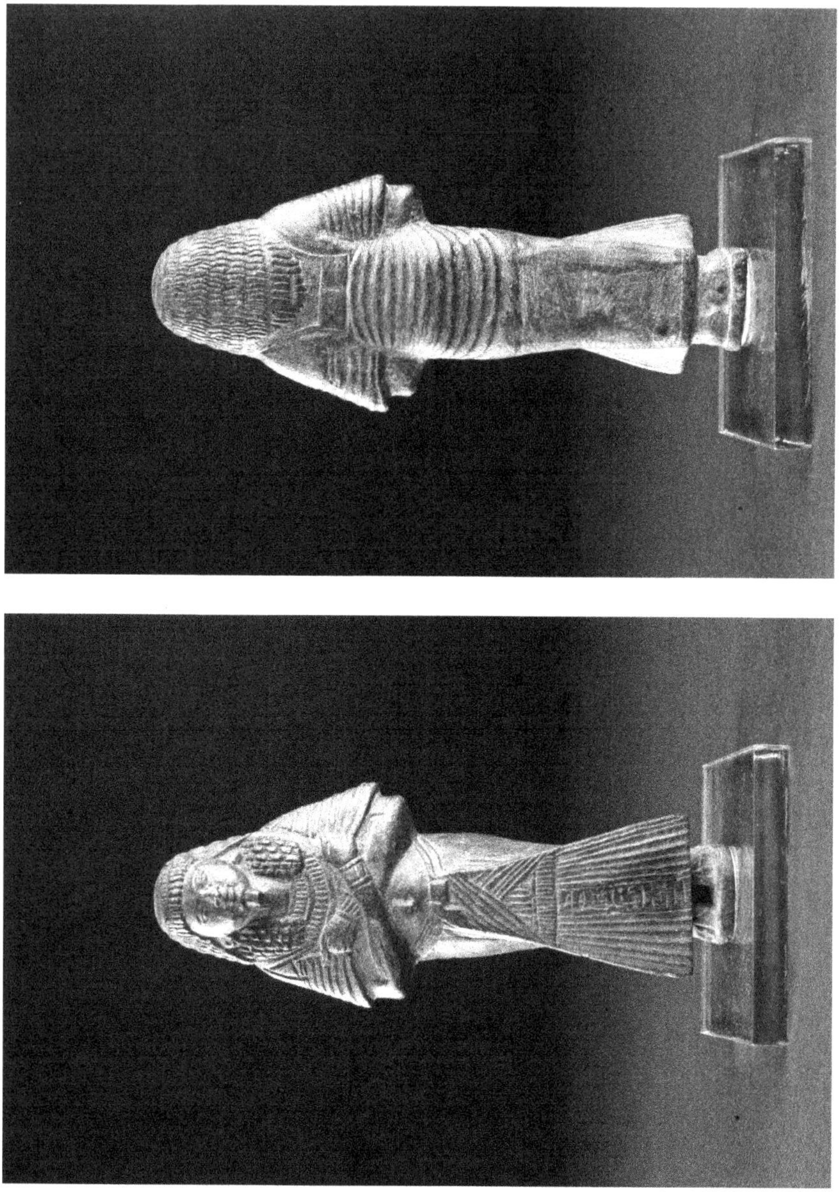

Fig. 5. Shabti of Neb-nofer dressed in clothing suitable to daily life. Probably Nineteenth or Twentieth Dynasty. The Archaeological museum in Zagreb. Inv. 307. © Archaeological Museum, Zagreb, Filip Beusan.

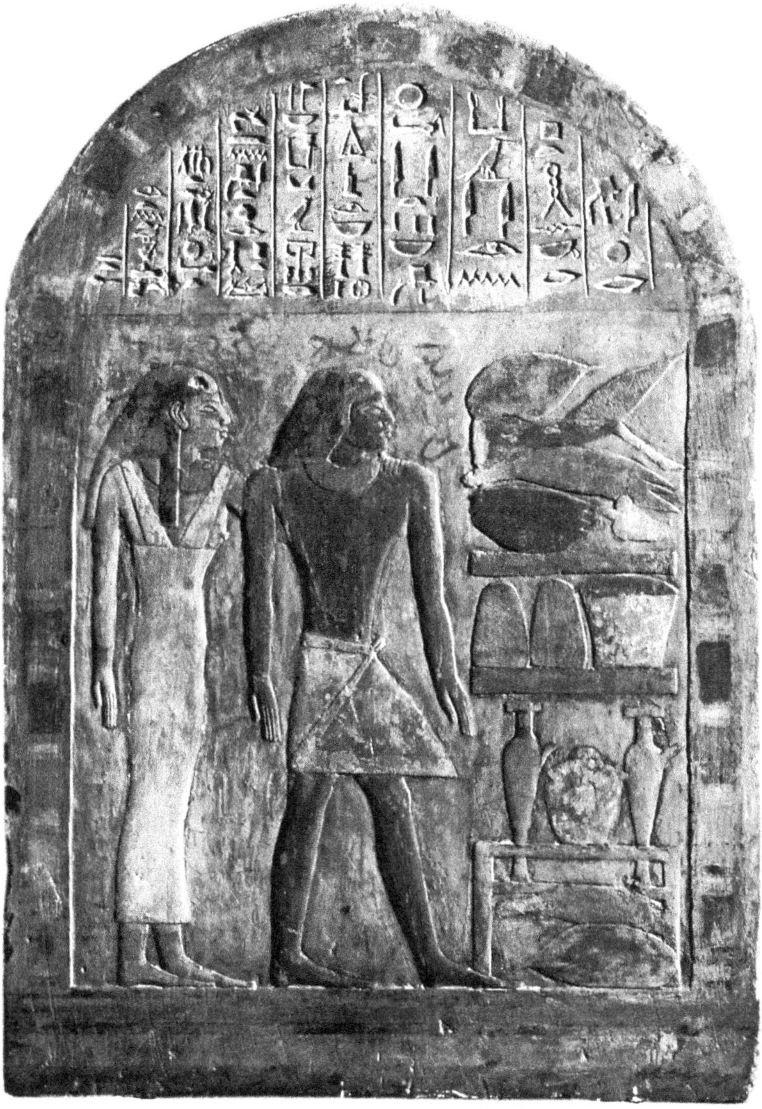

Fig. 6. A funeral stele of Kay. The Middle Kingdom. The Archaeological museum in Zagreb. Inv. 583. © Archaeological Museum, Zagreb.

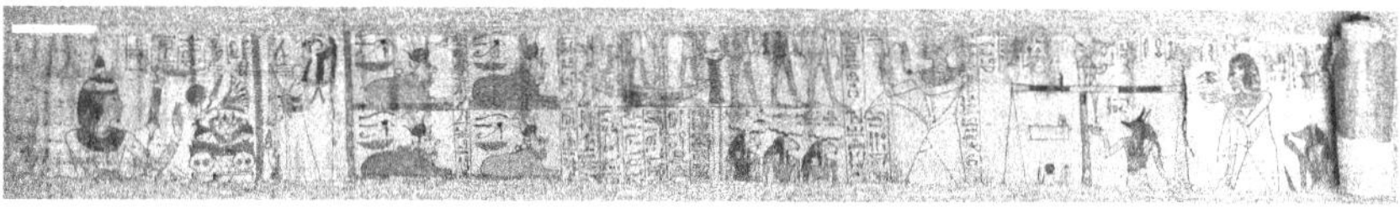

Fig. 7. Fragment of the Book of the Dead. The New Kingdom. The Archaeological museum in Zagreb. Inv. 600. © Archaeological Museum, Zagreb, Filip Beusan.

in 1973,[30] and by purchases of smaller private collections.[31] The collection contains approximately 2,300 artifacts of which the majority is small art like scarabs, amulets, shabtis (fig. 5), and statuettes of gods. But there are also valuable examples of stelae (fig. 6), Books of the Dead (fig. 7), mummies (fig. 4), and coffins (fig. 8).[32] Most of the artifacts date from the Middle Kingdom (fig. 9), the New Kingdom (figs. 10, 11), the Late period (figs. 8, 12, 13), and the Graeco-Roman period (figs. 14–18). The provenance of the artifacts is mostly unknown.

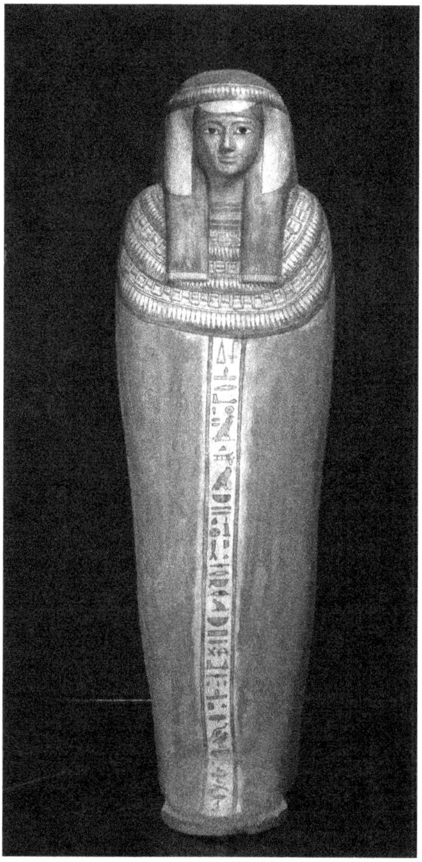

Fig. 8. Coffin of the mummy of Kaipamaw from TT192, El-Asasif on the western bank of Luxor. Twenty-Second Dynasty. The Archaeological museum in Zagreb. Inv. 687. © Archaeological Museum, Zagreb, Filip Beusan.

The Ancient Department

The Archaeological Museum in Zagreb also houses a variety of artifacts connected with the worship of Egyptian cults in the territory of Roman Illyricum (mostly from provinces Dalmatia and Pannonia with several exceptions from other provinces of the southeastern region of the Roman Empire). At the moment, there are at least thirty-six such objects in the department.[33] They are mostly statuettes of gods (Isis, Serapis, Hermes-Thoth, Isis-Fortuna, and Harpocrates), many other artifacts as-

30. Tomorad 2003a, 142.
31. The detail list of the all acquisitions in: Tomorad 2003a, 33–37; 2005, 4–5; 2006a, 7–10; forthcoming.
32. Monnet Saleh 1970; Gorenc 1979; Uranić 2005; Uranić 2009.
33. The detail list in Tomorad forthcoming.

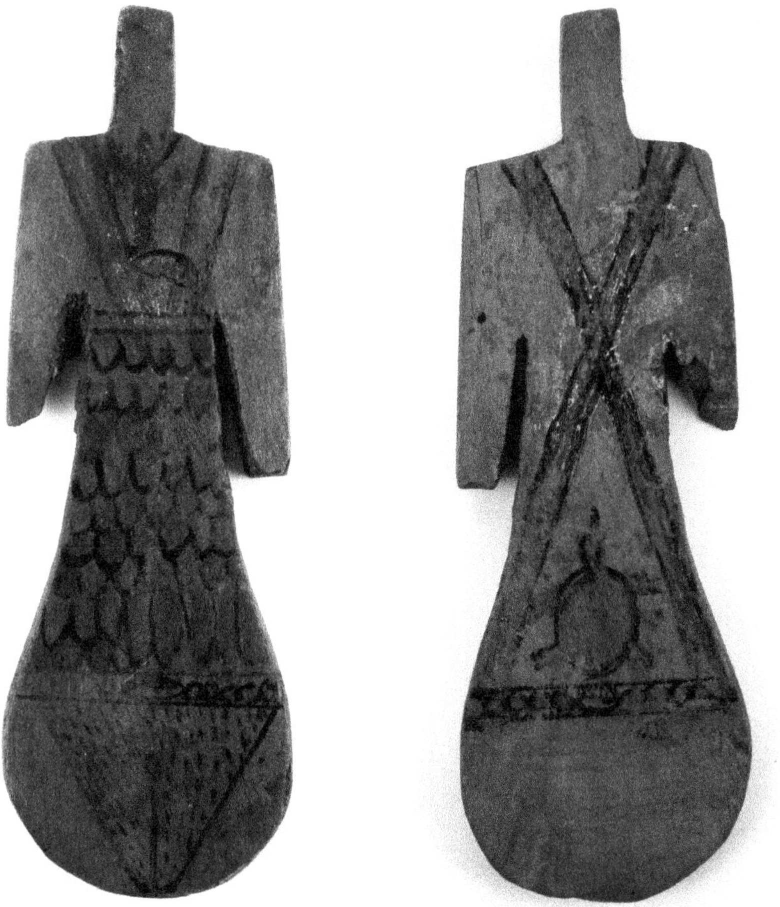

Fig. 9. Wooden doll. Middle Kingdom. The Archaeological museum in Zagreb. Inv. 188. © Mladen Tomorad.

sociated with the worship of the Egyptian deities.[34] The majority of these artifacts were acquired during the course of archaeological excavations since the nineteenth century. The bronze Hermes-Thot, Isis-Fortuna, and Harpocrates statuettes, sphinx, and other smaller artifacts originating from Graeco-Roman Egypt came into the possession of the Museum through the purchase of the Koller collection in 1868.[35] The several inscriptions excavated in Varaždinske Toplice during the archaeological excavations in 2011 and 2012 are still in situ. The number of the artifacts related to

34. Brušmid 1904; Brunšmid 1905; Brunšmid 1907; Brunšmid 1914; Tomorad 2003a, 40–42; 2005, 7; 2006a, 10–11; forthcoming.
35. Tomorad 2005, 7; forthcoming.

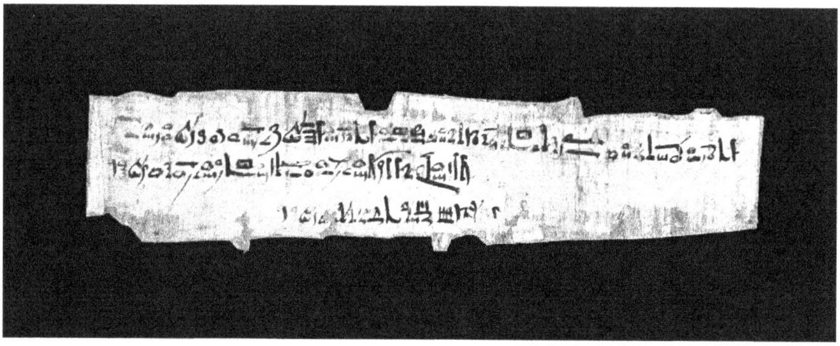

Fig. 10. A fragment of hieratic medical papyrus. New Kingdom. The Archaeological museum in Zagreb. Inv. 597–3. © Archaeological Museum, Zagreb, Filip Beusan.

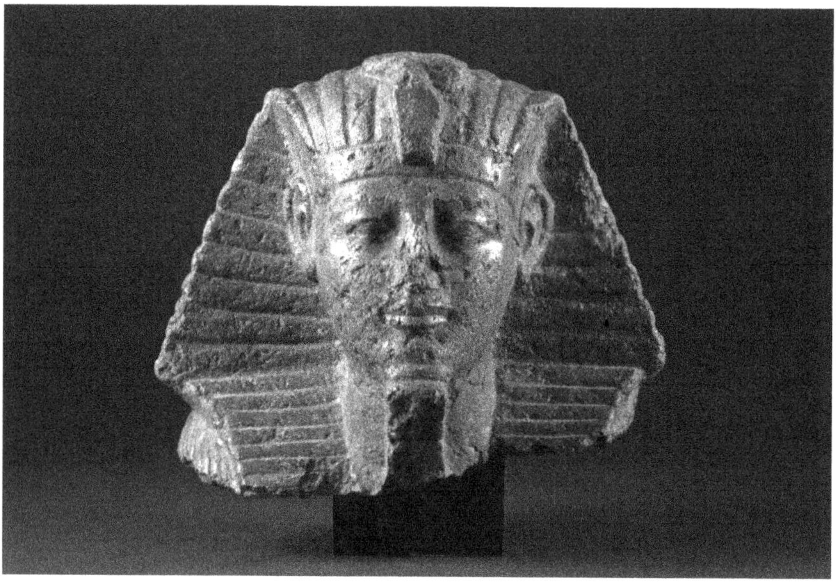

Fig. 11. Head of a sphinx. New Kingdom, probably reign of Amenhotep II. The Archaeological museum in Zagreb. Inv. 674. © Archaeological Museum, Zagreb, Filip Beusan.

Egyptian cults from Andautonia is uncertain; there are at least two related to the cult of Isis-Fortuna and Jupiter-Ammon, but the material is still unpublished.

The Numismatic Department

The Numismatic Department of the Archaeological Museum in Zagreb comprises a very large collection of coins. Two collections are associated with ancient Egyptian civilization: the collection of Ptolemaic coinage, and the collection of coinage from the

Alexandrian mint of the Roman province of Aegyptus. There are at least 175 specimens of Ptolemaic coins from all periods of the Ptolemaic dynasty (figs. 16, 17).[36] Most of them were purchased from various private collections (e.g., Benko Horvat),[37] but there are also specimens that were excavated in several places in Croatia.[38] The numismatic collection of the Roman imperial Alexandrian mint (emperors from Augustus to Constantine I) is very large and comprises at least 520 coins. These coins bear the images of various Roman emperors and their co-rulers or the images of various Egyptian Hellenistic deities (such as Apis, Isis, Osiris, Harpocrates) originating from the other African, and eastern provinces of the Roman Empire.[39] In this department are also Roman coins not minted in Alexandria bearing images of Egyptian gods, but their number is uncertain.

The Mimara Museum in Zagreb

The Mimara Museum was founded by the City of Zagreb as the institution that holds the large private collection (3,750 artifacts) of Ante Topić Mimara (Korušca, 1898–Zagreb, 1987).[40] Mr. Topić Mimara donated his art collection to the Socialist Republic of Croatia and the Council of the City of Zagreb on 6 October 1973 and 29 October 1986.[41] The artifacts of the Egyptian provenance are kept in two collections: The Collection of Ancient Civilizations and The Glass Collection.

The Collection of Ancient Civilizations of the Mimara Museum contains 617 artifacts dating from prehistory to the formation of the first medieval states. The Egyptian collection contains 32 artifacts of Egyptian origin dating from the Predynastic period to Late Antiquity.[42] The collection contains three artifacts from the Naqada I–III cultures[43] (fig. 19) and eight Coptic artifacts,[44] which makes this collection unique in Croatia.

The Glass Collection contains 470 Egyptian artifacts with the chronological range from the New Kingdom (fig. 2) to Late Antiquity.[45] This is the only glass collection with artifacts of Egyptian provenance in Croatia.

36. Tomorad forthcoming.
37. Tomorad forthcoming.
38. Brunšmid 1897; Mirnik 1981: 36–49; 1982; 1987; 1993; 2000; forthcoming.
39. The detail list in: Tomorad 2005, 9–11; 2006a, 14–16; forthcoming.
40. Tomorad 2003a, 63.
41. Tomorad 2003a, 64.
42. The detail list in Tomorad 2003a, 64–67; 2005, 11–12; 2006a, 16–17; forthcoming.
43. Tomorad 2009a: 541–44; 2013b; Tomorad forthcoming.
44. Tomorad 2003, 65, 67; 2005, 12; 2006a, 17; forthcoming.
45. The detail list in: Ratković–Bukovčan 2001; Tomorad 2005, 12–13; 2006a, 18; forthcoming.

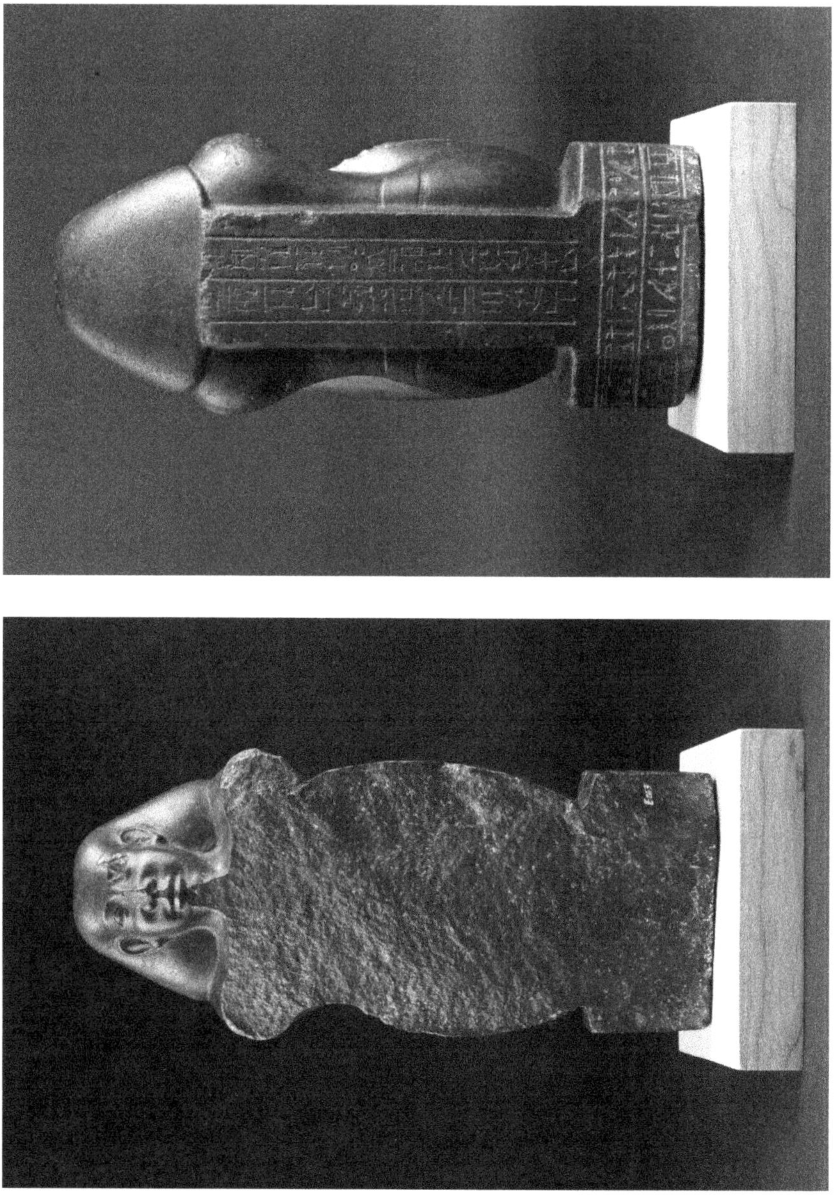

Fig. 12. A block statue of Djedptahiufankh. Twenty-Sixth Dynasty. The Archaeological museum i n Zagreb. Inv. 669. © Archaeological Museum, Zagreb, Filip Beusan.

The Archaeological Museum in Dubrovnik

The large Egyptian collection of the Archaeological Museum in the Museum of Dubrovnik is made up of donations of now mostly unknown persons. The only known donators are Tonko Kuraica, Ivo Nordeli, and the brothers Frane (Dubrovnik, 1821–?)[46] and Nikola (Dubrovnik, 1823–Vienna, 1892)[47] Amerling who donated probably the majority of artifacts. Frane Amerling lived in Cairo in the second half of the 19th century. Nikola (Niko) Amerling lived in Alexandria from 1842 onwards, and he left Egypt after the British occupation in 1882.[48] Brothers Amerling were both involved in the founding of the Museum to which the Amerling family donated many other artifacts gathered around the world. In 1872, they donated a collection of ancient Egyptian and Oriental artifacts to the local Dubrovnik museum.[49] According to the records in the inventory book, all the artifacts originated from Egypt. The only recorded year of the donation is 1872.[50] The time of arrival and the donors can be determined for only three artifacts (Inv. 638, 639, 3808).[51] It can be concluded from the archive that the Amerling family donated a large collection in 1872, and as the Amerling brothers were frequently in Egypt, it can be assumed that they are the probable donators of the majority of artifacts. The archive records showed that one large collection was donated by Ivo Nordeli who is not mentioned as a direct donor in the collection's inventory.[52] Unfortunately, the precise datas are not preserved so the origins of the collection remains unknown.

The Egyptian collection today contains 191 smaller artifacts and a mummy whose authenticity and age has not been determined.[53] The majority of artifacts date to the Late and Ptolemaic periods, but it is impossible to determine the provenance of the artifacts. During his examination of the collection I. Uranić identified 172 genuine and 30 fake objects;[54] it was also established that one artifact originated from Etruria (Inv. 3809).[55] Scientific anylisis of the artifact will be done in the next few years.

The Archaeological Museum of Istria in Pula

The Archaeological Museum of Istria in Pula houses 39 Egyptian artifacts. These artifacts can be divided in three large groups. The first group consists of fifteen artifacts connected to the worshippers of Egyptian cults in the Hellenistic and Roman periods.

46. Tomorad 2003a, 56.
47. Tomorad 2003a, 56.
48. Tomorad 2003a, 56.
49. Tomorad 2003a, 56; 2005, 14; 2006a, 19; forthcoming.
50. Tomorad 2003a, 56.
51. Tomorad 2003a, 63.
52. Tomorad 2003a, 63.
53. The detail list in: Uranić 2002; Tomorad 2005, 14–16; 2006a, 19–21; forthcoming.
54. Uranić 2002. Around Christmas 2002 the whole collection was stolen. Before this robbery it had 197 artifacts. In January 2003 most of the artifacts were returned to the museum.
55. Uranić 2002, 191.

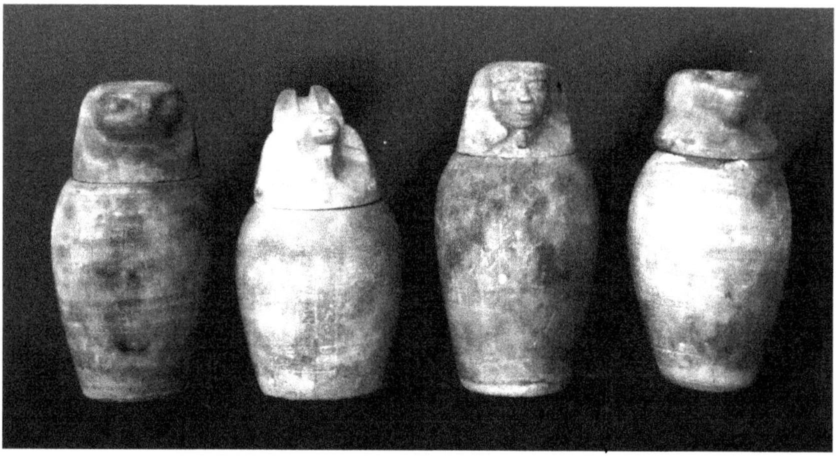

Fig. 13. Canopis jars of Ketjen. Twenty-Sixth Dynasty, the reign of Psamtek I. The Museum of the City of Varaždin. Inv. AO5280–5283. © Museum of the City of Varaždin.

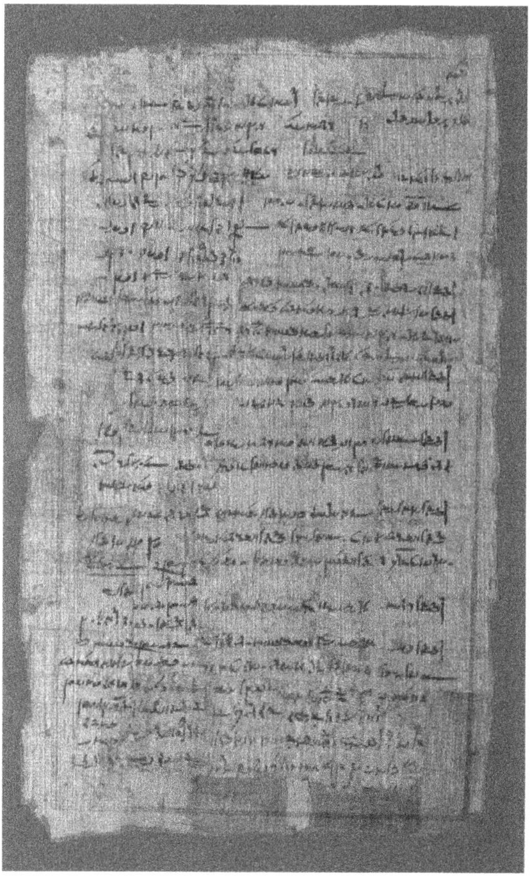

Fig. 14. Unpublish demotic papyri. The Ptolemaic period. The Archaeological Museum in Zagreb. Inv. 599. © Mladen Tomorad.

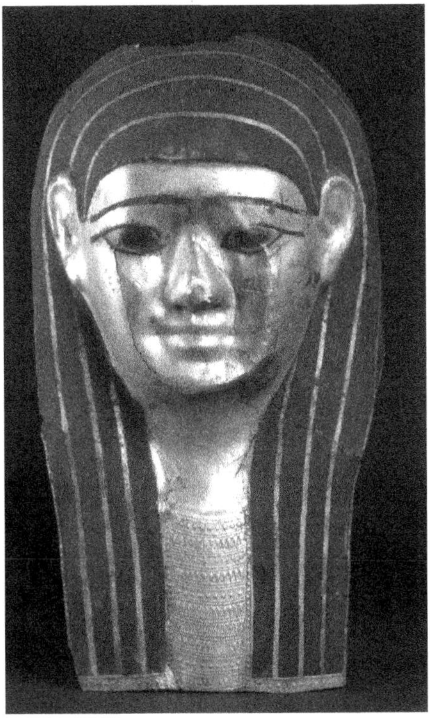

Fig. 15. A funeral mask of Shepenun. The Archaeological Museum in Zagreb. Inv. 667. © Archaeological Museum, Zagreb, Filip Beusan.

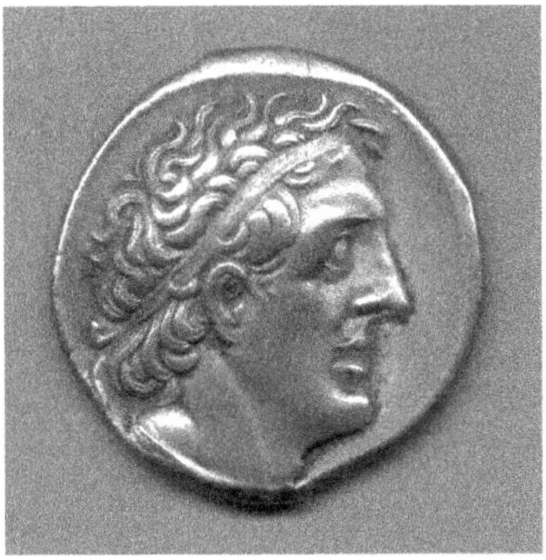

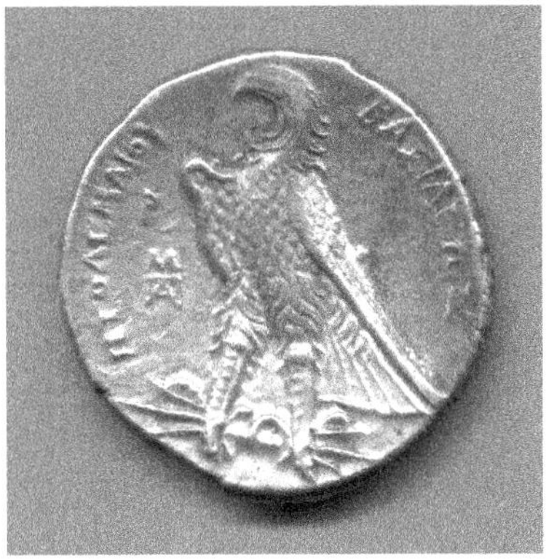

Fig. 16. A coin of Ptolemy I Soter. The Archaeological Museum in Zagreb, Numismatic department. Inv. A8370. © Mladen Tomorad.

The artifacts of this group were found during archaeological excavations in the area of Istria and are associated with the cults of Serapis, Isis, Isis-Fortuna, Jupiter-Ammon, Hathor, and Achelous.[56] The second group consists of seven bronze artifacts of mostly votive character.[57] The third group consists of seventeen artifacts, mostly Egyptian shabtis and amulets, that were part of the collection of an unknown Austrian donor.[58]

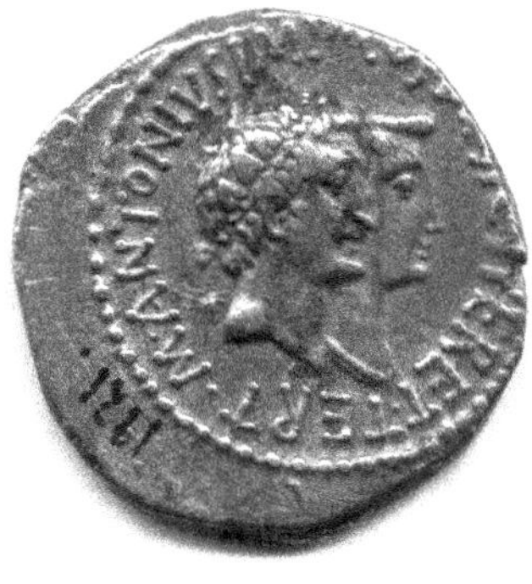

Fig. 17. A coin of Mark Anthony and Cleopatra VII, between 36 and 30 BC. The Archaeological Museum in Zagreb, Numismatic department. Inv. B1921. © Mladen Tomorad.

56. Jurkić–Girardi 2001, 5–17; Tomorad 2003a, 48–49; 2005, 16–17; 2006a, 24–25; 2007a, 43; forthcoming.

57. Džin 2001, 18–21; Tomorad 2003a, 49; 2005, 17; 2006a, 25; 2007a, 44; forthcoming.

58. Uranić 2001; Tomorad 2003a, 49–50; Tomorad 2005, 17–18; Tomorad 2006a, 25; Tomorad 2007a,

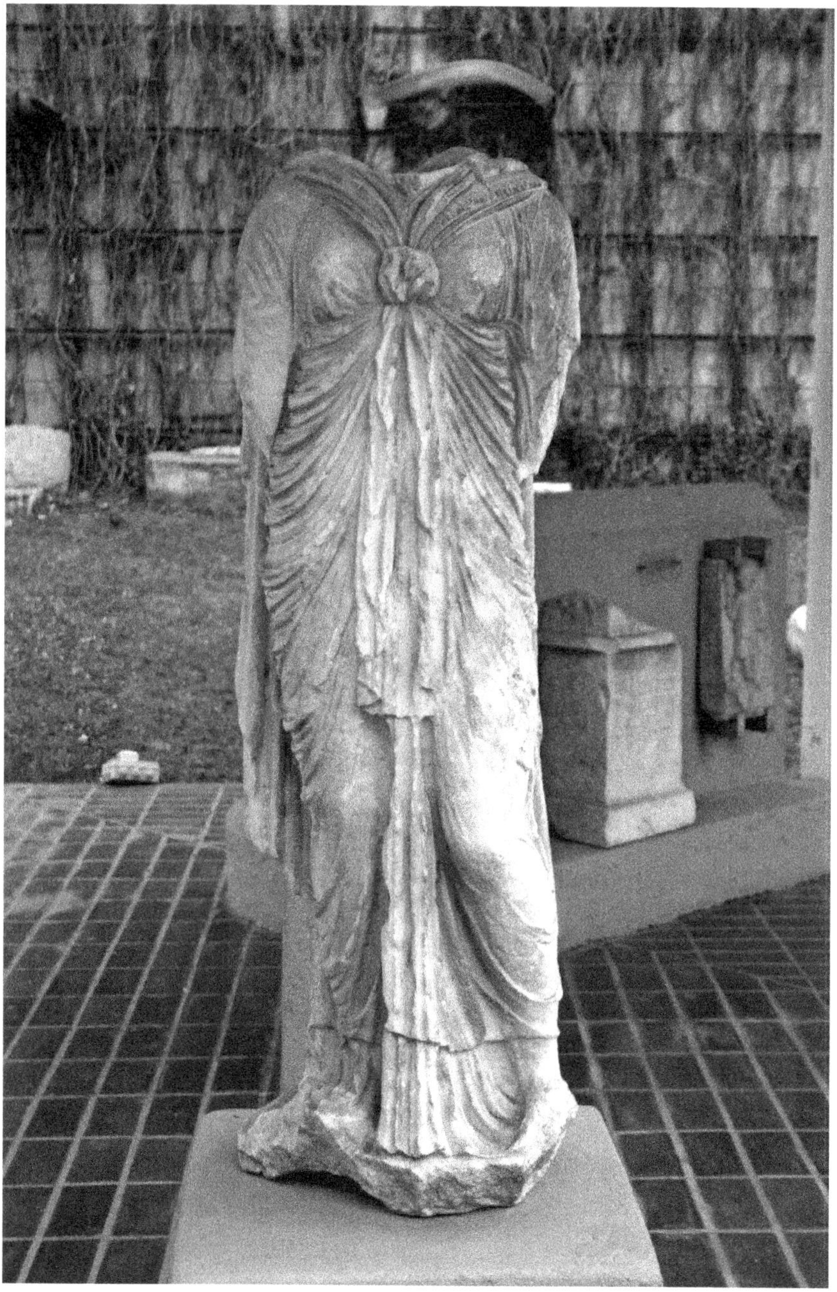

Fig. 18. White marble statue of Isis, from Nin (Aenona), Croatia. First–second century AD. The Archaeological Museum in Zagreb, Ancient department. Inv. A34. © Mladen Tomorad.

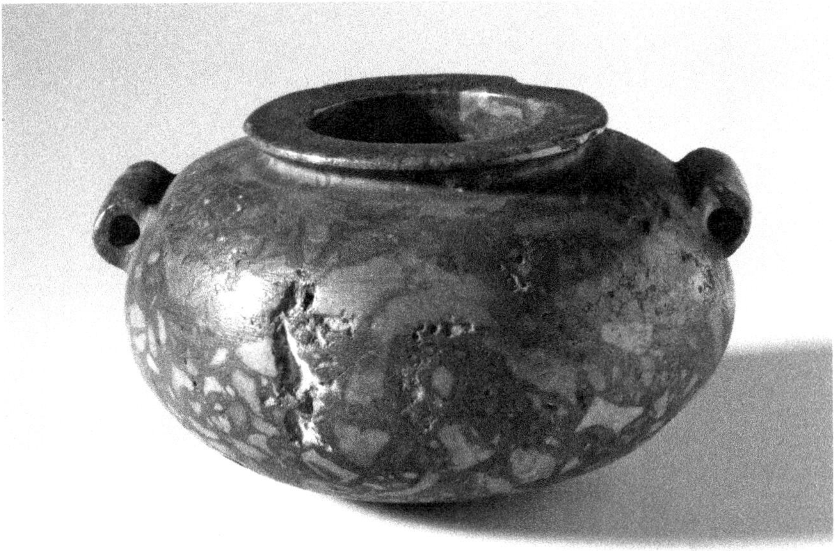

Fig. 19. Stone vessel from red breccia. Late Naqada I–Naqada II. The Collection of Ancient Civilizations, Museum "Mimara." Inv. ATM 230. © Museum Mimara, Zagreb.

The Archaeological Museum in Split

The Archaeological Museum in Split holds between seventy-two and seventy-nine artifacts connected with the diffusion of Egyptian cults in Roman province of Dalmatia[59] and were found in the area of mid-Dalmatia and its islands. The artifacts were acquired in the archaeological excavations, through purchases and by donations from private persons (for example, Lanza from Split, Marchi, Machiedo from Hvar, and Lukanović from Šibenik).[60] The Archaeological Museum, the Department for the History of Building and Architecture, and Diocletian's Palace in Split contain at least eleven sphinxes or their parts brought by the Emperor Diocletian during the building

45; Tomorad forthcoming.

59. Selem 1963a; 1969; 1972; 1997; Tomorad 2003a, 52–55; 2005, 18–19; 2006a, 22–24; forthcoming. During my latest examination of the collection in late May 2013 seven artifacts were missing. They are: a funeral stele with the theophoric name Serapioni, a funeral stela with theophoric name Isiacae Firminae, an Egyptian scarab (I-1835), gema with Harpocrates (I-888), gema with Serapis and Jupiter-Ammon (I-875), statuette of Harpocrates (H-5606), and an oil lamp with Serapis (Fc-443). These are either misplaced or lost. Today they are at least seventy-two artifacts in the collection.

60. Tomorad 2003a, 52; 2005, 18; 2006a, 22; forthcoming.

of his palace (fig. 1).[61] The Museum also has an Egyptian head made of the reddish granite that was found in the northern part of the palace.[62]

The Archaeological Museum in Zadar

The collection of the Archaeological Museum in Zadar possesses at least sixteen Egyptian cult artifacts found during the excavations in the territory of Zadar (ancient Iader) and surrounding area.[63]

The Museum of the City of Varaždin

The Archaeological Department of the Museum of the City of Varaždin was founded in the first half of the twentieth century. The museum currently holds seven ancient Egyptian artifacts (fig. 20; also fig. 13), six of them were once part of the smaller Egyptian collection of the noble Pasthory-Varady family,[64] and one scarab which came to the museum after 2007.[65] The Pasthory-Varady collection was probably amassed during the nineteenth century when one of the family members stayed in Egypt during his diplomatic service. After his return to the country, the artifacts were kept in Križovljan castle, and later were moved to the Museum.[66] The time when these artifacts arrived to the Museum cannot be determined with certainty, although it can be assumed that this took place in the first half of the nineteenth century.[67] A predynastic cup from the Badarian culture[68] is the oldest Egyptian artifact stored in any Croatian institution, which makes this collection very valuable.

The Museum of Slavonia in Osijek: The Archaeological Collection

The Archaeological Department of the Museum of Slavonia at Osijek holds nineteen artifacts connected to the Egyptian cults worshipped in the Roman province of Pannonia.[69] They were acquired during the archaeological excavations in the area of Osijek (ancient Mursa) and eastern Slavonia. The greatest attention was given to the

61. The location of the one sphinx and one fragment of the another sphinx, which were discovered during the archaeological excavations of the palace in 1995 and 1996, is unknown. These artifacts could be in situ or in some other institution in Split.

62. Novak 1932; Karaman 1937; Rismondo 1953; Selem 1963b; 1970; 1997, 97–106; Tomorad 2003a, 55; 2005, 18–19; 2006a, 24, 30–31; forthcoming.

63. Selem 1997, 50–59; Giunio 2002, 29–37; Tomorad 2003, 51–52; 2005, 20; 2006a, 27–28; forthcoming.

64. The detail list with scientific analysis in: Tomorad 2002; Tomorad and Uranić 2006.

65. Tomorad forthcoming.

66. Tomorad 2002; 2003a, 71; Tomorad and Uranić 2006, 88.

67. Tomorad 2002; 2003a, 71; 2005, 20; 2006a, 30; forthcoming; Tomorad and Uranić 2006, 88.

68. Tomorad 2002, 550–51; 2009a, 540–41; Tomorad and Uranić 2006, 88–89.

69. The detail list in Selem 1972; 1980; 1997, 141–45; Filipović 1997a, 49–51; 1997b, 65–79; Tomorad 2003a, 73–74; 2005, 21–22; 2006a, 29; forthcoming.

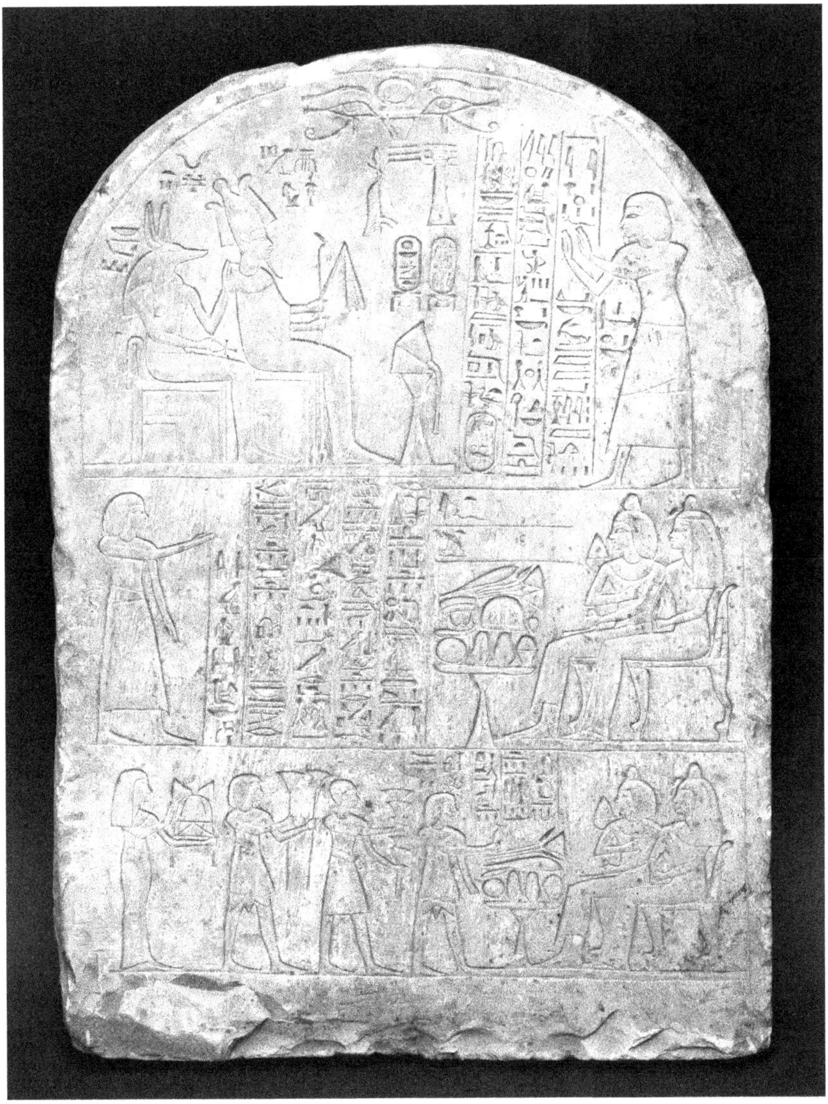

Fig. 20. Stele of Merymery. Eighteenth Dynasy, reign of Amenhotep III. The Museum of the City of Varaždin. Inv. AO5279. © Museum of the City of Varaždin, Varaždin.

discovery of a white limestone stele with a representation of Egyptian divinities (so-called the Padihorpakhered stele)[70] which was discovered in the area of Osijek's upper town in the late nineteenth century.[71] Part of this collection is still unpublished.

70. The Museum of Slavonia, Inv. 2590.

71. Höger 1942, 22–25; Selem 1972, 39–40; Selem 1980, 20–21; 1997, 142; Tomorad 2003a, 73.

The Benko Horvat Archaeological Collection, The Museum of Contemporary Art in Zagreb

The large private archaeological collection of Benko Horvat, which dates from the eleventh century BC to the eleventh century AD, was donated to the city of Zagreb in 1946.[72] It contains 381 artifacts,[73] among which eleven artifacts of Egyptian provenance can be found.[74] Today it is stored in the Galleries of the city of Zagreb (today the Museum of Contemporary Art), and in the Numismatic department of the Archaeological Museum in Zagreb.

The Collection of the St. Euphemia Monastery at Kampor on the Island of Rab

The St. Euphemia monastery on the island of Rab owns a diverse collection that also contains artifacts from the ancient Near East and Egypt. The collection was donated to the monastery by Ivo Kugli after the Second World War. There is no information preserved on the date of the donation, but it is known that the Egyptian artifacts were purchased in Aquileia from a Jew who fled to the United States of America to escape the Gestapo.[75] The provenance of the artifacts is unknown; they could originate from ancient Egypt or from surrounding areas of ancient Aquileia. It is not even established if they are originals or fakes. The collection consists of ten to twenty-one artifacts. The exact number at the moment is hard to determine because some of the artifacts are broken in pieces, so without full analysis we cannot determine if these pieces belong to the same or different artifacts. Analysis is at the moment not possible for various reasons.[76]

The Franciscan Monastery in Sinj: The Archaeological Collection

The Archaeological collection of the Franciscan monastery in Sinj contains six Egyptian artifacts. It consists a Serapis bust made of terracotta, a shabti from Čitluk made of green enameled terracotta, a shabti from Čitluk made of brown terracotta, a bronze Isis statuette, and two scarabs.[77] One of of the scarabs, made of a dark stone, was brought by father Ante Jadrijević from Egypt before the outbreak of the World War II.[78]

72. Tomorad 2003a, 70.
73. Koščević 2000.
74. Koščević 2000; 2003a, 70; 2005, 22; 2006a, 28–29; forthcoming.
75. Bonifačić 1985; Tomorad 2003a, 75; Tomorad 2005, 22; 2006a, 26; forthcoming.
76. Tomorad 2003, 75; Tomorad 2005, 22; 2006, 26–27; forthcoming.
77. Cambi 1971, 85–107; Selem 1979, 79–92; 1997; Tomorad 2003a, 75–76; 2004a; 2005, 22; 2006a, 31; 2006b; 2011; forthcoming.
78. Cambi 1971, 85–107; Selem 1979, 79–92; 1997; Tomorad 2003a, 75–76; 2004a; 2005, 22; 2006a, 31; 2006b; 2011; forthcoming.

Small Egyptian Collections in Regional Museums and Institutions in Croatia

In the Museum of the City of Požega, the fragment of a bone handle with a carved relief of an Isis or Hathor is kept. It was discovered during the May 1979 in the village Sesvete in the Požega Valley.[79] This artifact is still unpublished.

In August of 2001, a marble stele with a pair of lions (commonly connected with the cult of Serapis) was excavated from the lake located in the area of Gabajeva Greda in gravel pit near the river of Drava at the depth of 25 m. It was found by the gravel pit supervisor and amateur archaeologist Ivan Zvijerac. After the discovery, it was stored on the water dredge, and was transferred to the Museum of Koprivnica in late September 2001.[80]

The other artifact related to the diffusion of the ancient Egyptian cults in Pannonia is held by the Museum of the city of Križevci. It is a marble stele with a *kalathos* and two lion figures made of white marble, which was found in Križevci during the excavation of the new St. Rochus graveyard during 1950s. It corresponds iconographically to the imagery of the Egyptian god Serapis.[81]

In the Dr. Zlatko Dragutin Tudjina Museum of Pregada one small Egyptian amulet of the god Bes can be seen. It came to the museum as donation from the private collection of Mr. Tudjina from Munich.[82]

A single Egyptian artifact, the so-called "head of a citizen" (Twenty-Sixth Dynasty; Inv. MGZ 4759), was donated to the city of Zagreb by the famous German actress Tilla Durieux. Today it is housed in the Museum of the City of Zagreb.[83]

In the Museo del territorio parentino in Poreč, one small statuette of Isis-Fortuna, which was excavated in Loron during 1994–1998, is kept.[84]

In the private lapidary, located in the courtyard of the house in the J. Malevac Street no. 12 in Novigrad (Emonia) in Istria, are two fragments of a small altar dedicated to Isis.[85]

One monolithic stone block with a relief of Jupiter-Ammon can be seen in the Lapidarium of the island of Veliki Brijun. It was discovered in Pula and transferred to the island from the Archaeological Museum of Istria in Pula in 1949.[86]

In the Naval and History Museum of Hrvatsko primorje in Rijeka, an uncertain number of Ptolemaic coins are kept. They were discovered in the surrounding region and they are still unpublished.

In the archaeological collection of the Franciscan monestery on the island of Košljun, ten Egyptian artifacts discovered during the archaeological excavations in

79. Tomorad 2003a, 138.
80. Tomorad 2003a, 73; 2005, 22; 2006a, 33; forthcoming.
81. Tomorad 2003, 73; 2005a, 22; 2006a, 34; forthcoming.
82. Tomorad forthcoming.
83. Kadić 1984; Tomorad 2003a, 69; 2005, 21; 2006a, 34; forthcoming.
84. Jurkić–Girardi 2005, 204–205; Tomorad forthcoming.
85. Tomorad 2003a, 75; 2005, 23; 2006a, 32; forthcoming.
86. Jurkić–Girardi 2005, 147; Tomorad 2006a, 32;forthcoming.

town Krk are kept. They are: a shabti of the lady Mehytweskhet (Twenty-First–Twenty-Second Dynasty), a pseudo-shabti from the Hellenistic period, three scarabs from the Hellenistic period, and five amulets of cats from the Graeco-Roman period.[87]

One fragment of votive sculpture with an inscription dedicated to Serapis is located in the Lapidarium of the City Museum of Senj. It was discovered in 1898 at a nearby site and it has been kept in this regional museum since 1962.[88]

In the Museum of the City of Šibenik three artifacts related with the diffusion of the Egyptian cults in Dalmatian are kept. An altar made of white limestone with an inscription dedicated to Isis was found during the excavations in Varvaria; it was previously kept in the Lapidary of the Varvaria locality in Bribirska Glavica.[89] Still unpublished bronze statuette of Hermes-Thoth discovered in Danilo (Municipium Riditarum) is in the possesion of Dragica Klarić, and now kept in this museum. One bronze piece of the Ptolemaic coin with the head of Jupiter-Ammon and Isis cult symbol was discovered in the cape Ploče.

A female alabaster artifact connected with the Isis cult is housed in a small local museum in Bostan. It was found in 1968 during the archaeological excavations in that area.[90]

A female alabaster bust with plain Isaic features (veil, Isaic knot, and scarf) is kept in the Archaeological Museum Narona in Vid near Metković.[91]

The collection of the Narodno sveučilište in Imotski holds a bronze statuette of Isis–Fortuna found near the Šarampov Bridge in Prološac at Imotski. The statuette was purchased for the collection soon after it was discovered in 1986.[92]

In the dr. Grga Novak archaeological collection and its lapidary in Hvar, one Egyptian artifact is stored. It is a bronze statuette representing the god Nefertem discovered on the island of Hvar. A few other smaller Egyptian artifacts can be seen in the museum but they are on loan from the Archaeological Museum in Split.[93]

There is the possibility that other artifacts related to ancient Egyptian civilization or to the diffusion of Egyptian cults during antiquity are in other museum collections or in situ.[94]

---

87. Detailed analysis of the artifacts in Tomorad 2015a, 177, 185–95, nos. 11–20; Tomorad 2015b; Tomorad and Sliwa 2015.

88. Giunio 2002, 28.

89. Kuntić–Makvić 1982; Selem 1997: 59–61; Tomorad 2003a: 74; 2005a: 23; 2006a: 32; forthcoming.

90. Tomorad 2006a, 34; Tomorad, forthcoming.

91. Cambi 1971, 98–99; Selem 1972; 1997, 112–13; 2003a, 76; 2005, 23; Tomorad 2006a, 33; forthcoming.

92. Tonković 1991, 53–54; Selem 1997, 93; Tomorad 2003a, 76; 2006a, 33; forthcoming.

93. Tomorad 2003a, 74; 2005, 23; 2006a, 33; forthcoming.

94. Several artifacts related to ancient Egyptian civilization are mentioned in the main inventory book of the National Museum in Zagreb, which was divided into several museums in 1939. The largest part of the Egyptian artifacts are today in the Archaeological Museum in Zagreb, but many artifacts (Ptolemaic coinage, ancient Egyptian oil lamps, statuettes of gods, and so on) seem to be lost or in the possesion of some other museums in Zagreb (probably in the ethnographic museum or in the museum of arts and crafts). I

Private Collections of Egyptian Antiquities

The number of private collections of the Egyptian antiquities today in Croatia is unknown. However, they can be divided into two groups: (1) private collections included in the various museum and institutions; (2) collections kept by private persons, often in their homes. These collections are mostly unpublished, not systematically studied, and they are unknown to the public. According to the law, every private collection has to be reported, examined, and evaluated, but the law is not abided by in practice.

In the area of the towns of Zagreb, Hvar, Kutina, Požega, Sisak, and Split (e.g., private collection Carrara-Bratanić[95]), private persons are in possession of larger or smaller collections of Egyptian antiquities. Some of them are known to the public, but many more are completely unknown. The largest-known private collection is owned by Dražen Kovačić and Žarko Bošnjak. Their collection was exhibited in June 1991 in the Museum of Moslavina in Kutina.[96] This collection has approximately five hundred artifacts, and the exhibition showed about one hundred of them, ranging from the Naqada period to the Roman era. The artifacts in the exhibit were objects of everyday life, death masks, amulets, jewelry, fragments of sarcophagi, and votive stelae. The origin of the collection is unknown.

The Croato-Aegyptica Electronica (CAE) Project

The ultimate purpose of this project is to build up a targeted and selected database of relevant institutional and private collections of ancient Egyptian antiquities in Croatia. The first phase of the project's development started in late 2001 when the project was presented in the paper "Egyptian Antiquties in Croatia: Computerized Processing of Sources and Literature") at the international scientific conference "Historical Research, Study of History and Computerization" December 10–12, 2001 at the Faculty of Humanities and Social Sciences, University of Zagreb, Zagreb, Croatia. During the next two years (2002–2003) the first team of researchers and project development was formed consisting of M. Tomorad, I. Uranić, G. Zlodi, H. Gračanin, I. Malus Tomorad, and M. Gračanin. During the same period, with the help of P. Selem, we gained support from all the museums and other institutions to start studying their collections, and for future publishing of all material online as a digital catalogue. After the succesful application (2003) to the Ministry of Science, Education, Technology, and Sport of the Republic of Croatia in early 2004, we gained

---

tried to locate them several times in the last ten years but without any success. Even some Egyptian artifacts from the Archaeological Museum in Zagreb seem to be lost, at least they are not in the Egyptian department but they may be in the basement of the museum in the reserves of the other museum departments.

To the best of my knowledge in the house Glimb in Split one epigraphic inscription related to the Isaic cult was part of the wall. Today its location is uncertain and it is possibly lost. Such artifacts could exist in many other ancient towns along the Dalmatian coast and inland.

95. Selem 1971, 113–17.

96. Bobovec 1991; Tomorad 2003a, 78; 2005, 23; 2006a, 36; forthcoming.

sufficient financial funds to start the project. After solving the problem of funding, our team started the second phase of project development. During the first half of 2004, the first project website, titled Croato-Aegyptica Electronica, was created. M. Gračanin designed and programmed the whole site. A few hundred pages of texts written by M. Tomorad, I. Uranić, H. Gračanin, and I. Malus Tomorad were added to the site. In May 2004, the Croatian version of the web site was launched at http://infoz.ffzg.hr/cae. The English version, which is slightly different from the Croatian version, was launched at the end of June 2004. The CAE database has been accessible online since July 2004. In September 2004, the site obtained its own domain [www.croato–aegyptica.hr] and the first version of the database was incorporated in it (selection of the artifacts from the Archaeological Museum in Zagreb; 120 artifacts).[97] The CAE website was the first Croatian educational and information web portal about the history of any civilization in the world. It included information regarding: (1) the project Croato–Aegyptica Electronica; (2) the history of every Egyptian museum collection in Croatia; (3) links to the most important Egyptological web sites; (4) the development of Egyptology; (5) ancient Egyptian chronology from Prehistory to the Arab conquest of Egypt; (6) ancient Egyptian towns and sites; (7) Egyptian mythology; (8) ancient Egyptian history; (9) famous monuments in Egypt; and (10) everyday life in ancient Egypt. The news database was constructed using the free software programs PHP and My SQL as powerful open-source programs were used to develop our daily updated news. They are divided into five categories: Egyptological discoveries on the field, exhibitions (past, current, and future), lectures, conferences and symposiums and new Egyptological books in Croatian. News section of the web site, which is currently not working, had news about new discoveries in Egypt; other news dealing with Egyptology; announcements about past, current, and future exhibitions; information about conferences and symposiums dealing with ancient Egypt; information about new books, catalogues, and guides about ancient Egyptian history in Croatia; lectures about ancient Egypt in Croatia.[98] The whole site soon became very popular, which resulted in it being nominated for the Croatian scientific award for the popularization of science for the year 2004.

In 2006, the project stopped receiving the required financial support, raising various problems. In 2007, the project news part of the web site was hacked. In early 2010 we lost our domain with the introduction of new regulations at CARNet. At the same time in early 2010 the server of the Faculty of Humanities and Social Sciences, where it was implemented, crashed and our database has not been available since that time. In April 2011, M. Tomorad stopped working at the Faculty of Humanities and Social Sciences and became assistant professor at the Department of History of the Croatian Studies, University of Zagreb. As the main editor and the head of the project,

97. Tomorad 2004b.

98. Tomorad 2004b; 2006b, 131–42, 172–86, 99–200; 2007b; 2009b.

M. Tomorad moved the whole "old" website to the new web address at the portal of Croatian Studies [http://www.hrstud.unizg.hr/sites/cae/].

Our online CAE database, which was accessible online from July 2004 to January 2010, offered various kinds of information on the artifacts (collections; inventory number; origin; date; material; technique; description; inscriptions with transliteration and translation; various images, etc.). It was built using the M++ application, which is based on MS Access, Visual Basic script and C++ with more than twenty thousand code lines. From the early spring of 2004 to late 2008 we managed to analyze and enter into the database artifacts from the Museum Mimara in Zagreb (Collection of the Ancient Civilizations); the Archaeological Museum in Zagreb (artifacts from the Egyptian and Antiquties department); the Museum of the Contemporary Art in Zagreb (the Benko Horvat collection; the Archaeological Museum of Split; the Archaeological Museum of Istria in Pula; the Archaeological Museum of Zadar; the Museum of Slavonia in Osijek; the City Museum of Varaždin, and a variety of town and regional museums with minor collections.[99] As of today, our CAE database has about three thousand analyzed artifacts. The database as the final product, available through various media, will guarantee a comprehensive insight into the rich Croatian Egyptological material for domestic and foreign researchers and cultural institutions, offering a practical and quick search through the entire inventory and a data display suitable for the general public.

Since 2014, the project has been sponsored by the University of Zagreb. During 2014 the new web site "Stara povijest" [www.starapovijest.eu] was created with a lot of new texts about ancient history and archaeology. In the second half of 2015, the name of the project changed to Croato-Aegyptica. During 2015/2016 the completely new online digital catalogue Croato-Aegyptica was developed and prepared by G. Zlodi and M. Tomorad. The main online catalogue is written in Croatian, with a selection of artifacts translated into English. Regarding our future plans, the project's development can be divided in several phases: (1) analyzing and implementing the rest of the collections into the database; (2) development of the new Croatian/English web site with new texts, images, and maps. Most of the material has already been prepared by a whole new team of collaborators with the help of foreign Egyptologists and Orientalists; (3) transferring the newly formed website to the online Egyptological journal; (4) development and implementation of the completely new online digital catalogue CAE prepared by G. Zlodi, I. Uranić, and M. Tomorad; (5) implementation of the CAE database into GEM (The Global Egyptian Museum);[100] (6) transliterating and

99. Tomorad 2007a; 2009b.

100. The Global Egyptian Museum [http://www.globalegyptianmuseum.com/] was formed at the beginning of 2003. Today the whole virtual museum has almost twenty thousand artifacts from museums all over the world. In the beggining it was formed under the aegis of the CCER and today under CIPEG-ICOM and the Center for Documentation of Cultural and Natural Heritage (Cultnat) in Egypt. In late October 2012, M. Tomorad started exchanging e-mails with the people from Cultnat who are responsible for this project and in the near future we hope we will solve all technical details related to the implementa-

translating all Egyptian inscriptions on our artifacts; (7) documentation of all private collections of Egyptian antiquities in Croatia; *8) publishing a series of catalogues as books and CD-ROMs, (9) online interactive historical maps of the ancient Egypt (from prehistoric periods to the end of Byzantine rule in Egypt).

Summary

Most of the Egyptian antiquities in Croatia came from various private collections in the second half of the nineteenth century. Today, the biggest collection is kept in the Archaeological Museum of Zagreb. The nucleus of the Egyptian department of Archaeological Museum in Zagreb is connected to the donation in 1862 of the well-known Zagreb mummy with its linen Etruscan wrappings (Liber linteus Zagrabiensis). The bulk of the collection consists the objects from the private collection of the Austrian baron Franz Koller that was bought for the National Museum of Croatia in 1868. Today it comprises about 2,300 artifacts of Egyptian origin. The Archaeological Museum of Zagreb also owns the great number of other artifacts related to the history of ancient Egyptian civilization. There are almost 700 ancient Egyptian coins from the Graeco-Roman period in the Numismatic department. The Antique Department holds statues, statuettes, and epigraphic monuments related to the diffusion of Egyptian cults during the Graeco-Roman periods, originating mostly from the Roman provinces of southeastern Europe. During the last 150 years, these collections have been supplemented by a variety of smaller or larger purchases and donations by private individuals, so the number of artifacts increases constantly.

In other museums and other institutions in Croatia there are also almost twenty-five other smaller or larger collections in which Egyptian artifacts can be found. The most important collections can be seen in the Mimara of the Ante Topić Mimara in Zagreb, the Archaeological Museum of Dubrovnik, the Archaeological Museum of Split, the Archaeological Museum of Istria in Pula, the Archaeological Museum of Zadar, the Museum of Slavonia in Osijek, and the Museum of the City of Varaždin. According to our information, there are at least 3,840 artifacts in museums and institutions and an unknown number of artifacts (at least 500) in private collections in Croatia.

The basic aim of the Croato-Aegyptica Electronica (CAE) project is to select relevant material presenting the Egyptian cultural heritage in Croatia both in the form of institutions and private collections (ca. 4,000–5,000 artifacts). From its initial phase in 2003 to the summer of 2016, around three thousand artifacts were analysed and entered into our CAE database. In the next phase, the multilingual online digital catalogue, as the final product, will include all Egyptian collections, both museum-based and private, in Croatia from the Predynastic period to the Arab conquest of

tion of our database. For now, we have only received information that they are interested in our database and nothing more.

Egypt in the seventh century AD. The plan for the future is to integrate the CAE database into Global Egyptian Museum [http://www.globalegyptianmuseum.org/], which is under the aegis of the International Committee for Egyptology (CIPEG) and the Center for Documentation of Cultural and Natural Heritage of Egypt (Cultnat) [http://www.cultnat.org/].

References

BOBOVEC, A. 1991. *Egipatska kolekcija Kovačević–Bošnjak.* Kutina: Gradski muzej.

BRUNŠMID, J. 1897. "Nekoliko našašća novca na skupu u Hrvatskoj i Slavoniji. Našašće italskih i afrikanskih novaca u Mazinu." *Vjesnik hrvatskog arheološkog društva* n.s. 2, 42–49, 58–67, 79–80.

———. 1904. "Kameni spomenici hrvatskog narodnoga muzeja u Zagrebu." *Vjesnik hrvatskog arheološkog društva* n.s. 7.

———. 1905. "Kameni spomenici hrvatskog narodnoga muzeja u Zagrebu." *Vjesnik hrvatskog arheološkog društva* n.s. 8.

———. 1907. "Kameni spomenici hrvatskog narodnoga muzeja u Zagrebu." *Vjesnik hrvatskog arheološkog društva* n.s. 9.

———. 1914. "Antikni figuralni bronsani predmeti u hrvatskom narodnom muzeju u Zagrebu." *Vjesnik hrvatskog arheološkog društva* n.s. 13.

BULIĆ, F., and LJ. KARAMAN. 1927. *Palača cara Dioklecijana u Splitu.* Zagreb.

CAMBI, N. 1971. "Nove potvrde egipatskih kultova u antičkoj provinciji Dalmaciji." *Vjesnik za arheologiju i historiju dalmatinsku* 65–67, 85–107.

DŽIN, K. 2001. "Egipatske votivne figurice u lararijima." Pp. 18–21 in K. DŽIN (ed.), *Egipatska religija i antička Istra.* Pula: Arheološki muzej Istre.

FILIPOVIĆ, S. 1997a, "Arheološki odjel." Pp. 49–51 in *Muzej Slavonije Osijek 1877–1997: Blago muzeja Slavonije.* Osijek: Muzej Slavonije.

———. 1997b. "Antička arheologija." Pp. 65–79 in *Muzej Slavonije Osijek 1877–1997: Blago muzeja Slavonije.* Osijek: Muzej Slavonije.

GIUNIO, K. 2002. "Egyptian Gods on the Eastern Adriatic Coast." Pp. 21–63, pls. 3–17 in H. Győry (ed.) *Aegyptus et Pannonia I – Acta Sympsii anno 2000.* Budapest: Comité de l'Égypte Ancienne de l'Association Amicale Hongroise-Égyptienne.

GORENC, M. 1979. *Egipat. Serija vodiča Arheološkog muzeja u Zagrebu.* Zagreb: Arheološki muzej.

HÖGER, M. 1942. "Ein ägyptisches Denkmal im Osjeker Museum." *Osječki zbornik* 1, 22–25.

JURKIĆ-GIRARDI, V. 2001. "Egipatska religija i antička Istra." Pp. 5–17 in K. Džin (ed.), *Egipatska religija i antička Istra.* Pula: Arheološki muzej Istre.

———. 2005. *Duhovna kultura antičke Istre, knjiga I: Kultovi u procesu romanizacije antičke Istre,* I. Zagreb : Školska Knjiga.

KADIĆ, H. 1984. "Zagrebački mali Egipćanin–egipatska brončana statueta iz nekadašnje zbirke Lubienski–Durieux." *Vijesti muzealaca i konzervatora Hrvatske,* fasc. 1–2, 2.

KARAMAN, LJ. 1937. "Staroegipatska sfinga otkopana u Splitu." *Jugoslovenski istorijski časopis,* 615–17.

KUNTIĆ-MAKVIĆ, B. 1982. "Žrtvenik iz Varvarije posvećen božici Izidi." *Arheološki radovi i rasprave* 8–9, 151–57, pl. I.

LJUBIĆ, Š. 1871, "Sbirke Narodnoga zemaljskoga muzeja, I. Arheologički razdjel, A. Kollerova egjipatska sbirka." *Viestnik narodnoga zemaljskoga muzeja u Zagrebu* 1, 30–54.

———. 1889a. *Popis Arheološkog odjela Narodnog Zemaljskog Muzeja u Zagrebu*. Vol. 1: *Egipatska sbirka*. Zagreb: Narodni muzej.

———. 1889b. *Popis Arheološkog odjela Narodnog Zemaljskog Muzeja u Zagrebu*. Vol. 3: *Numizmatička sbirka*. Zagreb: Narodni muzej.

MENALO, R. 2003. *Egipatska zbirka Dubrovačkog muzeja*. Dubrovnik: Dubrovački muzeji - Arheološki muzej.

MIRNIK, I. 1981. *Coin Hoards in Yugoslavia*. BAR International Series 95. Oxford: B.A.R.

———. 1982. "Skupni nalazi novca iz Hrvatske III: Skupni nalaz afričkog brončanog novca i aes rude iz Štikade." *Vjesnik Arheološkog muzeja u Zagrebu* 3. s. XV, 149–67, pls. 1–6.

———. 1987. "Circulation of North African etc. Currency in Illyricum." *Arheološki vestnik* 38, 369–92.

———. 1993. "Le trésor monétaire de Bosanska Krupa." Pp. 113–16, pl. II in T. Hackens and G. Moucharte (eds.), *Proceedings of the XIth International Numismatic Congress Brussels September 8th–13th 1991*. Louvain-la-Neuve: Association Professeur Marcel Hoc pour l'encouragement des recherches numismatiques.

———. 1996. "Arheološki muzej u Zagrebu (Archaeological Museum in Zagreb)." Pp. 17–40 in D. Balen and Z. Dukat (eds.), *Muzeopis 1846–1996*, Zagreb: Arheološki muzej.

———. 2000. "Skupni nalaz novca iz Krupe (Coin Hoard from Krupa)." *Bosna Franciscana* 12–VIII, 196–211.

MIRNIK, I., and I. URANIĆ. 1999. "Geneza Kollerove Egipatske zbirke Arheološkog muzeja u Zagrebu." Pp. 197–208 in *Zbornik radova 'Naš museum', Zagreb*. Zagreb: Arheološki muzej.

MONNET SALEH, J. 1970. Les antiquités égyptiennes de Zagreb. Catalogue raisonné des antiquités égyptiennes conservées au Musée Archéologique de Zagreb en Yougoslavie, Paris: Mouton.

NOVAK, G. 1932. "Sfinge u Dioklecijanovoj palači." *Novo doba* 170, 2–3.

RISMONDO, V. 1953. "Sfinge u Dioklecijanovoj palači." *Književni Jadran*, 24.

RATKOVIĆ-BUKOVČAN, L. 2001. *Buđenje staklarstva (The Dawn of Glassmaking)*. Zagreb: Muzej Mimara.

RENDIĆ-MIOČEVIĆ, A. 1982. "Egipatski skarabeji." *Vjesnik Arheološkog muzeja u Zagrebu* 3. s. XV, 276.

———. 1986. "Liber linteus Zagrabiensis." *Vjesnik Arheološkog muzeja u Zagrebu* 3. s. XIX.

———. 1993. "Egipatska zbirka," Pp. 122–27 in S. Rendić–Miočević (ed.), *Arheološki muzej u Zagrebu. Izbor iz fundusa*, Zagreb.

SELEM, P. 1963a. "Egipatska božanstva u Arheološkom muzeju u Splitu." *Vjesnik za arheologiju i historiju dalmatinsku* 61, 94–107, pls. X–XV.

———. 1963b. "Dioklecijanove sfinge." *Telegram* 13, 4.

———. 1969. "Egipatski šauabtiji i amuleti u Arheološkom muzeju u Splitu." *Vjesnik za arheologiju i historiju dalmatinsku* 63–64, 125–44, pls. XIV–XXI.

———. 1970. "Stanje istraživanja sfinga carske palače u Splitu." *Adriatica*, 639–56.

———. 1971. "Egipatski šauabtiji iz zbirke Carrara–Bratanić." *Vjesnik za arheologiju i historiju dalmatinsku* 55–57, 113–17, pl. XXVII-XXXI.

———. 1972. "Egipatski bogovi u rimskom Iliriku." *Godišnjak, Akademija nauka i umjetnosti Bosne i Hercegovine – Centar za balkanološka istraživanja* 9.7, 5–104.

———. 1979. "Nekoliko zapažanja o difuziji egipatskih kultova po rimskoj Dalmaciji." *Vjesnik za arheologiju i historiju dalmatinsku* 72–73, 79–92, pl. 1–2.

———. 1980. *Les religions Orientales dans la Pannonie Romaine: partie en Yougoslavie*. Études préliminaires aux religions orientales dans L'Empire Romain 85. Leiden: Brill.

———. 1997. *Izidin trag*. Split: Splitski književni krug.

Tomorad, M. 2001. "Šauabtiji u Dalmaciji i Panoniji." *Historijski zbornik* 53, 1–14.

———. 2002. "Egipatske zbirke u Hrvatskoj s posebnim osvrtom na egipatsku zbirku Gradskog muzeja Varaždin." Pp. 543–58 in A. Mohorovičić and V. Stipetić (eds.), *Zbornik radova međunarodnog simpozija Stvaralački potencijali u funkciji društveno–ekonomskog i kulturnog razvoja sjeverozapadne Hrvatske, Varaždin 21. – 22. studeni 2002*, Zagreb-Varaždin: Hrvatska akademija znanosti i umjetnosti.

———. 2003a. Egipat u Hrvatskoj: egipatske starine u Hrvatskoj znanosti i kulturi, Zagreb.

———. 2003b. "Zagrebačka egipatska mumija i lanena knjiga." Pp. 54–59 in *Meridijani* 77. Zagreb.

———. 2004a. "Shabtis from Roman Provinces Dalmatia and Pannonia." *Journal of Egyptological Studies* 1, 89–116.

———. 2004b. "Croato-Aegyptica Electronica. Database of the Egyptian Antiquities in Croatian Museum and Private Collections." *PalArch* 3.2, 7–11.

———. 2005. "The Egyptian Antiquities in Croatia." *PalArch* 2.1, 1–33.

———. 2006a. "Model računalne obrade i prezentacije staroegipatskih predmeta u muzejskim zbirkama u Hrvatskoj." PhD diss., University of Zagreb.

———. 2006b. "Shabtis from Roman Provinces Dalmatia and Pannonia and Their Role in Egyptian Cults during Roman Empire." Pp. 279–309, pls. 69–78 in H. Györy (ed.), *Aegyptus et Pannonia III – Acta Symposii anno 2004*, Budapest: Comité de l'Égypte Ancienne de l'Association Amicale Hongroise-Égyptienne.

———. 2007a. "Egyptian Artefacts in the Archaeological Museum of Istria in Pula (Croatia)." *Journal of Egyptological Studies* 2, 43–58.

———. 2007b. "Croato-Aegyptica Electronica: model obrade i analize staroegipatskih predmeta u muzejskim i privatnim zbirkama u Hrvatskoj, dokumentacijski i komunikacijski pristup." *Muzeologija* 41–42, 218–39.

———. 2009a. "Egyptian Prehistoric and Early Dynastic Artefacts in Croatian Museum Collections." Pp. 539–45 in D. Agičić (ed.), *Spomenica Josipa Adamčeka*, Zagreb: FFPress.

———. 2009b. "Croato-Aegyptica Electronica: Database of the Egyptian Antiquities in Croatian Museum and Private Collections." Pp. 183–90 in J. Popielska-Grzybowska (ed.), *Proceedings of the Third Central European Conference of Young Egyptologists. Egypt 2004, Perspectives of Research*. Pułtusk: The Pułtusk Academy of Humanities.

———. 2011. "Shabtis in the Museum and Private Collections in Croatia." *Egyptological* 1, http://www.egyptological.com/2011/06/shabtis-in-croatian-private-collections-and-museums-3441/.

———. 2013a. "Ancient Egyptian Funerary Statuettes in Croatian Collections." *Opuscula archeologica Radovi arheološkog zavoda* 36, 81–88.

———. 2013b, "Redating of Three Ancient Egyptian Artefacts from Naqada II–III and the Archaic Period in the Mimara Museum in Zagreb." *Prilozi Instituta za arheologiju u Zagrebu* 29, 135–43.

———. 2015a. "The Early Penetration of Ancient Egyptian Artifacts and Dissemination of the Cults of Egyptian Divinities in Istria and Illyricum (1st Millennium B.C.–1st Century A.D.)." Pp. 165–200 in Tomorad M. (ed.), *A History of Research into Ancient Egyptian Culture Conducted in Southeast Europe*. Oxford: Archaeopress.

———. 2015b. "The End of Ancient Egyptian Religion: The Prohibition of Paganism in Egypt from the Middle of the 4th to the Middle of the 6th Century A.D." *The Journal of Egyptological Studies* 4, 147–64.

———. forthcoming. *Staroegipatska civilizacija, sv. II: Uvod u egiptološke studije*. Zagreb: Hrvatski studiji.

Tomorad, M., and J. Sliwa. 2015. "Tri staroegipatska skarabeja iz Arheološke zbirke franjevačkog samostana na Košljunu, Hrvatska (Three Ancient Egyptian Scarabs from the Archaeological Collection of the Franciscan Monastery on Košljun, Croatia)." *Prilozi Instituta za arheologiju* 32, 243–50.

TOMORAD, M., and I. URANIĆ. 2006. "The Egyptian Collection of the Museum of the City of Varaždin, Croatia." *Trabajos de Egiptología (Papers on Ancient Egypt)* 3, 87–98.

TONKOVIĆ, S. 1991. "Brončana statua Izide–Fortune iz Prološca." *Imotski. Obavijesti Hrvatskog arheološkog društva* 23.3, 53–54.

URANIĆ, I. 1996. "Egipatska zbirka." Pp. 89–95 in D. Balen and Z. Dukat (eds.), *Muzeopis 1846–1996*, Zagreb: Arheološki muzej.

———. 1999. Bogovi, duhovi i demoni starog Egipta – Gods, Spirits and Demons of Ancient Egypt. Zagreb: Arheološki muzej.

———. 2001. "Duhovi i demoni starog Egipta." Pp. 22–28 in K. Džin (ed.), *Egipatska religija i antička Istra*. Pula: Arheološki muzej Istre.

———. 2002. "Dubrovačka zbirka egipatskih starina." *Vjesnik Arheološkog muzeja u Zagrebu* 3 s. XXXIV, 181–204.

———. 2003. "Egipatski predmeti." P. 12 in A. Rendić-Miočević (ed.), *Na tragovima vremena (iz arheološke zbirke Mateja Pavletića)*. Zagreb: Arheološki muzej.

———. 2005. *Egipatska zbirka: Vodič*. Zagreb: Arheološki muzej.

———. 2009. *Aegyptiaca Zagrabiensis*. Musei Archeologici Zagrebiansis Catalogi et Monographiae 4. Zagreb: Arheološki muzej.

———. 2012. *Mumije, znanost i mit (Mummies: Science and Myth)*. Zagreb: Arheološki muzej.

General Index

Museums, Institutions, and Organizations